PHOTOSHOP CS3

Visual QuickPro Guide

Elaine Weinmann

Peter Lourekas

Peachpit Press

Photoshop CS3: Visual QuickPro Guide
Elaine Weinmann and Peter Lourekas

Peachpit Press
1249 Eighth Street
Berkeley, CA 94710

510/524-2178
510/524-2221 (fax)

Find us on the Web at: www.peachpit.com

Copyright © 2008 by Elaine Weinmann and Peter Lourekas

Cover design: Peachpit Press
Interior design: Elaine Weinmann
Production: Elaine Weinmann and Peter Lourekas
Illustrations: Elaine Weinmann and Peter Lourekas, except as noted

Colophon

This book was created with Adobe InDesign CS3 on two Power Macintosh G5s. The primary fonts used were ITC Stone Serif, ITC Officina Sans, and Myriad.

ISBN-13: 978-0-321-55310-2

ISBN-10:   0-321-55310-1

9 8 7 6 5 4 3 2 1

Printed and bound in the United States of America

Acknowledgments

Nancy Aldrich-Ruenzel, publisher, supports the core strengths of Peachpit Press while cultivating new subject areas and technologies. This book was in the idea stage for many years, and we're grateful to her for helping to nurture it to fruition.

Victor Gavenda, our technical editor at Peachpit, ever so carefully tests the book in Windows, wears another hat as our editor-editor, and always manages to crack us up, even at the eleventh hour.

Lisa Brazieal, expert production editor at Peachpit, irons out the preflight kinks in our files as she readies them for press, then sends them to Courier Printing.

Nancy Davis, editor-in-chief; Gary-Paul Prince, promotions manager; Keasley Jones, associate publisher; and many other terrific, hardworking people at Peachpit contribute their respective talents.

Elaine Soares, photo researcher at the Image Resource Center of Pearson Education, the parent company of Peachpit Press, procured the stock images used throughout the book and responded promptly to all of our requests.

Rebecca Pepper did a thorough and thoughtful job of copy editing.

Steve Rath generated the index.

Leona Benten did the final round of proofreading.

Krista Behrend of Datacolor provided us with technical and product support for our Spyder3Elite display calibrator.

For creating a great product that's a pleasure to use and write about, and for helping beta testers like ourselves untangle the mysteries of Photoshop by way of the online forum, kudos to John Nack, senior product manager for Adobe Photoshop; Vishal Khandpur, senior prerelease program associate for Adobe Photoshop; and other members of the Adobe Photoshop CS3 beta team.

Most important, our love and gratitude to Alicia and Simona, for just being who they are (a pleasure!).

Elaine Weinmann and Peter Lourekas

Introduction

Why a "Pro" book on Photoshop?

Photoshop has so many features, we couldn't stuff instructions for all of them into our *Visual QuickStart Guide* on the subject. Such a rich application deserves a sequel. In this QuickPro, we cover many topics that are too complex for beginning users to tackle, and expand on topics that we touched upon in our *QuickStart Guide,* such as Camera Raw, selection and retouching techniques, painterly effects, and layer masking, to name but a few. We'll show you not only how individual features work, such as the mechanics of creating selections or masks, but how they work in the context of completing real world, multistep tasks.

Is there a prerequisite to using this book?

Since you're reading a *QuickPro* book, we assume that you have a basic proficiency and working knowledge of Photoshop. If you want brush up on some of your basic skills or incorporate more shortcuts into your workflow, see Chapter 4, Using Photoshop, and the Quick Summary reference guides to essential tasks that are scattered throughout this book. For example, there's a guide to choosing colors on page 80, and a summary of Layers palette features on pages 82–83 (see the table of contents for more).

How this book is organized

The chapters in this book are organized in a logical progression, from essential to specialized. The following breakdown will give you a bird's-eye view of how the Adobe Photoshop application and its pals, Adobe Bridge and the Adobe Camera Raw plug-in (both of which ship with Photoshop), fit into the "bigger picture." It will also give you an idea of how this book is organized, from calibrating your display to choosing color settings to using Bridge and Camera Raw, and then, of course, to the many image-editing and image-processing controls in Photoshop.

Chapter 1: Color Management

Calibrating your display and choosing color management settings are essential steps toward ensuring that your input (digital photos or scans) will match the image that you see and edit onscreen, as well as the final output. Don't skip this chapter!

Chapter 2: Bridge

Adobe Bridge serves as a conduit among all the programs in the Adobe Creative Suite. In addition to being the most convenient vehicle for opening files into Camera Raw or Photoshop, Bridge also lets you rate, sort, examine, and compare image thumbnails; assign keywords and other metadata to your files; and locate files by rating and other criteria. If one of your goals is to streamline your work sessions, taking the time and effort to become more familiar with Bridge will pay dividends in the long run.

Chapter 3: Camera Raw

Raw files from a digital camera must be converted by the Camera Raw plug-in ("Camera Raw" for short) before they can be opened and edited in Photoshop. But the ever-improving Camera Raw is more than just a converter; it's also a powerful adjustment tool. We'll show you how to use it to apply cropping and straightening; adjust exposure; correct color casts and chromatic distortion; remove noise, dust marks, and red-eye; and apply sharpening—among other tasks—and then open your photos into Photoshop. You should take advantage of the Camera Raw plug-in, not just because it has a user-friendly interface and a smorgasbord of controls, but also because the settings remain editable, so it preserves the original photos (like film negatives). If you shoot digital photos and you haven't explored Camera Raw thoroughly, don't skip this comprehensive chapter.

Chapters 4 to 15: Photoshop

From Chapter 4, which summarizes the fundamental features of Photoshop, through the last chapter in the book, you'll be immersed in Photoshop, in all its power and glory. Topics range from color and tonal corrections; in-depth montaging, masking, tinting, retouching, and fine art techniques; creating type, paths, and shapes; and saving and loading presets to recording and playing actions, as well as output-related tasks, such as output sharpening, creating a Web photo gallery, and choosing print and export settings. We've tried to strike a balance between technical (geeky) topics and creative (arty) image-editing techniques.

Bridge

You should open your digital photos from Bridge into Camera Raw, then from there into Photoshop. Open other files types from Bridge directly into Photoshop.

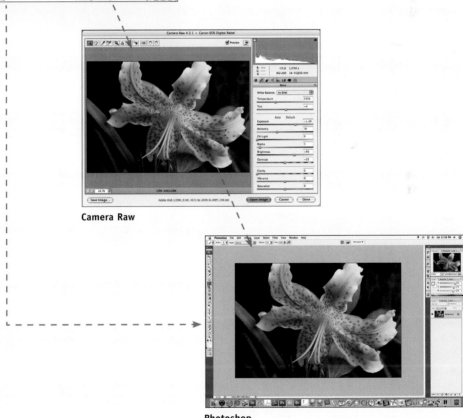

Camera Raw

Photoshop

The philosophy behind this Pro guide

As Photoshop continues to evolve, upgrade by upgrade, its feature set also expands. The sheer number of tools and commands can be intimidating—not to mention the huge choice of tool and command settings. It can be a challenge even for an experienced user to sort out the best features from the rest. And to add to the confusion, some of them overlap or are downright redundant. To perform a simple process like cropping, for example, should you use the Crop tool in Camera Raw or Photoshop, or the Crop, Trim, or Crop and Straighten command in Photoshop? Or suppose you want to lift a figure or object from its background and put it on a new background. Should you use the Extract command, or select it by using a selection tool or command, or a Quick Mask?

Although Photoshop may offer more than one way to reach a goal, one might be marginally successful and tedious, whereas another might let you get the job done with little effort. What makes one method or sequence superior to another? Speed, power, accuracy, and flexibility. Whether your goal is simply to correct problems in a photograph (such as under- or overexposure) or to be adventurous with filters and creative montaging, with some forethought and planning—and a little guidance so you reach for the right tool or command the first time around—you'll reach your goal with more economical steps and less aggravation.

Our photos, or yours?

One approach, when following the instructional steps in this book, is to use the images that we've made available for you to download (see the directory on pages xiii–xvi). If you do so, you'll be able to monitor your progress closely by viewing the figures in the book. Another approach is to use photos from your own inventory or that you download from a stock house, in which case

you'll be able to practice on high-resolution files. You'll find our instructions to be generic enough to work with "outside" images, provided you have access to a reasonably diverse assortment. Possible categories include landscapes, exterior and interior architecture, still lifes, portraiture, sports, wildlife, and special events.

You can have it your way

Every photographer has a unique perspective, and every photography or design project poses unique challenges. Although we recommend some features or methods over others, we also readily admit that there is no one best way to use Photoshop. Feel free to branch off from the techniques described in this book to develop methods that work for your specific photographs, assignments, workflow, and personal style.

Pep talk

Learning software can be fun, but it can also be maddeningly confusing and frustrating. Not only do you need to learn how commands and features work (no easy accomplishment in itself), but to become really proficient, you need to learn when, for what purpose, and in what sequence to use them. With patience, perseverance, and practice, fundamental editing steps and sequences will become second nature, and you will evolve into a pro Photoshop user. You'll even experience occasional moments of clarity (between moments of cursing under your breath!) when a formerly baffling feature becomes comprehensible and everything, well, clicks.

Whether you want to become more technically proficient in Photoshop to give your photos a more professional edge or you want to explore it in new ways to unleash your artistic side, we hope this book helps you reach your personal goals, and makes your experience of using the program more rewarding and enjoyable.

Chapters at a glance

CONTENTS

Contents

9 Sharpening

10 Tinting & Blending

11 Fine Art Media

12 Creative Type

13 Paths & Shapes

REGISTER THIS BOOK!

Purchasing this book entitles you to more than just a couple of pounds of paper. If you register the book with Peachpit Press, you're also entitled to download copies of most of the images used throughout the book, which you can use to practice with as you follow the step-by-step tutorials. To get started, follow this link: www.peachpit.com/photoshopcs3vqp

This takes you to the book's page at the Peachpit Press website. Once there, click Register your book to log in to your account at peachpit.com (if you don't already have an account, it takes just a few seconds to create one, and it's free!).

After logging in, you'll need to enter the book's ISBN code, which you'll find on the back cover. Click Submit, and you're in! You'll be taken to a list of your registered books. Find *Photoshop CS3 Visual QuickPro Guide* on the list, and click Access to protected content to get to the download page.

Please note that these images are low-resolution, not suitable for printing, and they are copyrighted by their owners, who have watermarked them to discourage unauthorized reproduction. They are for your personal use only, not for distribution.

INSTRUCTORS! READERS!

The Adobe Creative Suite upgrades approximately every year and a half. Although that pace leaves us huffing and puffing, we also welcome the challenge and innovations that each revision cycle presents us with. At the very least, our jobs are never boring! Moreover, compulsive perfectionists that we are, each upgrade also presents us with yet another opportunity to improve, refine, and redesign our books.

Is there a topic that you would like us to cover, or cover more in depth, or clarify, or explore from a different angle? Have you discovered a special workflow or sequence of commands that you'd like to share with us—and potentially with other readers? Let us know via email, by visiting the book's Web page (see above, "Register this Book!") and clicking the Feedback link.

Downloadable images

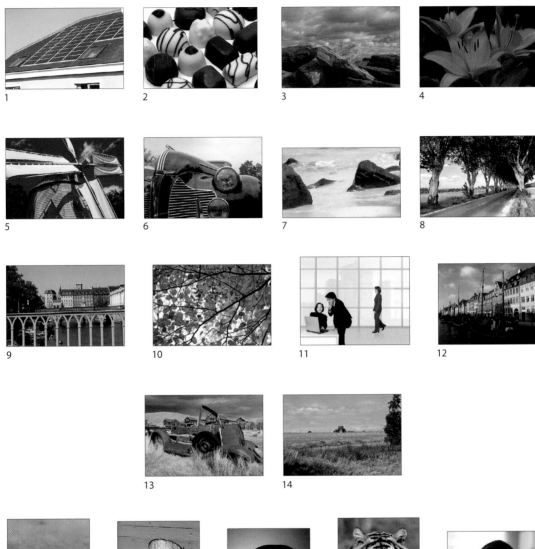

1

2

3

4

5

6

7

8

9

10

11

12

13

14

15

16

17

18

19

20

21

22

23

24

25

26

27

28

29

30

31

32

33

34

35

36

37

38

39

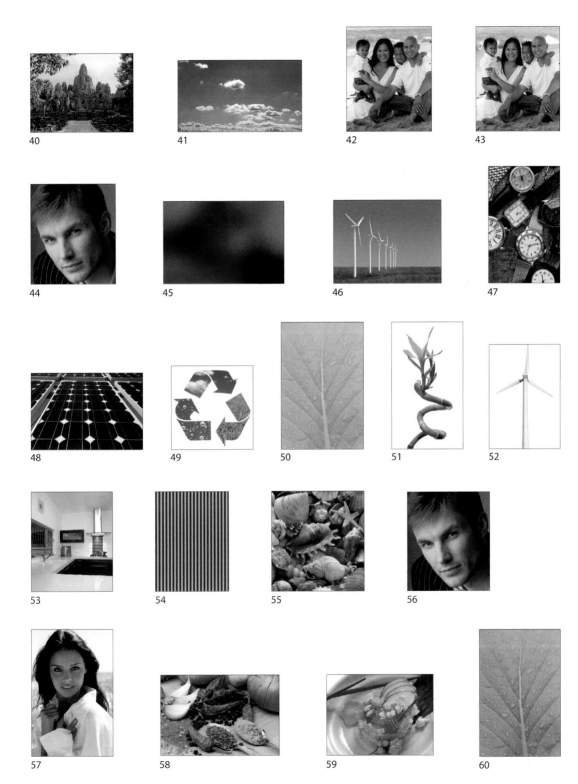

40

41

42

43

44

45

46

47

48

49

50

51

52

53

54

55

56

57

58

59

60

61

62

63

64

65

66

67

68

69

70

71

72

73

74

75

76

77

78

79

80

81

82

83

84

Although you may be tempted to start editing your images right away, you should make sure your display is properly calibrated and choose the appropriate color management settings first.

What is color management?

Each device in your workflow reads colors differently, from the camera, to the display in Photoshop, and finally to print or to a website. As a result, the colors you see through the viewfinder in your camera may not look the same on your computer display, let alone on a printout. A color management system can solve most of these color inconsistencies by acting as a color interpreter. It knows how each device and program interprets color and adjusts colors, if necessary, to keep them as consistent as possible when you shift your file among devices and programs. With the proper color management settings in place, your colors will display and output more accurately.

Each device can capture and reproduce only a limited range (gamut) of colors, which is referred to as its **color space**. The mathematical description of the color space of each device is stored in a type of file known as a **color profile** and is the key feature of any color management system. Each input device, such as a camera, embeds a color profile into the image files it produces. Photoshop then uses this **embedded profile** to determine how to display the document colors, or if a file doesn't have a profile, Photoshop uses data from the current **working space** instead (a color space that you've chosen for Photoshop) to display document color.

To help you maintain color consistency throughout your workflow, in this chapter we'll show you how to set the color space of your digital camera to Adobe RGB, calibrate your display, choose a color space for Photoshop, acquire the proper profiles for your intended printer and paper type, and finally, use those profiles to view a soft proof of your document onscreen. In Chapter 15, color management will come into play once again as you learn how to choose the correct output profile for an inkjet printer.

1

(COLOR MANAGEMENT)

IN THIS CHAPTER

Setting your camera to the Adobe RGB color space

Most digital SLR cameras and most of the higher-end, advanced amateur digital cameras have an onscreen menu that enables you to customize how the camera processes digital images. In this task, we'll demonstrate how to set a camera to the Adobe RGB color space using the example of a Canon EOS 40D, but you can follow the same basic procedure to set the color space for your camera model.

If you shoot in JPEG format, you should choose **Adobe RGB** as the color space for your camera, regardless of which model it is. If you shoot raw files, these steps are optional, because you'll assign the Adobe RGB color space when you convert your photos via the Adobe Camera Raw plug-in.

To set a camera to the Adobe RGB color space:

1. On the back of the camera, click the Menu button to access the menu on the LCD screen, then press the right arrow to select the Shooting Menu tab.**A**

2. Press the down arrow to select the **Color Space** category (in a Nikon camera, this category is called **Optimize**; in a Canon Digital Rebel, it's called **Parameters**).**B** Press the Set button to move to the submenu on the right (in a Nikon camera, press the proper arrow key instead).

3. Press the down arrow to select **Adobe RGB** (in a Nikon, you have to choose a Color Mode category to get to Adobe RGB).**C–D**

4. Press the Set button, then press the **Menu** button to exit the Menu screen.

A On the Canon Menu screen, we chose the **Shooting Menu** tab.

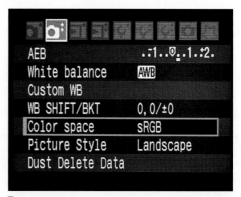

B We used the down arrow to select the **Color Space** category (then will press Set to get to the submenu).

C We chose **Adobe RGB** from the submenu (then will press Set to assign that option).

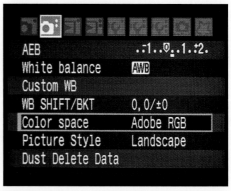

D Adobe RGB is now established as the color space for this camera.

Calibrating your display

Display types

There are two basic types of computer displays: CRT (cathode ray tube, as in a traditional TV set) and LCD (liquid crystal display, or flat panel). The display performance of a **CRT** fluctuates due to its analog technology and the fact that its display phosphors (which produce the glowing dots that you see onscreen) fade over time. A CRT display can be calibrated reliably for only around three years.

An **LCD** display uses a grid of fixed-sized liquid crystals that filter color coming from a back light source. Although you can adjust only the brightness on an LCD (not the contrast), the LCD digital technology offers more reliable color consistency than a CRT, without the characteristic flickering of a CRT. The newest LCD models provide good viewing angles, display accurate color, use the desired daylight temperature of 6500K for the white point (see below), and are produced under tighter manufacturing standards than CRTs. Moreover, in most cases the color profile that's provided with an LCD display (and that is installed in your system automatically) describes the display characteristics accurately.

➤ Both types of displays lose calibration gradually, and you may not notice it until the colors are way off, so try to stick to a regular monthly calibration schedule to maintain color consistency.

Understanding the calibration settings

Three basic characteristics are adjusted when a display is calibrated: The **brightness** (white level) is set to a consistent working standard; the **contrast** (dark level) is set to the maximum value; and finally, a **neutral gray** (gray level) is established using equal values of R, G, and B. To adjust these three characteristics, calibration devices evaluate the white point, black point, and gamma in the display.

➤ The **white point** data enables the display to project a pure white, which matches an industry-standard color temperature. Photographers usually use D65/6500K as the temperature setting for the white point.

➤ The **black point** is the darkest black a display can project. All other dark shades will be lighter than this darkest black, thereby ensuring that shadow details display properly.

➤ The **gamma** defines how midtones are displayed onscreen. A gamma setting of 1.0 reproduces the linear brightness scale that is found in nature. Yet human vision responds to brightness in a nonlinear fashion, so this setting makes the screen look washed out. A higher gamma setting redistributes more of the midtones into the dark range, where our eyes are more sensitive, producing a more natural-looking image. Photography experts recommend using a gamma setting of 2.2 in both Windows and the Mac OS.

Buying a calibration device

The only way to properly calibrate a display is by using a hardware calibration device. It will produce a profile with the proper white point, black point, and gamma data settings for your display. The Adobe color management system, in turn, will use this data to display colors in your Photoshop document with better accuracy.

If you're shopping for a calibration device, you'll notice a wide range in cost, from a colorimeter that will run you between $100 and $300 to much more costly, but more precise, high-end professional gadgets, such as a spectrophotometer. Instead of relying on subjective "eyeball" judgements, the colorimeters and step-by-step wizard tutorials that are included with these devices enable you to calibrate your display more accurately.

Among moderately priced calibrators, our informal reading of hardware reviews and other industry publications has yielded the following as some current favorites: Spyder3Pro and Spyder3Elite by Datacolor; Eye-One Display 2 by X-Rite; and hueyPro, which was developed jointly by Pantone and X-Rite.

The steps outlined below will loosely apply to all three of the hardware **display calibrators** that are mentioned on the previous page. We happen to use Spyder3Elite.

To calibrate your display using a hardware device:

1. Set the room lighting to the usual level that you use for work. If you have a CRT, let it warm up for 30 minutes, to stabilize the display.

2. Increase the brightness of your display to its highest level. In the Mac OS, if you have an Apple-branded display, choose System Preferences > Displays and drag the Brightness slider to the far right. For a third-party display, or any display in Windows, use either an actual button on the display or a menu command in the OnScreen Display (OSD).

3. Launch the calibration application that you've installed, then follow the straightforward instructions in the "step-by-step wizard" screens. Proceed from one screen to the next, choosing options as you go. A

   The important information that you need to tell the application is: what type of display you have (CRT or LCD); the white point you want to use (choose D65/6500K); and the gamma you want to use (choose 2.2 for both Windows and Macintosh). If you're calibrating a CRT display, you may see a few more instructional screens requesting more display setting choices.

4. After entering your display information, you'll be prompted to drape the hardware calibration sensor (the colorimeter) over the monitor. For an LCD, remember to clip on the baffle that's included with the device to prevent the suction cups from touching and potentially damaging the screen. Follow the instructions to align the sensor with the image onscreen (A, next page). Click OK or Continue to initiate a series of calibration tests, which will take from 5 to 10 minutes to complete.

5. After removing the calibration sensor, you'll be prompted to name your new display profile (B, next page). Include the date in the profile name, so you'll be able to tell which profile is the latest. The application will place the new profile in the correct location for use by your Windows or Macintosh operating system. The wizard will step you through one or two more screens (C, next page), then you're done. Upon launching, Photoshop will automatically be aware of the new display profile.

A We launched the **Sypder3Elite** application, then answered questions on two consecutive screens to tell the wizard software what features are present on our LCD monitor, clicking Next to get from one screen to the next. The resulting settings appeared on this **Current Settings** screen.

A When this **Measuring Display** screen appeared, we aligned the **colorimeter** with the onscreen image, then clicked **Continue** to start the actual calibration process. (Note: Although the Spyder3Elite instructions state that the sensor can be attached with suction cups to or draped over the LCD monitor, we play it safe by doing the latter.)

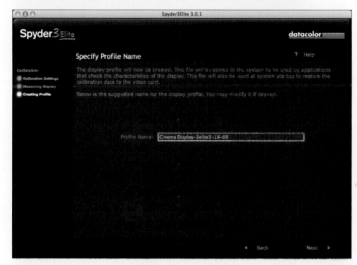

B When the calibration was finished, we clicked Next, and this **Specify Profile Name** screen appeared. We included the monitor name and the current date in our profile name.

C After clicking Next again, this **SpyderProof™** screen appeared. We clicked **Switch** to compare the pre- and postcalibration results, then clicked Next a last time to exit the software.

Choosing a color space for Photoshop

The next step is to choose a color space for Photoshop. If you use Photoshop primarily for print work (whether you use a desktop printer or output your work to a commercial press), you can choose a **color settings preset** by following the simple instructions below.

To set the color space to Adobe RGB (1998):

1. Choose Edit > **Color Settings** (Ctrl-Shift-K/Cmd-Shift-K). The Color Settings dialog opens.**A**

2. Choose Settings: **North America Prepress 2** (foreign readers, choose an equivalent for your output device and geographic location). This preset changes the RGB working space to Adobe RGB (1998) and sets the color management policies to the safe choice of Preserve Embedded Profiles, so each file you open in Photoshop will keep its own profile.

3. Click OK.

DOCUMENT-SPECIFIC COLOR

Photoshop supports **document-specific color,** meaning that each document keeps its own color profile. The profile controls how colors in the file look when you preview and edit them onscreen, and how they're converted upon output. If a document lacks an embedded profile, Photoshop will generate a preview based on the current working space. An RGB document without an embedded profile will be assigned the current working space (Adobe RGB, if you follow the instructions on this page), whereas a CMYK document without a profile will be assigned the current CMYK working space.

Note: The Adobe RGB color space includes more colors in the CMYK print range than the sRGB color space, which is designed for online output. For some reason, Adobe feels compelled to keep sRGB as the default RGB working space in the Color Settings dialog, which can spell disaster for print output.

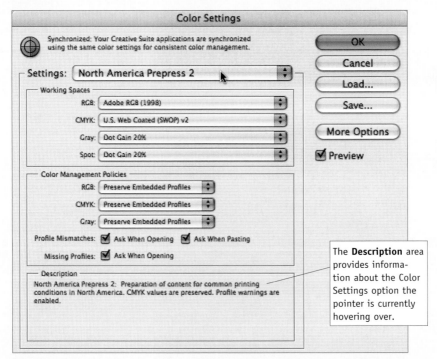

A **North America Prepress 2** is chosen from the **Settings** menu in the **Color Settings** dialog.

For commercial printing, you can ask your print shop to recommend a Settings menu preset for you to use, or a list of suggested settings. Even better, find out if they can supply you with a **color settings** (.csf) **file** containing the correct Working Spaces and Color Management Policies settings for their press. If they send you a .csf file, all you need to do is install it in the proper location, as per the instructions below. Thereafter, you'll be able to access it via the Settings menu in the Color Settings dialog.

To install custom color settings as a preset for the Creative Suite:

1. In Windows, put the file in C:\Documents and Settings\[user]\Application Data\Adobe\Color\ Settings.

   In the Mac OS, put the file in Users/[user name]/ Library/Application Support/Adobe/Color/ Settings.

2. To access your newly saved settings file, relaunch Photoshop, choose Edit > **Color Settings,** then choose the .csf file name from the **Settings** menu.

If your print shop gives you a list of recommended settings for the Color Settings dialog box—but not an actual .csf file—you can choose and then **save** that collection of **settings** as a **.csf** file, as per the instructions below.

To save custom color settings as a preset:

1. Choose Edit > **Color Settings** (Ctrl-Shift-K/ Cmd-Shift-K). The Color Settings dialog box opens.

2. Enter the required settings by choosing menu options and checking appropriate options.

3. Click **Save.** In the Save dialog, enter a file name (we recommend that you include the printer type in the name), keep the .csf extension and the default location (the Settings folder), then click Save.

4. The Color Settings Comment dialog opens. Enter the name of the print shop and the printer type, to help you identify the preset, then click OK.

5. Note that the new settings preset is now listed on the Settings menu. Click OK to exit the Color Settings dialog box.

Acquiring a printer profile

Thus far, you've learned how to set your camera to the Adobe RGB color space, calibrate your display, and specify Adobe RGB as the color space for Photoshop. Next, you need to acquire the necessary **printer profile** (or profiles) so you can incorporate color management into your specific printing scenario.

To download a printer profile:

1. Most printer manufacturers have a website from which you can download either a profile for a specific printer/paper combination or a printer driver that contains a collection of specific printer/paper profiles. Be sure to choose a profile that matches the particular printer/paper combination that you plan to use.

   If you have an Epson photo inkjet printer, you can follow the images on this page to navigate through the epson.com website.**A–D**

   You could also download a profile for a specific printer/paper combo from the website for a paper manufacturer, such as illford.com or crane.com/museo.

   Note: The profiles for the newest printer models may not be available yet on these sites. Check back periodically.

2. After visiting the website, follow the installation instructions for whichever file you downloaded. To use the newly installed profile to proof a document onscreen, see the following page.

A On the Epson home page for your geographic region, click **Drivers & Support**, then click **Printers**.

B Click **Printers**, then **Ink Jet**, then scroll down and click your printer model on the list of printers.

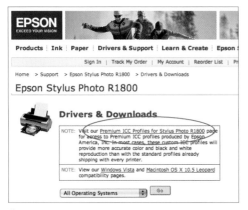

C On the page for the printer model, click the link below Drivers & Downloads. On the **Drivers & Downloads** page, click the **Premium ICC Profiles for [printer name]** link.

D On the **Premium ICC Printer Profiles** page, click the **profile** for your chosen paper type.

Proofing a document onscreen

In this final step in the color management setup, you'll create a custom preset for soft proofing, using settings for your specific inkjet printer and paper, then use that preset to view a **soft proof** (onscreen simulation) of how your colors will look in print.

To simulate an inkjet print onscreen:

1. Open the document, then from the View > **Proof Setup** submenu, choose Custom. The Customize Proof Condition dialog opens.**A**

2. You'll choose custom proofing settings for your output device. Check Preview, then from the **Device to Simulate** menu, choose the color profile for your inkjet printer and paper (this is the profile you either downloaded from a website or that your printer driver installed).

3. Uncheck **Preserve RGB Numbers** to have Photoshop simulate how the colors will look when converted to the chosen profile. This option is available only if the color mode of the output profile that you chose from the Device to Simulate menu matches the mode of the current file (e.g., if your image is in RGB Color mode and will be output on an RGB printer).

4. From the **Rendering Intent** menu, choose the **Perceptual** or **Relative Colorimetric** option to control how colors will change as the image is shifted from one profile to another. You can evaluate each intent via the preview. (For a description of the intents, see the sidebar on the next page.)

Check **Black Point Compensation** to improve the printing of blacks. With this option on, the full dynamic range of the image color space is mapped to the full dynamic range of the printer's color space. With this option off, blacks in the image may display or print as grays. We recommend checking this option when outputting a file on an inkjet printer.

5. *Optional:* For Display Options (On-Screen), check Simulate Paper Color to preview the white of the printing paper, as defined in the printer profile. For this simulation to be effective, the chosen printer profile must include the specifications for your printing paper.

6. To save your custom settings, click **Save**, enter a name (keep the .psf extension and the default location as the Proofing folder), then click Save. Your proofing preset will be available on the Customize Proof Condition menu, and also at the bottom of the View > Proof Setup submenu.

7. Click OK. View > **Proof Colors** will be checked automatically, enabling you to view the soft proof onscreen. Also, the Device to Simulate profile will be listed in the document title bar.

Note: A soft proof is merely an onscreen simulation of your print output. Colors in the actual file won't be converted to the chosen profile until you change the document color mode (e.g., from RGB to CMYK) or send the file to print.

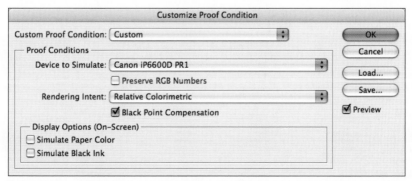

A To establish which printer the soft proof will simulate, in the **Customize Proof Condition** dialog, choose your printer model as the **Device to Simulate**.

You can also have Photoshop create a **soft proof**, or onscreen simulation, of how the colors in your RGB file will look when printed with **CMYK** inks by a commercial press.

To proof colors for commercial printing:

1. Open your document, then from the View > **Proof Setup** submenu, choose **Custom.** The Customize Proof Condition dialog opens.

2. Check Preview, then from the **Device to Simulate** menu, choose the color profile for the type of commercial press and paper stock the job will be printed on. Click OK.

3. The View > **Proof Colors** feature will be checked automatically. You can uncheck it to turn off soft-proofing at any time (Ctrl-Y/Cmd-Y).

➤ The Working CMYK option on the Device to Simulate menu in the Customize Proof Condition dialog is automatically set to the current CMYK Working Space that is specified in Edit > Color Settings.

Moving on

If you followed the instructions in this chapter, you've successfully completed the first (and most lengthy) part of the color management setup. You set your camera to the Adobe RGB color space, calibrated your display, chose Adobe RGB as the color space for Photoshop, acquired the proper profile for your inkjet printer and paper type, and created a soft-proof setting using that profile. You'll need to focus on color management once more when you prepare your file for printing. In Chapter 15, you'll learn how to let Photoshop handle color conversions for an inkjet printer, using the printer profiles that were used for the soft proof.

The benefit of using color management is that it helps ensure color consistency among all the devices in your workflow—from camera to display to printer. As you use Photoshop to enhance your photos, you can be confident that the colors in your printout will closely match what you see onscreen.

In the next chapter, you'll learn how to download your digital photo files, then use Adobe Bridge to locate, sort, organize, examine, and manage them. And don't miss Chapter 3, the chapter on the powerful Camera Raw plug-in, which lets you apply extensive adjustments to your photos before you open them into Photoshop.

THE RENDERING INTENTS

➤ **Perceptual** changes colors in a way that seems natural to the human eye, while attempting to preserve the overall appearance of the image. It's a good choice for continuous-tone images.

➤ **Saturation** changes colors with the intent of preserving vivid colors, but in so doing compromises color fidelity. It's a good choice for charts and business graphics, which normally contain fewer colors than continuous-tone images.

➤ **Absolute Colorimetric** maintains color accuracy only for colors that fall within the destination color gamut (i.e., the color range of your printer), but in so doing sacrifices the accuracy of colors that are out of gamut.

➤ **Relative Colorimetric,** the default intent for all the Adobe predefined settings in the Color Settings dialog, compares the white, or highlight, of your document's color space to the white of the destination color space (the white of the paper, in the case of print output), and shifts colors where needed. This is the best Rendering Intent choice for documents in which most of the colors fall within the color range of the destination gamut, because it preserves most of the original colors.

You shot some photos with your new digital camera. Now what? In the beginning of this chapter, you'll learn how to download images from a digital camera to a computer. The remainder of the chapter is devoted to the **Adobe Bridge** application, which lets you preview and open images into Photoshop and Camera Raw* (and also works with the other programs in the Adobe Creative Suite). You'll learn how to customize the Bridge window for your needs; rate, filter out, compare, and stack image thumbnails; open files into Photoshop; embed metadata into your files; use the Find command to locate files; and choose Bridge preferences.

Downloading photos

When you shoot digitally, your camera stores the photos in a removable memory card, such as a CompactFlash (CF) or Secure Digital (SD) card. This is usually a more practical solution than shooting with your camera (and yourself) tethered to a computer. To get the photos from your camera into a computer, you can remove the memory card and insert it into a card reader device, then download the photos via a USB or Firewire cable, depending on which connection your card reader supports (Firewire is faster).

For downloading photos, we use the **Photo Downloader** application, which is included with Bridge 2 and later (see the next page). We recommend using Photo Downloader instead of the default system application in Windows or Macintosh for several reasons: it's fully integrated with Bridge; it lets you download raw digital photos; it provides simple but useful file management and naming controls; and it lets you embed copyright information into your photo files.

OTHER WAYS TO GET IMAGES INTO PHOTOSHOP

You're not limited to using images from a digital camera, although doing so will let you take advantage of the powerful, nondestructive adjustment controls in the Camera Raw plug-in. Other options are to scan imagery, such as original artwork or photographs, on a flatbed scanner; scan transparencies on a slide scanner; download stock photos from an online resource; place or drag and drop files from Adobe Illustrator; or create images, patterns, or textures from scratch by using various tools and filters.

To open images into Camera Raw, see page 36.

USING BRIDGE

2

IN THIS CHAPTER

To download photos via Photo Downloader:

1. Take the card out of your camera and insert it into the appropriate slot in your card reader.

2. Plug the card reader into your computer. If the default system application for acquiring photos launches, exit/quit that application.

3. Launch **Bridge**.

4. Choose File > **Get Photos from Camera**.

   The Photo Downloader dialog opens. If an alert dialog appears and you want to make Photo Downloader the default capture application, click Yes; if not, click No.

5. From the **Get Photos From** menu in the Source area, select your card reader or camera.

6. Click **Advanced Dialog** to switch to the larger Advanced dialog **A** in order to view more options.

7. In the **Save Options** area, do the following:

   To change the save location, click **Browse/ Choose,** then navigate to the desired folder. Click OK/Choose again to select that folder and get back to the Photo Downloader dialog.

   To create a new subfolder for the photos within the folder you just selected, choose a naming convention from the **Create Subfolder(s)** menu (**A**, next page) or choose Custom Name and type a folder name in the field below. If you don't want to create a subfolder, choose None.

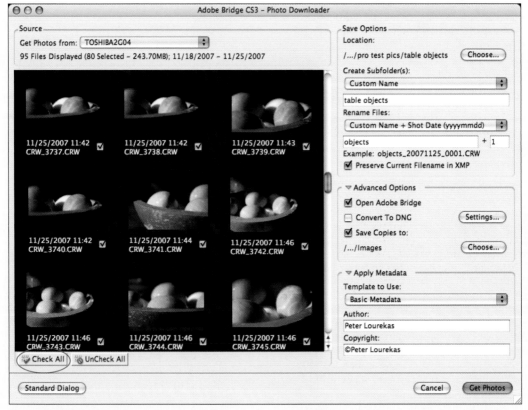

A In the **Advanced Dialog** of the **Photo Downloader**, you can apply metadata to the photos to be downloaded, then check the box below specific photos to be downloaded or click **Check All** (as was done here) to download them all.

To assign names and short sequential numbers to your files to replace the long default numbers that your camera assigned, on the **Rename Files** menu, choose **Custom Name**, then enter a name and a starting number.**B** Use a short but descriptive name to help you locate the files via searches; and consider including the shot date to create unique file names to prevent your files from being overwritten unintentionally. A sample of the name displays in the Example field.

Note: Some camera models create a small .thm file for each raw photo, which contains nonessential image data and will be hidden in Bridge by default. If you want to download these files, keep the box checked below all the .thm thumbnails.**C**

8. Check **Preserve Current Filename in XMP** to preserve the option to access the original file names in the future.

9. In the Advanced Options area, check **Open Adobe Bridge** to have the photos display automatically in a new window in Bridge when the download is completed.

Continued on the following page

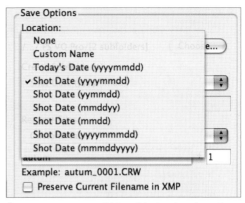

A You can name your folder with the shot date of the photo by choosing a **Shot Date** option on the **Create Subfolder** menu. A subfolder will be created for each shot date found among the selected photos, and photos will be placed into folders labeled with corresponding dates.

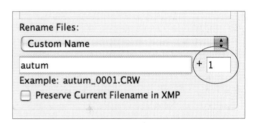

B Via the **Custom Name** option, you can rename your photos and include an identifying number. By default, the dialog will display the next number after the one that was assigned to the last download. Either keep that number to continue the sequential numbering or enter a new starting number.

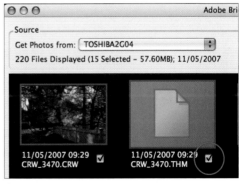

C If your camera model creates **.thm** files and you want to download them along with your photos, keep the box below the thumbnails checked.

WHAT IS DNG?

Have you wondered what the best file format is for saving digital photos — for the present and future — so you'll be able to access and print them over, say, a 20-year period or longer? Currently, there is no one standard raw format; each camera maker has its own proprietary method for creating raw files. And should a manufacturer discontinue its proprietary method, raw photos from their cameras might then be incompatible with commonly used image-editing software.

DNG, an open-standard file format that was developed by Adobe, may some day become a popular long-term solution. It preserves all the raw, unprocessed pixel information that the camera records. Adobe has made the coding for DNG publicly available ("open standard") to other interested companies in the hope that it will be adopted for a wide range of hardware devices and software applications. In the future, hopefully, DNG files will be universally readable.

10. *Optional:* If you like to be selective about which raw photos you convert to the DNG format (we do), you can do so by using the Save Options dialog in Camera Raw. Or if you prefer to convert all the raw photos you're downloading to this format now, check Convert To DNG. (To learn more about DNG, see the sidebar on the previous page). This format is not recommended for digital photos captured as JPEG or TIFF.

The DNG Conversion Settings dialog opens.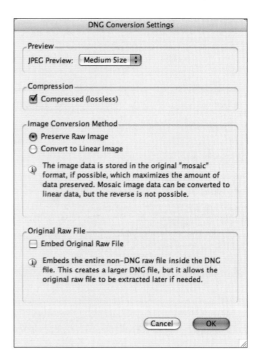A Do the following:

To enable a thumbnail to display for a DNG file, it must contain a JPEG preview. Choose a size from the JPEG Preview menu. Medium Size produces an adequate preview without greatly increasing the file size.

Check Compressed (Lossless) to decrease the file size with no loss of image detail.

For the Image Conversion Method, click Preserve Raw Image to maximize the amount of original data that's preserved and available for reediting.

For Original Raw File, we don't check Embed Original Raw File (which would embed the large raw file into the DNG file) because doing so would increase the file size substantially, and because we trust that Adobe and other companies will continue to provide support for the DNG format. Check this option only if you must preserve access to the original raw image.

Click OK.

11. In the Photo Downloader dialog, be sure to check **Save Copies To,** then click Browse/Choose to send copies of your photos to a designated external hard drive. This is your emergency backup!

12. In the **Apply Metadata** area, if you've created a metadata template already (see page 27), choose it from the Template to Use menu; otherwise, manually enter Author and Copyright info to be added to the metadata of all the photos you're downloading. (The metadata info displays in the Metadata panel in Bridge.)

13. Do either of the following:

To download all the photos from your memory card, click **Check All.**

To download select photos, below the thumbnail window, click **UnCheck All,** then check the box below each photo you want to download. Or click, then Shift-click a sequence of photos (and any corresponding .thm files), then check the box for one of them; a check mark will appear below all the selected photos.

14. Click **Get Photos** to start the downloading process. When the downloading is finished, the Photo Downloader application will quit automatically. If you checked the Open Adobe Bridge option, your photos will now display in a new window in Bridge; if not, launch Bridge (see the following page).

15. Before you move on to managing your photos in Bridge, archive your photos to a disk. Insert a blank DVD-R disk into your computer and burn copies of your photos to the DVD as a permanent archive. (In the Mac OS, you can do this via drag-and-drop in the Finder.) For more information, see the Help file for your system.

A In the **DNG Conversion Settings** dialog, choose options to control how your raw photos will be converted and archived to the DNG format.

Taking a look at Adobe Bridge

With its ability to display large thumbnail previews of files from all the Adobe Creative Suite applications, **Adobe Bridge** is the best vehicle for opening files into Photoshop—and for opening raw photos into Camera Raw—plus it offers a host of other useful features.**A** You can use Bridge to display, arrange, examine, rate, and sort thumbnails; organize thumbnails into expandable stacks; rate or reject images; assign keywords and other metadata to make your files more searchable; embed copyright notices; rotate images; and view data (metadata), such as the specific shooting conditions the digital camera recorded into your photos.

To launch Bridge:

Do one of the following:

In Photoshop, near the middle of the Options bar, click the **Go to Bridge** button 🖼 (Ctrl-Alt-O/Cmd-Option-O).

Double-click the **Bridge** application icon **Br** in Program Files\Adobe\Adobe Bridge CS3 in Windows, or Applications/Adobe Bridge CS3 in the Mac OS.

In the Mac OS, click the **Bridge** icon **Br** on the **Dock.**

The Adobe Bridge window opens.

FEATURES OF THE BRIDGE WINDOW

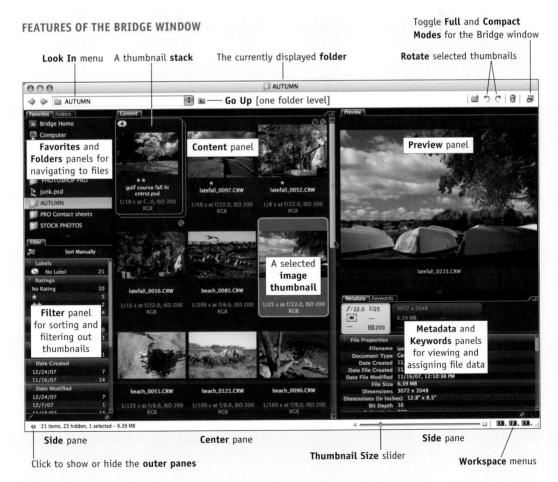

A You can use **Bridge** to locate, preview, rate, sort, and apply metadata to your images and, of course, open them into Photoshop or Camera Raw. The **Default** workspace is shown above.

Choosing a workspace for Bridge

One way to reconfigure the Bridge window quickly is by choosing a **predefined workspace**.

To choose a predefined workspace for Bridge:

From one of the three **workspace** menus in the lower right corner of the Bridge window,**A** choose one of the predefined workspaces, or use the assigned shortcut that's listed on the menu.

If you're baffled by the choices, pick one of our two favorites:

To view the largest possible number of image thumbnails in a given folder at a time, laid out like a contact sheet, choose **Light Table.B–C**

A Choose a predefined workspace from one of the three **workspace** menus.

This is a good layout to use for the first round of comparing and rejecting images.

➤ To hide or show file data (thumbnail labels and metadata) in the Content panel, press Ctrl-T/Cmd-T.

Or to display a large preview of the currently selected image or images, choose the **Vertical Filmstrip** workspace (**A–B**, next page).

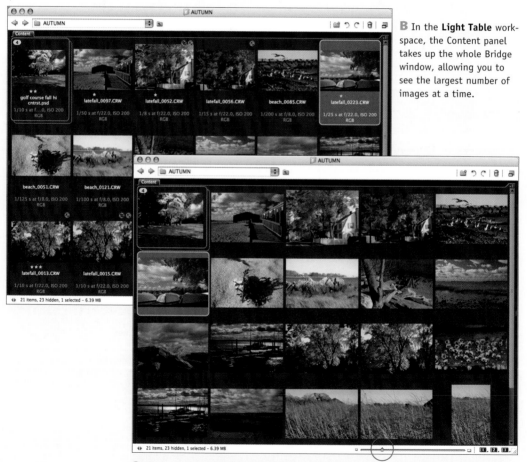

B In the **Light Table** workspace, the Content panel takes up the whole Bridge window, allowing you to see the largest number of images at a time.

C This is also the Light Table workspace, with two changes: we hid the file information (Ctrl-T/Cmd-T) and enlarged the thumbnails via the slider.

A In the **Vertical Filmstrip** workspace, you can cycle through thumbnails in the current folder by pressing the up or down arrow key, view a large preview of the current image, and examine details in the Preview panel by using an onscreen loupe.

B We double-clicked the vertical bar to hide the left pane in this **Vertical Filmstrip** workspace to make the preview larger.

If the predefined workspaces aren't to your liking, you can **customize** the **workspace** so it contains the thumbnail and preview sizes and support panels that you like to work with. Even better, take a minute to save your custom workspace (or workspaces) so you can choose it quickly in future work sessions.

To customize the Bridge workspace:

1. Choose the **Default** workspace. You can customize any workspace, but this is a good one to start with.

2. Do any of the following:

   Resize the overall Bridge **window.**

   Drag the horizontal bar between panels to make an area taller or shorter, or a vertical **bar** to make a side pane or the center pane wider or narrower.**A**

   Resize the thumbnails by using the **Thumbnail Size** slider at the bottom of the Bridge window.

To save a custom workspace:

1. From one of the three **workspace** menus ▣, ▣, ▣, in the lower right corner of the Bridge window, choose **Save Workspace.** The Save Workspace dialog opens.

2. Enter a **Name** for the workspace, choose a **Keyboard Shortcut** (or choose None), check Save Window Location as Part of Workspace and/or check Save Sort Order as Part of Workspace (both are optional), then click Save.

3. You can choose any predefined or saved workspace from one of the **workspace** menus. Thereafter, it will be the default for that button; click the button to redisplay that workspace.

   Any changes you make to the current workspace, such as resizing a panel, will be saved to the button that you assigned the workspace to. (To demonstrate, click a different workspace button, then click the button for the modified workspace.) To redisplay a saved workspace without your temporary changes, choose the name from the workspace menu instead of just clicking the button.

A This is one of the **custom workspaces** that we use. You can create workspaces to suit your needs.

Previewing thumbnails

To display a folder of thumbnails:

1. To navigate to a folder, do one of the following:

   In the **Folders** panel, navigate to the file you want to open. Scroll upward or downward, expand or collapse any folder via the arrowhead, or click a folder icon.

   From the **Look In** menu at the top of the Bridge window, choose from the list of **Favorites** or **Recent Folders.**

   Click a folder in the **Favorites** panel.

   ➤ To move up a level in the current folder hierarchy, click the Go Up button 🔼 at the top of the Bridge window.

2. To display the contents of a subfolder, double-click the folder thumbnail in the Content panel. Note: Any image that has a number in the upper left corner is part of a stack (group of thumbnails). You can click the top image thumbnail in a stack to preview just that image. To learn more about stacks, see page 21.

➤ When a folder of images displays for the first time in Bridge, it takes time for the previews to be generated, so don't judge them too hastily. The initial preview for a raw photo reflects the Camera Default settings in Camera Raw; it will update if you edit the photo in Camera Raw.

To examine images in the Preview panel:

1. In the **Content** panel, click an image thumbnail. It will now have a colored border; note also the large preview in the Preview panel and the file data in the Metadata panel.

2. To **compare** thumbnails in the Preview panel, Ctrl-click/Cmd-click two or more thumbnails. **A**

   ➤ Ctrl-click/Cmd-click a selected thumbnail to deselect it and remove it from the Preview panel.

3. To examine a small detail, click a thumbnail in the Preview panel to make the loupe appear. **B** Click the area you want to examine, or drag the loupe. By default, pixels display in the loupe at 100% view; the zoom level is listed below the preview. Press + to zoom in the loupe display or – to zoom out.

   ➤ Click the loupe to remove it.

➤ If you're using a loupe in two different thumbnails, you can Ctrl-drag/Cmd-drag either loupe to move them in unison.

B Use the **loupe** on any image in the **Preview** panel to examine small details.

A Ctrl-click/Cmd-click to select multiple **thumbnails** in the **Content** panel.

Rating and sorting thumbnails

Even master photographers discard many more photos than they actually use. Using **Ratings**, the **Filter** panel, **sorting**, and **stacks**, you can rate or categorize your images and narrow the choices down to just the best of the lot.

To rate and sort thumbnails:

1. Click a thumbnail or select multiple thumbnails that you consider to be "in the running," then press Ctrl-1/Cmd-1 to assign a **star** rating to them.**A** You could also set up a hierarchy of levels, using Ctrl/Cmd 1, 2, 3, 4, or 5 to assign that number of stars.

2. Press Alt-Backspace/Option-Delete to apply the **Reject** rating to any selected thumbnails that you want to remove from view but not yet delete. Use the View > **Show Reject Files** command to show or hide rejected thumbnails.

3. In the **Ratings** category on the **Filter** panel, check a star rating to see only images with that rating, or Shift-click a star rating to see all the thumbnails with that star rating and higher. (Shift-click the first star rating to remove all the star check marks.) You can also narrow the thumbnail selection by checking other categories in this panel.

4. On the **Filter** panel, do any of the following:

SHORTCUTS FOR RATING THUMBNAILS	
Apply the Reject rating to selected thumbnails	Alt-Delete/Option-Delete (NOT Ctrl/Cmd-Delete!)
Remove a Reject or star rating	Ctrl-O/Cmd-0
Assign a star rating	Ctrl/Cmd-1, 2, 3, 4, or 5
Apply the current Filter panel choices as you display other folders	Click the Keep Filter When Browsing button 📌
Remove all check marks from the Filter panel for the current folder	Click the Clear Filter button ⊘ or press Ctrl-Alt-A/Cmd-Option-A

From the **Sort** menu, ⇕ choose a sorting order (such as By Date Created).

Click the arrowhead to sort thumbnails in **Ascending Order** ▲ or **Descending Order**.▼

Click a **keyword** to display only thumbnails that were assigned that keyword (see page 29).

5. You also can rearrange thumbnails by dragging. To group multiple thumbnails into stacks, see the following page.

➤ To apply ratings in Slideshow mode, see pages 22–23.

A These thumbnails were assigned **reject**, **1-star**, and **2-star** ratings and then were sorted according to **Rating**.

Using stacks

Another good way to limit how many thumbnails display at a given time is by organizing them in **stacks** by category (such as landscapes, head shots, or multiple shots of the same subject).

To create a stack:

1. Shift-click or Ctrl-click/Cmd-click to select multiple thumbnails. The first one you click will become the "stack thumbnail" (the one that displays on top of the stack).

2. Press Ctrl-G/Cmd-G or right-click/Control-click and choose Stack > **Group as Stack.** The number in the upper left corner of a stack indicates how many thumbnails it contains.

To select thumbnails that are in a stack:

Do either of the following: **A**

To **select and display** all the thumbnails in a stack, click the stack number. Click it again to collapse the stack. The stack stays selected.

To **select** all the thumbnails in a stack while keeping the stack **collapsed**, Alt-click/Option-click the stack thumbnail.

To rearrange thumbnails that are in a stack:

To **rearrange** a thumbnail in an expanded stack, click it to deselect the other selected thumbnails, then drag it to a new position (as shown by the colored drop zone line).

To promote a different thumbnail to the top of the stack, click the thumbnail to be promoted, then choose Stacks > **Promote to Top of Stack.**

To move a whole stack:

1. Alt-click/Option-click a stack that's in its collapsed state, to select it.

2. Drag the image thumbnail (not the border).

➤ If you drag the top thumbnail of an unselected stack, you'll move just that thumbnail, not the whole stack.

To add a thumbnail to a stack:

Click a thumbnail, then drag it into a stack.

To remove thumbnails from a stack:

1. Click the stack number to expand the stack.

2. Click a thumbnail (to deselect the other thumbnails), then drag it out of the stack.

To ungroup a whole stack:

1. Click the stack number to expand and select all the thumbnails in the stack.

2. Right-click/Control-click and choose Stack > **Ungroup from Stack** (or choose Stacks > Ungroup from Stack). The stack number and border will disappear. The ungrouped thumbnails will be repositioned according to the current sorting criterion.

SHORTCUTS FOR STACKS	
Group as stack	Ctrl-G/Cmd-G
Ungroup from stack	Ctrl-Shift-G/Cmd-Shift-G
Open stack	Ctrl-right arrow/Cmd-right arrow
Close stack	Ctrl-left arrow/Cmd-left arrow
Expand all stacks in folder	Ctrl-Alt-right arrow/Cmd-Option-right arrow
Collapse all stacks in folder	Ctrl-Alt-left arrow/Cmd-Option-left arrow
Select all thumbnails in stack, keep stack collapsed	Alt-click/Option-click the stack thumbnail

A The **stack** of image thumbnails in the top row is **collapsed**, whereas the one below it is **expanded**.

Using Slideshow mode

In **Slideshow** mode, images in the currently selected folder are displayed in succession as full-screen previews on an uncluttered background.**A** You can rate or rotate images in this mode as you view the images.

To preview images in Slideshow mode:

1. Open a folder or click a thumbnail and then, to put Bridge into Slideshow mode, do either of the following:

   Press Ctrl-L/Cmd-L or choose View > **Slideshow.**

   To choose options for the slideshow first, choose View > **Slideshow Options** (Ctrl-Shift-L/Cmd-Shift-L). Choose options in the Slideshow Options dialog (**A**, next page), then click **Play.**

2. While the slideshow is playing, you can use the shortcuts listed onscreen to perform various commands; or if you find the list to be obtrusive, press H to hide it and use the sidebar on the following page as a reference guide.

   For example, you can press **L** to open the **Slideshow Options** dialog, then preview the effect of different **When Presenting, Show Slides** options on the current slide.

   Or to open a raw photo into **Camera Raw**, press **R**. The slideshow will resume playing when you click Done in the Camera Raw dialog.

3. To exit Slideshow mode, press **Esc.**

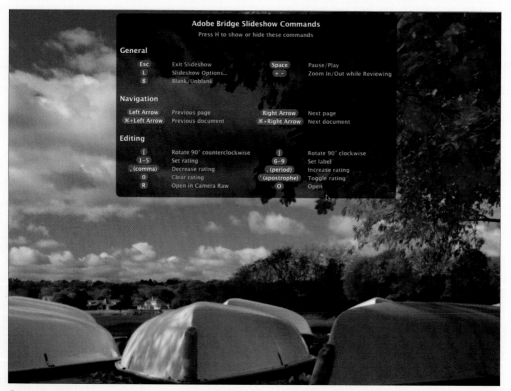

A In **Slideshow** mode, the current image fills the whole screen. Press **H** to show or hide the list of commands.

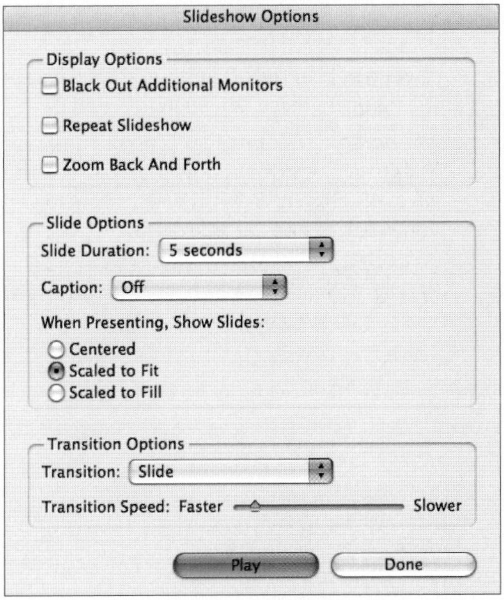

Slideshow Options

Display Options
- ☐ Black Out Additional Monitors
- ☐ Repeat Slideshow
- ☐ Zoom Back And Forth

Slide Options
Slide Duration: 5 seconds
Caption: Off
When Presenting, Show Slides:
- ○ Centered
- ◉ Scaled to Fit
- ○ Scaled to Fill

Transition Options
Transition: Slide
Transition Speed: Faster ————△———— Slower

[Play] [Done]

A Choose **Display, Slide,** and **Transition** options for your slideshow in the **Slideshow Options** dialog.

SHORTCUTS FOR SLIDESHOW MODE

Enter Slideshow mode	Ctrl-L/Cmd-L
Hide/show shortcuts	H
Apply rating	1–5
Apply label	6–9
Increase rating by 1	. (period)
Decrease rating by 1	, (comma)
Clear current rating	0 (zero)
Open file in Camera Raw, then continue the slideshow	R
Open file	O
Open Slideshow Options dialog	L
Blank/unblank screen	B
Pause or Play	Spacebar
Zoom in or out	+ or –
Previous slide or PDF page	Left arrow
Next slide or PDF page	Right arrow
Jump from PDF page to previous (or next) slide	Ctrl-left (or right) arrow/ Cmd-left (or right) arrow
Rotate 90° Counterclockwise	[
Rotate 90° Clockwise	]
Exit Slideshow mode	Esc

Opening files into Photoshop

You can **open** as many files into **Photoshop** as the currently available RAM and scratch disk space allow. (Note: To open a raw or JPEG digital photo into Camera Raw, see pages 34 and 36.)

To open files from Bridge into Photoshop:

1. Select one or more image thumbnails (Shift-click or Ctrl-click/Cmd-click to select multiple thumbnails), then press Ctrl-O/Cmd-O or right-click/Ctrl-click and choose **Open**. Photoshop will launch, if it isn't already running, and the image(s) will appear onscreen.

2. If the **Embedded Profile Mismatch** dialog appears,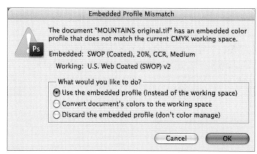 it means the file's color profile doesn't match the current working space. Click **Use the Embedded Profile (Instead of the Working Space)** if you must keep the document's current profile, or for better consistency with your color management workflow, click **Convert Document's Colors to the Working Space** to convert the profile to the current working space. Click OK.

   Note: If you double-click a thumbnail, the file or selected files will open into Photoshop or Camera Raw, depending on the file type and the current status of the **Prefer Adobe Camera Raw for JPEG and TIFF Files** or **Double-Click Edits Camera Raw Settings in Bridge** option in Bridge Preferences.

➤ For existing Photoshop files: If you want to minimize/close the Bridge window as you open a PSD file, hold down Alt/Option as you double-click the thumbnail. To reopen the Bridge window at any time, click the Go to Bridge icon ![icon] on the Options bar in Photoshop.

DECIPHERING THE BADGES

You may see one or both of these icons in the upper right corner of some or all of your image thumbnails:

BADGE	WHAT IT SIGNIFIES
![badge]	The file was opened and **modified** in Camera Raw
![badge]	The file was opened and **cropped** in Camera Raw

A If the **Embedded Profile Mismatch** dialog appears, click whether you want to use the embedded profile or convert the file to the current working space.

Developing a workflow for managing digital photos in Bridge

Basic setup tasks

➤ Create and **save custom workspaces** for different purposes that incorporate the panels, panel sizes, and thumbnail sizes that you use most often. For example, you could choose the Default workspace, enlarge the thumbnails and the Preview panel, and save that configuration as one custom workspace, then choose the Vertical Filmstrip workspace, customize it to your liking, and save that configuration as another workspace.

➤ Create **metadata templates**, including a basic, all-purpose template for embedding your contact and copyright information.

➤ Enter **IPTC metadata** via the Metadata panel, and keywords vias the **Keywords** panel.

A suggested workflow

The following is the workflow we typically follow in Bridge. You don't have to perform all of these tasks. Develop a sequence that works for you.

➤ Use the **Photo Downloader** to rename the photos, embed copyright info, and choose an external hard drive for your backup copies (you can also convert files to the DNG format at this time).

➤ Choose Bridge Preferences > Thumbnails and click **High Quality Thumbnails.**

➤ **Display** your **folder** of downloaded photos, then get up and do a few stretches while Bridge generates the thumbnail previews.

➤ Embed creator contact and copyright information in all the photos by applying your **metadata template.**

➤ Choose the **Light Table** workspace via one of the Workspace menus to display as many photo thumbnails as possible.

➤ Select the obvious rejects, press Alt-Backspace/Option-Delete to apply a **reject** rating to them, then choose View > **Show Reject Files** (to remove the check mark) to hide them from view.

➤ Switch to the **Default** workspace, then enlarge the thumbnails and the Preview panel (or choose a saved workspace that has similar characteristics).

➤ Assign a **reject** rating or **star** ratings to thumbnails: first to the obvious losers and winners, and then to the maybes.

➤ Choose the **Vertical Filmstrip** workspace (or a saved workspace that has similar characteristics), then select, view, compare, and examine shots of the same scene or subject one, two, or three at a time. Use the **loupe** to examine small details.

➤ **Raise** or **lower** any of the star **ratings** as you discover subtle differences among the photos.

➤ Assign descriptions and keywords to selected thumbnails via the **Metadata** panel (IPTC Core category) or the **Keywords** panel.

➤ Filter thumbnails by **Rating** or another criterion via the **Filter** panel.

➤ Organize thumbnails into **stacks** based on common similarities, such as their subject matter.

➤ Open one or more photos into **Camera Raw** (see the next chapter) for exposure corrections and other adjustments.

MOVING FILES OR FOLDERS IN BRIDGE

If you need to move or copy a file or folder from one location to another in Bridge, right-click/Ctrl-click and choose **Move To** or **Copy To.** Choose a folder from the submenu or select Choose Folder to open a navigation dialog.

Working with metadata

Data about the camera settings you use is embedded into your digital photos by the camera; other data (called "metadata") is embedded into your files by Bridge; and you can assign still other data ("user data") manually, such as contact information for viewers, and searchable descriptions and keywords. To view and assign metadata, you'll use the **Metadata** panel.

To view the metadata for a file:

1. Click a file thumbnail.

2. The placard **A** at the top of the **Metadata** panel will list the camera settings that were used to capture the photo, as well as file specifications, such as the pixel dimensions and file size.*

   The **File Properties** category **B** will list other information about the file, such as the name, format, date created, and date modified. Click an arrowhead to expand or collapse a category.

   If a digital photo is selected, the Camera Data (EXIF) category will list the camera settings that were used to capture the photo, in more detail than in the placard. This data was embedded into the photo by your camera.

➤ Data that you enter in the Author and Copyright fields in the Photo Downloader is listed in the IPTC Core panel.

➤ Once a photo is edited in Camera Raw, the settings are listed in a separate Camera Raw category, and are updated each time further edits are made in Camera Raw.

➤ The metadata sticks with a file, and with copies of the file that are created via File > Save As.

If you don't see the placard, choose Show Metadata Placard from the Metadata panel menu.

CONFIGURING THE METADATA PANEL

➤ To change the point size of the listings in the Metadata panel, choose **Increase Font Size** or **Decrease Font Size** from the panel menu.

➤ To hide all categories that don't contain any metadata, choose Preferences from the panel menu, then check **Hide Empty Fields.**

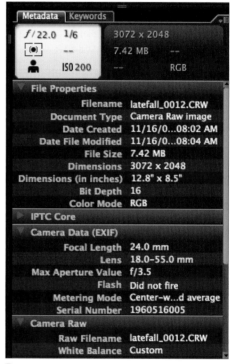

B Use the **Metadata** panel to view detailed information about the currently selected thumbnail.

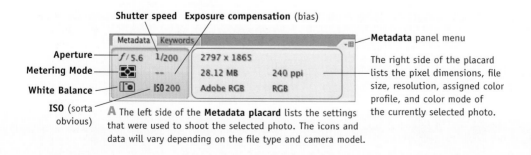

Shutter speed   Exposure compensation (bias)

Aperture
Metering Mode
White Balance
ISO (sorta obvious)

Metadata panel menu

The right side of the placard lists the pixel dimensions, file size, resolution, assigned color profile, and color mode of the currently selected photo.

A The left side of the **Metadata placard** lists the settings that were used to shoot the selected photo. The icons and data will vary depending on the file type and camera model.

Instead of repetitively entering user data for individual photos, you can put general information, such as contact (creator) information and a copyright notice, in a custom **metadata template** and then apply the template to multiple photos at once.

To create a metadata template:

1. Do either of the following:

   From the Metadata panel menu,▾▤ choose **Create Metadata Template.**

   Choose Tools > **Create Metadata Template.**

2. In the Create Metadata Template dialog,**A** enter a **Template Name.**

3. Click in the Creator, Copyright Notice, or other fields and enter general data that applies to the majority of your photos (you can press Tab to jump from field to field).

4. Click Save.

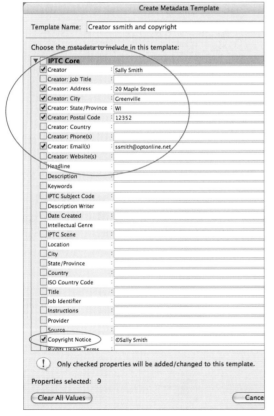

A In the **Create Metadata Template** dialog, enter the creator or copyright notice information that you want to apply to the majority of your photos.

The fastest way to **apply metadata** is via a **template.** (To assign additional data subsequently by using the Metadata panel, see the following page.)

To apply a metadata template:

1. Click, then Shift-click, consecutive thumbnails, or Ctrl-click/Cmd-click nonconsecutive thumbnails.

2. From the **Metadata** panel menu (or the Tools menu), do either of the following:

   Choose a template name from the **Append Metadata** submenu to add that metadata. Any existing metadata will be preserved.

   Choose a template name from the **Replace Metadata** submenu to add metadata to blank fields and replace existing metadata with the template metadata (this option removes data).

3. The Metadata panel will update to reflect the changes.

➤ You can also assign a metadata template in the Photo Downloader dialog (of course, you have to create the template first).

To edit a metadata template:

1. From the **Edit Metadata Template** submenu on the Metadata panel menu or Tools menu, choose the name of the template that you want to edit.

2. The Edit Metadata Template dialog opens, and it's exactly like the Create Metadata Template dialog. Edit the existing data or enter additional data, then click Save.

METADATA PANEL OR FILE INFO COMMAND?

We think the easiest way to embed user data is via the **Metadata** panel in Bridge, but if you prefer to use the File Info command, select a file or files, then choose File > **File Info.** On the left side of the dialog, click a category to display related entry fields, then enter data. Data entered in any of the four IPTC panels or Description panel will also be listed in the IPTC Core category in the Metadata panel. That is, data entered or edited in one location will update in the other.

Via the **IPTC* Core** category of the Metadata panel, you can embed user-created metadata into your files manually. For example, you can assign information pertaining to a specific photo shoot (such as the location, country, or description) or assign keywords to make your files easier to sort, run searches for, and filter out by category.

Before assigning any metadata manually, examine your photos, assign star and reject ratings to them, and apply a basic metadata template to all. Then you'll be ready, as per the following instructions, to assign Description and Keywords data to progressively smaller numbers of photos—a general category to the largest bunch, then narrower and more specific categories to smaller groups.

To add metadata to files manually:

1. Display and select multiple related photos.

2. In the **Metadata** panel, expand the **IPTC Core** category by clicking the arrowhead.

3. Click to the right of **Description**, then enter descriptive data about the selected photos.**A**

4. In the **Keywords** field, enter keywords, separated by commas, to help you identify, locate, and filter out your photos. Click in (or press Tab to get to) any other fields, and enter data.

5. To embed your data into the selected images, click the **Apply** button ☑ in the lower right corner of the panel.

➤ Any keywords that you enter in the Keywords field will also be listed separately in the Other Keywords category in the Keywords panel, and those keyword listings will be checked for the images you selected.

➤ You can control which fields display in the IPTC Core and other categories in the Metadata panel via Bridge Preferences > Metadata. To conserve space in the panel, keep the Hide Empty Fields option checked.

*_IPTC is an information standard that is used for transferring and publishing text and images._

A Enter user data in the **IPTC Core** category in the **Metadata** panel.

USING THE FILTER PANEL

Since keywords that are applied to an image display in the Keywords category on the Filter panel, you can filter the display of images by clicking specific keywords in that category.

Via the **Keywords** panel, you can create main-level keyword categories (such as events, people, places, things, themes, etc.), then create and assign nested subkeywords within those categories.

To create keywords:

1. To create a new main-level keyword category, in the Keywords panel, click the **New Keyword** button, ✚ then type a keyword.

2. To create a nested subkeyword, click a main level keyword (e.g., the one you just created), click the **New Sub Keyword** button, ⬕ then type a word. You can also create sub-subkeywords.

➤ You can move (drag) subkeywords into other main-level keyword categories.

To assign keywords:

1. Select one or more thumbnails. (A list of keywords that are already assigned to the selected images appears at the top of the panel.)

2. Check the box for one or more subkeywords.**A** (Although you can assign a main-level keyword, we don't see much use for doing so.)

➤ Read about the Keywords preferences on page 32.

➤ If you import an image that contains keywords, they'll appear in three locations: under Other Keywords in the Keywords panel, under Keywords in the Filter panel, and in File > File Info. To add an imported keyword as a permanent subkeyword to the Other Keywords list, select it, then right-click/Control-click and choose Persistent from the context menu.

A In the **Keywords** panel, create main-level keyword categories and subkeywords that pertain to the images you're working with, to help you search for, display, and identify them.

+--+
| **SHORTCUTS FOR THE KEYWORDS PANEL** |

Rename a main-level keyword or subkeyword	Click the word, choose Rename from the Keywords panel menu, then type a name (this won't change already embedded data)
Delete a main level keyword or subkeyword	Click the word, then click the Delete Keyword button 🗑 (this won't change already embedded data either)
Find a keyword or subkeyword	Type the word in the search field at the bottom of the panel

Searching for files

You can locate files in Bridge simply by checking the keywords under the Keywords category in
the Filter panel, or by entering criteria in the **Find**
dialog, such as the file name or specific keywords.

To find files via Bridge:

1. In Bridge, press **Ctrl-F/Cmd-F.** Or to start with
   a keyword as a search criterion, click a keyword
   on the Keywords panel, then choose **Find** from
   the panel menu. The Find dialog opens.**A**

2. From the **Look In** menu, choose a folder to be
   searched through. To select a folder that's not
   on the list, choose **Browse**, locate the desired
   folder, then click OK/Choose.

3. From the menus in the **Criteria** area, choose
   search criteria (e.g., file name, date created,
   label, rating, camera settings), choose a parame-
   ter from the adjoining menu, then enter data in
   that field. To include more criteria in the search,
   click ⊕, then choose or enter parameters.

4. From the **Match** menu, choose **If Any Criteria
   Are Met** to find files based on one or more
   criteria, or choose **If All Criteria Are Met** to
   narrow the selection to files that meet all the
   chosen criteria.

5. Check **Include All Subfolders** to search all
   subfolders within the folder you chose in step 2.

6. *Optional:* Check Include Non-indexed Files
   (May Be Slow) to search through files that

Bridge hasn't yet indexed (any folder Bridge has
yet to display). This will slow down the search.

7. Do either of the following:

   To copy the search results and send them to
   a **temporary** Search Results folder, click **Find.**
   The images will display in the Content panel,
   and the **Search Results** folder will appear on
   the Recent Folders list, which you can access
   from the Look In menu at the top of the Bridge
   window. Each time you perform a search and
   click Find, another generic Search Results listing
   will appear on the menu, with no hint as to its
   content (this can be confusing).

   To save a copy of the search results to a
   permanent file group, click **Save as Collection.**
   In the Save Collection dialog, enter a name,
   choose a location (preferably the current folder),
   then click Save; the files will display in the
   Content panel. Navigate to the folder you chose
   for the collection; a **Collect** icon will display in
   the Content panel.**B** Double-click the icon to
   rerun the search and view the search results.

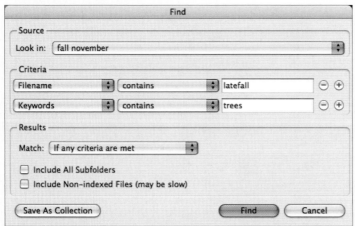

A Use the **Find** dialog to search for and locate files using various criteria.

B When you use the
Save as Collection
option, a **Collect**
icon appears in the
Content panel.

Choosing preferences for Bridge*

General Preferences (Ctrl-K/Cmd-K) A

Appearance

Choose a value between Black and White for the overall **User Interface Brightness** (for the side panes) and for the **Image Backdrop** (the background behind the Content and Preview panels).

Choose an **Accent Color** for highlighted items.

Behavior

Check **When a Camera Is Connected, Launch Adobe Photo Downloader** (Mac OS only) to make Photo Downloader the default system utility for acquiring photos.

Check **Double-click Edits Camera Raw Settings in Bridge** to have a raw file open automatically into Camera Raw (hosted by Bridge) when you double-click its thumbnail.

For **Number of Recent Items to Display**, enter the maximum number of folders (0–30) that can be listed at a time on the Look In menu in Bridge.

Favorite Items

Check which items and folders you want listed in the **Favorites** panel. (You can also add selected favorite files and folders via File > Add to Favorites.)

If you're using Bridge 2.0, you'll see fewer panels and options in this dialog.

Thumbnails Preferences B

Performance and File Handling

Note: To implement changes to the Performance and File Handling preferences, you must purge the folder cache (Tools > Cache submenu).

Check **Prefer Adobe Camera Raw for JPEG and TIFF Files** to have files in those formats open into Camera Raw when you select them and press Ctrl-R/Cmd-R.

For **When Creating Thumbnails Generate**, for the Preview panel, click whether you want Quick Thumbnails, High Quality Thumbnails, or Convert to High Quality [thumbnails] When Previewed.

For **Do Not Process Files Larger Than**, enter the maximum file size (the default is 400 MB) that you will permit Bridge to display as a thumbnail. Large files process slowly.

Details

For **Additional Lines of Thumbnail Metadata**, check which file information you want listed below each image thumbnail in the Content panel.

Check **Show Tooltips** to allow tool tips to display when you rest the pointer on Bridge features, including information about image thumbnails.

Continued on the following page

A **General** Preferences, in **Bridge**

B **Thumbnails** Preferences, in **Bridge**

Playback Preferences

Choose options to control whether audio and video files will play and/or loop when previewed via the Preview panel. The Stack Playback Frame Rate controls the speed at which a group of 10 or more thumbnails is viewed (when you click the play button).

Metadata Preferences

Check which metadata categories you want displayed in the Metadata panel.

Keywords Preferences

Automatically Apply Parent Keywords

With this option on, checking a box for a sub-keyword also applies the main-level keyword, and to apply just the subkeyword, you would have to Shift-click it. We keep this option off.

Write, Read Hierarchical Keywords

Tell Bridge what punctuation was used to separate keywords in files that you've exported or imported.

Labels Preferences

Check whether to **Require the Control/Command Key** [to be pressed] **to Apply Labels and Ratings** to selected file thumbnails. You can change the label names here, too, but not the colors.

File Type Associations Preferences

These settings tell Bridge which application to use when opening files of each type. Don't change these settings unless you know what you're doing!

Cache Preferences

Check **Automatically Export Caches to Folders When Possible** to have Bridge export the cache for image thumbnails to the folders the images are stored in.

Click **Choose** to specify a new location for the central database.

Click **Purge Cache** to purge all thumbnail caches from the central database to free up space or if you encounter thumbnail display problems.

Inspector Preferences

Select items for display in the Inspector panel in Version Cue, which lists information about Version Cue projects.

Startup Scripts Preferences

Depending on your workflow, check only the scripts that you need to have run automatically when you launch Bridge; or if you're using the Adobe Creative Suite, keep the first 11 scripts checked. Relaunch Bridge to implement any changes.

Advanced Preferences

Note: Changes to the Advanced Preferences take effect upon relaunch.

Miscellaneous

Check **Use Software Rendering** to turn off hardware acceleration for the Preview panel or Slideshow only if the previews aren't display-ing properly or your slideshows aren't playing smoothly.

Check **Use High-Quality Previews** to enable high-quality previews to display in the Preview panel and in Slideshow mode (in case you didn't check the High Quality Thumbnails option in the Thumbnails panel). In our testing, this setting didn't make a difference.

International

Choose a **Language** for the Bridge interface and for the **Keyboard.**

GET REAL...

To learn more about Bridge and Camera Raw, we recommend *Real World Camera Raw with Adobe Photoshop CS3,* by the late, brilliant Bruce Fraser and by Jeff Schewe, published by Peachpit Press.

RESETTING BRIDGE PREFERENCES

If you need to reset the Bridge preferences, exit/quit the application. Hold down Alt/Option, then double-click the application icon. In the alert, check **Reset Preferences,** then click OK.

The Adobe Camera Raw plug-in lets you apply powerful correction commands to photos before opening them in Photoshop, and is a digital darkroom in and of itself. Learning how to use this plug-in is essential if you want to maximize the potential of your digital photos. In this chapter, you'll choose Camera Raw preferences; correct white balance, exposure, contrast, and luminance problems; apply split toning; sharpen, crop, straighten, and retouch; blend dual exposures; process multiple photos; import photos as Smart Objects; and more!

Why use Adobe Camera Raw?

Advanced amateur and pro digital SLR cameras let you capture photos as raw files, which has many advantages over capturing photos in the JPEG or TIFF format. For JPEG and TIFF, the camera applies internal processing to the original pixels, such as sharpening, white balance, and color adjustments. With raw files, you get only the raw data that the camera captured onto its digital sensor, so you have full control over subsequent image correction. Raw files must be converted by the Camera Raw plug-in before they can be opened and edited in Photoshop. Camera Raw can process raw files from most of the current camera manufacturers, as well as JPEG and TIFF files.

With Camera Raw, you not only get a converter, you also get a powerful adjustment tool. Camera Raw adjustments (e.g., exposure, white balance, hue/saturation, noise reduction) are less destructive than similar commands in Photoshop, so more of the original pixel data in your photos is preserved. Furthermore, many Camera Raw features, such as the sharpening controls, produce better results and are easier to use.

The Camera Raw conversion redistributes tonal values from the highlight areas of the tonal range (which contain an abundance of pixel data) to the shadow areas (which usually contain insufficient pixel data). This helps prevent posterization and a loss of detail in the shadow areas that may result when you apply tonal adjustments in Photoshop.

Camera Raw edits made to raw files are stored as a series of instructions, which in turn are saved in either a sidecar file or in the Camera Raw database, whereas instructions for edits made to JPEG and TIFF files are saved in the file itself. Regardless of the file

Continued on the following page

Note: Settings listed in the captions in this chapter were chosen for photos that are approximately 3000 x 2000 pixels.

CAMERA RAW

3

IN THIS CHAPTER

type, when you open a photo from Camera Raw into Photoshop, the instructions are applied to a copy of the file, and the original digital file is left intact. This is one of the key advantages to using the Camera Raw plug-in: No matter what type of corrections you perform, like a traditional film negative, the original capture file is preserved. You can reopen a photo into Camera Raw and modify or remove any of your corrections at any time.

Although the instructions in this chapter apply to raw and JPEG files, if your camera has the capability to shoot raw files, we suggest that you choose that option. Regardless of your format choice, however, we recommend that you process your photos and apply tonal and color corrections in Camera Raw before opening them in Photoshop. (A third file format option, camera-generated TIFF files, are as large as raw files and have none of the advantages of raw files.)

Choosing preferences for Camera Raw

Although the Camera Raw interface is well designed, the preference settings that govern which file types open in Camera Raw—only raw files or raw, JPEG, and TIFF files—and which program is hosting Camera Raw (Photoshop or Bridge) are downright confusing. To simplify your workflow, we suggest that you let all your images open automatically into Camera Raw from Bridge. To establish the necessary preferences for this to occur, follow the steps below:

To choose preferences for opening files:

1. In Photoshop, press Ctrl-K/Cmd-K to open the Preferences dialog, then click **File Handling** on the list of categories on the left side. Under File Compatibility, uncheck **Prefer Adobe Camera Raw for JPEG Files** and **Prefer Adobe Camera Raw for Supported Raw Files**.

2. In Bridge, press Ctrl-K/Cmd-K to open the Preferences dialog, click **Thumbnails** on the list of categories, then check **Prefer Adobe Camera Raw for JPEG and TIFF Files**. Also click the **General** category and check **Double-Click Edits Camera Raw Settings in Bridge**.

   Note: To open a JPEG or TIFF file directly into Photoshop (and bypass the Camera Raw plug-in), select the thumbnail, then press Ctrl-O/Cmd-O.

CAMERA RAW, LIGHTROOM, OR PHOTOSHOP?

The Camera Raw sliders and options are virtually identical to those in the Develop module in the Adobe Photoshop Lightroom application (the interfaces are similar, too). Both programs preserve the original digital files when you apply corrections. If you work with a large volume of photos and need the file management power of Lightroom, you could conceivably perform all of your file management and correction work in that program instead of in Camera Raw. You can base your decision to use Camera Raw or Lightroom on how many and what kind of adjustments you usually apply to your photos. If you want to edit the photos in Photoshop, it makes sense to apply your initial corrections in Camera Raw.

► Note that Camera Raw and Lightroom work only on one-layer photos, and corrections (other than those made with the Retouch tool) affect the whole layer. In Photoshop, you can put imagery on multiple layers and selectively edit portions of any layer.

STAY CURRENT

Of the many proprietary raw "formats," some are unique to a particular manufacturer (such as Nikon or Canon) and some are unique to a particular camera model. To verify that you're using all the latest **interpreters** for the raw formats that Camera Raw supports, periodically visit **www.adobe.com** and download any Camera Raw updates that are available for your camera.

To choose preferences for the Camera Raw plug-in:

1. In Bridge, choose Edit (Bridge CS3, in the Mac OS) > **Camera Raw Preferences.** Or if the Camera Raw dialog is open, click the **Open Preferences** dialog button ≡ at the top of the dialog (Ctrl-K/Cmd-K). The Camera Raw Preferences dialog opens.**A**

2. In the **General** area, choose a **Save Image Settings In** option. We recommend choosing **Sidebar ".xmp" Files** (this won't increase the file size significantly). Leave the **Apply Sharpening To** setting as **All Images,** to permit Camera Raw to sharpen your photos.

3. Choose **Default Image Settings.** We suggest leaving Apply Auto Tone Adjustments unchecked, as this option would give Camera Raw the go-ahead to apply its Auto settings to your photos automatically.

Also leave the two "Make Defaults" options unchecked unless you use more than one camera body of the same model or want the default settings to be used for a specific ISO setting.

4. The **Camera Raw Cache** holds the thumbnail and preview data. Leave this on the default setting (1.0 GB) unless you're blessed with a lot of extra space on your hard disk.

5. For **DNG File Handling,** we recommend checking both options. The first allows metadata to be written into your DNG files, and the second causes the previews to update automatically when edits are made in Camera Raw.

6. Check both **JPEG and TIFF Handling** options if you use both Lightroom and Camera Raw and you want the adjustments you apply to your photos to be readable by both programs.

7. Click OK.

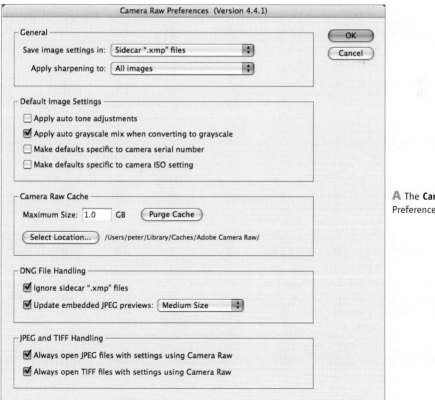

A The **Camera Raw** Preferences dialog

Opening files into Camera Raw

On this page, you'll learn how to **open** a **file** into the **Camera Raw** dialog (**A**, next page). Elsewhere in this chapter you'll apply corrections using basic and specialized adjustment tabs (**B**, next page) and a few of the Camera Raw tools (**C**, next page).

Note: To open multiple files into Camera Raw for viewing and rating, and possibly to synchronize their settings, see pages 62–63.

To open a digital photo into the Camera Raw plug-in:

1. In **Bridge**, locate the raw or JPEG file that you want to open. Each digital camera manufacturer attaches a unique extension to its raw files, such as .nef for Nikon, .crw or .cr2 for Canon, and .dcr for Kodak. If a photo has been opened and edited previously in Camera Raw, it will have a badge ⬆ above its thumbnail. **Double-click** the thumbnail to open the file into Camera Raw.

2. The Camera Raw dialog opens. Information about your photo (taken from the metadata the camera attached to the photo) is listed in the following locations: the camera model in the title bar at the top of the dialog, the file name below the preview, and the camera settings that were used to take the photo (aperture, shutter speed, ISO sensitivity, and focal length) below the histogram on the right side.

   The underlined color space/bit depth/dimensions/resolution link below the preview gets you to the Workflow Options dialog.

   To correct the photo, you'll work your way through some or all of the eight tabs: Basic, Tone Curve, Detail, HSL/Grayscale, Split Toning, Lens Corrections, Camera Calibration, and Presets. We'll step you through most of the tabs in this chapter. Once you're satisfied with how the photo looks, you'll click Open. Camera Raw will convert and open a copy of the image into Photoshop using your chosen settings, without altering the original data.

Now that you've opened a photo into Camera Raw, you can **magnify** it to get a closer look and/or move it around in the preview window.

To use the zoom features in Camera Raw:

1. Do any of the following:

   Choose the **Zoom** tool 🔍 (Z), then click the preview to zoom in or Alt-click/Option-click to zoom out.

   Below the image preview, click the – or + zoom level button, or from the **Zoom Level** menu, choose a preset zoom percentage.

   Press **Ctrl–/Cmd–**(hyphen) to zoom out or **Ctrl-+/Cmd-+** to zoom in.

   To change the zoom level to **100%**, double-click the **Zoom** tool; or to change the zoom level to **Fit in View**, double-click the **Hand** tool.

2. When the image preview is magnified, you can use the **Hand** tool (H) 🖐 to move it in the preview window. (With another tool chosen, you can hold down Spacebar for a temporary Hand tool.)

The Camera Raw interface

A THE CAMERA RAW DIALOG

Camera model

Toggle between **Full-Screen mode** and the previous dialog size

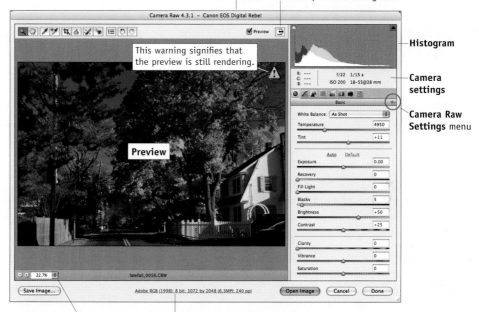

This warning signifies that the preview is still rendering.

Preview

Histogram

Camera settings

Camera Raw Settings menu

Zoom controls

Click to open the **Workflow Options** dialog (see page 38).

B THE CAMERA RAW TABS

Tone Curve   HSL/Grayscale   Lens Corrections   Presets

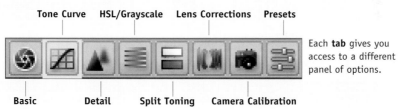

Each **tab** gives you access to a different panel of options.

Basic   Detail   Split Toning   Camera Calibration

C THE CAMERA RAW TOOLS

Hand: Moves a magnified preview in the window

Color Sampler: Places up to 9 RGB color sampler points in the preview

Straighten: Straightens the photo along a line you drag

Red Eye Removal: Corrects red-eye in portrait photos

Rotate Counterclockwise: Rotates the photo 90° counterclockwise

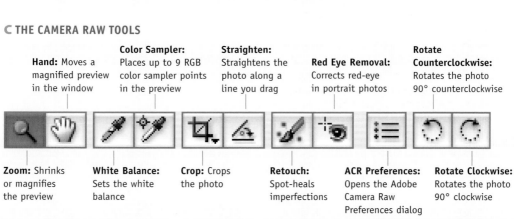

Zoom: Shrinks or magnifies the preview

White Balance: Sets the white balance

Crop: Crops the photo

Retouch: Spot-heals imperfections

ACR Preferences: Opens the Adobe Camera Raw Preferences dialog

Rotate Clockwise: Rotates the photo 90° clockwise

Choosing workflow options

Via the **Workflow Options** dialog, you can establish a default color space, bit depth (number of bits per channel), dimensions, and resolution for your photos before opening them into Photoshop—without altering the original digital files.

To choose default workflow options:

1. With a photo open in the Camera Raw dialog, click the underlined link below the preview that lists the color space, file dimensions, etc. The **Workflow Options** dialog opens. **A**

2. From the **Space** menu, choose the color profile to be used for converting the raw file to RGB: Adobe RGB (1998), ColorMatch RGB, ProPhoto RGB, or sRGB IEC61966-1 ("sRGB," for short). If you followed our instructions in Chapter 1, you assigned Adobe RGB as the default color space for color management, and we recommend that you choose that option here, too.

3. From the **Depth** menu, choose a color depth of 8 Bits/Channel or 16 Bits/Channel (see page 77). Note: If you have a large hard drive and a fast system with a lot of RAM, you can more easily work with 16 Bits/Channel images. With the extra pixels, more of the original tonal levels will be preserved as you edit the photo in Photoshop.

4. If you want to resize the photo to a preset size (in megapixels, or MP), choose from the **Size** menu. If a crop marquee is present, the crop size will be listed as the default image size (the size without a – or +). If you choose a larger size than the original, the image will be resampled. To help prevent pixelization, avoid choosing the largest size.

   ➤ Experts currently disagree on whether Camera Raw or Photoshop does a better job of resampling. Until they reach a consensus, you can take your pick.

5. Enter a **Resolution** (e.g., for an image that is 2000 x 3000 pixels or larger and is to be printed on an inkjet printer or a commercial press, enter a resolution between 240 and 300). This value affects only the print output size of the file.

6. Click OK. The new workflow information will be listed below the preview and will be applied to the current photo and to all future photos that you open into Camera Raw.

   ➤ To have all future photos open from Camera Raw into Photoshop as Smart Objects when you click Open Object, check Open in Photoshop as Smart Objects in the Workflow Options dialog (see page 66). We keep this option off.

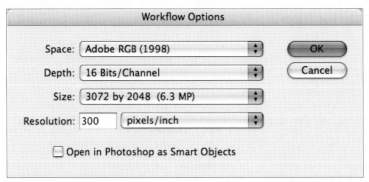

A Use the **Workflow Options** dialog to assign color space, bit depth, dimensions, and resolution settings to the current photo, and to establish new default settings.

Cropping and straightening photos

Among the qualities that great photos have in common are interesting subject matter, a winning composition, sharp focus in the key details, and proper exposure and lighting to create the right mood. The controls discussed on this page—**cropping** and **straightening** in Camera Raw—afford a chance to make improvements if you didn't compose a shot perfectly before clicking the shutter.

After opening a photo in Camera Raw, the next step (before applying any adjustments) is to decide whether it needs cropping, and to straighten it out if it's askew. By stripping away nonessential areas, you can eliminate distracting features, create an intimate close-up, or draw the viewer's attention to a key area. With the Crop tool in Camera Raw, you can control which part of a photo opens into Photoshop. (But fear not: Whether cropped or not, all the original raw pixels will be preserved.)

To marquee a photo for cropping:

1. Choose the **Crop** tool (C). 🔁
2. Do either of the following:

   Drag a marquee in the preview window.

   To create a marquee based on a fixed proportion, from the Crop tool menu or the context menu, choose a **preset** (or choose Custom and enter values), then drag in the preview window. (To turn this tool behavior off, choose Normal.)

3. *Optional:* To move the crop marquee, drag inside it; or to resize it, drag a handle.

   Note: Only the area within the marquee will import into Photoshop.

To remove a crop marquee:

1. Choose the **Crop** tool (C). 🔁
2. Press **Esc**, or choose **Clear Crop** from the Crop tool menu or from the context menu. You can even reopen the photo and undo the crop (Photoshop doesn't offer this editability).

To straighten a crooked photo:

1. Choose the **Straighten** tool (A). 🔼
2. Drag across the preview, along an edge in the image that you want to align to the horizontal or vertical axis. **A** A crop marquee will appear, aligned to the angle you drew. **B** When you open the image in Photoshop, that edge will be aligned with the document window. **C**

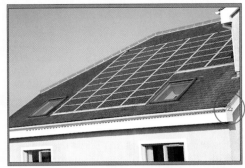

A With the **Straighten** tool, drag along an edge that you want to align to the horizontal or vertical axis.

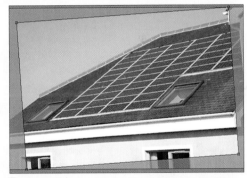

B A crop marquee appears, based on the angle drawn.

C The **straightened** image is opened into Photoshop.

TIPS FOR CROPPING PHOTOS

➤ To change a horizontal crop of a fixed size to a vertical crop of the same fixed size, drag a handle across the center of the crop marquee.

➤ A preset choice of 2 to 3 for the Crop tool has the same proportions as a 4˝ by 6˝ image; 4 to 5 is the same as an 8˝ by 10˝, etc.

Correcting the white balance

With cropping out of the way (pun intended), it's time to study the photo, diagnose its deficiencies and weaknesses, and decide which Camera Raw options are best suited to fix them. Look for and correct the broadest problems first, such as under- or overexposure. A good exposure correction will enhance the details in both the shadow and high-light areas and light up the key details in the com-position. Another common problem, a color cast, can be corrected via the temperature controls.

The **Basic** tab is the best place to begin making corrections (it's in the first slot for good reason). For the first round of adjustments, we recommend using the sliders in the order they appear.

To apply white balance adjustments:

1. Click the **Basic** tab 🎛 and double-click the Hand tool to make Fit in View the zoom level for the preview.

2. To see the effect of one of the preset tempera-ture settings, from the **White Balance** menu, choose a preset that best describes the lighting conditions under which the photo was taken (**A–C**, next page). The presets are available only for raw files.

3. When you're done exploring the presets, restore the original camera settings by choosing **As Shot** from the White Balance menu.

4. Use the **Temperature** slider **A–C** to add blue or yellow (make the photo look cooler or warmer). This adjustment is a relatively subjective pro-cess. If it's an outdoor shot, consider the time of day: A sunset shot will naturally have a warm tone, whereas a scene shot at midday will more likely have a neutral, blue-gray tonality. An interior shot could be warm, cool, or neutral, depending on the light source. Portraits need the most careful adjustment, to make sure the skin tones look natural.

➤ Although the white balance can be adjusted based on a sampled area (by clicking the White Balance tool 🖊 on a grayish-white area that contains some details), deciding which area to click on can be tricky, so we prefer to use the Temperature and Tint sliders instead.

➤ If your photo is very underexposed, fix the exposure first by using the Exposure slider (see page 42) and then adjust the white balance.

A Lowering the **Temperature** setting made the image look overly **cool** (note the blue cast on the white surfaces and in the highlight areas).

B Raising the **Temperature** made the image look too **warm** (the chocolates look too yellowish).

C The **As Shot** setting on the **White Balance** menu produced the best warm/cool balance.

ADJUSTING THE WHITE BALANCE

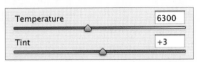

A This photo is underexposed and the clouds have a slightly greenish cast; the As Shot settings are shown above. We'll correct the white balance first and then the exposure. But rather than changing the Temperature, we'll let a white balance preset do the work for us.

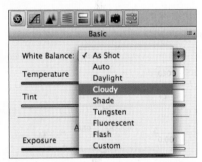

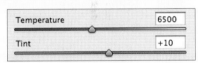

B Since the light conditions were affected by the cloudy sky, we chose the **Cloudy** preset from the **White Balance** menu. The higher Temperature and Tint values in this preset removed the greenish cast.

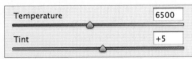

C The Cloudy preset added a slight reddish cast to the clouds, which we corrected by lowering the **Tint** value.

Correcting the exposure

To demonstrate how to correct common exposure problems via the **Basic** tab, we'll use two photos, one **underexposed**, the other **overexposed.**

To correct an underexposed photo:

1. Open an underexposed photo into Camera Raw, then click the **Basic** tab.🌑 The sliders are set automatically to the default values for your camera model (the word "Default" is dimmed).

   ➤ To see which slider adjustments Camera Raw recommends, click Auto; then before proceeding, reset the sliders to their default settings by clicking Default.

2. Study the **histogram** to see how much the shadow pixels are being clipped (clustered at the left edge). Unless the subject matter happens to be very dark or light, there should be a fairly uniform distribution of pixels from left to right in the histogram. The goal is to redistribute pixels to conform to the Adobe RGB color space, which you're using for color management.

3. Turn the clipping warnings on to view a representation of any shadow or highlight clipping in the preview:

   In the top left corner of the histogram, click the **Shadow Clipping Warning** button (U). Clipped shadows are represented by blue areas. **A**

   And in the top right corner, click the **Highlight Clipping Warning** button (O). Clipped highlights are represented by red areas.

4. To lessen the clipping of shadow pixels, do the following:

   To lighten the photo and recover detail in the midtones, increase the **Exposure** value (**A–B**, next page). A value change of plus or minus 1 is equivalent to widening or reducing a camera aperture by one full f-stop.

   To recover shadow details, use the Fill Light and Blacks sliders as a twosome. Move the **Fill Light** slider a third of the way to the right and the **Blacks** slider to the left, until only a trace remains of the blue shadow clipping color.

5. Increase the **Brightness** to lighten and restore detail to the midtones. If you also want to decrease the contrast and reduce the intensity of the shadows, reduce the **Contrast** slightly (**C**, next page).

6. Set the **Vibrance** to around +10 to increase the color saturation slightly. This feature doesn't cause oversaturation. We've found that most of our photos benefit from a Vibrance adjustment of around +10 to +15.

DRAG OR SCRUB

To change a setting in a Camera Raw tab, you can either drag the slider **manually** (to the left to reduce the value or to the right to increase it) or use the **scrubby** slider.

PREVIEW ON, PREVIEW OFF

Check **Preview** (P) to preview the collective changes from all the tabs; uncheck it to preview changes from all the tabs except the current one.

TOGGLE THE ORIGINAL/CURRENT SETTINGS

➤ To reapply all the built-in defaults for the current camera model, from the Camera Raw Settings menu, choose **Camera Raw Defaults**; then, to reapply the settings that were chosen during the current editing session and assess your editing progress, choose **Custom Settings**.

➤ Double-click a slider in any tab to restore the default setting for that **slider**. Press Ctrl-Z/Cmd-Z to reinstate the last slider position.

Shadow Clipping
Warning button

Highlight Clipping
Warning button

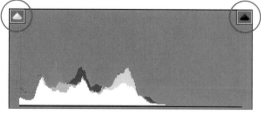

A Click either or both of the **Clipping Warning** buttons above the histogram (a white frame around a button indicates that the warning is on). This is the histogram for the original photo that is shown in **A** on the next page. Most of the pixels are clustered to the left side of the graph, which signifies that the photo is underexposed.

CORRECTING UNDEREXPOSURE

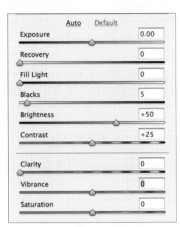

A To correct this underexposed photo, we'll use the sliders in the **Basic** tab.

B A new **Exposure** setting (shown above) lightened the entire photo, and a new **Fill Light** setting lightened the shadows and darker midtones. The blue clipping warning disappeared, proving that our adjustments corrected the shadow clipping.

C Next we raised the **Brightness** to lighten the midtones, increased the **Contrast**, and increased the **Clarity** to darken the edges of shapes. Finally, we raised **Vibrance** to boost the color saturation. (To lighten the photo even more, we'll use the Tone Curve tab, as shown on pages 46–47.)

To correct an overexposed photo:

1. Open an overexposed photo into Camera Raw,**A** then click the **Basic** tab.

2. The **histogram** shows that the highlight pixels are clustered at the right edge (are being clipped).**B**

3. To display possible shadow or highlight clipping, click the **Shadow Clipping Warning** (U) and **Highlight Clipping Warning** (O) buttons.

4. To minimize the clipping of highlight pixels, do either of the following:

   To darken the photo and recover details in the highlights, reduce the **Exposure** and increase the **Recovery** until you see less of the red highlight warning color.

   Alt-drag/Option-drag the **Exposure** and/or **Recovery** slider and release the mouse when tiny areas of white (representing all three color channels) display on a black background **C** (and **A**, next page).

You can also Alt-drag/Option-drag the **Blacks** slider to display a clipping preview against a white background, and release the mouse when tiny areas of black display. Color areas, if any, represent clipping in those channels.

5. If you need to darken and restore details in the lighter midtones, reduce the **Brightness** slightly (**B**, next page).

6. Finally, to adjust the color intensity and contrast in the photo, work with the **Contrast**, **Clarity**, and **Vibrance** sliders as a trio. If you want to strengthen the contrast, increase the Contrast setting; and to darken the edges of shapes and restore contrast to the midtones, increase the Clarity setting slightly. Or to soften the contrast (particularly in the midtones), reduce the Contrast; then increase the Clarity until the edges of the shapes are darkened sufficiently (**C**, next page).

   For either scenario, also adjust the **Vibrance** to boost the color saturation, to add some zing.

A This photograph is **overexposed**.

B In this Camera Raw **histogram** for the overexposed photo shown above, pixels are clustered at the right edge, which is an indication of highlight clipping.

C In the **Basic** tab, we Alt/Option dragged the **Recovery** slider until only a few white highlight areas remained in the clipping preview.

A We lowered the **Exposure** setting and readjusted the **Recovery** setting to darken the entire photo and recover detail in the highlights. These corrections overdarkened the midtones, however, so we'll remedy that next.

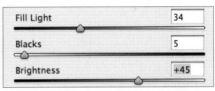

B Increasing the **Fill Light** setting lightened the shadows and darker midtones (note that the shadows in the trees and at the far side of the pool are now lighter). We also reduced the **Brightness** slightly to recover more detail in the highlights and lighter midtones.

C Finally, we reduced the **Contrast** to further lighten the midtones, increased the **Clarity** to sharpen the edges, and increased the **Vibrance** to restore some color saturation.

Using the Tone Curve tab

After using the Basic tab, **A** the next step is to tweak the adjustments in specific tonal ranges. In the **Tone Curve** tab (unlike in the Basic tab), you can adjust the brightness of the highlights or the lighter or darker midtones individually.

To adjust the curve, you could place points manually (as you would in the Curves dialog), but we prefer to use the Parametric sliders—one for each of the four tonal ranges. We'd rather move sliders than spend time trying to guess which part of the curve to bend. Plus, the results are more fail-safe, because you can't misshape the curve, which creates posterization.

To make targeted adjustments using the Parametric sliders:

1. Click the **Tone Curve** tab, 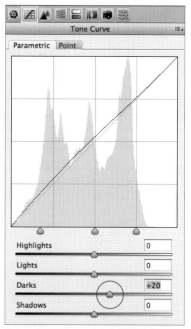 then click the nested **Parametric** tab. Behind the curve is a static image of the current histogram. **B**

2. Increase the value for the **Highlights, Lights, Darks, C** or **Shadows** to lighten that tonal range (and thereby raise the corresponding part of the curve above the diagonal line); or reduce the value to darken that tonal range (and thereby lower that part of the curve below the diagonal line) (**A–B**, next page).

A This photo was adjusted by using the **Basic** tab (see pages 42–43).

C The **Darks** adjustment in the **Tone Curve** tab produced this change.

B By using the sliders in the **Tone Curve** tab (nested **Parametric** tab), you can fine-tune the exposure without throwing off the tonal balance that you achieved via the Basic tab. For our photo, we increased the **Darks** setting to lighten and restore detail to the lower midtones (the background behind the flowers).

3. *Optional:* To expand or contract the tonal range that a slider adjustment affects, move the corresponding region control, located below the graph. The left region control affects the Shadows, the middle control affects the Lights and Darks, and the right control affects the Highlights. C–D The more a control bends the curve away from the diagonal line, the more adjacent tonal ranges are affected; the closer the curve gets to the diagonal, the less adjacent ranges are affected.

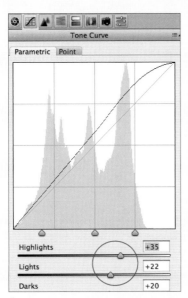

A Increasing the **Lights** and **Highlights** raised the upper part of the curve.

B The **Lights** and **Highlights** adjustment lightened the flowers without diminishing the details in those areas. The contrast between the sunlit and darker areas was preserved as the tonal distribution was improved.

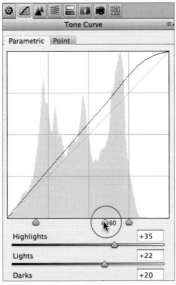

C Moving the **middle region control** to the right lowered the middle of the curve and narrowed the range and impact of the Lights slider.

D Just to demonstrate how the region controls work, we moved the **middle region control** to the right; this decreased the contrast slightly in the lighter midtones.

Reviving color

If your photo has decent contrast but the colors are undersaturated and dull, make a few basic exposure corrections via the Basic tab and then try using the controls in the **HSL/Grayscale** tab to brighten it. By improving the color, you'll also improve the contrast. (If you were to use only the Basic tab sliders to correct the color, the photo would probably end up looking washed out.)

To increase color saturation and luminance:

1. Open an undersaturated photo into Camera Raw.**A**

2. To brighten the midtones by lightening them, do either of the following:

   In the **Tone Curve** tab, ▨ **Parametric** nested tab, increase the **Lights** and/or **Darks** setting.**B**

   In the **Basic** tab, ◉ increase the **Brightness** setting.

3. In the **Basic** tab, do any of the following:

   If it's hard to distinguish individual colors in the shadows or lower midtones, increase the **Fill Light** value.

   Reduce the **Contrast** setting slightly (too much contrast would darken the color), and to make the colors richer, set the **Vibrance** to around +20.

4. Go to the **HSL/Grayscale** tab, ▤ then use the sliders in the nested **Saturation** tab to boost the saturation of individual colors (**A–B**, next page), and in the **Luminance** tab to increase their brightness (**C–D**, next page).

   Note: The default Brightness and Contrast settings for a raw photo are +50 and +25, respectively; for a JPEG photo, the default setting for both sliders is 0.

REVIVING LANDSCAPE COLORS

In a landscape photo, use the **Oranges**, **Yellows**, and **Blues** sliders to rebalance the color intensity, reducing the brightness of the sky and enriching the color in the midtones and highlights. Lowering the Blues luminance has an effect similar to shooting a sky with a polarizing filter.

REVIVING COLOR IN A LANDSCAPE

A The colors in this photo look dull and undersaturated.

B In the **Tone Curve** tab, we set the **Lights** value to +28 to lighten and brighten the colors in just the upper midtones, taking care not to overlighten the sky.

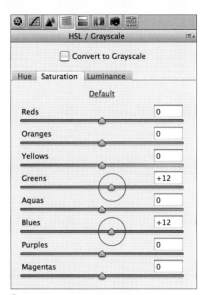

A In the nested **Saturation** tab of the **HSL/Grayscale** tab, we increased the saturation of the **Greens** and **Blues**.

B The blue sky and the green foliage now look a bit brighter, but the colors still need a further boost.

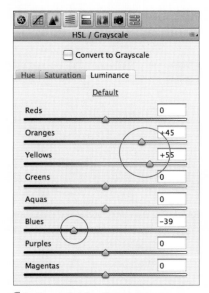

C In the nested **Luminance** tab, we increased the luminance (lightness) for the **Oranges** and **Yellows** but lowered it for the **Blues**.

D Now the darker blue sky is complemented by the richer colors in the lower half of the photo, and both provide a good contrast to the white clouds, white bark on the tree, and white trim on the houses.

Using the Detail tab

With the basic adjustments completed, you can now explore some of the more specialized features in Camera Raw, such as those in the Detail, Split Toning, and Lens Corrections tabs.

We think highly of the **sharpening** controls in the **Detail** tab of Camera Raw because they're very powerful yet easy to work with. And, of course, as with all Camera Raw adjustments, you can change the settings or undo the sharpening at any time without altering the original pixel data.

Note: The "capture" sharpening that you apply via Camera Raw shouldn't be your only round of sharpening. After editing and resizing your document in Photoshop—and before printing—you should apply another round of sharpening by using the Smart Sharpen or Unsharp Mask filter.

To sharpen a photo via the Detail tab:

1. Click the **Detail** tab, ▲ and choose a zoom level of 100% to help you assess the effects of your sharpening adjustments in the preview.

2. If the words "Preview Only" display in the Detail tab, go to Camera Raw Preferences and choose **Apply Sharpening To: All Images.**

3. With the **Hand** tool (H), drag an area of detail to be monitored into view in the preview (press the Spacebar for a temporary Hand tool).

4. For subject matter that needs a lot of sharpening, such as hard objects or architecture, set the **Amount** to 100;**A–B** if less sharpening is needed, try a value of around 50–60. For a portrait, keep the Amount between 50 and 70.

A We'll apply sharpening to enhance the detailed surfaces and clearly defined shapes in this photo of a vintage windmill.

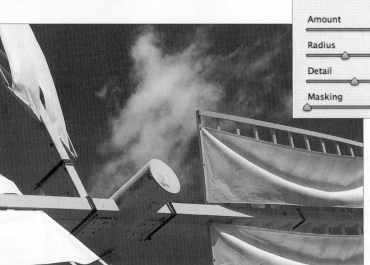

B Our first step was to zoom in to 100% view, then Alt-drag/Option-drag the **Amount** slider to 100 to set the strength of the sharpening.

➤ To judge a sharpening setting in a mono-chromatic grayscale preview without the distraction of color, Alt-drag/Option-drag a slider.

5. The **Radius** controls how many pixels surrounding the edges will be modified; keep this setting between 1 and 1.4.

6. Alt-drag/Option-drag the **Detail** slider until the grayscale preview displays the amount of edge detail that you want to revive in moderate to

high-contrast areas.**A** At a low setting (25–50), only high-contrast areas will be affected, whereas at a high setting (50 or higher), most areas will be affected.

7. To limit the sharpening to just high-contrast edges, Alt-drag/Option-drag the **Masking** slider to the right until the black-and-white preview displays areas of black (low-contrast areas that won't be sharpened) and white lines along the edges of shapes (areas of contrast).**B** As you

Continued on the following page

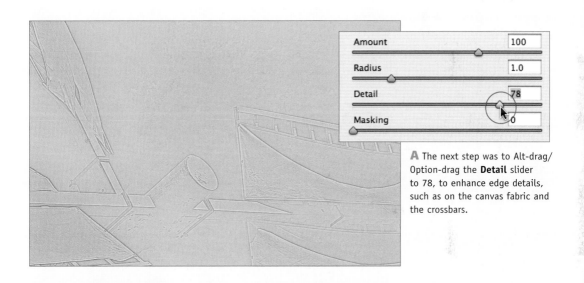

A The next step was to Alt-drag/Option-drag the **Detail** slider to 78, to enhance edge details, such as on the canvas fabric and the crossbars.

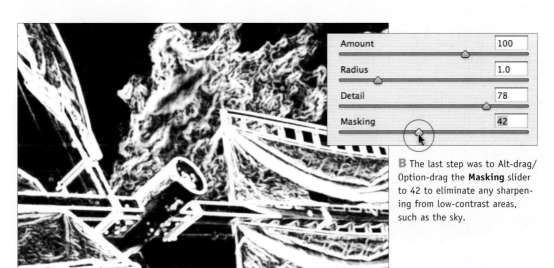

B The last step was to Alt-drag/Option-drag the **Masking** slider to 42 to eliminate any sharpening from low-contrast areas, such as the sky.

drag the slider to the right, areas of black will increase in the display and areas of white will be limited to only high-contrast edges. **A–B**

➤ Try not to oversharpen your photo. Sharpen it only to the point where crisp edges start to become evident at 100% view. Remember, this is just the first round of sharpening; you'll apply stronger sharpening, more selectively, in Photoshop.

➤ Until now, limiting sharpening to just the edges of shapes required performing multiple steps in Photoshop. By using the Masking slider in Camera Raw and the visual feedback it provides, you can apply sharpening where needed without sharpening areas of low contrast or areas that have artifacts or stray pixels (noise).

➤ To learn how to use the Luminance and Color sliders in the Detail tab to reduce color and luminance noise, see our *Visual QuickStart Guide* to Photoshop.

A This is the unsharpened photo.

B And this is the same photo after using the **sharpening** controls in the **Detail** tab.

Using the Split Toning tab

The **Split Toning** tab lets you reduce an image to grayscale and apply one or more color tints ("tones") to make it look richer and more luminous, or to give it an aged quality. You can apply one tint to the highlight areas and a different one to the shadow areas. In our testing, this technique works well on photos of metallic objects or images that have subdued color.**A**

To convert a photo to grayscale and apply a color tint:

1. After adjusting the exposure in the image, click the **HSL/Grayscale** tab, ▦ then check **Convert to Grayscale**.

2. Click the **Split Toning** tab.▬

3. Move both **Saturation** sliders about halfway across the bar to make it easier to judge the colors you'll apply in the next step (this is just a temporary change).

4. Move the **Highlights Hue** slider to tint the highlights **B** and/or the **Shadows Hue** slider to tint the shadows.

5. Readjust the **Saturation** for each hue. Avoid oversaturating the highlights, or the coloring effect will be too pronounced.

6. *Optional:* Reduce the **Balance** setting to apply more of the Shadows tint to the entire photo, or increase it to apply more of the Highlights tint to the entire photo.**C–D**

A We think the elegant geometric shapes and linear details in this photo of an antique car will stand out more if the dark colors are tinted with the same hue; we'll do this via the **HSL/Grayscale** tab.

B We tinted the **Highlights** with blue first.

C Then we tinted the **Shadows** with brown. Finally, an adjustment to the **Balance** setting to favor the shadow color more lends the photo an antique feel.

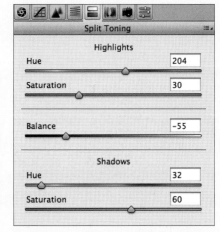

D These are our final **Split Toning** settings.

Using the Lens Corrections tab

The **Lens Corrections** tab lets you correct for two different problems. Depending on the lens and aperture being used, sometimes a camera lens can't properly focus all the wavelengths of colored light to exactly the same spot. The result may be a color fringe around some of the shapes in the photo, most noticeably along the edges of high-contrast areas. To correct this problem in Camera Raw, you can resize the offending color channel by using one of the **Chromatic Aberration** sliders.

The second problem, over- or underexposure near the edges of a photograph, which is usually created by a wide-angle or telephoto lens, can be corrected by using the **Lens Vignetting** sliders— or in some cases you may want to add a vignette intentionally to focus the viewer's attention toward the center of your photo.

To fix chromatic aberrations:

1. Click the **Lens Corrections** tab. 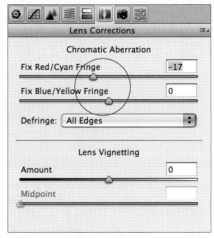 and zoom in to a high-contrast area in the photo.

2. Under **Chromatic Aberration**, do any of the following:

   Reduce the **Fix Red/Cyan Fringe** setting to remove a red fringe from high color-contrast edges,**A–C** or increase it to remove a cyan fringe. (The image may "jump" in the preview while the color channel is being scaled.)

   Reduce the **Fix Blue/Yellow Fringe** setting to remove a yellow fringe from high color-contrast edges, or increase it to remove a blue fringe.

   ► These sliders can help correct a landscape photo in which dark objects, such as foliage, contrast with a light background, such as sky.

3. From the **Defringe** menu, choose **All Edges**.

A Note the red fringe around the rock on the left, which is visible against the light color of the water.

B We reduced the **Fix Red/Cyan Fringe** value in the **Lens Corrections** tab.

C Our **Chromatic Aberration** adjustment reduced the red fringe.

To correct or apply vignetting:

1. Click the **Lens Corrections** tab.

2. Under **Lens Vignetting:**

   If your camera lens created a dark area (vignette) around the edges of the photo that you want to remove, increase the **Amount.** Or conversely, if you want to focus attention to the center of your photo by softly darkening the outer border, reduce the Amount.

   Also, reduce the **Midpoint** setting to widen the vignette toward the center of the photo, **A–B** or increase it to shrink it outward toward the edges.

A Adding a dark vignette around the edges of this photo will help focus the viewer's attention to the area that we want to showcase: the center.

B In the **Lens Corrections** tab, we moved the **Amount** slider all the way to the left to create a dark edge. Then, to widen the darkening vignette (expand it inward), we set the **Midpoint** value to 8.

Combining multiple exposures

You've probably had the experience of trying to shoot a subject against a bright sky or in front of a window. If you set the exposure properly for the figure or object in shadow, details will be lacking in the bright sunlit areas (and vice versa). To simulate what the human eye sees naturally, the solution is to shoot dual exposures and then combine them into one image. If you didn't bracket your shots, you can simulate **two exposure versions** for a single raw photo with Camera Raw. If you did bracket your shots, follow the instructions in the sidebar on the next page. In either case, the last step is to blend the best of the two exposures via a layer mask.

To simulate two exposures with one photo:

1. Open a raw photo **A** into Camera Raw.*

2. In the **Basic** tab, 🔅 use the exposure sliders to create a proper exposure for the shadows and lower midtones, **B** then in the **Tone Curve** tab, ✎ use the **Parametric** sliders to refine the adjustment in the four tonal regions.

3. Hold down Shift and click **Open Object.*** The photo will open in a new document window in Photoshop, on a Smart Object layer.

JPEG and TIFF photos aren't likely to contain enough pixel data for this technique to work successfully.

**If Open in Photoshop as Smart Objects is checked in the Workflow Options dialog, just click Open Object.*

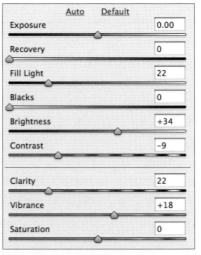

A The range of lighting in this scene was too wide to be captured in this single exposure: the alley of trees is slightly underexposed, whereas the sky and background are slightly overexposed. We'll use Camera Raw to create an exposure for each area, then combine them to create the best of both worlds.

B We used sliders in the **Basic** tab to recover shadow details (in the trees), then Shift-clicked **Open Object** to open the photo into Photoshop as a **Smart Object** layer.

4. Right-click/Control-click below the Smart Object layer name and choose **New Smart Object Via Copy** from the context menu (don't use Ctrl-J/Cmd-J, the Duplicate Layer command).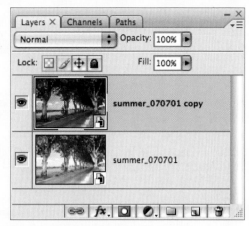

5. Double-click the thumbnail on the Smart Object copy to reopen the photo in Camera Raw. Because you used the **New Smart Object Via Copy** command, this Smart Object isn't linked to the original Smart Object, and changes made in Camera Raw will affect only this copy. This time, use the **Basic** and **Tone Curve** tabs to create a proper exposure for the upper midtones and highlights, then click OK. Upon your return to Photoshop, your edits will be applied to the copy of the Smart Object layer that you created.

6. Follow the instructions on the next page to blend the two layers.

A The **New Smart Object Via Copy** command created a nonlinked copy of the original Smart Object.

COMBINING BRACKETED SHOTS

To combine bracketed shots, follow steps 1–3 on the previous page to open the first photo as a Smart Object. In Bridge, select the next bracketed photo and choose File > Place > **In Photoshop**. It will open in Camera Raw. Apply any corrections, then click OK. The second photo will become a new Smart Object layer in the current Photoshop document. Finally, follow the steps on the next page.

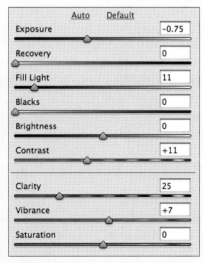

	Auto	Default	
Exposure			-0.75
Recovery			0
Fill Light			11
Blacks			0
Brightness			0
Contrast			+11
Clarity			25
Vibrance			+7
Saturation			0

B We opened the **copy** of the **Smart Object** in Camera Raw, used sliders in the Basic tab to properly expose the upper midtones and highlights in the background and sky, then clicked OK to return to the Photoshop file.

To blend two exposures via a layer mask:

1. If the bulk of the properly exposed areas are on the topmost layer, click the **Add Layer Mask** button ⬛ at the bottom of the Layers palette to create a white mask; 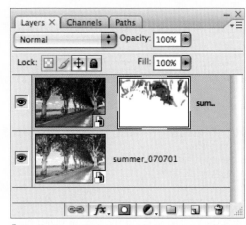A or if the lower layer contains more of the properly exposed areas, Alt-click/Option-click the **Add Layer Mask** button to create a black mask.

2. Choose the **Brush** tool 🖌 (B or Shift-B), a Soft Round tip, Normal mode, and an opacity of 70–80%. If you created a white mask, paint with black, or if you created a black mask, paint with white (press [or] to change the brush diameter). Draw strokes to reveal some of the corrected areas.**B** If you need to remask any areas, press X and paint with the reverse color.

3. Make any other edits, then save your file.**C**

A On the **layer mask** thumbnail for the copy of the Smart Object layer, you can see the dark brush strokes that we applied to reveal areas from the layer below.

B We added a layer mask to the copy of the Smart Object layer, then painted with the **Brush** tool (70% opacity) and **black** as the Foreground color to reveal some of the corrected midtone and shadow areas from the underlying layer.

C In the final image, the exposure information from the two Smart Object layers is combined, so it has a wider tonal range than the original photo (compare it with **A** on page 56). The sky looks richer now, and you can see more details in the trees in the distance. Note: As a last step, we applied a Hue/Saturation adjustment layer to tone down the acid green in the grassy field.

Retouching photos

Camera Raw has its own healing tool for removing small imperfections: the **Retouch** tool. It's useful for removing spots caused by dust or debris on the camera lens or to heal blemishes in a portrait, but we suggest that you save more complex retouching tasks for the healing tools in Photoshop.

To remove spots with the Retouch tool:

1. Open a photo that has an area that needs retouching. Choose the **Retouch** tool ✄ (B) and zoom to 100%.

2. Drag in the preview; a red and white **target** circle will display.**A** Drag inward or outward to scale the circle and cover the spot or blemish. Release the mouse, and a green and white source circle will appear, linked to the target circle.

3. Drag the **source** circle over an area to copy those pixels to the target circle.**B**

4. From the **Type** menu, choose **Heal** (our preference) to blend source pixels into the luminosity of the target pixels or **Clone** to produce an exact copy of the source pixels. Pause to preview.

5. You can also drag the edge of either circle to **scale** them both simultaneously, **add** more circle pairs to correct other blemishes, or **reposition** them by dragging at any time. They'll remain available even after you exit the dialog because the original raw pixels aren't altered.

   To **hide** the circles, uncheck Show Overlay or click a different tool.

   To **remove** a pair of circles, click inside one circle, then press Backspace/Delete; or to remove all pairs, click **Clear All.**

ASSEMBLY-LINE RETOUCHING

If you have a series of photos with the same dust spots in the same, er...spots,**C** you need to actually fix them in only one photo. Use the **Retouch** tool, but don't change where the program places the green and white source circle. Keep the tool selected, click Select All, click **Synchronize,** choose **Spot Removal** from the Synchronize menu, then click OK. Because you didn't change the source circles, Photoshop will attempt to place them in appropriate spots in the other photos. Study all the photos to verify that the green and white source circles were placed correctly, and reposition them, if necessary.

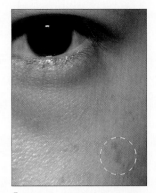

A With the **Retouch** tool, drag to create a **target** circle over a blemish...

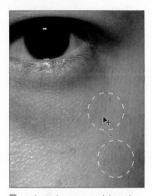

B ...then drag to position the **source** circle. Pixel data will copy automatically from the source circle to the target circle.

C We can use the **Retouch** tool to fix the **dust spots** in this photo, then synchronize the edit to correct the same dust spots in other photos of the same shoot and subject.

Red-eye (red eyes) in portrait photos result from light emitted by a camera-mounted or built-in electronic flash reflecting off the retina. If your camera doesn't have a built-in red-eye control (or you forgot to use it), a click of the **Red Eye Removal** tool in Camera Raw can fix it. It's even easier to use than the Red Eye tool in Photoshop.

To remove red-eye from a portrait:

1. Zoom in on the eye area in a portrait.

2. Choose the **Red Eye Removal** tool 🛇 (E).

3. Drag across the red area on one of the pupils.**A–B** The tool will remove all traces of red.

4. To better view the slider adjustments, hide the overlay rectangle by unchecking **Show Overlay** or pressing V.

5. Adjust the **Pupil Size** for the recolored pupil. You don't want the pupil to be enlarged.

6. Adjust the **Darken** value to control the darkness of the pupil. Try a value of 30–50%. Light eyes will need a lower setting than dark eyes.

7. Repeat steps 3–6 for the other eye.

➤ To resize the overlay rectangle and thereby enlarge its effect, drag one of its edges with the Red Eye Removal tool.

➤ To remove one overlay rectangle, click it with the Red Eye Removal tool, then press Backspace/Delete. To remove both rectangles, click Clear All.

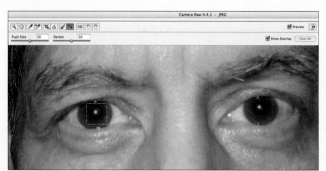

A With the **Red Eye** tool, we dragged a marquee over one of the eyes.

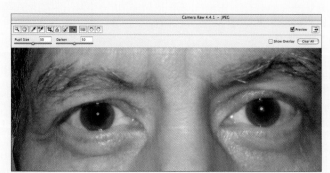

B The tool removed the red area (shown here with the Overlay hidden). We can now use the sliders to adjust the size and darkness of the pupil.

Using Camera Raw presets

By saving your carefully chosen **Camera Raw settings** as a **preset**, you'll be able to reestablish those settings quickly when needed simply by choosing that preset. A saved preset can also be applied to a series of photos from the same shoot or that were taken under the same studio lighting conditions that need the same or similar corrections. A settings preset can be applied to a single photo or multiple selected photos in Camera Raw, or to multiple selected thumbnails in Bridge.

To save Camera Raw settings as a preset:

Method 1

1. Open a photo into Camera Raw that has been corrected with the settings that you want to save as a preset (or use Camera Raw to apply corrections to a photo).

2. Choose **Save Settings** from the Settings menu. The Save Settings dialog opens. **A**

3. Check which settings you want saved in the settings file (if you want to display check marks for just one category of settings, choose that category from the Subset menu). Click Save. In the next Save Settings dialog, enter a Name (preferably one that describes the type of settings being saved). Keep the .xmp extension and also keep the location as the Settings folder, then click Save.

Method 2

1. Follow step 1 in Method 1.

2. Click the **Presets** tab, then click the **Add Preset** button. The New Preset dialog opens.

3. Enter a **Name** for the preset, then check which settings you want saved in the settings file (if you want to display check marks for just one category of settings, choose that category from the Subset menu). Click OK.

You can apply a **user-defined preset** (a saved collection of settings) to any photo in Camera Raw.

To apply a Camera Raw preset:

With a photo open in Camera Raw, do either of the following :

Click the **Presets** tab, then click the preset you want to apply.

From the **Apply Preset** submenu on the Camera Raw Settings menu, choose the desired preset.

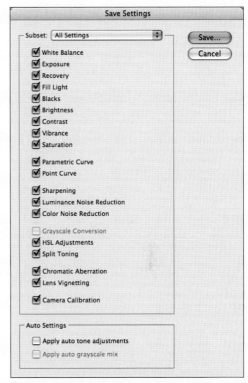

A In the **Save Settings** dialog, check which of your custom Camera Raw settings are to be saved in the preset.

Processing multiple photos via Camera Raw

In theory, you could open multiple files from the same photo shoot into Camera Raw (they'll appear in the filmstrip panel on the left side of the dialog), choose settings for one of the photos, and then click **Synchronize** to apply those **settings** to all the photos. In actuality, it's unlikely that all the adjustments needed for one photo will work like a charm on the rest—even if they're from the same shoot. However, for applying some initial settings, such as basic white balance, exposure, and HSL adjustments, the Synchronize option can be a very useful timesaver.

To synchronize the Camera Raw settings of multiple files:

1. In Bridge, select two or more raw file thumbnails that were shot under the same lighting conditions and that require the same corrections, then double-click one of them.

2. The photos will display on the filmstrip panel in the Camera Raw dialog (**A**, next page).

3. Click one of the thumbnails, and make the necessary adjustments to it—including cropping, if you want to crop all the photos the same way.

4. Click **Select All** at the top of the filmstrip panel or Ctrl-click/Cmd-click multiple thumbnails, then click **Synchronize** (**B**, next page). The Synchronize dialog opens. It has the same options as the Save Settings dialog, which is shown on the previous page.

5. Check the settings you want to apply; or choose a category of settings from the **Synchronize** menu, then remove or add any check marks.

6. Click OK. The current settings in the category you chose will be applied to all the thumbnails that you selected.

USING THE RATING FEATURES

If you open multiple files in Camera Raw, before performing any adjustments, you can magnify and scroll through the images to get a closer look, and if you like, also select and rate them. If you do so, the following shortcuts will come in handy:

TASK	METHOD
Scroll through the images sequentially	Press the up or down arrow on the keyboard
Apply star ratings	Select one or more image thumbnails, then press Cmd-./Ctrl-. (period)
Remove stars one by one from selected thumbnails	Press Cmd-,/Ctrl-, (comma)
Select only the images that have star ratings	Alt-click/Option-click the Select All button
Mark (or unmark) selected images with an X for deletion	Press Delete

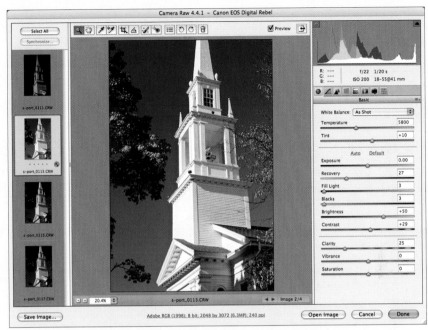

A If you open multiple raw photos into **Camera Raw** via Bridge, the image thumbnails will display in the **filmstrip** panel on the left side of the dialog. Click the thumbnail for one of the photos that you want to apply corrections to, then make the needed corrections.

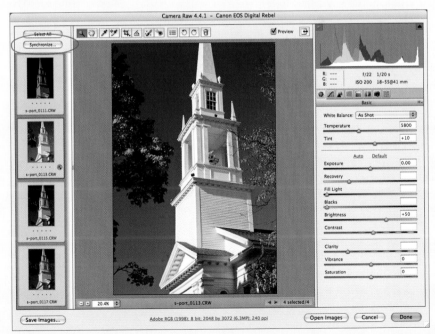

B Ctrl-click/Cmd-click other thumbnails that you want to apply the same corrections to or click Select All, then click **Synchronize**.

The user-created **settings presets** that are listed in the Presets tab of the Camera Raw dialog are also accessible in Bridge and can be applied to multiple files in one pass via **batch processing.** If you like, you can assign a series of presets to your selected files, each one controlling a few slider settings, simply by choosing one preset after another.

To batch-process multiple photos via Bridge:

1. In Bridge, do either of the following:

   Shift-click or Ctrl-click/Cmd-click multiple photo thumbnails, then from the Edit > **Develop Settings** submenu, choose the desired preset or presets. Those settings will be applied to the selected photos.

   Click the thumbnail for a photo that you know contains the desired settings, then press Ctrl-Alt-C/Cmd-Option-C (Edit > Develop Settings > **Copy Camera Raw Settings**). Click one or more other thumbnails, then press Ctrl-Alt-V/ Cmd-Option-V (Edit > Develop Settings > **Paste Settings**).**A** The Paste Camera Raw Settings dialog opens. Check the settings you want to paste or choose a tab name from the Subset menu, remove or add any check marks, then click OK.

▶ To remove all Camera Raw settings from a selected thumbnail in Bridge, choose Edit > Develop Settings > Clear Settings or right-click/ Control-click the thumbnail and choose the command from the Develop Settings submenu on the context menu.

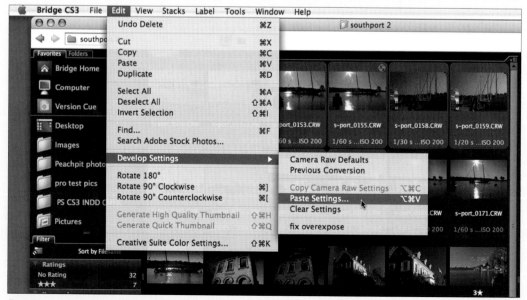

A In Bridge, you can **copy** the Camera Raw settings from one photo and **paste** them to multiple selected thumbnails.

Saving files via Camera Raw

Via the **Save Options** dialog in Camera Raw, you can rename your photos and convert them to the DNG (digital negative), JPEG, TIFF, or PSD (Photoshop) format without having to open them in Photoshop. DNG is an up-and-coming format that Adobe has developed for long-term archival of raw photos (see the sidebar on page 13). Camera Raw lets you save files in this format, whereas Photoshop does not.

To save a photo via Camera Raw:

1. Open a raw file (not a digital JPEG or TIFF photo) into Camera Raw, or if you opened multiple files into the Camera Raw dialog, select the ones that you want to save.

2. Click **Save Image**. The Save Options dialog opens.**A**

3. Choose a **Destination** (location), and choose **File Naming** options, which can include the file name, current date, and sequential numbering.

4. Choose a file **Format**, then check the desired options for that format. If you want to preserve the ability to edit your raw files in Camera Raw, save it in the Digital Negative (DNG) format.

➤ Via the Embed Original Raw File option, you can embed the entire original raw file into the DNG file. We recommend doing this only if you also plan to edit your raw photos in the conversion software that came with your camera.

5. Click Save.

➤ Via the Save Options dialog, you can also save versions of a photo with different adjustments (such as different exposure settings). Simply change the file name and choose a format.

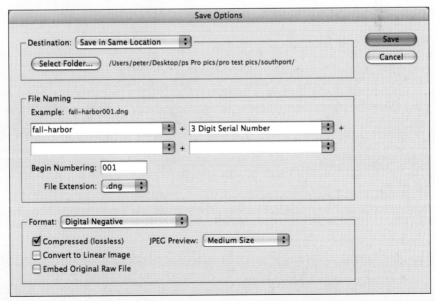

A One purpose of the **Save Options** dialog is for saving photos in a different format, such as Digital Negative (DNG).

Working with photos as Smart Objects

If you open or place a Camera Raw photo into Photoshop as a **Smart Object**, you'll be able to readjust its Camera Raw settings at any time.

To open a Camera Raw photo into a new Photoshop file as a Smart Object:

> With a photo open in Camera Raw, hold down Shift and click **Open Object.** A new file will open in Photoshop, with the image on a Smart Object layer.

To place a Camera Raw file into an existing Photoshop file as a Smart Object:

1. Open a Photoshop document.

2. In Bridge, click the thumbnail for a raw photo.

3. Choose File > Place > **In Photoshop.** The Camera Raw dialog opens.

4. Make adjustments to the photo, then click OK. It will appear on its own layer in the Photoshop document, in a transform box.

5. Apply any scale or shape transformations (enlarge the document window to access the handles, if necessary), then press Enter/Return or double-click in the transform box to accept the image. It will become a Smart Object layer.

To edit a Smart Object image in Camera Raw:

1. Double-click a **Smart Object** layer thumbnail to reopen an embedded copy of the photo into the Camera Raw dialog.

2. Make any desired adjustments, then click OK to apply your edits to the Smart Object layer. The original photo won't be affected by your edits.

   Note: When you scale a Smart Object layer, Photoshop uses the pixel data from the original photo, so the image quality isn't diminished — provided you don't enlarge it beyond the size at which it was originally captured.**A–C** To see what the original dimensions are, click the thumbnail in Bridge, then look in the File Properties category of the Metadata panel.

If Open in Photoshop as Smart Objects is checked in the Workflow Options dialog, just click Open Object.

SCALING A PHOTO THE BEST WAY

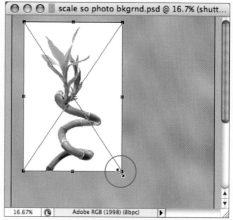

A To **scale** a **Smart Object** layer, Shift-drag a corner handle on the transform box with the Move tool.

B This photo was opened in Photoshop as an ordinary layer. When we enlarged it, it lost definition.

C This time, the photo was enlarged after being placed as a **Smart Object** layer: The details remained crisp and the image quality remained high.

This chapter begins with a summary of fundamental Photoshop features. Topics include using the palettes **A** and screen modes; changing the image size, file format, and bits/channel mode; cropping and rotating images; choosing and saving colors; using the Layers and History palettes; and creating and managing presets.

USING PHOTOSHOP

A Each palette in Photoshop has a unique icon, which displays when the palette is in its collapsed state. Try to memorize the **icons** for the **palettes** you use often, so you'll be able to identify them quickly as you work.

4

Brushes

Channels

Character

Clone Source

Color

Histogram

History

Info

Layer Comps

Layers

Navigator

Paragraph

Paths

Styles

Swatches

Tool Presets

USE THE AVAILABLE INFO

➤ If you're unsure what an icon means or a palette or dialog option does, rest the pointer on it, and a descriptive **tool tip** will pop up onscreen (if tool tips are hidden, check Show Tool Tips in Preferences > Interface).

➤ Some dialogs have a **Description** field that lists information about the option your pointer is hovering over.

➤ Keep an eye on the **Info** palette for color breakdowns (including readouts from any color samplers), document data (e.g., dimensions, size, resolution, profile), and tool hints (tips for using the currently selected tool).

➤ Also keep an eye on the **Histogram** palette —or on the histogram in a dialog—to monitor changes to the tonal levels in your document.

Using the palettes

Most edits made in Photoshop require the use of one or more palettes. Photoshop CS3 has a clever system for storing and accessing palettes so they're easily expandable and collapsible and don't intrude on the document window when you're not using them. As expected, with enhanced flexibility, you also get greater complexity.

By default, some of the most commonly used palettes are grouped into vertical **docks** (dark gray areas) on the far right side of your screen **A** —except for the Tools palette, which occupies its own dock on the left side. Each dock can hold as many or as few palettes or palette groups as you wish. We'll show you how to reconfigure the docks to suit your working style.

Show or hide a palette: To show a palette, choose the palette name from the Window menu. The palette will display either in its default group and dock or in its last location. To bring a palette to the front of its group, click the tab (palette name). Some palettes can also be shown or hidden via a keyboard shortcut (look for them on the Window menu).

Show or hide a palette (that's in icon form): Click the palette icon or name. If Auto-Collapse Icon Palettes is checked in Preferences > Interface and you open a palette from an icon, it will collapse back to the icon when you click away from it. With the preference off, the palette will stay expanded. To collapse it, click the collapse/expand button ⏩ on the palette bar, or the palette tab or icon.

Expand or collapse a palette (non-icon) **or group vertically:** Double-click the palette tab; or click the light gray bar (above the palette tabs); or click the palette or group minimize/maximize button. ▬

Use a palette menu: Click the ▾☰ icon to open a menu for the frontmost palette in the group.

Close a palette or group: To close (but not collapse) a palette, click the close button ✕ on its tab, as in Layers ✕ . To close a palette group, click the ✕ on the gray bar. To close a group that's an icon, expand the dock first by clicking the collapse/expand button,⏩ then click the ✕.

Collapse or expand a whole dock into icons with names: Click the collapse/expand button ⏩ or the dark gray bar at the top of the dock.**B** To further collapse the dock to just icons (no names), drag the vertical edge of the dock inward horizontally;**C** or to expand it, do the reverse.

A There are two **docks** at the right edge of our screen: Palettes in the left dock are **collapsed** to icons with names; palettes in the right dock are **expanded** and are organized into three groups.

B When we clicked the **collapse/expand** button to collapse the right dock to icons, the palette groups were preserved.

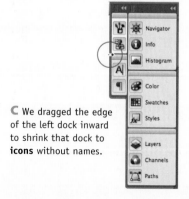

C We dragged the edge of the left dock inward to shrink that dock to **icons** without names.

Widen or narrow a dock and palettes (non-icon): Position the mouse over the vertical edge of the dock (✦⬚ cursor), then drag sideways.

Lengthen or shorten a palette, group, or dock: Position the mouse over the dark gray line at the bottom of the palette or dock (⬚ cursor), then drag upward or downward. Palettes and palette groups in the dock will scale accordingly.

Move a palette to a different slot, same group: Drag the palette tab (name) horizontally.

Move a palette to a different group: Drag the palette tab over the bar of the desired group, and release the mouse when the blue drop zone border appears.**A**

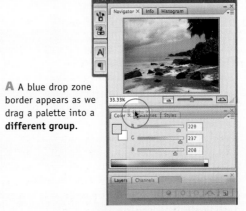

A A blue drop zone border appears as we drag a palette into a **different group.**

Move a palette group upward or downward in a dock: Drag the gray bar, and release the mouse when the blue drop zone line appears in the desired location.**B**

Create a new dock: Drag a palette tab or gray bar sideways over the vertical edge of the dock,**C** and release the mouse when the blue vertical drop zone bar appears.

Make a palette or group freestanding: Drag the palette tab, icon, or group bar out of the dock. To move a freestanding group, drag the group bar.

B A blue horizontal drop zone bar appears as we **move** a palette group **upward** in its dock.

Reconfigure a dock (icon): Drag the group bar over the edge of a dock to create a new dock; drag it between groups to restack it; or drag it over another gray bar to add it to that group. The blue drop zone will indicate the new location for the palette or group.

➤ When you open a palette from the Window menu, it appears either as a freestanding palette or in a dock, depending on its last location.

➤ To reset the palettes to their default locations and show/hide states, choose Default Workspace from the Workspace menu on the Options bar. To reset just the palette locations, choose Window > Workspace > Reset Palette Locations.

➤ To create a custom workspace that remembers palette locations and which palettes are showing or hidden, choose Save Workspace from the Workspace menu on the Options bar.

➤ For any tool that uses a brush, you can click the Toggle Palette button 📑 on the Options bar to show/hide the Brushes palette. For the Type tool, this button displays the Character palette.

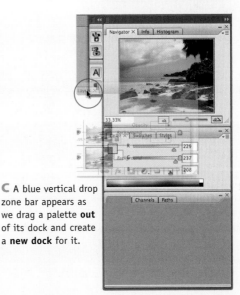

C A blue vertical drop zone bar appears as we drag a palette **out** of its dock and create a **new dock** for it.

Hiding and showing palettes

When you need to fully maximize your screen space, **hide** all the currently **open palettes**, then make them reappear only when you need to use them. If you hide the palettes when your document is in Maximized screen mode, the document window will resize dynamically to the maximum screen width; redisplay the palettes and the document window will resize again as needed.

To hide or show the palettes:

Do any of the following:

Press **Tab** to hide or show the Tools palette and all open palettes.

Press **Shift-Tab** to hide or show just the palettes and keep the Tools palette open.

To make hidden palette docks reappear:

With the palettes hidden as per the instructions above, move the pointer to the very edge of your monitor (or to the very edge of the application window in Windows). The palette docks (not freestanding palettes) will redisplay temporarily.**A–B** Move the pointer away from the palettes and they'll disappear again.

➤ If you want to conserve screen space but don't want to hide the palettes, collapse the ones you use least frequently to icons.

CHANGING VALUES QUICKLY

➤ Use the **scrubby slider** to change values quickly in a palette or dialog: Drag slightly to the left or right on the name or icon. Examples include some fields on the Options bar, the Opacity and Fill settings on the Layers palette, and the Input and Output Levels settings in the Levels dialog.**C**

➤ When the pointer is in a palette or dialog field, you can change the value by pressing the up or down **arrow key**.

➤ To access a **pop-up slider** (e.g., to change an Opacity percentage), click the arrowhead. To close a slider, click anywhere outside it or press Enter/Return. If you click an arrowhead to open a slider, you can press Esc to restore the last setting.

C A **scrubby slider**

A If the palettes are hidden and you position the pointer at the very edge of the monitor...

B ...the palette docks will **reappear temporarily**. Move the pointer away from the palettes and they'll disappear again. Easy come, easy go.

Changing screen modes

The **screen modes** control which Photoshop interface features are showing or hidden and what type of background displays behind your image. Our favorite is Maximized screen mode.

To change screen modes:

From the **Screen Mode** menu at the bottom of the Tools palette, A choose a screen mode, or press **F** to cycle through these choices:

Standard Screen Mode (the default mode) to display the document window, menu bar, Options bar, and palettes, with the Desktop and other application windows visible behind everything. When working in this mode, enlarge the document window to display a gray background behind the image, and to obscure as much of the Desktop as possible. B

Maximized Screen Mode to display the image on the gray (default color) background of an expanded document window, which will fill the space between the Tools palette, Options bar, and palettes. This mode is dynamic, meaning that if you make a palette dock wider or narrower, the document window will resize accordingly and the image will recenter itself in the remaining available space.

Full Screen Mode with Menu Bar to display the image on a gray (default color) background, obscuring the Desktop, with the menu bar, Options bar, and palettes visible, but without dynamic resizing.

Full Screen Mode to display the image on a black (default color) background, with the palettes and Options bar visible but the menu bar (and the Dock, in Mac) hidden, and without dynamic resizing.

➤ In the latter two modes mentioned above, you can reposition the image on the background with the Hand tool.

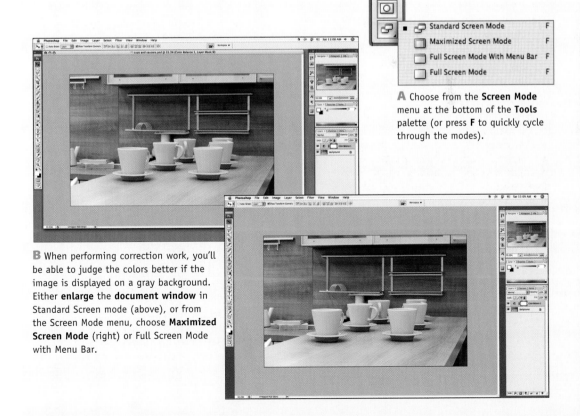

A Choose from the **Screen Mode** menu at the bottom of the **Tools** palette (or press **F** to quickly cycle through the modes).

B When performing correction work, you'll be able to judge the colors better if the image is displayed on a gray background. Either **enlarge** the **document window** in Standard Screen mode (above), or from the Screen Mode menu, choose **Maximized Screen Mode** (right) or Full Screen Mode with Menu Bar.

Tools on the Tools palette

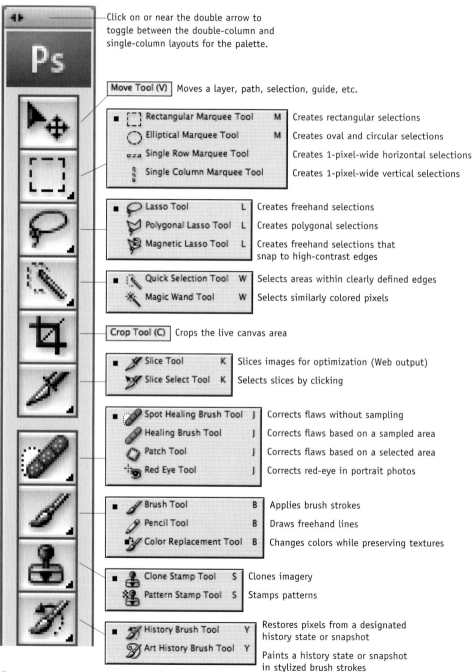

Click on or near the double arrow to toggle between the double-column and single-column layouts for the palette.

Move Tool (V) Moves a layer, path, selection, guide, etc.

- Rectangular Marquee Tool — M — Creates rectangular selections
- Elliptical Marquee Tool — M — Creates oval and circular selections
- Single Row Marquee Tool — Creates 1-pixel-wide horizontal selections
- Single Column Marquee Tool — Creates 1-pixel-wide vertical selections

- Lasso Tool — L — Creates freehand selections
- Polygonal Lasso Tool — L — Creates polygonal selections
- Magnetic Lasso Tool — L — Creates freehand selections that snap to high-contrast edges

- Quick Selection Tool — W — Selects areas within clearly defined edges
- Magic Wand Tool — W — Selects similarly colored pixels

Crop Tool (C) Crops the live canvas area

- Slice Tool — K — Slices images for optimization (Web output)
- Slice Select Tool — K — Selects slices by clicking

- Spot Healing Brush Tool — J — Corrects flaws without sampling
- Healing Brush Tool — J — Corrects flaws based on a sampled area
- Patch Tool — J — Corrects flaws based on a selected area
- Red Eye Tool — J — Corrects red-eye in portrait photos

- Brush Tool — B — Applies brush strokes
- Pencil Tool — B — Draws freehand lines
- Color Replacement Tool — B — Changes colors while preserving textures

- Clone Stamp Tool — S — Clones imagery
- Pattern Stamp Tool — S — Stamps patterns

- History Brush Tool — Y — Restores pixels from a designated history state or snapshot
- Art History Brush Tool — Y — Paints a history state or snapshot in stylized brush strokes

A The top part of the **Tools** palette

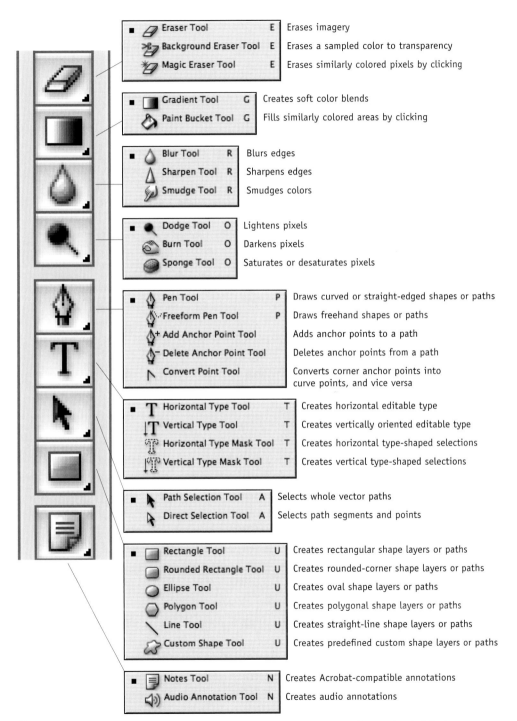

Eraser Tool	E	Erases imagery
Background Eraser Tool	E	Erases a sampled color to transparency
Magic Eraser Tool	E	Erases similarly colored pixels by clicking

Gradient Tool	G	Creates soft color blends
Paint Bucket Tool	G	Fills similarly colored areas by clicking

Blur Tool	R	Blurs edges
Sharpen Tool	R	Sharpens edges
Smudge Tool	R	Smudges colors

Dodge Tool	O	Lightens pixels
Burn Tool	O	Darkens pixels
Sponge Tool	O	Saturates or desaturates pixels

Pen Tool	P	Draws curved or straight-edged shapes or paths
Freeform Pen Tool	P	Draws freehand shapes or paths
Add Anchor Point Tool		Adds anchor points to a path
Delete Anchor Point Tool		Deletes anchor points from a path
Convert Point Tool		Converts corner anchor points into curve points, and vice versa

Horizontal Type Tool	T	Creates horizontal editable type
Vertical Type Tool	T	Creates vertically oriented editable type
Horizontal Type Mask Tool	T	Creates horizontal type-shaped selections
Vertical Type Mask Tool	T	Creates vertical type-shaped selections

Path Selection Tool	A	Selects whole vector paths
Direct Selection Tool	A	Selects path segments and points

Rectangle Tool	U	Creates rectangular shape layers or paths
Rounded Rectangle Tool	U	Creates rounded-corner shape layers or paths
Ellipse Tool	U	Creates oval shape layers or paths
Polygon Tool	U	Creates polygonal shape layers or paths
Line Tool	U	Creates straight-line shape layers or paths
Custom Shape Tool	U	Creates predefined custom shape layers or paths

Notes Tool	N	Creates Acrobat-compatible annotations
Audio Annotation Tool	N	Creates audio annotations

A The midsection of the **Tools palette**

Continued on the following page

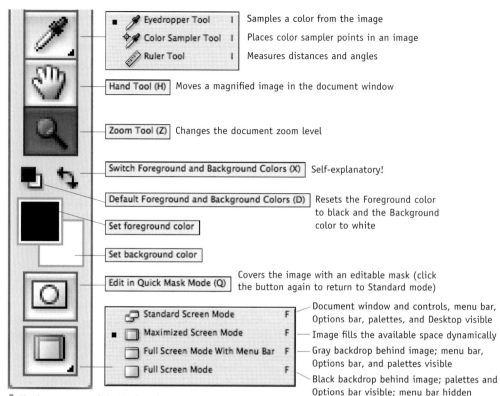

A The bottom part of the **Tools palette**

GETTING PROGRAM UPDATES

To find out if there's an update for Photoshop, Bridge, or any other Adobe products, choose Help > **Updates.** Click **Show Details** to see a listing of available updates and software components that are already installed on your system, then click **Download and Install Updates.** Click **Preferences** to specify whether you want downloads to happen automatically or prefer to be notified via an alert (and how often), and check which programs you wish to receive updates for.

Changing the image size

There are three ways to choose a file resolution:

➤ When opening a raw digital photo, you should set the output resolution in the **Camera Raw** dialog (see page 38).

➤ For a JPEG photo or other image that you need to change the resolution for, use the **Image Size** dialog after opening the file in Photoshop.

➤ When **scanning**, set the input resolution to control how many pixels the device will capture.

Changing the image size without resampling

Via Image > **Image Size** (Ctrl-Alt-I/Cmd-Option-I), you can change the resolution of your file and/ or its width and height. If you do so with the **Resample Image** option unchecked **A** (without resampling), the image quality will remain at its current level. This method is recommended for digital photos and scanned images.

By default, JPEG photos from a digital camera have a low resolution (72–180 ppi) and very large width and height dimensions, with a sufficient number of pixels for high-quality output (prints as large as 8˝ x 10˝)—provided you increase the resolution to the proper value. When you increase the resolution to suit your output device, the pixel dimensions will remain constant and the print dimensions will become smaller.

Unlike photos from a digital camera, s**canned** images usually have a high resolution and small size dimensions but also contain a high enough pixel count to produce large, high-quality prints. In this case, you should change the width and height with Resample Image unchecked (thereby keeping the resolution and pixel count constant).

Changing the image size with resampling

If your file contains too few pixels to meet the resolution requirement of your target output device, you'll have to increase the resolution with Resample Image checked.**B** This will add pixels to the file (increase its pixel dimensions) and increase its storage size accordingly. You should increase the resolution only to a level that is necessary to achieve the desired output quality.

When you downsample a file (decrease its resolution with Resample Image checked), pixels are discarded permanently. For a **Web** graphic, downsampling isn't an issue; users will view it on a computer display, which is a low-resolution device. For print output, try to avoid resampling, because it reduces the image sharpness (although you can use a sharpening filter to remedy blurring from a minor amount of resampling).

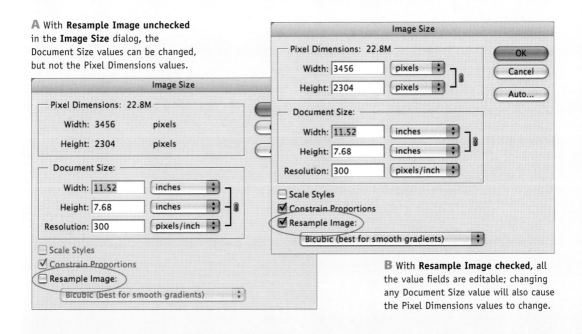

A With **Resample Image unchecked** in the **Image Size** dialog, the Document Size values can be changed, but not the Pixel Dimensions values.

B With **Resample Image checked,** all the value fields are editable; changing any Document Size value will also cause the Pixel Dimensions values to change.

Choosing a file format

When using File > Save, Save As, or Save a Copy to save a file, remember that **Photoshop (PSD), Large Document (PSB),** * **TIFF,** and **Photoshop PDF** are the only formats that preserve the following Photoshop features:

➤ Multiple layers and layer transparency

➤ Shape layers

➤ Smart Objects

➤ Adjustment layers

➤ Editable type layers

➤ Layer effects

➤ Alpha channels

➤ Grids and guides

All of the above-mentioned file formats, plus the PICT, JPEG, and Photoshop EPS formats, preserve ICC color profiles.

To prepare your document for printing from another application, or to export it to an application that can't read Photoshop layers, read about the **PDF, EPS,** and **TIFF** formats on pages 335–339. Or for Web output, read about the **GIF** and **JPEG** formats on pages 340–345.

Large Document (PSB) files can be opened only in the CS versions of Photoshop.

KEEP YOUR FILES IN RGB COLOR MODE

There are many reasons to keep your files in **RGB Color** mode (the mode in which digital photos are captured):

➤ Editing is faster in RGB Color mode.

➤ RGB is the only mode in which all the Photoshop tool options and filters are accessible.

➤ RGB is the mode of choice for online output, for export to video and multimedia applications, and for desktop inkjet printing.

The only time you'll need to convert your files to CMYK Color mode is for commercial printing. If and when you do so, remember to convert a copy of the file — not the original!

Note: If you work with high-resolution CMYK scans and you have a profile for the specific CMYK press and paper combination that your files will be printed on, you may want to keep your files in CMYK Color mode.

Choosing a bits/channel mode

To get good-quality output, you need to capture or input a wide range of tonal values. One of the greatest challenges to a photographer is capturing detail in the shadow areas of a scene. The wider the dynamic color range of the camera, the more subtleties of color and tone it can capture. Most advanced amateur and professional digital SLR cameras capture from 12 to 16 bits of accurate data per channel, and the resulting photos contain an abundance of pixels in all levels of the tonal spectrum.

Consumer-level scanners capture 10 bits of accurate data per channel, whereas high-end professional scanners can capture up to 16 bits of accurate data per channel. Like the better digital cameras, scans from a high-resolution device will contain an abundance of pixels in all the tonal ranges.

In Photoshop, you have a choice of three bit depths, available on the Image > **Mode** submenu: **8**, **16**, and **32 Bits/Channel** mode. At the present time, 16 Bits/Channel mode offers the most advantages. 32 Bits/Channel mode may be the mode of choice for high-end photographic work in the future, but at the moment Photoshop doesn't support it sufficiently to make it a practical choice.

Another factor in getting good-quality output is the ability to preserve the full tonal range of your images as you edit them in Photoshop. Because they contain more pixels, 16-bit images are better able to withstand the wear and tear of editing and resampling.**A–B** The Levels and Curves commands, for example, remove pixel data and alter the distribution of pixels across the tonal spectrum. After editing, the reduction in image quality will be visible on high-end print output of an 8-bit image, but not of a 16-bit image, because the latter has more pixels in all parts of the tonal spectrum.

To summarize, the following are some basic facts about 16-bit files that you should know:

➤ Photoshop can open 16-bit files in CMYK or RGB mode.

➤ 16-bit files can be saved in the following widely used formats: Photoshop (.psd), Large Document (.psb), PDF (.pdf), PNG (.png), TIFF (.tif), and JPEG2000.

➤ 16-bit images can be successfully edited and adjusted in Photoshop, with just a few restrictions. Most of the filters on the Blur, Noise, Render, Sharpen, and Other submenus on the Filter menu are available, as is the Distort > Lens Correction filter. Filters on the other submenus aren't available, and you can't use the Art History Brush tool.

➤ When you print your file, you need to convert your 16-bit images to 8-bit (Image > Mode > 8 Bits/Channel).

If system or storage limitations prevent you from working with your images in 16 Bits/Channel mode, try this two-stage approach: Perform your initial tonal corrections (such as Levels and Curves adjustments) on the original 16 Bits/Channel version, then convert the file to 8 Bits/Channel for further editing.

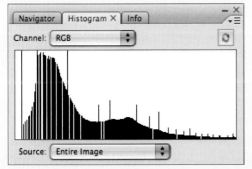

A After a Levels command adjustment, this **8-bit** image shows signs of tonal degradation: spikes and gaps.

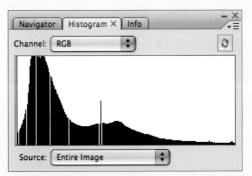

B After the same Levels adjustment in the **16-bit** version of the same image, the histogram shows that the smooth tonal transitions were preserved.

Cropping an image

You can crop your photos in Camera Raw (see page 39) or by using the **Crop** tool in Photoshop.

To crop an image using a marquee:

1. Choose the **Crop** tool (C). 🔲

2. Drag a marquee over the part of the image you want to keep.**A**

3. On the Options bar, do the following:

   If you're cropping a layer (not the Background), you can click **Cropped Area: Delete** to delete the cropped-out areas or click **Hide** to save those areas with the file (they'll extend beyond the visible canvas area but can be moved back into view later with the Move tool).

   Check **Shield** to cover the area outside the crop marquee with a dark shield to help you see which part will remain after cropping. You can change the shield color by clicking the **Color** swatch, or change the shield's **Opacity** value.

   For the Perspective option, see Photoshop Help. We prefer to use the Lens Correction filter to correct perspective problems (see our *Visual QuickStart Guide* to Photoshop).

4. Do any of these optional steps:

   To **resize** the marquee, drag any handle (double-arrow pointer). Shift-drag a corner handle to preserve the proportions of the marquee; Alt-drag/Option-drag a handle to resize the marquee from its center; hold down Shift and Alt/Option to do both.

   To **reposition** the marquee, drag inside it.

   To **rotate** the marquee, position the cursor just outside it (curved arrow pointer), then drag in a circular direction. This is a quick way to both crop and straighten a photo. To change the axis point around which the marquee rotates, drag the center point away from the center of the marquee before rotating. The image orientation will change after the next step.

5. Do one of the following:

   Press Enter/Return.**B**

   Double-click inside the marquee.

   Right-click/Control-click the image and choose Crop.

➤ To cancel a crop marquee, press Esc.

➤ To create presets for the Crop tool, see page 91.

CROPPING TO A SPECIFIC SIZE

To crop an image to a specific size (say, 4 x 6 inches), choose the **Crop** tool (C), then on the Options bar, enter the desired **Width** and **Height** values. (You can click the Swap Width and Height button ⇄ to swap the two values.) For Web output, lower the image Resolution value to 72 ppi; for print output, enter the current image Resolution value to prevent it from changing when the image is cropped. Finally, drag a crop marquee on the image.

A With the **Crop** tool, drag a marquee across part of an image, and resize the marquee as needed.

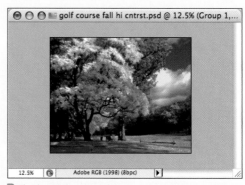

B The image is cropped.

Rotating an image

The **Rotate Canvas** commands rotate all the layers in an image. (To rotate just one layer at a time, use a rotate command on the Edit > Transform submenu instead.)

To rotate an image by an exact amount:

Do either of the following:

Choose Image > Rotate Canvas > **180°, 90° CW** (clockwise), or **90° CCW** (counterclockwise).

Choose Image > Rotate Canvas > **Arbitrary.** The Rotate Canvas dialog opens. Enter an **Angle** value, click °**CW** (clockwise) or °**CCW** (counter-clockwise), then click OK.

You didn't have a tripod handy for that unforget-table moment? Did a sloppy job of scanning? You can straighten out your photo with the **Ruler** tool.

To straighten a crooked image:

1. Choose the **Ruler** tool 📏 (I or Shift-I), formerly the Measure tool.

2. Drag along a feature of the image that you want to orient horizontally or vertically,  and note the angle (A) value on the Options bar.

3. Choose Image > Rotate Canvas > **Arbitrary.** The angle you dragged will appear in the **Angle** field.

4. Click OK. 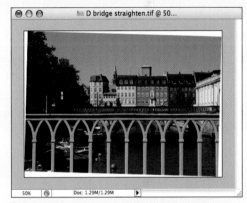 You can crop the image to remove any background color areas that resulted from the rotation.

A We dragged the **Ruler** tool from left to right along the crooked railing.

B The Rotate Canvas > **Arbitrary** command rotated the image along the angle we drew with the Ruler tool.

C We used the **Crop** tool to remove the white areas. Now the image looks level.

QUICK SUMMARY: CHOOSING COLORS

The current **Foreground color** is applied when you create type and when you use some tools and commands, such the Brush or Pencil tool. The current **Background color** is applied by other edits, such as when you apply a transform command to, or move a selection on, the Background.

The two colors are displayed in the Foreground and Background color squares on the Tools palette **A** and Color palette. There are many ways to choose a Foreground or Background color:

➤ Enter values or click a color in the **Color Picker.B**

➤ Sample a color in the image with the **Eyedropper tool.**

➤ Click a user-saved or preset swatch on the **Swatches palette.**

➤ Enter values or move sliders on the **Color palette.C**

➤ Choose a premixed color from a matching system via the **Color Libraries** dialog (click Color Libraries in the Color Picker to access it).

The **Default Foreground and Background Colors** button (D) makes the Foreground color black and the Background color white.

A The color controls on the **Tools** palette

The **Switch Colors** button (X) swaps the current Foreground and Background colors.

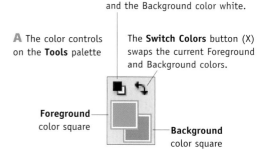

Foreground color square

Background color square

B To open the **Color Picker**, click the Foreground or Background color square on the **Tools** palette.

New color   Current color

Start by clicking the color square you want to mix a color for, if it's not already selected.

Foreground color square (selected)

Background color square

Choose a **model** for the sliders.

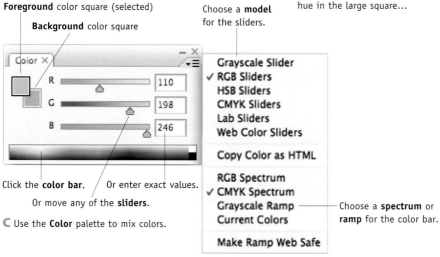

Click a **hue** on the color slider, then click a variation of that hue in the large square...

...or enter values in the **HSB, RGB, Lab,** or **CMYK** fields.

Click the **color bar.**   Or enter exact values.

Or move any of the **sliders.**

C Use the **Color** palette to mix colors.

Choose a **spectrum** or **ramp** for the color bar.

QUICK SUMMARY: USING THE SWATCHES PALETTE

TASK	METHOD
Choose a color from the Swatches palette	To choose a color for the currently selected color square (Foreground or Background), click a color swatch; to choose a color for the unselected color square, Ctrl-click/Cmd-click a swatch.
Add a color to the Swatches palette (colors on the palette are available for all documents)	Mix or choose a Foreground color by using the Color palette, Color Picker, or Eyedropper tool, then click the New Swatch of Foreground Color button on the palette. (Or to name the swatch as you create it, click the blank area below the swatches on the Swatches palette or right-click/Control-click any swatch and choose New Swatch; enter a name, then click OK.)
Delete a swatch from the Swatches palette	Alt-click/Option-click the swatch to be deleted (scissors pointer),**A** or right-click/Control-click a swatch and choose Delete Swatch. This can't be undone.
Save the current swatches on the palette as a library	Choose Save Swatches from the palette menu (keep the .aco extension when you enter a name in the dialog).
Save changes to an existing user-created library	Follow the instructions above, except retype the same name for the library. When the alert dialog appears, click Replace.
Load a user-created library or a preset swatch library	From the Swatches palette menu, choose a library name, then either click Append to append the new swatches while keeping the existing ones on the palette or click OK to replace the current swatches with the new ones (an alert may appear, giving you the option to save the current swatches).
Restore the default swatches	Choose Reset Swatches from the Swatches palette menu, then click OK. An alert may appear, giving you the option to save the current swatches.
Save the current swatches for use in another Adobe Creative Suite program	Choose the Save Swatches for Exchange command on the Swatches palette menu.

RGB OR CMYK?

To mix a specific process color for print output, enter **C, M, Y,** and **K** percentages from a printed color swatch book for a matching system, such as the PANTONE® Formula Guide.

For Web output, enter **R, G,** and **B** values (0–255). White (the presence of all colors) is produced when all the sliders are positioned at the far right, black (the absence of all colors) is produced when all the sliders are at the far left, and gray is produced when all the sliders are aligned vertically with one another at any other location.

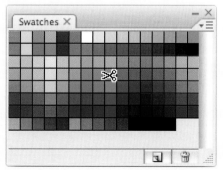

A Alt-click/Option-click a swatch to **delete** it.

Using the Layers palette

Every new image contains either a Background or a transparent layer, on top of which you can add layers of many types, such as:

➤ **Image** layers, which can contain all opaque pixels or a combination of opaque, transparent, and semitransparent pixels.

➤ **Fill** and **adjustment** layers, which apply editable color or tonal adjustments to underlying layers.

➤ **Editable type** layers, which you create with the Horizontal Type or Vertical Type tool.

➤ **Smart Object** layers, which are created when you bring an Illustrator vector file, another Photoshop file, or a raw file into a Photoshop document via File > Place, or when you convert

a standard layer. Double-click a Smart Object layer and the object reopens in its original application for editing; save and close it and the object updates in Photoshop. Apply a filter to a Smart Object layer and it becomes an editable and removable Smart Filter.

➤ **Shape** layers, which contain vector shapes.

You'll undoubtedly use the **Layers** palette **A** in most Photoshop sessions. It lets you create, select, show and hide, duplicate, group, restack, link, merge, flatten, and delete layers; change the layer blending mode, opacity, and fill opacity; apply layer effects; attach layer and vector masks; move layer content; and copy layers between files.

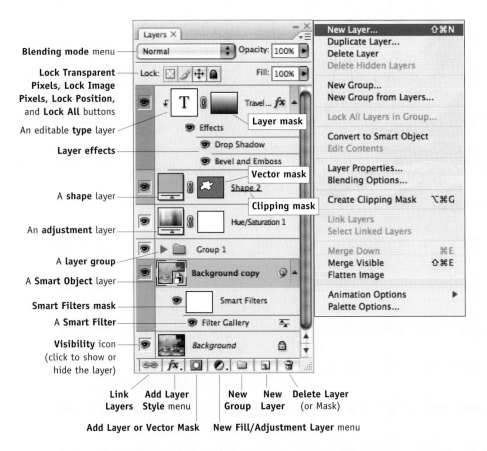

A This figure shows almost every conceivable **Layers** palette feature. As you work, your palette list may become as long as this one, but it won't look as complex because you'll probably use fewer types of layers and masks at a given time.

QUICK SUMMARY: USING THE LAYERS PALETTE

TASK	METHOD
Create a new layer, 100% opacity and fill	Click the New Layer button
Create and choose options (name, identifying color, etc.) for a new layer	Alt-click/Option-click the New Layer button or press Ctrl-Shift-N/Cmd-Shift-N
Copy selected pixels to a new layer	Press Ctrl-J/Cmd-J; or right-click/Control-click in the document window and choose Layer via Copy
Duplicate the Background, a layer, or a layer group	Click the Background, a layer, or a layer group, then press Ctrl-J/Cmd-J. Or drag it over the New Layer button
Select multiple layers	Shift-click or Ctrl-click/Cmd-click to the right of the layer names
Select all layers (not the Background)	Press Ctrl-Alt-A/Cmd-Option-A (or choose Select > All Layers)
Select all layers of a similar kind (e.g., all image layers or all adjustment layers)	Right-click/Control-click a layer and choose Select Similar Layers
Select a layer or layer group below the pointer that contains visible pixels	Choose the Move tool (V), check Auto-Select and choose Group or Layer on the Options bar, then click visible pixels
Open the Layer Style dialog	Double-click next to a layer name
Convert the Background to a layer	Alt-double-click/Option-double-click the Background (or double-click it with no modifier key to choose options)
Create a Background if there is none	Click a layer, then choose Layer > New > Background from Layer
Create a layer group from existing layers	Select multiple layers, then press Ctrl-G/Cmd-G
Ungroup a group and keep the layers	Click the layer group, then press Ctrl-Shift-G/Cmd-Shift-G
Delete a group and its contents	Right-click/Control-click a layer group and choose Delete Group, then click Group and Contents
Delete a layer, bypassing the prompt	Click a layer, then Alt-click/Option-click the Delete Layer button
Hide or show all layers except one	Alt-click/Option-click a visibility icon; or right-click/Control-click the visibility column and choose Show or Hide All Other Layers
Reposition a layer group in the document	Choose the Move tool (V), check Auto-Select and choose Group on the Options bar, then drag in the document window (to move just one layer in a group, choose Layer instead)
Choose palette options	Right-click/Control-click a layer thumbnail; choose from the menu
Change the color behind the visibility icon	Right-click/Control-click the visibility column and choose a color (this can be done to color code layer groups)
Merge layers	Click the upper of two layers (the bottom one must be an image layer) or select multiple layers, then right-click/Control-click and choose Merge Down or Merge Layers (Ctrl-E/Cmd-E) or Merge Visible (Ctrl-Shift-E/Cmd-Shift-E)
Flatten layers (discards hidden layers)	Right-click/Control-click a layer and choose Flatten Image
Copy and merge layers	Select multiple layers, then hold down Alt/Option and choose Merge Visible from the palette menu

Using fill and adjustment layers

The command in a **fill layer** (such as a Gradient Fill layer) or **adjustment layer** (such as a Levels adjustment layer) affects all the layers below it. We like to use them because they're flexible, meaning you can change their settings as often as you like, restack or hide/show them at any time, and even drag-copy them between files. When you're done using an adjustment layer, you can either merge it downward to make the changes permanent or toss it out. Now, how easy is that?

To create a fill or adjustment layer:

1. Click the layer that you want the fill or adjustment layer to appear above.

2. From the **New Fill/Adjustment Layer** menu ⊘. at the bottom of the Layers palette, choose a command.**A**

3. The dialog for the chosen command opens. Choose the desired settings, then click OK. The fill or adjustment layer will appear on the Layers palette; it will have a unique thumbnail icon for its particular command **B** and an editable mask.

To change the settings for a fill or adjustment layer:

1. On the Layers palette, double-click the fill or adjustment layer **thumbnail** (the thumbnail on the left).

2. Make the desired changes in the dialog, then click OK.

When you **merge down** a fill or adjustment layer, the changes are applied permanently to the underlying layer.

To merge a fill or adjustment layer:

Do either of the following:

Click the fill or adjustment layer to be merged downward, then press **Ctrl-E/Cmd-E.**

Right-click/Control-click near the fill or adjustment layer name and choose **Merge Down.**

➤ Adjustment layers don't contain pixels, so you can't merge them with one another. However, you can merge multiple adjustment layers into an image layer (or layers) by using either the Merge Visible or Flatten Image command on the Layers palette menu.

A From the **New Fill/Adjustment Layer** menu, choose an adjustment command.

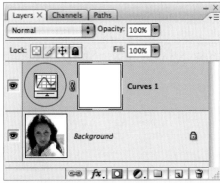

B Each **adjustment** command has a unique icon in its layer thumbnail.

CHANGING LAYER CONTENT

You can keep a fill or adjustment layer right where it is but change the command that it contains (e.g., change Levels to Curves or change Hue/Saturation to Color Balance). Click a fill or adjustment layer, then from the Layer > **Change Layer Content** submenu, choose a replacement command. Choose the desired settings, then click OK.

In the course of correcting an image, you can use multiple adjustment layers to address different specific tonal and color problems. If you nest the **adjustment layers** in a **group**, the Layers palette will be better organized, plus you'll have the option to add a layer mask that applies to all the layers in the group.

To create a layer group:

On the Layers palette for an image that contains two or more sequential adjustment layers, click the topmost adjustment layer, Shift-click the bottommost layer,**A** then press **Ctrl-G/Cmd-G** (or from the Layers palette menu, choose New Group from Layers, then click OK).**B** The layers are now nested in a group. Click the triangle to expand or collapse the group listing.

➤ To quickly hide or show all the adjustment layers, click the visibility icon for the group.

One way to limit the effect of an individual fill or adjustment layer is by editing the layer mask for that layer. And with your fill or adjustment layers in a group, you can create (and edit) a **layer mask** just for the **group** that will affect all the layers nested within it.

To create a layer mask for a layer group:

1. Do either of the following:

Create a **new selection** on an image layer.

To load a selection that you've already saved, Ctrl-click/Cmd-click the alpha channel on the **Channels** palette.

2. On the **Layers** palette, click the adjustment group, then click the **Add Layer Mask** button.🔲 A mask thumbnail will appear on the group layer.**C**

3. *Optional:* Edit the layer mask, such as by applying a gradient or by using the Brush tool.

➤ Although each adjustment layer in a group has its own layer mask, the mask effect may be limited by any dark areas that you add to the group mask.

CLIPPING ONE ADJUSTMENT LAYER

To restrict (clip) the effect of an adjustment layer to just the image or adjustment layer below it, Alt-click/ Option-click the line between the two. (Use the same command to undo the clipping effect.)

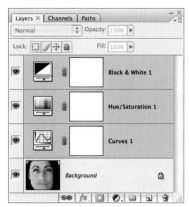

A We selected three **adjustment layers** on the Layers palette...

B ...then pressed Ctrl-G/Cmd-G to put the selected layers in a **group**.

C A **mask** that we added to the **group** is controlling the visibility of the corrections for all the adjustment layers in the group.

Choosing a mode for the History palette

As you work on a document, your edits are recorded and listed on the **History** palette. **A**
In Preferences > Performance > **History & Cache: History States,** you can control the maximum number of states that the palette may list. If this number is exceeded, prior states are deleted from the palette to make room for the new ones. Each open document has its own list of states, but the states will remain on the palette only until you close the document

A fast way to undo multiple edits is by clicking a prior state on the **History** palette. You can work with the palette in either of two modes. To change modes, choose History Options from the palette menu, then check or uncheck **Allow Non-Linear History.** With the palette in **linear** mode (Allow Non-Linear History unchecked), if you click an earlier state and resume editing from or delete that state, all subsequent (dimmed) states will be discarded. Simple.

In **nonlinear mode,** if you click (or delete) an earlier state, subsequent states won't be deleted or become dimmed. In this mode, if you resume image editing with an earlier state selected, your next edit will show up as the latest state on the palette. The latest state will incorporate the earlier stage of the image plus your newest edit, and all the states in between will be preserved. If you change your mind, you can click any in-between state whenever you like and resume editing from there. To learn more about this mode, see pages 88–90.

➤ The Make Layer Visibility Changes Undoable option in the History Options dialog makes the clicking on or off of the visibility icon on the Layers palette register as a history state. If you want to prevent those states from taking up space on the palette, keep this option off.

➤ To undo an unintentional file save, click a pre-Save state on the History palette.

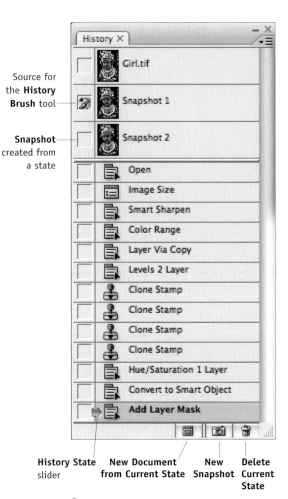

Source for the **History Brush** tool

Snapshot created from a state

History State slider

New Document from Current State

New Snapshot

Delete Current State

A The **History** palette lists edits made to a document (with the most recent edit at the bottom), lets you create snapshots of various editing stages, and lets you undo multiple steps.

Making snapshots of history states

A snapshot is like a copy of a history state, with one major difference: unlike a state, the snapshot will remain on the palette for the current editing session, even if the state from which it was created is deleted. You can click a snapshot thumbnail at any time to revert your document to that stage. All snapshots (and states) are deleted when you close your document.

You should get in the habit of creating snapshots periodically as you work and before running any actions on your document. To **create snapshots** manually, follow one of the methods below. In Method 2, you'll be able to choose whether the snapshot will be made from the full document, from merged layers, or from just the current layer.

To create a snapshot of a state:

Method 1 (without choosing options)

1. On the History palette, click the state that you want to create a snapshot of.

2. If the Show New Snapshot Dialog by Default option is off in the History Options dialog, click the **New Snapshot** button at the bottom of the History palette. If the aforementioned dialog option is on, Alt-click/Option-click the New Snapshot button. A new snapshot thumbnail will appear below the last snapshot in the upper section of the palette. **A** Click the last state on the palette to resume editing.

Method 2 (choosing options)

1. *Optional:* To create a snapshot of a layer, click that layer on the Layers palette.

2. Right-click/Control-click a history state and choose **New Snapshot**. The New Snapshot dialog opens.

3. Type a **Name** for the snapshot.

4. Choose an option from the **From** menu:

    Full Document creates a snapshot from all the layers on the Layers palette and is useful if you want to preserve all the edits at a particular stage of your document.

    Merged Layers merges all the layers on the Layers palette at that state into the snapshot.

    Current Layer makes a snapshot from only the currently selected layer in its current editing state.

5. Click OK.

To make a snapshot become the current state:

Do either of the following:

Click a **snapshot thumbnail.** If the Allow Non-Linear History option is off and you edited the document after taking that snapshot, the document will revert to the snapshot stage of editing and all the states will be dimmed; when you resume editing, all dimmed states will be discarded. If Allow Non-Linear History is on, subsequent states will remain on the palette.

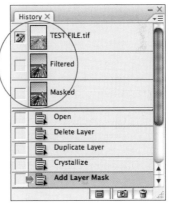

A Create **snapshots** to preserve editing states for the current work session.

CHOOSING SNAPSHOT OPTIONS

Choose **History Options** from the History palette menu and then, in the History Options dialog, check or uncheck any of the following options:

▶ **Automatically Create First Snapshot** to have Photoshop create a snapshot each time you **open** a file (this helpful option is checked by default).

▶ **Automatically Create New Snapshot When Saving** to have Photoshop create a snapshot each time you **save** a file. The time of day that the snapshot was created will be listed next to the snapshot thumbnail.

▶ **Show New Snapshot Dialog by Default** to have the New Snapshot dialog appear whenever you click the New Snapshot button, enabling you to choose options.

Working with nonlinear histories

The History palette's **nonlinear mode** gives you
the flexibility to go back to prior edit states without losing any of the recent edit states. In this
exercise, you'll set the History palette to nonlinear
mode, create three different edit states, and then
go back to compare the three states. This way, you
won't have to create a lot of duplicate or merged
layers in order to compare your edits.

To compare History edits in nonlinear mode:

1. Choose **History Options** from the **History** palette menu, check **Allow Non-Linear History**,
   then click OK.

2. Perform an edit in your document, then click
   the state prior to that edit.**A–D**

3. Create a new edit or a variation of the first
   one. Again, click the state prior to the first edit
   to restore the document to its preedited state
   (**A–D**, next page, and **A–B**, page 90).

4. Create a third edit. All three edits will be listed
   on the History palette. Click each edit state to
   compare them, then click the one you prefer
   and continue working on your document.

A We'll try out three different ways to create a
"find edges" version of this photo and use the
nonlinear mode of the History palette to compare the results.

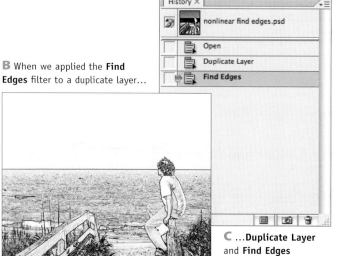

B When we applied the **Find
Edges** filter to a duplicate layer...

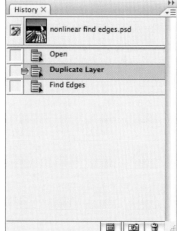

C ...**Duplicate Layer**
and **Find Edges**
appeared as listings on
the **History** palette.

D Because the palette is in nonlinear
mode, when we clicked the **Duplicate
Layer** state to restore the photo to its
prefilter stage, the more recent state
didn't become dimmed.

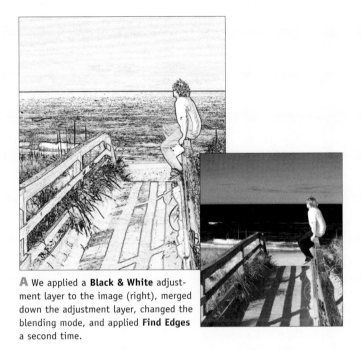

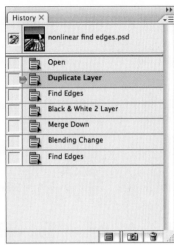

A We applied a **Black & White** adjustment layer to the image (right), merged down the adjustment layer, changed the blending mode, and applied **Find Edges** a second time.

B Next, we clicked back on the **Duplicate Layer** to restore the image to its prefilter state.

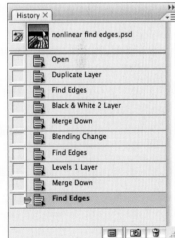

C We applied a **Levels** adjustment layer to the photo (right), merged down the adjustment layer, then applied **Find Edges** once more.

D This is the **History** palette after the third application of Find Edges.

See also the figures on the following page

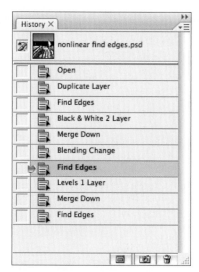

A We clicked the second Find Edges state to display and compare it with the third Find Edges state...

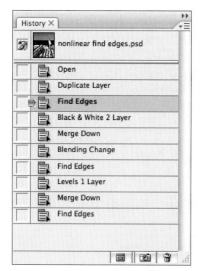

B ...and then we clicked the first Find Edges state to compare it with the second one. This is the History palette in action.

MEMORY USAGE AND THE HISTORY PALETTE

► The History palette uses some system memory, which you can free up periodically by choosing Edit > **Purge** > **Histories**.

► To clear all states (but not snapshots) from the History palette for just the current document, right-click/Control-click any state (it doesn't matter which one) and choose **Clear History.** This command can be undone.

Using presets

For any tool, you can save a collection of the current Options bar settings as a **tool preset.** Thereafter, when you use that tool, you can choose your preset from either the Tool preset picker on the Options bar or the Tool Presets palette. Having a variety of tool presets at your disposal saves you setup time when you use specific tools, even if the differences among the presets are minor.

If you check **Current Tool Only** on the Tool Presets palette or on the Tool preset picker, only those tool presets that pertain to the current tool will display on the palette and picker, and you'll have fewer presets to wade through. With Current Tool Only unchecked, the tool presets for all tools will display. Regardless of this setting, when you click a tool preset, the tool that the preset is used with becomes selected automatically.

To create a tool preset:

1. Customize a tool, such as the Brush, Crop, or Type tool.**A** Choose a preset from the appropriate picker (such as a brush tip for the Brush tool or a gradient for the Gradient tool), choose settings from Options bar (such as dimensions and a resolution for the Crop tool), and choose a Foreground color, if applicable, to save with the preset.

2. Do either of the following:

    On the Options bar, click the **Tool preset picker** thumbnail or arrowhead to open a temporary Tool Presets palette.**B**

    Open the **Tool Presets palette.**✂

3. Click the **New Tool Preset** button ⬛ on the picker or palette. The New Tool Preset dialog opens.**C**

4. If the default **Name** doesn't describe the preset adequately, change it. Also, if the dialog displays an Include Color option (such as for the Brush or Pencil tool), you can check it to save the current Foreground color with that preset.

5. Click OK. The new tool preset will appear on, and can be chosen from, both the picker and the palette.**D**

6. To preserve your tool presets for future use in any document, save them to a tool presets library by choosing **Save Tool Presets** from the picker or palette menu. You can also load any previously saved preset library via either menu.

A Choose options for a tool.

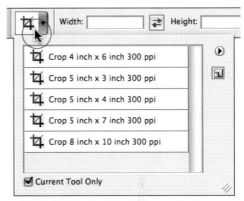

B Click the thumbnail or arrowhead to open the **Tool preset** picker (a temporary Tool Presets palette), then click the **New Tool Preset** button (on the right).

C Be sure to use a descriptive name for the new tool preset.

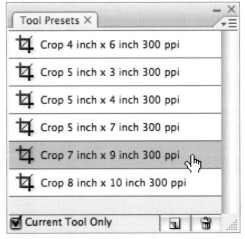

D The new preset appears on the **Tool Presets** palette.

As an evolving pro user, you're probably already familiar with many of the preset pickers in Photoshop, such as the Brush and Gradient preset pickers that can be accessed via the Options bar. The Swatches and Brushes palettes are preset pickers, too. Each item on a **picker** is called a **preset**, and each collection of presets that you can load onto a picker or palette is called a **library.**

To create a preset:

Each kind of preset is created in a different way, such as a pattern, color swatch, gradient, custom brush, custom shape, contour (for layer effects), or graphic style. The following are a few examples:

➤ Customize a brush via the Brushes palette or Brush preset picker, then click the **New Preset** button ⬚ on the palette or picker.

➤ Add a swatch to the Swatches palette by clicking the **New Swatch of Foreground Color** button. ⬚

➤ Create a gradient by clicking **New** in the Gradient Editor dialog.

➤ Create a style by clicking the **New Style** button ⬚ on the Styles palette or by clicking **New Style** in the Layer Style dialog.

➤ Create a pattern via Edit > **Define Pattern** or by clicking the **Save Preset Pattern** button ⬚ in the Filter > Pattern Maker dialog.

If you've created some **presets** that you want to preserve for future use, save them in a **library.**

To save all the presets currently on a picker as a new library:

1. From the palette or picker menu, choose **Save** [preset type].

2. Enter a name, keep the default extension and location, then click **Save.**

3. To make the new library appear on the palette or preset picker menu and on the menu in the Preset Manager, you must relaunch Photoshop.

Once your presets have been saved in a library, you can easily **load** them onto the appropriate **palette** or **picker** when needed.

To load a library of presets:

1. From the lower portion of the palette or the picker menu, choose the desired library name.

2. When the alert dialog appears, click **Append** to add the additional presets to the palette or

picker, or click **OK** to replace the current presets on the palette or picker with those in the library.

Note: If you made changes to the current palette, another alert dialog will appear. Click Save if you want to save your changes.

➤ Photoshop includes default presets, as well as an assortment of preset libraries that you can load as needed from the lower portion of the appropriate palette or picker menu.

The **Preset Manager** is a central dialog in which you can organize, append, replace, and reset your preset libraries and control which libraries load onto individual palettes and pickers at startup. Changes made to an individual preset picker are reflected in the Preset Manager, and vice versa.

To use the Preset Manager:

1. Do either of the following:

   Choose Edit > **Preset Manager.**

   From the menu on any palette or picker that contains presets, such as the Brush Preset picker or Brushes palette, choose **Preset Manager.**

2. In the Preset Manager (**A**, next page), choose from the **Preset Type** menu.

3. Do any of the following:

   To add presets to the current library, from the menu ⓘ, choose a **library name** (**B**, next page), then in the alert dialog, click Append (**C**, next page), or click OK to have them replace the current library.

   To append (to the current presets) a library that is not currently listed on the menu, click **Load**, locate the library, then click Load again.

   To restore the default library for the chosen type, from the menu ⓘ, choose **Reset** [preset type], then click Append to append the default presets to the current library, or click OK to replace the current library with the default presets.

4. Respond to any alert prompt that appears regarding saving changes to the current presets.

5. Click **Done.**

➤ To change how the presets are displayed, choose a thumbnail or list view from the Preset Manager menu.

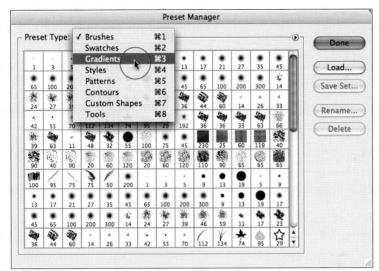

A In the **Preset Manager** dialog, choose the **Preset Type** that you want to work with.

B From the menu in the dialog, choose a library, then in the alert dialog, click **Append** to add the presets to the existing presets on the picker or click **OK** to replace them.

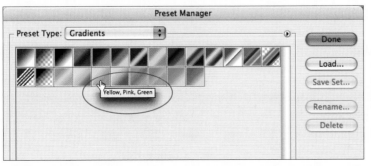

C The **library** will appear in the Preset Manager dialog and on the respective picker or palette when you exit the dialog.

Streamlining your workflow

This page lists some of the features of Photoshop that you can incorporate into your workflow to increase flexibility and boost your productivity.

Keep your edits flexible

➤ Copy imagery to duplicate or separate **layers;** use **adjustment layers** to try out tonal and color adjustments; use **fill layers** to apply colors; apply editable and removable **layer styles;** and use **layer comps** to show variations of a document to clients without having to open and close individual files.

➤ Place Camera Raw images or vector objects from Illustrator into Photoshop as **Smart Objects** for easy round-trip edits and updates.

➤ If you can afford the processing lag, apply filters as editable and removable **Smart Filters** to layers that you've converted to Smart Objects.

➤ Use **layer** and **vector masks** to hide or show areas of a layer.

Save, reuse, recycle

➤ Save your Camera Raw settings as **presets** for future use.

➤ Create and save **presets** for brushes, swatches, gradients, type, patterns, shapes, contours, styles, and tools. Save your presets in **libraries** for safekeeping and easy access.

➤ Save collections of layer effect, opacity, and blending mode settings as **styles** in the Styles palette for use in any Photoshop file.

➤ Store selections as **alpha** (grayscale) **channels,** then load them as selections when needed.

➤ Save repetitive sequences of editing or processing steps as **actions.**

➤ Create and save theme-oriented **workspaces,** with optional color-coded menu labels.

Use context menus

When you **right-click/Control-click** in the document window, depending on where you click and which tool happens to be selected, a list of **context-sensitive** commands pops up onscreen. Some palette thumbnails, names, and features have related context menus, too. **A–B** To make life simpler, we've included context menu choices in many of the instructions in this book.

Keep a spare

➤ **Duplicate** a **layer** (or a file, for that matter) and edit the copy.

➤ Create snapshots on the History palette as you work, or save snapshots of your files as separate documents via the **Create Document from Current State** button on the History palette.

Keep a record

➤ Get a notebook and use it to **take notes.** We're not kidding! Jot down the progression of features that you use, and even specific settings, for future reference. Do quick sketches of design concepts, make a record of images that inspire you as you go about your daily life, or write down possible new scenarios for streamlining your workflow. Someone in our household (being diplomatic here) has a pet peeve against writing notes on napkins, so we keep notebooks for many aspects of our lives—not just for Photoshop.

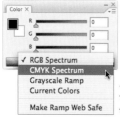

A The **context menu** for the color bar on the Color palette

B The **context menu** for a **selection**

To edit, adjust, copy, or move only part of a layer, **A** you must select that area first to isolate it. To hide or reveal part of a layer, you can use a mask. Creating selections and masks is prep work—and the more careful the prep, the better the results. Like house painting, some Photoshop work sessions can involve doing quite a bit of prep work before you get to the actual job of "painting."

It's not easy to distinguish among the many selection and masking controls in Photoshop, let alone decide which tasks they're best suited for. Without this knowledge, you could spend hours trying one selection technique after another and get nowhere; with the right tool in hand, you'll be better equipped to reach your goal. For techniques that will help you strategize at the beginning of your work sessions and make informed choices instead of guesses, see the summary of selection and masking methods that begins on the following page.

Following that summary, you'll learn how to use the Quick Selection and Magnetic Lasso tools, then tackle some challenging selection and masking tasks, such as selecting a complex object in a landscape, using adjustment layer masks, selecting feathery edges and hair, extracting imagery from a layer, and creating a selection based on a color range. Hopefully, you'll exit this chapter with some useful new techniques up your sleeve.

Creating selections and masks, though exacting work, is far from an exact science. Even more variables are thrown in when you consider that every image—not to mention Photoshop user—is unique. As you work with increasingly complex assignments, adopt a pro mindset, taking the liberty to veer from "standard" practice. If it works, it works.

SELECTING & MASKING

5

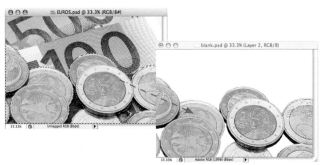

A One purpose for creating **selections** is to **move** imagery between files.

Choosing a selection method

SELECT IRREGULARLY SHAPED AREAS BASED ON COLOR OR TONAL VALUES

Magic Wand tool ✨ **A** *(see pages 104, 109, 112)*
Click to select color areas based on Options bar settings: a Tolerance range (how many shades or colors the tool may select) and whether you want to select Contiguous areas and/or Sample All Layers. This tool is useful for selecting a background in a photo, such as sky or water, or a solid color.

Quick Selection tool ✨ **B** *(see page 101)*
Click or drag to select well-defined but irregular areas, such as a figure on a plain background. The tool detects color boundaries automatically.

Magnetic Lasso tool ✨ **C–D** *(see pages 102–103)*
Let the mouse hover over the border of a shape, and the tool will create fastening points where it detects a high-contrast edge. You can also click to create fastening points. Use this tool to select objects or figures that are clearly delineated from their background in tonality or color. It produces more accurate results than the Lasso tool.

Color Range command *(see page 118)*
For selecting areas by color, this dialog is more powerful than the Magic Wand tool. Hide any layers you don't want to sample from, then choose Select > Color Range. With Sampled Colors chosen on the Select menu (the default option), click or drag with the eyedropper in the preview or document window. Add Shift to add to the selection or Alt/Option to subtract from it, or move the Fuzziness slider. You can also preview the selection in several modes, such as in grayscale, and, via the Select menu, limit the selection to a specific color family or tonal range, such as Reds or Highlights.

SELECT STRAIGHT-EDGED OR GEOMETRIC AREAS

Rectangular Marquee tool ▢
Elliptical Marquee tool ○
Drag to create a rectangular or elliptical selection. To specify a specific width-to-height ratio or dimensions, choose from the Style menu on the Options bar, then enter Width and Height values. Start dragging, then hold down Alt/Option and keep dragging to draw from the center of the selection; or use Shift to constrain the selection to a square or circle.

Polygonal Lasso tool ✨ *(see pages 184 and 284)*
Click to create corners in a straight-edged selection.

A We selected the tabletop by clicking once with the **Magic Wand** tool.

B We selected the egg yolk with one quick drag of the **Quick Selection** tool.

C We selected the cookie cutter by moving the **Magnetic Lasso** tool over its edges.

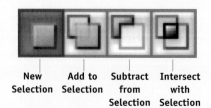

New Selection	Add to Selection	Subtract from Selection	Intersect with Selection

D Click one of these options for your selection tool on the Options bar (New Selection is the default setting).

SELECT IRREGULAR AREAS

Lasso tool ⚲ A *(see pages 100 and 148)*

Drag to create an irregularly shaped nonmagnetic selection. You can use this tool to create a new selection, such as a loosely defined, feathered area for an adjustment, or to modify an existing selection that you created with a different tool (see the next page). Alt/Option toggles the Lasso to a temporary Polygonal Lasso, and vice versa. While using the Polygonal Lasso, you can press Delete to reverse your steps.

Extract dialog B–C *(see pages 114–116)*

The Filter > Extract dialog is useful for selecting intricate shapes, such as figures or animals, that are hard to trace manually. You define a rough selection area with a masking tool and then, when you exit the dialog, the extracted pixels appear on their original layer, surrounded by transparency. Cleanup work is usually needed. This command works better than the Eraser and Background Eraser tools; also see an alternative method on pages 104–109.

CREATE A SELECTION BY PAINTING A MASK

Quick Mask mode D *(see pages 150, 154, 160)*

Click the Edit in Quick Mask Mode button 🔲 on the Tools palette, with or without creating a selection first. Choose the Brush tool, then paint a mask with black as the Foreground color. Protected areas have a light red, nonprinting "rubylith" shield. To remove unwanted areas of the mask, press X to switch the Foreground color to white, and paint again. When you're done painting the mask, click the Edit in Standard Mode button; the mask will convert automatically to a selection.

CREATE A VERY PRECISE SELECTION

Pen tool ✎ E *(see page 291)*

When you need the most precise and smooth selection possible, such as for a high-resolution image, you can trace shapes with the Pen tool (click the Paths button 🔳 on the Options bar for the tool); then to convert the path to a selection, Ctrl-click/Cmd-click the path on the Paths palette. Or to convert a selected path to a vector mask, choose Layer > Vector Mask > Current Path.

➤ To select shape edges in order to sharpen them selectively, see pages 203–206.

Note: For more page references, see the index. Many of the Photoshop selection tools and techniques are also covered in our Visual QuickStart Guide.

A We selected the cookie by dragging with the **Lasso** tool.

B We highlighted this figure by using tools in the **Extract** dialog.

C Upon exiting the dialog, the unextracted imagery became transparent.

D We put the image in **Quick Mask** mode, then with the Brush tool, painted a mask on the cookie.

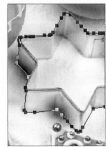

E A path, in the shape of the cookie cutter, is being stored on the **Paths** palette. A path can be converted to a selection at any time.

CLEAN UP OR MODIFY A SELECTION

Refine Edge dialog A *(see pages 106, 109, 204–205)*

With a selection active and a selection tool chosen, click Refine Edge on the Options bar (or choose Refine Edge from the context menu). This very versatile dialog lets you refine the smoothness, sharpness, and precision of a selection edge; expand a selection outward or contract it inward; eliminate a fringe; and apply feathering—plus it lets you preview the refinements on different backgrounds.

Lasso tool* ⌁

This tool is useful for enlarging selection areas or for removing stray selection areas after using the Magic Wand tool. Shift to add; Alt/Option to remove; or Alt-Shift/Option-Shift to select the intersection of the existing and new selection areas.

Quick Mask mode

Click the Edit in Quick Mask Mode button ▣ on the Tools palette, then paint with the Brush tool and black as the Foreground color to subtract from a selection, or with white to add to it.* This method is also useful for eliminating stray selection areas after using Magic Wand tool.

Grow, Similar commands *(see pages 104 and 109)*

Based on the current Tolerance setting of the Magic Wand tool, the Grow command selects additional contiguous areas, and the Similar command selects additional noncontiguous areas.

Convert a selection to a path *(see page 290)*

For precise reshaping, convert a selection to a path by clicking the Make Work Path from Selection button ◠ on the Paths palette. Reshape the path (see pages 295–298), then to convert it back to a selection, Ctrl-click/Cmd-click the thumbnail on the Paths palette. Note: A path (vector) becomes less precise when converted to a selection (pixels).

Invert a selection *(see page 109)*

To swap the currently selected and unselected areas, press Ctrl-Shift-I/Cmd-Shift-I (Select > Inverse).

Transform a selection marquee *(see page 179)*

Choose Select > Transform Selection, then manipulate the handles on the transform box to scale (Shift-drag for proportional scaling), skew (Ctrl-drag/Cmd-drag a side handle), distort (Ctrl-drag/Cmd-drag a corner handle), or apply perspective to (Ctrl-Alt-Shift/Cmd-Option-Shift drag a corner handle) the selection marquee. To accept the edits, double-click inside the marquee.

Use a stylus and graphics tablet, if available.

MOVING AND COPYING SELECTIONS

TASK	METHOD
Move just the selection marquee	Drag inside it with a selection tool
Move the selection contents*	Drag inside the marquee with the Move tool (V) ⯈
Copy the selection contents on the same layer	Alt-drag/Option-drag inside the marquee with the Move tool
Copy the selection contents to a new layer	Press Ctrl-J/Cmd-J

*If you move selection contents on a layer, the exposed area is replaced with transparency. If you move a selection on the Background, the exposed area is filled with the current Background color.

MIND YER LAYERS!

Before or after you create a selection, click a layer or the Background to let Photoshop know which tier of your document your edits will affect.

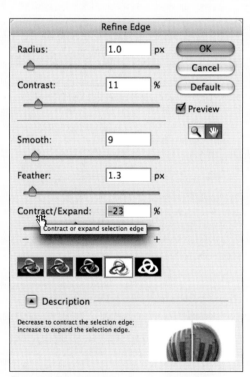

A Via the **Refine Edge** dialog, you can modify the edge of an active selection in many different ways.

USE LAYER MASKS

Layer masks *(see pages 58, 107, 142–143, 174–178)*
Vector masks *(see pages 300–303)*
Filter effects masks *(see page 278)*

The purpose of a mask is to hide or reveal parts of a layer, such as to limit adjustments to a specific area or to soften the seams between image layers. For a quick summary of how to create and use masks, see the sidebar at right. Black areas in a mask hide pixels fully, white areas reveal pixels fully, and gray areas function as a partial mask. Layer masks are used extensively throughout this book.

You can attach a mask to any kind of layer—be it image, adjustment, Smart Object, or type—but not to the Background. Adjustment, fill, and shape layers automatically have a mask, as do Smart Object layers that contain Smart Filters. If you add a layer (pixel) mask while a selection is active, the selection shapes will become white or black areas in the mask, depending on whether you click or Alt/Option click the Add Layer Mask button. You can edit a mask by using a filter (such as a blur filter) or an adjustment command (such as Levels). A mask that is created when no selection is active will be blank, but black or white areas can be added to it (e.g., by using the Brush or Gradient tool).

A mask won't change the image permanently unless you apply it. Masks can also be hidden or discarded at any time.

SAVE SELECTIONS

Alpha channels *(see page 106)*

To store an active selection on the Channels palette as an alpha channel, click the Save Selection as Channel button. An alpha channel can be displayed onscreen in grayscale by clicking the alpha channel name or as a rubylith shield by clicking the visibility icon. In an 8-bit image, an alpha channel can store up to 256 shades of gray; in a 16-bit image, it can store up to 32,000 shades. Note that alpha channels use mega amounts of storage space, so we usually store our selections as layer masks.

You can distort, blur, or sharpen the shapes in an alpha channel by various means, such as by using the Brush tool or filters. To load an alpha channel onto your image as a selection, Ctrl-click/Cmd-click the channel thumbnail. You can combine an alpha channel selection with an existing selection as you load it (see the sidebar at right).

QUICK SUMMARY: USING MASKS

TASK	METHOD
Create a mask for a layer or layer group; the selection area reveals layer content	Create a selection (optional), then click the Add Layer Mask button
Create a layer mask; the selection area hides layer content	Create a selection (optional), then Alt-click/Option-click the Add Layer Mask button
Display a layer mask in grayscale	Alt-click/Option-click the layer mask thumbnail
Display a layer mask as a Quick Mask	Click the layer mask thumbnail, then press \ (backslash)
Select the white areas in a mask	Ctrl-click/Cmd-click the layer mask thumbnail
Hide (or show) the effect of a layer mask	Shift-click the layer mask thumbnail
Invert a layer mask	Click the mask thumbnail, then press Ctrl-I/Cmd-I
Disable, delete, or apply a layer mask	Right-click/Control-click the mask thumbnail and choose from the context menu
Copy a mask to another layer	Alt-drag/Option-drag the layer mask thumbnail
Create a vector mask, before or after drawing a path	If the layer already has a layer mask, click the Add Layer Mask button; Ctrl-click/Cmd-click if it doesn't
Convert a path to a vector mask	Click a layer, then choose Layer > Vector Mask > Current Path. Shape layers automatically have a mask

LOADING AS A SELECTION

To load a layer mask, a path, a channel, or nontransparent areas of a layer as a selection, use these modifier keys as you click the thumbnail on the palette:

TASK	METHOD
Load it as a selection	Ctrl-click/Cmd-click
Combine it with an existing selection	Ctrl-Shift-click/ Cmd-Shift-click
Subtract it from an existing selection	Ctrl-Alt-click/ Cmd-Option-click
Select the intersection of existing and new	Ctrl-Alt-Shift-click/ Cmd-Option-Shift-click

Next, we'll review the two selection tools that you'll probably use quite often: Lasso and Quick Selection. They both select irregular areas via dragging, but in distinctly different ways.

Using the Lasso tool

We use the **Lasso** tool to select nongeometric areas; to create loose selections for limiting adjustments or other edits; and to clean up selections made with other tools, such as the Quick Selection or Magic Wand (e.g., to eliminate stray areas from a Magic Wand selection).

To create a free-form selection:

1. Choose the **Lasso** tool 🔾 (L or Shift-L).

2. Click a layer, then drag to select an area.**A** Don't worry if your initial selection isn't perfect —you can refine it later. When you release the mouse, the open ends of the selection will join automatically with a straight edge.

3. Do any of the following:

   To **add** to the selection, Shift-drag around the area to be added.

   To **subtract** from the selection, starting with the pointer outside the selection, Alt-drag/Option-drag around the area to be removed.

   To refine the selection, click **Refine Edge** on the Options bar, then adjust any of the settings.**B–D**

▶ To create a straight side with the Lasso tool, keep the mouse button down and Alt-click/Option-click to create corners. To resume drawing the free-form selection, release Alt/Option as you drag.

C Via a **Hue/Saturation** adjustment layer, we increased the **Saturation** for the **Blues** (our selection became the white area in the adjustment layer mask).

USING A FEATHERED LASSO SELECTION FOR A SATURATION ADJUSTMENT

A With the **Lasso** tool, we selected an area of water that we want to make brighter.

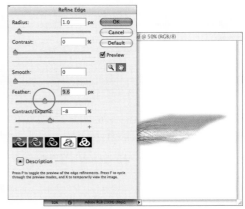

B We raised the **Feather** value of the selection via the **Refine Edge** dialog.

D The water is now a brighter blue. Because the edge of the selection was feathered, the adjustment faded gradually into adjacent (unadjusted) areas.

Using the Quick Selection tool

The **Quick Selection** tool creates a selection more quickly and with less effort than the Lasso tool, and the results are very precise if you use it on shapes that have distinct borders. All you have to do is drag across a shape. You can enlarge the resulting selection to include adjacent shapes, or push back into it to make it smaller.

To use the Quick Selection tool:

1. Click a layer, then choose the **Quick Selection** tool ⬚ (W or Shift-W).

2. If there is an existing selection in your document, deselect it by clicking the **New Selection** button ⬚ on the Options bar or by pressing Ctrl-D/Cmd-D.

3. Check **Auto-Enhance** on the Options bar for improved edge detection.

4. Choose an appropriate diameter for the tool for the area you want to select by pressing] or [, then drag within that area.**A** The selection will expand to the first distinct shape boundary that the tool detects. It will preview as you drag, then become more precise when you release the mouse.

5. Zoom in, then do the following:

   To **enlarge** the selection, click or drag in an adjacent area; the selection will enlarge to include it.

   ➤ You can use another tool to add or subtract from the selection, such as the Lasso tool.**B**

   To **subtract** from the selection, Alt-drag/Option-drag across the area to be subtracted.**C–D**

   To **contract** the selection inward, Alt-drag/Option-drag along the edge of the selection.

   ➤ To block an adjacent area from becoming selected as you enlarge a selection, Alt-click/Option-click that area, release Alt/Option, then drag to enlarge the selection area. The block will remain in effect only until you click that area again with the Quick Selection tool.

   ➤ To undo the last click or drag of the Quick Selection tool, press Ctrl-Z/Cmd-Z.

USING A QUICK SELECTION TO ISOLATE PART OF A LAYER

A To enable us to move the buckets and table to a different background, our first step was to select most of the background with the **Quick Selection** tool.

B We cleaned up some selection edges with the **Lasso** tool.

C With the **Quick Selection** tool and **Alt/Option** down, we dragged carefully on the handles of the pails to deselect them.

D We **inverted** the selection (Ctrl-I/Cmd-I), then with the Move tool, drag-and-dropped it into a different document.

Using the Magnetic Lasso tool

If the shapes you want to select have clearly defined edges and you want some hands-on control over creating the selection, we suggest using the **Magnetic Lasso** tool. Drag or move the tool along a shape, and a selection line snaps to where the tool detects a change in contrast. The stronger the contrast between the shape and the surrounding areas, the more precise the selection. This tool requires less dexterity than the Lasso.

To use the Magnetic Lasso tool:

1. Choose the **Magnetic Lasso** tool 🖉 (L or Shift-L).

2. Choose Options bar settings:

    Feather (0–250 pixels) to soften the edge of the selection. (The effect won't be visible until you edit the selected area.) The higher the file resolution, the larger the feather value required. For example, on a 300 ppi image, a Feather value of 5–7 would soften the edge slightly, whereas a Feather of 20–25 would soften a noticeably wider area. (To feather an existing selection, use the Refine Edge dialog.)

    Width (1–256 pixels) for the size of the area in pixels under the pointer that the tool considers when it places a selection line.**A–B** Try a wide Width (20 pixels or wider) for a high-contrast image that has strong edges, or a narrow Width (2–6 pixels) for an image that has subtle contrast changes or small shapes in close proximity.

    Contrast (1–100%) for the degree of contrast needed between shapes in order for the tool to read it as an edge. For a low-contrast image, use a low Contrast value (less than 10%).

    ➤ If you choose a low or high Width, do the same for the Contrast.

    Frequency (0–100) to control how often fastening points are placed as the selection is made (**A–C**, next page). The higher the Frequency, the more often points are placed. To select a highly irregular contour, try using a high Frequency (70 or higher). We usually use a Frequency value of 50 pixels.

    To use tablet pressure to control the Width, click the 🖉 button.

3. Click in the image to establish the first fastening point. Move the mouse, without pressing the

A At a **Width** setting of **10** pixels, the **Magnetic Lasso** tool correctly detected some parts of the man's profile but missed his forehead and brow.

B At a **Width** setting of **4** pixels, the tool detected the edge of his forehead and brow correctly.

FRIENDS AND RELATIONS

While using the **Magnetic Lasso** tool, you can do either of the following:

➤ Click, then Alt-click/Option-click to use a temporary **Polygonal Lasso** tool (to draw a straight edge). To get back to using the Magnetic Lasso, release Alt/Option and click.

➤ Alt-drag/Option-drag to use a temporary **Lasso** tool (to draw an irregular edge manually). To go back to using the Magnetic Lasso, release Alt/Option.

mouse button, along the edge of the shape that you want to select. A selection line will snap to the edge of the shape, and temporary points will appear (they'll disappear after step 4).

If the selection line starts to follow adjacent shapes that you don't want to select, click the edge of the shape that you do want to select to add a fastening point manually, then continue to move or drag the mouse. (To delete the last fastening point, press Backspace/Delete.)

Note: If you move or drag the mouse quickly on a large image, the selection border may not keep pace with you. Pause to let it catch up.

4. To close the selection, do one of the following:

Double-click anywhere over the shape.

Click the starting point (a small circle will appear next to the Magnetic Lasso tool pointer).

Press Enter/Return.

Alt-double-click/Option-double-click to create a new fastening point and close the selection with a straight segment.

➤ To decrease the Width value by 1 pixel while creating a selection, press [; to increase it, press].

➤ To cancel (remove) an incomplete Magnetic Lasso selection, press Esc.

MAKING THE MAGNETIC LASSO STRONGER

To temporarily heighten the contrast in an image to help the Magnetic Lasso tool work "smarter," choose **Levels** from the New Fill/Adjustment Layer menu ⬮ at the bottom of the Layers palette. In the Levels dialog, move the black Input Levels slider to the right **D** (and also the gray Input Levels slider, if needed), then click OK. Delete the adjustment layer after you're done using the Magnetic Lasso.

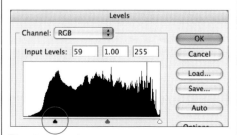

D To increase the contrast in an image via **Levels,** move the **black Input Levels** slider to the right.

A The **Magnetic Lasso** tool used with a **Frequency** setting of **75** produced too many fastening points.

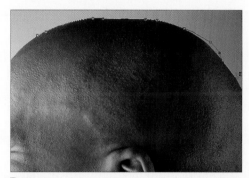

B The same tool used with a **Frequency** setting of **20** produced too few fastening points to accurately define the head shape.

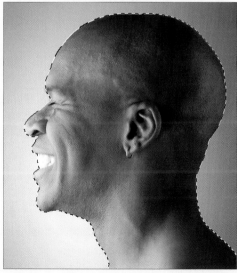

C We selected the head successfully using a **Width** setting of **4** and a **Frequency** setting of **50.**

Selecting complex shapes

Small, finely detailed shapes, such as leaves on trees in a landscape, are incredibly tedious to select manually with just a selection tool. We've devised an easier method in which you use adjustment commands and other features to differentiate and isolate delicate shapes from surrounding areas. Using this method, we'll step you through three demanding tasks: to select leaves on a tree, fur on an animal, and hair in a portrait.

In this first task, we'll show you how to select **leaves** on a **tree** by using the Black & White, Levels, and Similar commands, plus the Magic Wand and Lasso tools. Subsequent adjustments or edits can be limited to just the selected or unselected areas.

To select leaves on a tree:

1. Open an RGB image of a leafy tree (**A**, next page). To simplify the selection process, you'll convert the image to black and white temporarily and heighten the contrast between the shapes. From the New Fill/Adjustment Layer menu ◑ at the bottom of the Layers palette, choose **Black & White**. The Black & White dialog opens.

2. To heighten the contrast between the leaves and sky, do the following: (**B**, next page)

   To darken the leaves, move the **Yellows** slider almost all the way to the left. If the leaves contain green, also move the **Greens** slider to the left by the same amount.

   To lighten the sky, move the **Cyans** and **Blues** sliders almost all the way to the right.

   Click OK.

3. To pump up the contrast even more, from the New Fill/Adjustment Layer menu ◑ at the bottom of the Layers palette, choose **Levels**. The Levels dialog opens.

AN ALTERNATIVE APPROACH

To differentiate shapes from one another, we think the method described in the steps on this page is more flexible and yields better results than the following method, which you may have heard about or already use. But here it is, just for the record: Display and view each separate channel first to see which offers the most contrast between the shapes to be selected and the surrounding areas. Next, duplicate the chosen channel, increase the contrast on the duplicate via the Levels command, then use the Magic Wand tool to select the newly differentiated shapes. Finally, clean up the selection, save it as an alpha channel, then maybe use the Gaussian Blur filter to soften the edge transitions in the alpha channel.

---

4. Do the following: (**C**, next page)

   Move the **black Input Levels** slider to the right to further darken the leaf shapes.

   Move the **gray Input Levels** slider to the left to further lighten the background.

   Click OK.

   ➤ You can readjust the Black & White conversion or Levels contrast at any time.

5. Now you're ready to create the selection. Choose the **Magic Wand** tool (W or Shift-W). On the Options bar, set the Tolerance to around 40 and check Contiguous.

6. With the Levels adjustment layer still selected, click a dark area in the document window. To select additional leaves and branches, Shift-click more areas, then choose Select > **Similar**.

7. If your selection includes shapes that aren't part of the tree, choose the **Lasso** tool ◯ (L or Shift-L), then Alt-drag/Option-drag around those areas.

8. The final task is to fine-tune the selection edge. On the Layers palette, click the visibility icon for each of the adjustment layers to hide them.

Instructions continue on page 106

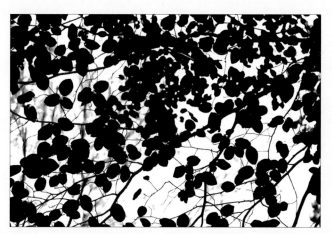

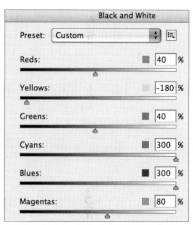

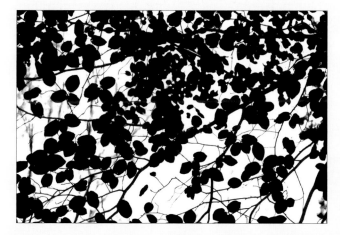

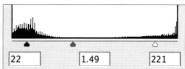

A We want to lighten and increase the saturation of just the leaves in this image, so we'll use the following method to select those areas.

B In the **Black & White** dialog, we moved the **Yellows** slider to –180 to darken the leaves and moved the **Cyans** and **Blues** sliders to +300 to lighten the sky.

C Next, we used a **Levels** adjustment layer to further darken the leaves and pump up the contrast between the leaves and sky.

9. Click **Refine Edge** on the Options bar. In the Refine Edge dialog, click **Default**. As you make the following adjustments, click the **On Black** preview button to gauge how much of the light background color appears in the selection, or click **On White** to gauge the edge sharpness:**A**

Set the **Radius** value to around 10–30 and the **Contrast** value to a slightly higher value to include soft-edged pixels while preserving the edge contrast.

Set the **Smooth** value to 1 and the **Feather** value to 0 to preserve the jagged edges on the leaves.

Set the **Contract/Expand** value to +7 to ensure that the fine edges of the leaves and branches stay visible, but not so much that sky areas appear.

Click OK.

10. Display the Channels palette, then click the **Save Selection as Channel** button. A new alpha channel containing your selection shapes will appear on the palette.**B**

11. Press Ctrl-D/Cmd-D to deselect the selection.**C**

To use the selection to limit an adjustment, follow the instructions on the next page.

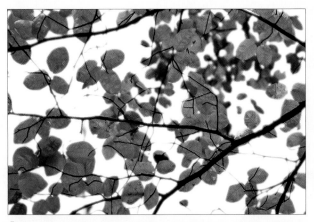

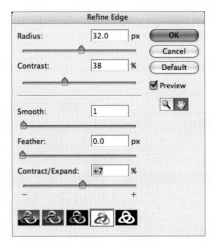

A Our chosen **Refine Edge** dialog settings (right) produced a cleaner, more clearly defined edge, as shown in this preview closeup.

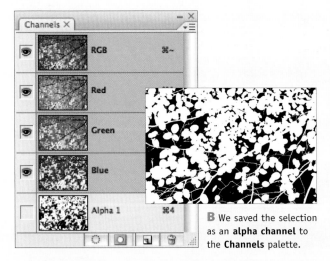

B We saved the selection as an **alpha channel** to the **Channels** palette.

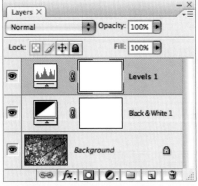

C The **adjustment layers** that we used to heighten the contrast appear on the Layers palette.

Using adjustment layer masks

An existing selection can be converted to an adjustment **layer mask** to protect part of the image from further edits.

To limit a tonal adjustment using a selection:

1. Either create a selection or, on the Channels palette, Ctrl-click/Cmd-click an alpha channel (saved selection) to load it as a selection. (We loaded the channel that we saved in step 10 on the previous page.)

2. Choose a command from the **New Fill/ Adjustment Layer** menu at the bottom of the Layers palette. **A** The adjustment layer has a layer mask, in which white represents the active, editable areas.

3. Make adjustments in the dialog, then click OK.

▶ Now that the selection has been converted to an adjustment layer mask, you should delete the alpha channel to reduce the file size.

To apply the effect of an adjustment layer to the unselected areas of an image, **invert** the **adjustment layer mask**.

To reverse the selected and unselected areas in an adjustment layer mask:

1. *Optional:* If you're following along with the leaves image, on the Layers palette, drag an adjustment layer over the New Layer button to duplicate it, and keep the duplicate selected.

2. Click the layer mask thumbnail, then press **Ctrl-I/Cmd-I** to invert the black and white areas in the mask. **B** (In our example, the adjustment layer is now affecting only the sky.)

3. Double-click the adjustment layer thumbnail on the duplicate adjustment layer, choose settings, then click OK. **C**

▶ You can change the command for a selected adjustment layer via the Layer > Change Layer Content submenu (the dialog for the replacement command will open).

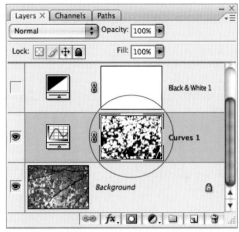

A We created a **Curves** adjustment layer. The layer mask (for the leaves) matches the new alpha channel that we created in the previous exercise.

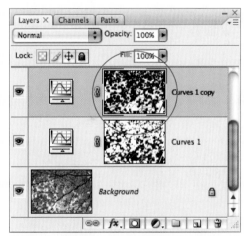

B We duplicated the Curves adjustment layer, then **inverted** the **layer mask** so the next round of adjustments will affect just the sky.

C We dragged the RGB curve upward for the first **Curves** adjustment layer to lighten only the leaves, and dragged the RGB curve downward for the second adjustment layer to darken only the sky. Compare this final image with **A** on page 105.

Selecting furry or feathered critters

Next, we'll show you how to select the fine edges of **fur** or **feathers** on pets or wildlife (or on any fuzzy-edged object), using steps similar to those in the previous exercise.

To select furry or feathered critters:

1. Open an RGB image of a furry or feathered beast, or any other fuzzy-edged subject. **A** From the New Fill/Adjustment Layer menu ⬤ on the Layers palette, choose **Black & White.**

2. In the Black & White dialog, move the sliders to increase the contrast between the fur and background, then click OK.**B** (Don't worry, the grayscale state of the image is just temporary.) Keep the layer selected.

3. To heighten the contrast further, create a **Levels** adjustment layer. In the Levels dialog, move the **black Input Levels** slider to the right and the **white Input Levels** slider to the left.**C**

   Move the **gray Input Levels** slider to the left to increase the contrast, or to the right to decrease it (**A**, next page). Click OK.

A We want to select the tiger so we can put it on a solid-color background.

B In the **Black & White** dialog, we moved the **Reds** slider to 300 to lighten the fur, moved both the **Greens** and **Blues** sliders to −150 to darken the background, and moved the **Yellows** slider to −44 to increase the contrast between the fur and background.

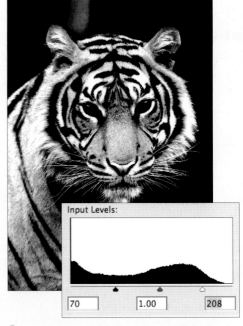

C In the **Levels** dialog, we moved the **black Input Levels** slider to the right to darken the background and the **white Input Levels** slider to the left to shift lighter shades to white and intensify the contrast.

4. The shape you want to select should now stand out distinctly from its background. To create the selection, choose the **Magic Wand** tool (W or Shift-W). On the Options bar, set the Tolerance to around 30–40 and check Anti-alias and Contiguous.

5. Click the background area. If necessary, choose Select > **Grow** to expand the selection.

6. Shift-click with the Magic Wand tool again, if necessary, to select the rest of the background. To clean up the selection, choose the **Lasso** tool (L or Shift-L), then Shift-drag around any unselected areas of the background that you want to add to the selection.

When the cleanup is done, choose Select > **Inverse** to reverse the selected/unselected areas.

7. On the Layers palette, hide the two adjustment layers, then click the Background. On the Options bar, click **Refine Edge.**

8. In the Refine Edge dialog, click **Default**, adjust the sliders to refine the selection on the edge of the fur,**B** then click OK.

9. On the **Channels** palette, click the **Save Selection as Channel** button to save the selection as an alpha channel. Now you can safely deselect the selection (Ctrl-D/Cmd-D), and save your file. To put the selection on a new background, follow the steps on the next page.

A In the **Levels** dialog, we moved the gray **Input Levels** slider to the left to increase the contrast and thereby preserve the finely detailed fur.

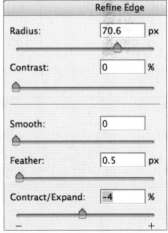

B In the **Refine Edge** dialog, we set the **Contrast, Smooth,** and **Feather** sliders to the settings shown above to preserve a sharp edge, moved the **Radius** slider to the right until we saw enough fine details on the edges of fur, and moved the **Contract/Expand** slider to the left to eliminate most of the remaining background pixels.

Creating a background for imagery

Follow these instructions if you want to **create** a **new background** for a selection of soft-edged imagery (in our example, a tiger). The black "cutout" in the layer mask that you create from the selection will reveal areas from the underlying layer.

To create a new background for selected imagery:

1. On the **Channels** palette, Ctrl-click/Cmd-click the new alpha channel (your saved selection) to load it as a selection.

2. On the Layers palette, click the Background. From the New Fill/Adjustment Layer menu at the bottom of the palette, choose **Solid Color**. The selection appears in the layer mask, and the Color Picker dialog opens.

3. Click a hue on the vertical spectrum bar, click a color variation in the large square, then click OK.

4. On the **Color Fill** layer, click the layer mask thumbnail, then press Ctrl-I/Cmd-I to **invert** the black and white areas in the mask. Now the black area on the Color Fill layer mask—a cutout in the shape of the selection—is revealing imagery from the underlying layer. **A**

5. Zoom in to 100% view to examine the edge of the fur or feathers. If there's still some background color showing along the edge, with the layer mask thumbnail still selected, choose Image > Adjustments > **Levels** (Cmd-L/Ctrl-L) (don't create an adjustment layer).

   ➤ If the background color is visible along only part of the edge of the image, drag a loose selection around that area with the Lasso tool before choosing the Levels command.

6. In the Levels dialog, move the **gray Input Levels** slider to the left until the background color along the edge is reduced, **B** but not so far that you start to lose details along the edge. Click OK. The Levels adjustment contracts the black area of the mask, thereby hiding more of the underlying layer.

A This closeup shows the tiger image as revealed through the **layer mask** on the **Color Fill** layer. Note that some of the original background is still visible on the edges.

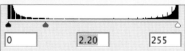

B We loosely selected the right side of the tiger with the Lasso tool, then in the **Levels** dialog, moved the **gray Input Levels** slider to 2.20 to shrink the black area of the mask and hide a bit more of the background.

Selecting hair in a portrait

In this example, we'll select the **hair** on a model in preparation for adding subtle "highlighting." The challenge will be to select all of her hair, including the delicate strands. As in the previous two exercises, we'll heighten the contrast by using a Black & White adjustment layer, increase the contrast further by using a Levels adjustment layer, and tweak the edge of the selection by using the Refine Edge dialog. In addition, we'll choose Lighter Color blending mode for the Black & White adjustment layer to keep the hair from being converted to grayscale.

Note: If you want to use this task as a tutorial, follow the trail of figures and captions on this page and the next two pages, using the image file that we have provided.

A Selecting the hair in this portrait will be a challenge because some of the background colors are close in value to the hair color.

B We held down Alt/Option and chose **Black & White** from the New Fill/Adjustment Layer menu. In the New Layer dialog, we chose **Lighter Color** from the Mode menu, then clicked OK. In the Black & White dialog, we moved the **Reds** slider to –200 and the **Yellows** slider to +300 to increase the contrast between the hair and the background.

C To distinguish the hair even more from its background, we created a **Levels** adjustment layer, and used the Input Levels slider settings shown above to slightly darken the edges of the individual hair strands (but not so much as to make them disappear).

See also the figures on the next two pages

A For the **Magic Wand** tool, we set the Tolerance to 60 and checked Contiguous on the Options bar. We clicked on the hair, lowered the Tolerance to 35, then Shift-clicked to select other areas of hair, including the small strands at the bottom.

B Using the **Quick Selection** tool (and a small brush diameter), we dragged to add unselected areas of hair to the selection. Where the tool pushed the selection into the background, we clicked or dragged with Alt/Option held down to push it back onto just the hair.

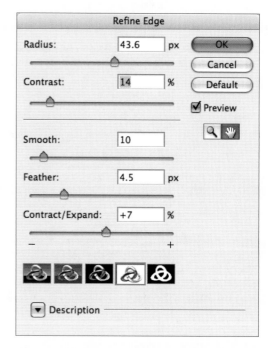

C With the selection active, we clicked **Refine Edge** on the Options bar. In the Refine Edge dialog, we moved the **Smooth, Feather,** and **Contract/Expand** sliders to the values shown at right to keep the fine hair strands selected, while minimizing the selection of background pixels (see also the figures on the next page).

A Continuing in the Refine Edge dialog, we moved the **Radius** slider until individual hair strands looked soft but well defined (we settled on a value of 43), and set the **Contrast** slider to 14 to sharpen the edge of the selection.

B We saved our final selection to an **alpha channel.** Compare an alpha channel from the original selection (upper left) with the softer, finer edge details that resulted from using the Refined Edge command (lower right).

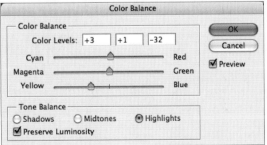

C To finish this exercise, we hid both adjustment layers, loaded the alpha channel selection, then used a **Color Balance** adjustment layer to lighten the highlights in the model's hair (we clicked Midtones and set Yellow to −10, then clicked Highlights and chose the settings shown above).

Using the Extract filter

The **Extract** filter offers a unique method for lifting a shape from its background, even a shape that has finely detailed edges. In the dialog, you mask and preview the shapes to be extracted and use special tools to clean up the edges. When you exit the dialog, the extracted imagery appears on the original layer, surrounded by transparency. Further cleanup work can be done with the History Brush tool, as we show you on page 116.

To extract a shape from its background:

1. Duplicate the image layer, then hide the original.**A**

2. Choose Filter > **Extract** (Ctrl-Alt-X/Cmd-Option-X). The resizable Extract dialog opens.

3. You'll mask the border of the object first, then click the interior to define the fill area. Choose the **Edge Highlighter** tool (B) from the toolbox on the left side of the dialog.**B** Under **Tool Options**, choose a small Brush Size (20–60 px) to highlight a shape that has smooth edges or a large brush (100–140 px) if the shape has wide, choppy edges, such as hair blowing in the wind.

4. Draw a border along the edge of the shape you want to extract, starting and stopping as needed (**A**, next page). Cover the edge of the figure or object, plus a sliver of the background. You can change the brush size as needed by pressing [or]. Complete the loop to close the shape. You don't need to highlight shape edges that meet the edge of the canvas.

   To use the Edge Highlighter tool as a "Smart" highlighter on a high-contrast edge, hold down Ctrl/Cmd and drag. The highlight width will change automatically to the minimum size necessary.

   ► To zoom in on the preview, press Ctrl-+ (plus)/Cmd-+. Or to zoom out, press Ctrl-– (minus)/Cmd-–. To move the image in a magnified preview with a temporary Hand tool, hold down the Spacebar and drag.

5. If you need to erase any unwanted edge highlighting, use the **Eraser** tool (E) with an appropriate brush size, then mark the edge again, if needed, with the Edge Highlighter tool.

A We want to select this man and then move him to a different background. His spiky hair will be too hard to select with the Magic Wand or Lasso tool.

 Edge Highlighter B

 Fill G

 Eraser E

 Eyedropper I

 Cleanup C

 Edge Touchup T

 Zoom Z

Hand H

B Tools in the **Extract** dialog

A With the **Edge Highlighter** tool in the Extract dialog, draw a highlight around the object or figure to be extracted.

B Fill the interior of the highlight with the **Fill** tool.

6. Choose the **Fill** tool (G), then click inside the highlighted area. **B** Note: If the entire image becomes filled, it's because you left gaps in the highlighted edge. Click again to undo the fill, use the Edge Highlighter tool to close the remaining gaps, then click once more with the Fill tool. Click the **Preview** button. **C**

7. In the **Preview** area on the right, choose any of the following:

   Show: Extracted to view the extracted image.

   Display: None to display the background as transparent; or **Black Matte**, **Gray Matte**, or **White Matte** to display the extracted shape on a background of black, gray, or white, respectively. The matte options will enable you to see if there are any edges that might need cleanup work.

Continued on the following page

C Click **Preview** to display the extraction results. As you can see from this closeup, some areas along the edge of the man's face, neck, and clothing need to be restored.

8. To refine the extraction, zoom in, then do any of the following (choose an appropriate brush size for the tool):

Drag with the **Cleanup** tool (C) to gradually mask (hide) pixels along the edge, or Alt-drag/Option-drag to restore them.**A–C**

Use the **Edge Touchup** tool (T) to gradually sharpen the edge of the selection.**D** Don't use this tool on thin strands, such as wispy hair, or it will eliminate too much detail.

9. Click OK. The extracted imagery will appear on the same layer, surrounded by transparency.

If you didn't do a full cleanup job while the Extract dialog was open, you can **restore** areas with the **History Brush** tool—provided you do so immediately.

To restore areas of extracted imagery:

1. Immediately after using the Extract command, choose the **History Brush** tool (Y or Shift-Y).

2. Display the **History** palette. Click in the left-most column for the **Layer via Copy** state (the one just above the Extract command) to designate it as the source for the History Brush tool; the History Source icon will appear.

3. Draw strokes in the document window where you want to restore pixels.**E**

4. Show the Background temporarily, then study it for a moment to see which details you want to restore. Hide the Background, then continue to draw strokes with the History Brush tool.

5. If you go overboard and restore too many pixels, choose the **Eraser** tool (E or Shift-E). On the Options bar, choose Mode: Brush, Opacity 70–80%, and a small, soft brush tip, then drag along any of the edges.

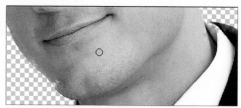

A We can see in the **Preview** that some parts of the face and neck won't be included in the extraction.

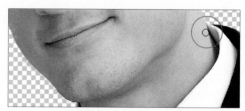

B We dragged the **Cleanup** tool along the left side of the face to restore pixels.

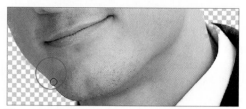

C We also restored pixels on the right side of the neck and shirt collar.

D A couple of quick swipes with the **Edge Touchup** tool restored the edge of the sleeve.

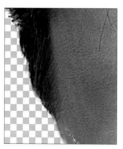

E If you missed a few spots with the Extract command, you can use the **History Brush** tool to restore them.

Moving imagery between files

Now you'll see how to **drag** and **drop** extracted or silhouetted imagery into another document. You can use the extracted imagery from the previous set of instructions or any imagery that's silhouetted on its own layer. As an optional step, you can apply the Photo Filter command to match the color temperature of the silhouette to its new background.

To drag and drop imagery to another file:

1. Open a document that contains a silhouette and a document that is to become the new background. Make sure that the latter has the same resolution as the former.

2. Choose the **Move** tool ⊕ (V), then drag the silhouetted image layer into the other document window.**A**

3. Check **Show Transform Controls** on the Options bar, then Shift-drag a corner handle if you want to **scale** the silhouette, or drag inside it to **reposition** it, then double-click inside it to accept the changes.

   ➤ If you don't see all the handles on the transform box, press Ctrl-0/Cmd-0 (zero) to enlarge the document window.

4. *Optional:* While holding down Alt/Option, choose Photo Filter from the New Fill/ Adjustment Layer menu. In the New Layer dialog, check Use Previous Layer to Create Clipping Mask (to restrict the adjustment to just the silhouette layer), then click OK. In the Photo Filter dialog, choose a Filter to make the image warmer or cooler, use the Density slider to control the level of adjustment,**B** then click OK.**C**

As in the steps on page 110, you can use a layer mask and the Levels command to **clean up** the **edge** of a **silhouette** after dropping it into a new file.

To remove edge pixels from an imported layer:

1. Ctrl-click/Cmd-click the thumbnail for an imported image layer to select just the imagery.

2. Click the **Add Layer Mask** button. The selection will become the white area in the layer mask. Keep the mask thumbnail selected.

3. Zoom in on the edges, then choose Image > Adjustments > **Levels** (Cmd-L/Ctrl-L). In the dialog, move the gray **Input Levels** slider to the right to reduce the white area and mask more pixels from the edge of the imported image.

A After using the Extract command and subsequent cleanup, we drag-and-dropped the imagery into another document.

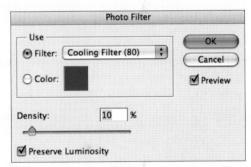

B We used a **Photo Filter** adjustment layer to make the man's skin warmer, to better match the color temperature of the skin tones of the other figures.

C The final extracted, imported, and adjusted image fits right into its new "office space."

Using the Color Range command

Via the **Color Range** dialog, you can select areas of an image by clicking in the preview or, as in these instructions, simply by choosing a tonal range from the menu.

To select a tonal range in an image:

1. Open an image, **A** then choose Select > **Color Range**.

2. From the **Select** menu in the Color Range dialog, **B** choose a color or tonal range. If desired, you can choose a Selection Preview option for the preview in the document window, such as Black Matte. Click OK. The selection displays in the document window.

3. *Optional:* With the selection active, make a correction, such as via an adjustment layer. **C** For further corrections, use the Color Range dialog to select a different tonal range, such as Midtones, and create another adjustment layer.

A In this image, the highlight areas look overexposed.

B We chose **Highlights** from the **Select** menu in the **Color Range** dialog.

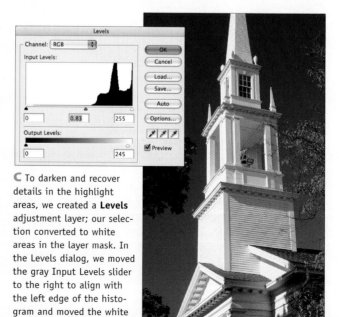

C To darken and recover details in the highlight areas, we created a **Levels** adjustment layer; our selection converted to white areas in the layer mask. In the Levels dialog, we moved the gray Input Levels slider to the right to align with the left edge of the histogram and moved the white Output Levels slider to 245.

In this chapter, you'll use various Photoshop features to remove noise, correct for under- and overexposure, enhance or correct contrast, simulate a neutral density filter, and neutralize a color cast.

If you shoot digital photos, as a first step we recommend performing as many color and tonal corrections in Camera Raw as possible (see Chapter 3). Camera Raw offers an impressive range of controls, the slider interface is easy to use, and the corrections are nondestructive. Then, for digital photos that have been processed through Camera Raw but need further refinement, as well as for scanned images, there are plenty of excellent color and tonal correction features in Photoshop to choose from. The challenge is to learn which command or tool can best solve a specific problem you're faced with, and to use it effectively.

We'll introduce you to color samplers and the Info palette first so you can monitor how the colors in your image change as you perform corrections. Then you'll learn how to correct exposure problems by using the Shadow/Highlight command, which, like Camera Raw, preserves all the tonal levels in an image. We'll also show you how to remove noise by using a filter, various ways to use the Curves command, and how to apply brush strokes to a neutral gray layer to enhance contrast gently.

The tasks in this chapter are presented in a logical progression, from broad corrections to subtle tweaks. If you're working with the photos we've supplied in a tutorial fashion, plunge in. If you're working with a photo of your own, study it and try to diagnose its weaknesses first. You can pick and choose among the many methods we offer, depending on the nature of the problems you need to correct.

➤ Related topics in other chapters include combining dual exposures on pages 56–58 and retouching portraits in Chapter 7.

Note! Remember to calibrate your monitor on a regular basis, and especially before following the instructions in this chapter.

COLOR & TONAL CORRECTION

IN THIS CHAPTER

Note: Settings listed in the captions in this chapter were chosen for photos that are approximately 3000 x 2000 pixels.

Using color samplers

Instead of relying on the single color readout that you get with the Eyedropper tool, you can get multiple readouts by placing up to four color samplers in your image with the **Color Sampler** tool. As you perform color and tonal corrections, pre- and postadjustment color breakdowns from the sampler locations will display as instant readouts on the Info palette. The color samplers will save with your file and can be displayed or hidden as needed.

To place color samplers in a document:

1. Choose the **Color Sampler** tool 🖉 (I or Shift-I).

2. Click in up to four locations in the document window; a color sampler will appear in each spot.**A** If you want to cover a wide spectrum of tonal values, place a sampler in a highlight area, a midtone area, and a shadow area, and perhaps place the fourth one on a specific color that you want to monitor closely.

➤ To add color samplers while the dialog for an adjustment command is open, Shift-click in the document window.

➤ If you flip or rotate the whole canvas, your samplers will move accordingly.

To move a color sampler:

Do either of the following:

Choose the **Color Sampler** tool 🖉 (I or Shift-I), then drag a color sampler.

Choose the **Eyedropper** tool 🖉 (I or Shift-I), then Ctrl-drag/Cmd-drag a color sampler.

When you **remove a color sampler** from a document, its readout, logically, disappears from the Info palette.

To remove a color sampler:

Do either of the following:

Choose the **Color Sampler** tool, then Alt-click/Option-click a sampler (the pointer will become a scissors icon).**B**

Choose the **Eyedropper** tool, then Alt-Shift-click/Option-Shift-click a sampler.

A Click in the document window with the **Color Sampler** tool to create up to four samplers.

B A color sampler is **deleted**.

MAKING COLOR SAMPLERS REAPPEAR

If you choose any tool except the Color Sampler, the Eyedropper, or a painting or editing tool, color samplers that you've placed in your document will disappear temporarily. If you want to redisplay them, choose one of the above-mentioned tools or open an adjustment dialog.

The **Info** palette displays color breakdowns of the pixel(s) currently under the pointer and at the location of up to four color samplers. You can use the palette to get instant feedback, such as while changing settings in an adjustment dialog.

To view color readouts on the Info palette:

1 Display the **Info** palette.

2. To change the **color mode** for any readout on the palette, click the dropper icon and choose from the menu.**A** (Actual Color displays data in the current document color mode.)

3. When an adjustment command dialog is open, the palette displays preadjustment data to the left of each slash, followed by the postadjustment data, as in "45/34%".**B**

When used with their default Sample Size setting of **Point Sample**, the Eyedropper and Color Sampler tools sample data only from the single pixel directly below the pointer. For color correction work, we recommend sampling from a slightly wider area. Choose the Color Sampler tool, then from the **Sample Size** menu on the Options bar,**C** choose **3 by 3 Average** (the setting we use) to sample an average color from an area 3 pixels square; or if you're working on a very high resolution image, choose one of the other Average options.

➤ Changing the Sample Size for the Color Sampler tool also changes that setting for the Eyedropper tool, and vice versa.

➤ When correcting an image on dual computer displays, choose the same sample size in both displays (different sample sizes would yield different-colored sampler data).

➤ If you hide a layer that a sampler is reading information from, the Info palette will update to reflect the change in data.

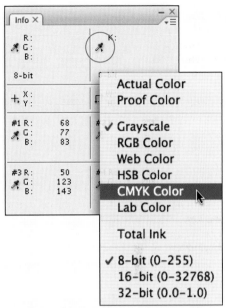

A To change the **color mode** for a readout, click its dropper icon and choose from the menu.

B When an adjustment dialog is open, the Info palette displays **pre-** and **postadjustment** values for the pixels under the pointer and for any color samplers that you've placed in your document (#1–#4).

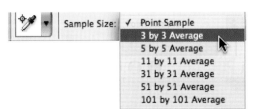

C From the **Sample Size** menu on the Options bar, choose a sampling area for the **Color Sampler** tool (your choice will also apply to the Eyedropper tool).

Using the Shadow/Highlight command

One good use for the Shadow/Highlight command is to illuminate shadow areas that result from strong side or back lighting. The Shadows and Highlights sliders are similar to two sliders in Camera Raw: The Shadows sliders recover shadow detail, as the Fill Light slider in Camera Raw does, and the Highlights sliders recover highlight detail, as the Recovery slider in Camera Raw does. Best of all, the Shadow/Highlight command produces minimal data loss while preserving the full range of tonal values.

To use the Shadow/Highlight command:

1. Click the Background, press Ctrl-J/Cmd-J to duplicate it, and keep the duplicate layer selected.**A**

2. *Optional:* Convert the duplicate layer to a Smart Object by choosing Filter > Convert for Smart Filters. The Shadow/Highlight command will be applied in the next step as a Smart Filter, which you can change the settings for at any time. Editing a Smart Filter takes more processing time, though, so be patient.

3. Choose Image > Adjustments > **Shadow/Highlight**. The Shadows/Highlights dialog opens, and it adjusts the image automatically using the default settings.

4. Check **Show More Options**.**B**

A Because of the low position of the sun at the time this image was shot, the shadow and midtone areas were **underexposed**.

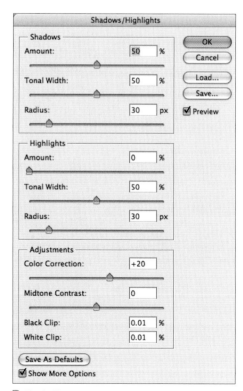

B Check **Show More Options** in the **Shadows/Highlights** dialog.

5. For the **Shadows**, increase the **Amount** slightly to lighten and recover details in the shadow areas. To keep the light from looking artificial, keep this value below 60%.

➤ You can use the scrubby sliders in this dialog.

6. To control which tonal levels will be adjusted, do the following:

Choose a **Tonal Width** value for the **Shadows** to control which part of the tonal range the command affects. **A–D** To limit the adjustment to just the darkest shadows, keep this value between 5–10%; or to allow the adjustment to affect the midtones, set it to 40–60%.

Continued on the following page

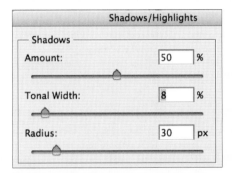

A The low **Tonal Width** setting is limiting the **Shadows** adjustment to the dark shadows.

B The shadows and dark midtones are still too dark, although the **Shadows** slider is near the middle of its range.

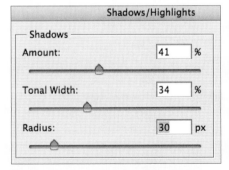

C This time, we reduced the **Amount** for the **Shadows** and increased the **Tonal Width**.

D The higher **Tonal Width** settings shown at left successfully corrected the exposure in both the shadows and the midtones.

Change the **Radius** value to expand or reduce the number of neighboring pixels affected by the adjustment.**A**

7. For the **Highlights**, increase the **Amount** to darken the highlights and recover some detail (at 0%, the slider has no effect). Also adjust the

Tonal Width and **Radius** to control whether just the highlights, or both the highlights and midtone levels, are adjusted.**B**

8. If an increased Amount for the Shadows caused oversaturation, correct it by reducing the **Color Correction** value in the **Adjustments**

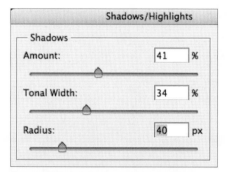

A In the **Shadows** area of the **Shadows/ Highlights** dialog, a **Radius** setting of 40 spread the Shadows correction into just the right amount of surrounding pixels. (A low Radius setting would have flattened the lighting, whereas a high Radius value — over 100 px for our file — would have created too much contrast by allowing too many pixels to be compared.)

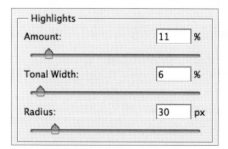

B In the **Highlights** area, we reduced the **Tonal Width** to restrict the adjustment to just the highlights (not the midtones) and raised the **Amount** to darken and recover details in the highlights. This also had the effect of subduing the yellow in the buildings in the foreground.

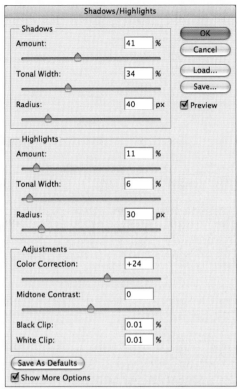

A For our final **Shadows/Highlights** adjustment, we set the **Color Correction** value to 24 to boost the color saturation, but left the **Midtone Contrast** value at 0.

area (or to boost the saturation, raise the Color Correction value).**A**

You can also increase the **Midtone Contrast** to intensify the contrast in the midtones, or lower it to do the opposite (this slider has the same effect as the gray Input Levels slider in the Levels dialog).

9. Uncheck then recheck **Preview** to compare the original and adjusted images, adjust any of the settings, then click OK.**B–C**

➤ If you created a Smart Filter layer and you want to edit the settings, double-click the Shadows/Highlights listing. To change the visibility or opacity of the adjustment, use the controls for the Smart Object layer. This will take less processing time than using the visibility or opacity control for the Smart Filter itself would.

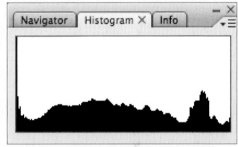

B There are no gaps or spikes in the **Histogram** for the final image, which proves that the Shadow/Highlight command preserved the full tonal spectrum.

C Overall, the **Shadow/Highlight** command improved the detail in the shadow areas.

Reducing noise

Digital noise (graininess or speckling) may result from using a high ISO setting in a camera or may be the unintended result of corrections made to recover details in underexposed shadow areas. The **Reduce Noise** filter removes both luminance noise (a grainy texture) and color noise (randomly colored dots). The filter also includes an option that removes artifacts (caused by the JPEG compression methods) from JPEG photos.

To reduce noise in shadow areas:

1. Zoom to 200%. With the **Hand** tool, move the image around in the window and inspect the shadow areas for stray red, green, or blue speckles or graininess.

   ➤ For a temporary Hand tool, hold down Spacebar.

2. Choose Filter > Noise > **Reduce Noise.**

3. In the Reduce Noise dialog, **B** check Preview. If you click in the document window, that area will appear in the preview window.

4. As you choose settings, try to strike a balance between removing noise, which will soften the image slightly, and keeping the edges sufficiently sharp. Click **Basic** and examine the result in the preview as you do the following (you can use the scrubby sliders):

   Choose a **Strength** value (try 6–8).

   Keep **Preserve Details** at a low value (around 5–10%) to reduce luminance noise and to avoid introducing more noise.

   Choose a **Reduce Color Noise** value (try 60–70%).

   Keep the **Sharpen Details** value low (10%) to avoid introducing artifacts.

5. Click **Advanced**, then click the **Per Channel** tab (**A**, next page).

6. From the **Channel** menu, choose **Blue** (the most noise is usually in this channel), then choose a Strength value of around 4–6 and a Preserve Details value of 50–60%. Next choose the **Red** channel and a Strength value of 1–2.

   ➤ For a portrait, try these Strength settings for the channels: Red 4, Green 2, and Blue 2. For a photo shot outdoors at twilight, try a Strength setting for the Blue channel of 6–8.

A In this closeup of an image shot at twilight, you can see some **noise** (tiny red, green, and blue dots).

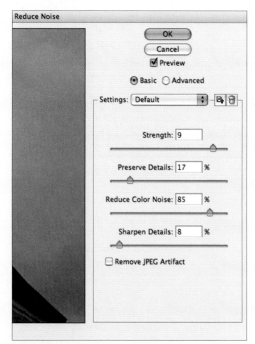

B In the **Reduce Noise** filter dialog, we clicked **Basic**, then chose these initial settings.

7. *Optional:* To save the current settings, click the Save a Copy of the Current Settings button, ✎ type a name, then click OK. You can choose saved settings from the Settings menu for any file.

8. Click and hold on the preview and then release to compare the original and adjusted images. Adjust the settings if needed, then click OK.**B**

9. We recommend that you resharpen the image via the Smart Sharpen filter to restore some lost definition (use a low Amount setting).

➤ To reduce the visibility of artifacts created by compression in a JPEG file, check Remove JPEG Artifact in the Basic options of the Reduce Noise dialog.

Using the Curves command

To adjust the tonal values, contrast, and white balance in a digital photo, whenever possible, start by using the nondestructive Basic and Tone Curve controls in Camera Raw. Then if you need to apply tonal and color corrections in Photoshop, use the command that the pros reach for: Curves. This command is useful in many scenarios, such as:

➤ When you need to correct a file that can't be processed through Camera Raw.

➤ When you want to correct an imbalance in a specific tonal or color range of an image with more precision than the Camera Raw sliders allow.

➤ When you want to limit which parts of an image are adjusted (by using the mask on the Curves adjustment layer).

➤ When you want to limit the adjustment to just the color or luminosity values of an image (by choosing a layer blending mode for the Curves adjustment layer).

We'll show you how to correct the color in a still life, a landscape, and a portrait by using a Curves adjustment layer. In each case, you'll use the dialog controls in the following order: make tonal adjustments to enhance contrast via the Curves sliders first; neutralize a color cast by using the gray eyedropper next; then fine-tune the color correction by subtly reshaping the curves for one or more of the individual color channels.

Continued on the following page

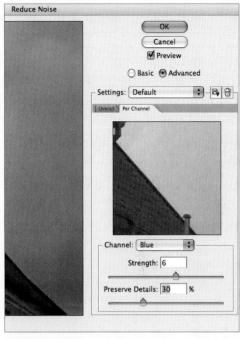

A Next we clicked **Advanced,** then chose settings for the **Blue** channel (and Red channel).

B The **Reduce Noise** filter successfully smoothed out the grainy texture.

Increasing contrast by using the Curves command

In these instructions, you'll apply basic tonal corrections to the **shadow**, **highlight**, and **midtone** areas of an image by using the **Curves** command.

To increase contrast by using the Curves command:

1. Open an RGB image, then create a **Curves** adjustment layer.

2. In the Curves dialog, click the **Curve Display Options** arrowhead, if necessary, to show more options, and check all four of the **Show** options.

Adjust the shadows and highlights

3. Examine the static histogram behind the curve. To increase the contrast in a dull image, drag the black and white **Input** sliders inward to align with the edges of the histogram.**B** Or to adjust the highlight and shadow clipping in high-contrast **Threshold** mode, Alt-drag/ Option-drag the black slider until a few areas of black appear,**C** then Alt-drag/Option-drag the white slider until a few areas of white appear.

Adjust the midtones

4. Do either of the following:

   To lighten the **midtones**, drag the middle of the curve upward; or to darken the midtones, drag the middle of the curve downward. A new point appears each time you move part of the curve.

   To boost the **contrast**, drag the part of the curve that represents the dark midtones downward slightly, and drag the part that represents the light midtones upward (**A–C**, next page).

Adjust a specific area of the image

5. Move the pointer over an area of the image that needs adjusting and then, to associate it with a part of the curve, press the mouse; a hollow circle will appear on the curve. Ctrl-click/Cmd-click to make a corresponding point appear on the curve, then move the new point upward to lighten that area, or downward to darken it (**D–E**, next page).

6. Click OK.

➤ Increasing contrast via the Curves command may also have the unintended effect of increasing color saturation. To limit a Curves adjustment to just tonal values (not colors), set the adjustment layer blending mode to Luminosity.

A This image could use a boost in tonal contrast.

B In the **Curves** dialog, we moved the black and white Input sliders slightly inward...

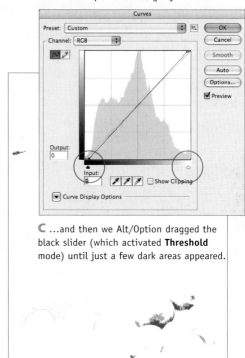

C ...and then we Alt/Option dragged the black slider (which activated **Threshold** mode) until just a few dark areas appeared.

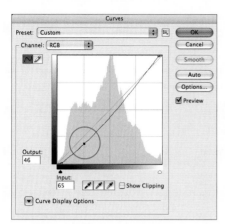

A We dragged the part of the curve that represents the dark midtones downward.

B The shadows and dark midtones are even darker now, especially in the foreground.

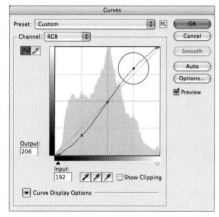

C We dragged the middle of the curve upward, and also the part of the curve that represents the light midtones.

▶ To heighten the contrast in an image, replicate the S shape that you see on the curve at left.

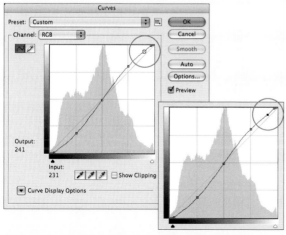

D When we pressed the mouse on a part of the image, a circle appeared on a corresponding tonal region of the curve; we lowered that part of the curve slightly (as shown in the insert).

E Making the midtones and highlights lighter improved the contrast, and lowering the top part of the curve restored some detail (as you can see on the wedge of cheese in the center).

Neutralizing a color cast

Suppose, after adjusting the tonal balance in an image, you still notice a **slight color cast.** To remove it, the first step is to locate a 50% midtone gray area in the image that's either neutral or close to it (a neutral gray has equal R-G-B values). If you can easily pinpoint such a gray, skip this task and go right to the instructions on the next page; if you can't, follow the instructions on this page first.

To pinpoint a neutral gray in an image:

1. Open an RGB image **A** and display the **Info** palette.ⓘ Choose **Actual Color** for the first readout on the palette (click the dropper icon to access the menu) and **Grayscale** for the second readout.

2. Choose the **Color Sampler** tool 🖌 (I or Shift-I).

3. On the Layers palette, click the Background, then press Ctrl-J/Cmd-J to duplicate it.

4. Press Ctrl-I/Cmd-I to **invert** the colors in the duplicate layer.

5. To help you locate a neutral gray, choose **Difference** as the layer blending mode. Any colors in the duplicate layer that match colors in the Background will display as black. Therefore, any inverted grays that are close to 50% neutral will still match the same grays in the background and will display as black.**B**

6. Move the pointer over black areas, noting the K readout on the Info palette. When you locate an area where the K value is at or near 99% (a neutral gray), click to place a color sampler.**C**

7. If you spot another black area in the image that's close to 99%, click to create a second color sampler, just as a second option.

8. Hide the duplicate layer, then follow the steps on the next page.

A This image has a yellowish **color cast.**

B We **inverted** the duplicate layer and changed the layer blending mode to **Difference.**

C With the **Color Sampler** tool, we placed sampler points on two areas that read as 98%K on the Info palette.

This exercise involves **neutralizing** a gray in the image by using the Curves command.

To neutralize a gray and remove a color cast with one click:

1. Open either an image that has an identifiable neutral gray or the image that you used for the instructions on the previous page.

2. Show the **Info** palette. ❶

3. Create a **Curves** adjustment layer. In the Curves dialog, click the gray (middle) eyedropper. 🖋

4. Do either of the following:

   Click the **identifiable** neutral gray area, then view the RGB readouts on the Info palette.

   Click the #1 sampler point in the image, then the #2 sampler point, viewing the readout for each on the Info palette to decide which one is removing the color cast more effectively. **A–B**

5. Once you verify that the readouts to the right of the slashes are as close in value as possible, signifying the presence of a neutral gray, **C–D** click OK. If you think the color needs still more tweaking, follow the captions on the next page.

A With the **gray eyedropper** chosen in the **Curves** dialog, we clicked a sampler point in the document.

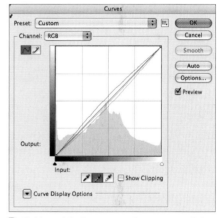

B Clicking with the gray eyedropper caused the curve for each color to be modified automatically and created a neutral gray.

C Converting gray areas to a **neutral gray** removed the yellow cast from the image. How simple was that?

Navigator	Histogram	Info ×
R: 134/ 123		K: 58/ 60%
G: 126/ 123		
B: 110/ 123		
8-bit		8-bit
X: 4.987		W:
Y: 1.037		H:
#1 R: 131/ 120		#2 R: 134/ 123
G: 126/ 123		G: 126/ 123
B: 111/ 124		B: 110/ 123

D On the **Info** palette, the RGB values from our Curves adjustment (to the right of each slash) are almost equal, which indicates that the color samplers are now reading neutral grays.

FINE-TUNE A COLOR CORRECTION VIA INDIVIDUAL CHANNELS IN CURVES

If you neutralized the midtone grays in your image as per the instructions on the previous page, but the colors still don't look quite as they should, try using the Curves command again, except this time modify the curve for **individual color channels.**

A The original image has a greenish cast. We used the technique described on page 130 to locate a neutral gray, then clicked to place a sampler point on the girl's sleeve (in the area shown by the circle).

B Clicking with the **gray eyedropper** from the **Curves** dialog neutralized the midtones but left the girl's face with a reddish cast.

DON'T TOUCH THAT DIAL!

► When you click in an image with the gray eyedropper, a midtone point is placed on the curve for the individual Red, Green, and Blue channels automatically. To avoid throwing off the neutralizing effect, don't move those points.

► When adjusting the color channels in the Curves dialog, keep the blending mode for the Curves adjustment layer on the default setting of Normal.

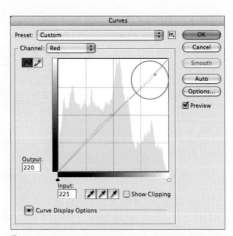

C In the **Curves** dialog, we lowered the upper part of the **Red** curve to reduce reds in the highlights.

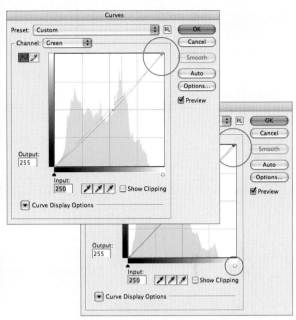

A Now the face looks less red. So far so good. Next, to balance the Green and Blue channels, we place another sampler point on a bright white area of the sleeve (in the area shown above).

B While noting the sampler point #2 data on the Info palette (see **C** on this page), we moved the white slider slightly inward on the **Green** curve in the **Curves** dialog, then did the same for the **Blue** curve, until the **G** and **B** readouts matched the **R** readout.

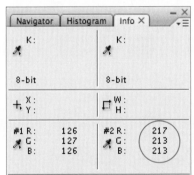

C Note the **Info** palette readout from sampler point #2 before we adjusted the Green and Blue curves...

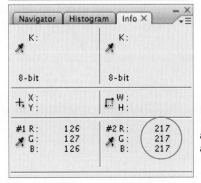

...and after we adjusted the Green and Blue curves.

D In the final image, the face looks less red and the shirt sleeve is a brighter white.

Simulating a neutral density filter

When shooting a landscape, sometimes the proper exposure setting for a sky can leave the foreground area underexposed (or vice versa). To resolve this conflict on site, photographers reduce light on the upper part of the lens by using a graduated **neutral density filter**. To simulate the effect of such a filter for a landscape photo in Photoshop, follow these instructions.

To simulate a graduated neutral density filter:

1. Open a landscape photo that contains a properly exposed ground and an overexposed sky.**A**

2. On the Layers palette, create a **Curves** adjustment layer.

3. In the Curves dialog, do the following:

   If the sky lacks strong highlights, align the **white Input** slider with the edge of the histogram to brighten the highlights.**B**

   Drag the part of the curve that represents the **light midtones** downward to darken the sky and make it more saturated.

   Click OK.**C** Don't fret about the foreground being too dark; you'll correct that next.

4. Keep the adjustment layer selected, and choose the **Gradient** tool ▮ (G or Shift-G).

5. On the Options bar, click the **Black, White** preset on the Gradient preset picker; click the **Linear** style button (**A**, next page); choose Mode: Normal; and choose Opacity 100%.

6. Starting from where the sky meets the ground, drag a short distance upward. You want the gradient in the layer mask to block the Curves effect from the lower part of the image (**B–C**, next page).

7. To control where the black part of the gradient mask ends, choose the **Move** tool ⊹ (V), and check **Show Transform Controls** on the Options bar. On the transform box for the gradient, drag the top center handle upward or downward until you're satisfied with where the Curves effect ends, then double-click inside the box to accept the edit (**D**, next page).

A The sky in this photo is too light relative to the foreground. We'll enhance it by using a Curves adjustment layer.

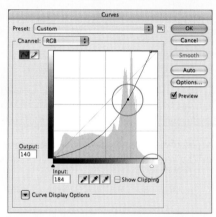

B In the **Curves** dialog, we moved the white Input slider inward and lowered the part of the curve that corresponds to the values in the sky.

C The **Curves** adjustment darkened the whole image.

8. If necessary, choose the **Brush** tool, ✏ a Soft Round tip, and an Opacity of 75%, press D, then carefully draw strokes over any shapes from the foreground that extend into the sky. The shapes will be added to the mask, as you'll see in the updated layer mask thumbnail. **E–F**

B We dragged the **Gradient** tool upward a short distance, starting from where the sky meets the ground.

A On the Options bar for the Gradient tool, we chose the **Black, White** preset on the Gradient preset picker and clicked the **Linear** style button.

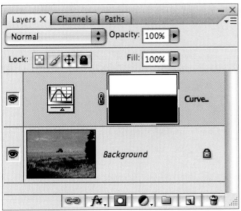

C The gradient appeared in the **layer mask** for the Curves adjustment layer.

D We dragged the top handle of the **transform** box for the gradient downward to change where the black part of the gradient mask ends.

E Finally, we painted with the **Brush** tool to mask out shapes from the foreground (the tractor and tree) that extend into the sky area.

F In the final image, the sky looks as rich and saturated as the rest of the photo. Mission accomplished.

Dodging and burning

For a subtle contrast enhancement, you can lighten or darken areas of an image by drawing strokes with the **Brush** tool on a removable, editable **neutral gray layer** (take a welcome break from using Curves!).

➤ Dodge to lighten, burn to darken.

To dodge or burn using a neutral color layer:

1. Open an RGB image.**A**

2. Click a layer, then Alt-click/Option-click the **New Layer** button ▣ on the Layers palette.

3. In the New Layer dialog, choose Mode: **Overlay**, check **Fill with Overlay-Neutral Color (50% gray)**, then click OK.

4. Press Ctrl-J/Cmd-J to duplicate the neutral gray layer.**B**

5. Choose the **Brush** tool ✐ (B or Shift-B), a large Soft Round tip, Normal mode, a very low tool Opacity of 6–10%, and a Flow setting of 50%. Press D to reset the Foreground and Background colors.

6. Click the lower neutral gray layer, then paint with black to burn (darken) some of the moderately dark shadow areas.**C–D**

A To create more contrast in this portrait, we'll dodge and burn areas with a brush on two neutral gray layers.

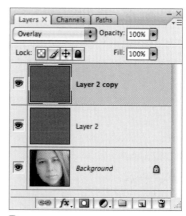

B We created a **neutral gray layer** and duplicated it.

C To darken the left side of the face, we clicked the lower of the two neutral gray layers, then painted with **black**.

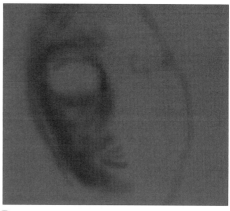

D These are the brush strokes that we applied to the lower neutral gray layer.

7. Click the upper neutral gray layer. Press **X** to swap the Foreground and Background colors, then paint with **white** to subtly dodge (lighten) some of the **highlight** areas.**A–B**

8. *Optional:* To remove any of your dodge or burn strokes, hide the Background, then Alt-click/ Option-click an unretouched area to sample the neutral gray. Redisplay the Background, choose an opacity of 100% for the Brush tool, then paint over areas you want to restore.**C–D**

9. *Optional:* To lessen the overall dodge/burn effect, click one of the neutral gray layers, then lower the layer Opacity (**A–B**, next page) or choose Soft Light as the layer blending mode.

A To lighten the right side of the face, we clicked the upper neutral gray layer, then painted with **white.**

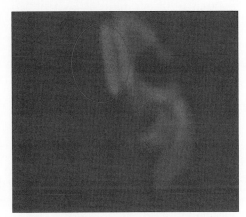

B This is a view of our light paint strokes on the upper neutral gray layer. Oops! We lightened too much of the forehead. That won't be hard to fix.

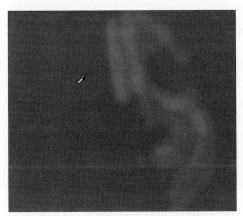

C We hid the Background and then, to sample the original neutral gray, Alt-clicked/Option-clicked an area where there weren't any brush strokes.

D We redisplayed the Background, chose an opacity of 100% for the Brush tool, then painted to remove some of the unwanted dodge strokes. Then we pressed D to reset the colors to black and white, lowered the brush opacity to 8%, and continued to dodge and burn more areas by hand.

See also the figures on the following page

A The original image was a bit humdrum.

B To soften the results of our **dodge** and **burn** strokes, we lowered the opacity of both neutral gray layers to 80%. Overall, our edits enhanced the contrast in the face and added subtle contouring.

Photographers have always found clever ways to enhance their portraits, from the hand tinting of early prints to the digital zapping of blemishes and wrinkles. In this chapter, you'll learn how to correct tonal imbalances, remove imperfections, and improve important facial features, such as the eyes and lips. You'll perform small retouching tasks, such as eliminating under-eye circles and whitening teeth, as well as broader edits, such as correcting a color cast and smoothing out the texture of skin (sometimes the camera is too darn honest!).

To meet these retouching challenges, you'll use a variety of selection and masking methods, and such features as adjustment layers, blending modes, blur filters, healing tools, and the Liquify command. As you work, keep these general guidelines in mind:

▶ Before performing any retouching work, evaluate the composition and if necessary, via cropping, eliminate a distracting background, trim off superfluous areas, or create an intimate close-up.

▶ When determining what kind of corrections to make, keep the "essence" of the subject, your intended audience, and the directives of your client or art director (if any) in mind.

▶ Make broad changes, such as applying color and tonal corrections, before attending to the small details, such as the facial features.

▶ Make as few cosmetic corrections as possible. By using the cloning, healing, distortion, and smoothing controls in Photoshop, you can change a person's shape, transfer them to a different scene, remove all the nooks, crannies, and pores from their skin (extreme smoothing), perform surreal color shifts (blue hair), or even stick their face on a different body. Take a moment to ask yourself if the alterations you're contemplating are necessary, artistic, appropriate—and legal!

▶ When using a brush, whether on a duplicate image layer or a layer mask, use a delicate touch (e.g., a Soft Round, low-opacity brush). If you have a stylus and graphics tablet, use them.

▶ After performing small touch-ups, evaluate the changes relative to the overall portrait; and conversely, after performing a large-scale correction, such as skin smoothing, make sure the important details are sharp and the eyes, the "window to the soul," look bright and alluring.

Note: For the figures in this chapter, settings were chosen for images that are approximately 3000 x 2000 pixels.

RETOUCHING PORTRAITS

7

IN THIS CHAPTER

Correcting a color cast in a portrait

Sometimes the skin tones in a portrait have a red or yellowish cast. Using the Curves dialog to set a neutral gray doesn't usually work as a solution to this problem because it's hard to find a neutral gray in a portrait. To **neutralize** a **color cast** in a portrait, we use a Hue/Saturation adjustment layer instead.

To adjust a color cast in a portrait:

1. Open an RGB image of a face.**A**

2. Via the **New Fill/Adjustment Layer** menu ⊘ on the Layers palette, create a **Hue/Saturation** adjustment layer.

3. In the Hue/Saturation dialog, do the following (drag the slider or use the scrubby slider):

   From the **Edit** menu, choose **Reds** (the range that usually needs correcting in a portrait), then lower the **Saturation** to remove red.**B–C**

   To add or remove yellow, choose **Yellows** from the **Edit** menu, then adjust the **Saturation** (**A–B**, next page).

4. *Optional:* You can make the adjustment more subtle by spreading it slightly into the adjacent color range (widen the "fall-off" area). With the Reds range chosen on the Edit menu, drag the rightmost triangle (inside the color bar) into the yellow area; and with the Yellows range chosen (if you adjusted it), drag the leftmost triangle into the red area (**C–D**, next page).

5. *Optional:* To beef up the skin tones, from the Edit menu, choose Master, move the Saturation slider slightly to the right, then click OK.

➤ To correct small areas of sunburned skin, see pages 162–163.

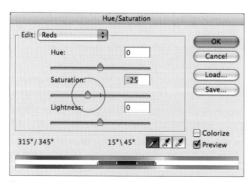

B In the **Hue/Saturation** dialog, we chose **Reds** from the Edit menu, then lowered the **Saturation** to –25.

A In this image, the skin has a very strong red color cast.

C The **reduction** in the **saturation** of **Reds** improved the photo considerably.

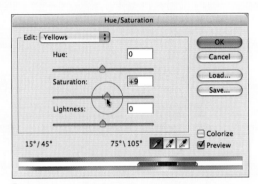

A Next, we chose **Yellows** from the **Edit** menu and raised the **Saturation** to +9, to add some warmth back to the blonde hair.

B This is the result after we increased the saturation of the **Yellows** range slightly, to +9.

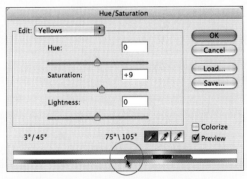

C To smooth the **transition** of the Yellows range into the Reds range (widen the fall-off), we dragged the leftmost triangle on the adjustment slider into the Reds area.

D Our corrections successfully removed the color cast from the woman's skin.

Smoothing skin

If you want to make **skin look smoother** without using a soft-focus effect on the whole portrait, try the following method. You'll use the Gaussian Blur filter and layer controls, such as Darken and Lighten blending modes, a Black & White adjustment layer, layer masks, and layer opacity.

To smooth skin:

1. Open an RGB image of a face.**A** Press Ctrl-J/ Cmd-J to duplicate the Background. Rename the new layer "blur darken."

2. Choose Filter > Blur > **Gaussian Blur.** In the Gaussian Blur dialog, move the Radius slider until the skin becomes smooth and blurry (check, then uncheck Preview to judge the blur), then click OK.**B** Don't worry that the face looks too blurry.

3. Choose **Darken** as the blending mode for the "blur darken" layer, then lower the layer opacity until a hint of the skin texture reappears (**A–B**, next page).

4. Alt-click/Option-click the **Add Layer Mask** button ◘ on the Layers palette to add a black mask, and keep the mask thumbnail selected.

5. Choose the **Brush** tool ✎ (B or Shift-B), a Soft Round tip, Normal mode, and 100% opacity, and press X to make the Foreground color white.

6. Paint on the image in areas where you want to reveal the smoothing effect. If you unintentionally paint over any important facial features, such as the eyes or eyebrows, press X to make the Foreground color black, and paint over your strokes. Press X again to switch back to white, and continue revealing skin areas.

   ► Press [to reduce the brush diameter to paint over small areas, such as between the eyes and brows or between the nose and lips, then press] when you need to enlarge it again.

7. Press Ctrl-J/Cmd-J to duplicate the "blur darken" layer. Double-click the new layer name, and rename it "blur lighten."

8. Change the blending mode of the "blur lighten" layer to **Lighten.** Lower the layer opacity to around 80%, or until any dark texture marks on the skin look softer (**C-D**, next page).

   The skin should now look smoother. To refine the effect, continue with the steps on page 144.

A We want to smooth the texture on this woman's skin. The first step is to smooth out the pores.

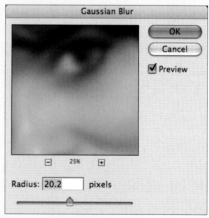

B In the **Gaussian Blur** dialog, we chose a **Radius** of 20.2 pixels.

B The **white** areas in the layer mask **reveal** the smoothing effect (cheeks, chin, and nose); the **black** areas in the mask **protect** the rest of the portrait (eyes, lips, and hair) from the smoothing effect. We lowered the opacity of the "blur darken" layer to 60%.

A To restore details in the shadow areas, we changed the blending mode of the "blur darken" layer to **Darken.** Then, with the layer mask selected, we applied brush strokes to reveal the smoothing effect on the skin (as shown above).

C We duplicated the "blur darken" layer, changed the blending mode of the new layer to **Lighten,** and changed the layer opacity to 52%.

D The two **blur** layers (one in **Lighten** mode and the other in **Darken** mode) made the skin look smoother.

Continued on the following page

9. Click the topmost layer on the Layers palette, then create a **Black & White** adjustment layer.

10. From the **Preset** menu in the Black & White dialog, choose **None**. Move the **Reds** slider to between +100 and +120 to eliminate skin imperfections in the midtones, and move the **Yellows** slider to between +80 and +100 to eliminate imperfections in the shadows, then click OK **A–B** (and **A**, next page).

11. Now the skin looks ghostly. To restore the skin tones, change the blending mode of the Black & White adjustment layer to **Luminosity**, and lower the layer opacity to around 30%.

12. To group the top three layers, select the adjustment layer, Shift-click the "blur darken" layer, then press Ctrl-G/Cmd-G (**B**, next page). Now you can control the visibility (or opacity) of the whole layer group via just a single control.

➤ Click the group visibility icon to hide or show the whole group; click the triangle for the group layer to expand or collapse the group listing.

13. Finally, to make the smoothing effect look more realistic and less "plastic," lower the opacity for the group layer until you've recovered just the right amount of skin texture (**C–D**, next page). Nice work!

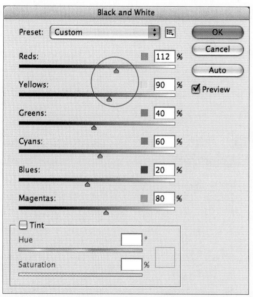

A In the **Black & White** dialog, we moved the **Reds** slider to +112 and the **Yellows** slider to +90.

B The **Reds** slider adjustment smoothed the dark skin marks.

SOFTENING OTHER TEXTURES

You can use the same method to soften a texture in a photo of any subject matter: one **blur** layer in **Darken** mode to preserve shadow details and another layer in **Lighten** mode to preserve highlight details. The **Black & White** adjustment layer will help neutralize the colors and refine the texture. And with the layers in a group, it will be easy to hide or show the overall adjustment and increase or reduce the intensity of the correction.

A The **Yellows** slider adjustment smoothed the shadow areas.

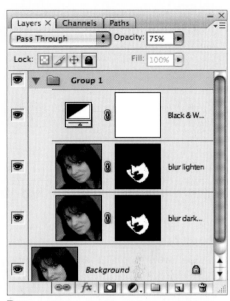

B We put the top three layers in a **group** (shown expanded) and lowered the opacity of the group layer to 75% to restore some of the skin texture.

C This is the original image, for comparison.

D And here she is with smoother skin.

Creating a soft-focus portrait

Photographers sometimes use a soft-focus effect to lend an ethereal—and flattering—look to a portrait. In Photoshop, you can achieve a similar **dewy glow** effect by using the Diffuse Glow and Gaussian Blur filters to soften the skin texture, choosing Soft Light layer blending mode, and then restoring some sharpness to the facial features by painting on the layer mask.

To create a soft-focus portrait:

1. Open an RGB image of a face. Press Ctrl-J/Cmd-J to duplicate the Background. Rename the new layer "diffuse."

2. Choose Filter > Distort > **Diffuse Glow.**

3. In the Filter Gallery, choose a zoom level that shows most of the image, then do the following:

   Set the **Graininess** to 1 (you don't want to add more texture).**B**

   Set the **Glow Amount** to around 8, or until the skin tone becomes a soft off-white.

   Set the **Clear Amount** to around 14, or until some skin color begins to reappear.

   Click OK.

A We want to soften the facial features and skin texture in this portrait.

B The **Diffuse Glow** filter (settings shown above) lightened the face and softened the features.

C Changing the blending mode of the Diffuse layer to **Soft Light** restored some detail and skin tone.

4. For the "diffuse" layer, change the blending mode to **Soft Light** (**C**, previous page).

5. Duplicate the Background again. Rename this new layer "blur," then drag the layer listing to the top of the stack.

6. Choose Filter > Blur > **Gaussian Blur.** In the dialog, drag the Radius slider to blur the edges, then click OK.**A**

7. Lower the opacity of the "blur" layer to 50%.

8. Click the **Add Layer Mask** button at the bottom of the Layers palette, and keep the mask thumbnail selected.

9. Choose the **Brush** tool (B or Shift-B), a Soft Round tip, Normal mode, and 50% opacity. Press X to make the Foreground color black. Paint on the image to mask the blur effect from the key features of the portrait, such as the eyes, nose, mouth, jewelry, and possibly a section of hair or a small detail on the clothing.**B–C** (If the results look too harsh, try using a lower-opacity brush.) Dahling, you look faa-bulous!

➤ To restore some color to the skin, lower the opacity of the "diffuse" layer to around 70%.

A A **Gaussian Blur** layer further softened the features (we chose a Radius of 15 pixels in the Gaussian Blur dialog).

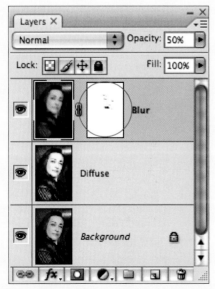

B We used two layers to achieve the final soft-focus effect (shown in **C**): a **Blur** layer (with brush strokes on the layer mask) and a **Diffuse** layer.

C The **Gaussian Blur** filter softened the edges and restored some skin tones. **Brush strokes** in the **layer mask** are blocking the blur effect from the pearl earring, nostrils, lips, pupils, and whites of the eyes.

Making eyes look brighter

If the **eyes** are the focal points in a portrait, it follows that getting the brightness and tonal contrast right in this area is one of the keys to good portraiture.

To select the eyes:

1. Open an RGB image of a face, then zoom in on the eyes. **A**

2. Choose the **Lasso** tool ⌇ (L or Shift-L).* Select the whites of one eye (don't include the tear duct), then Shift-drag to select the whites of the other eye. Alt-drag/Option-drag to subtract from the selection, if needed. **B**

3. On the Options bar, click **Refine Edge.** In the Refine Edge dialog, click Default, then click the On Black preview button. Adjust the Feather value to soften the edge of the selection, and adjust the Contrast/Expand value to loosely fit the selection to the eye shapes. You want the brightening effect to fade softly into the corners of the eyes. **C** Click OK.

4. Press Ctrl-J/Cmd-J to copy the selected area to a new layer, and follow the instructions below.

To brighten the eyes:

Method 1

Choose **Screen** as the layer blending mode (temporarily creepy), and lower the opacity to 30–40% (**A**, next page).

Method 2

1. With the new layer selected, choose **Convert to Smart Object** from the Layers palette menu. Note: This layer contains only a small area of image pixels, so a Smart Object and Smart Filter won't create a big processing lag.

2. Choose Filter > Distort > **Diffuse Glow.** In the Filter Gallery dialog, choose Graininess 1, Glow Amount 10 (adjust until any redness disappears from the eyes), and Clear Amount 9, then click OK. The eyes should now look softer and whiter. Diffuse Glow will appear as a Smart Filter listing on the Smart Object layer.

3. To soften the brightening effect, choose **Soft Light** as the layer blending mode. You can also lower the layer opacity to 60–80% (**B–C**, next page).

If you prefer to create the selection by using a Quick Mask, follow steps 2–5 on page 150.

A In the original image, the eyes look a bit dull.

B The first step was to select the eyes with the **Lasso** tool.

C Via the **Refine Edge** dialog, we applied a Feather value of 5.1 and contracted the selection by –4.

A We copied the selection to a new layer, chose **Screen** as the blending mode, and reduced the layer opacity to 30%.

B As an alternative method to the one used to produce the figure at left, we applied the **Diffuse Glow** filter, chose **Soft Light** as the layer blending mode, and lowered the layer **opacity** to 60%.

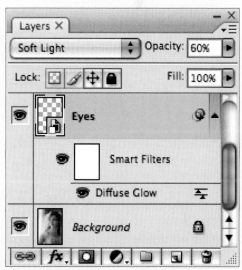

C Because we applied the Diffuse Glow filter to a Smart Object layer, we can double-click the filter listing at any time to edit the settings.

Recoloring eyes

Models can "change" their **eye color** by wearing colored contact lenses, and you can work similar magic by using the Color Balance dialog in Photoshop. The easiest colors to change are from blue eyes to hazel (green), hazel to blue, and blue to brown; it's harder to change brown eyes.

To recolor eyes:

1. Open an RGB image of a face,**A** and zoom in on the eyes.

2. Click the **Edit in Quick Mask Mode** button ⬜ on the Tools palette (Q).

3. Choose the **Brush** tool ✏ (B or Shift-B), a small Soft Round brush, Normal mode, and 100% opacity. Press D to make the Foreground color black.

4. Paint a Quick Mask over the iris of each eye, resizing the brush diameter as needed by pressing [or].**B** Don't paint over the pupils (you don't want to recolor them). To remove any unwanted Quick Mask strokes, press X and paint with white.

5. Click the **Edit in Standard Mode** button ⬛ (or press Q) to turn the mask into a selection, then press Ctrl-Shift-I/Cmd-Shift-I to invert it. Now just the irises are selected.**C**

6. Create a **Color Balance** adjustment layer.

7. In the Color Balance dialog, click **Tone Balance: Shadows,** and move any of the **Color Levels** sliders. Next, do the same thing for the **Midtones (A–C,** next page). There is no standard formula for choosing the right color.

   ➤ For the most natural appearance, allow flecks of other colors to appear in the irises. To achieve this, fiddle with the sliders in more than one of the Tone Balance ranges.

8. Click OK.

➤ You can use a Hue/Saturation adjustment layer for steps 6–7 above instead of Color Balance. In the Hue/Saturation dialog, choose Edit: Master, then fiddle with the Hue and Lightness sliders.

A We want to change the eye color of this model from blue to green.

B In **Quick Mask** mode, we painted a mask over the irises.

C When we clicked the **Edit in Standard Mode** button, the mask turned into a selection. We then inverted the selection.

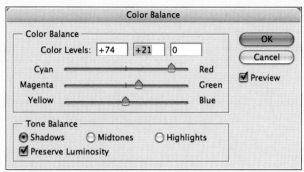

A In the **Color Balance** dialog, we chose these settings for the **Shadows**...

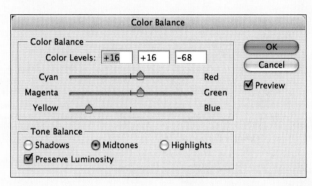

B ...and chose these settings for the **Midtones**.

DUAL ZOOMS

If you have dual computer displays, you can open another window for the same document in the second display. Choose 100% view for one of the windows and a higher zoom level for the other to do your detail work.

C Now the eyes are green.

Removing under-eye circles

Sometimes the area under the eyes needs some touch-up work, such as removing bags or dark circles. Although the Clone Stamp or Healing Brush tool might seem like an obvious choice for **retouching dark circles**, they can leave a visible seam. We think the Patch tool does a better job.

To remove under-eye circles:

1. Open an RGB image of a face.A Press Ctrl-J/ Cmd-J to duplicate the Background, then zoom in on the eyes.

2. Choose the **Patch** tool ○ (J or Shift-J). On the Options bar, click **Patch: Source.**

3. Drag a marquee around the area under one of the eyes that you want to repair.**B** If needed, Shift-drag to add to the selection or Alt-drag/ Option-drag to subtract from it.

4. Drag from inside the selection to an area of skin that you want to sample from, preferably an area of similar texture near the eye.**C** A second selection marquee will appear temporarily. When you release the mouse and the correction is done processing, the sampled imagery will appear inside the original selection.

5. Press Ctrl-D/Cmd-D to deselect.

➤ If you're not happy with the results, undo or click the "Patch Tool" state on the History palette, and try again.

A We want to preserve the dramatic contrast in this portrait as we lighten the area under his eyes.

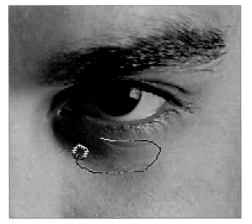

B With the **Patch** tool, we selected the area below the right eye...

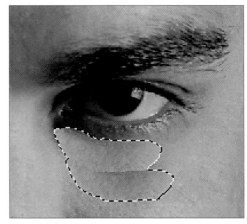

C ...then dragged from the selected area to a nearby area to **sample** those pixels.

6. Repeat steps 3–5 for the other eye.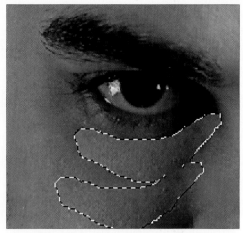

7. When your corrections are done, press Ctrl-E/ Cmd-E to merge the duplicate layer into the Background.**B**

8. *Optional:* If the Patch tool correction left some dark areas, choose the Lasso tool (L), choose a Feather value of 12 px on the Options bar, then select the area to be corrected. Create a Brightness/Contrast adjustment layer. In the dialog, move the Brightness slider slightly to the right, then click OK. Repeat for the other eye.

A We repeated same three steps (3–5) for the left eye.

B The under-eye circles are gone.

Changing lipstick color

Digital lipstick!

To apply lipstick:

1. Open an RGB image of a face, then zoom in on the lips. **A**

2. Click the **Edit in Quick Mask Mode** button ⬚ on the Tools palette (Q).

3. Choose the **Brush** tool ✎ (B or Shift-B), a small Soft Round brush, Normal mode, and 100% opacity, and press D to make the Foreground color black.

4. Paint a Quick Mask over the lips. Change the brush diameter as needed by pressing [or]. To remove areas of the Quick Mask, press X to paint with white.

5. Click the **Edit in Standard Mode** button ⬕ (Q) to turn the mask into a selection.

6. Press Ctrl-Shift-I/Cmd-Shift-I to invert the selection. Now just the lips are selected.

7. Create a **Color Balance** adjustment layer. In the Color Balance dialog, check **Preserve Luminosity**, move the sliders for each **Tone Balance** range (Shadows, Midtones, and Highlights), **B–C** then click OK.

8. *Optional:* To darken the lips, Ctrl-click/Cmd-click the layer mask to turn it into a selection, then create a Hue/Saturation adjustment layer. In the dialog, move the Saturation slider to around +7 and the Lightness slider to around –8, then click OK. **D** After performing this step, you may need to go back and edit the settings for the Color Balance adjustment layer.

A In the original image, the lips look very pale.

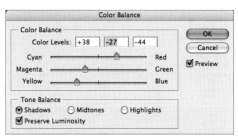

B In the **Color Balance** dialog, we clicked **Shadows** and moved the first two sliders to the Color Levels shown above. Then we clicked **Midtones** and moved the first slider to +20 and the second slider to –44.

C The lips have a new color but still look too pale.

D Via a **Hue/Saturation** adjustment layer, we changed the Saturation to +19 and the Lightness to –5. Now the lips are a luscious coral.

A VARIATION ON CHANGING THE LIPSTICK COLOR

A In the original image, the lip color is too dark and clashes with the chocolate color.

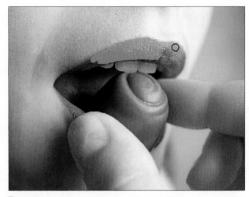

B We followed steps 2–6 on the previous page, including painting a mask over the lips in Quick Mask mode.

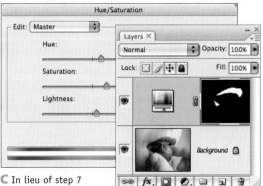

C In lieu of step 7 (previous page), we used a **Hue/Saturation** adjustment layer.

D The selection translated into white areas in the **adjustment layer mask**.

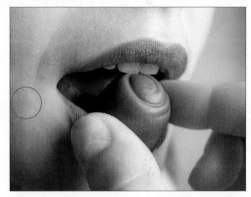

E The new lip color is more in keeping with the rest of the image. We'll make one further correction to remove the small pink spot (a lipstick smudge?) from the cheek.

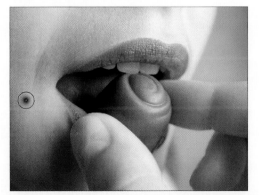

F We clicked the Background, then with the **Spot Healing Brush** tool 🖌 (50 px brush and Create Texture chosen on the Options bar), clicked once on the smudge. Poof!

G The corrections are done. Kiss-kiss.

Lightening dark hair roots

In this task, you'll **lighten dark roots** on **blond** hair—without using smelly chemicals.

To lighten dark roots in blond hair:

1. Open an RGB portrait of a blonde,**A** and zoom in on the area to be recolored.

2. Create a new blank layer, rename it "recolor," and choose **Soft Light** as the blending mode.

3. Choose the **Brush** tool ✏ (B or Shift-B), a small Soft Round tip, Normal mode, opacity 60%, and Flow 100%. To create strokes that fade gradually, on the Brushes palette, click Other Dynamics, choose Fade from the Control menu, and enter 80 in the adjacent field.

4. To sample the desired color for retouching, Alt-click/Option-click a light area of hair (not a highlight).

5. Draw strokes over the hair in the same direction as the strands.**B** You can build up the color by dragging once or twice more over the same strands (remember, the brush opacity is only 60%). Don't worry that the strokes look too obvious; they'll blend in after the next step.

   ➤ To remove any unwanted brush strokes from the "recolor" layer, use the Eraser tool.

6. Press Ctrl-J/Cmd-J to duplicate the "recolor" layer that you just worked on, then choose Color as the blending mode. Zoom back out, then lower the opacity of the duplicate layer to achieve the desired intensity of coloring.**C–D**

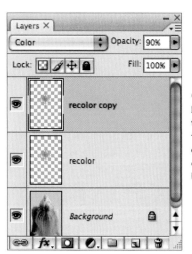

A We want to lighten the dark hair roots.

B We're drawing strokes over the dark strands.

C To blend the brush strokes into the Background image, we lowered the **opacity** of the topmost layer to 80%.

D Now the hair color looks more natural.

Using Liquify to trim or tighten

Liquify is a very powerful distortion command, but it can also be used to gently slim or reshape a waistline, chin, arms, or oddly shaped clothing. With a tool in the Liquify dialog, all you have to do is draw a stroke or two on the area that you want to reshape. If only dieting were this easy! A stylus and tablet would be useful for this exercise.

To trim a waistline:

1. Open an RGB image of a figure.**A** Press Ctrl-J/ Cmd-J to duplicate the Background, and keep the duplicate layer selected.

    ▶ The image shown at right (or any silhouette of a figure) will work particularly well for this exercise because we won't have to be concerned about distorting the background.

2. Choose Filter > **Liquify** (Ctrl-Shift-X/Cmd-Shift-X). The Liquify dialog opens.

3. Zoom in on the waist area (Ctrl-click/Cmd-click).

4. Click the **Push Left** tool ▓ (O).

5. For better control, under **Tool Options** on the right side of the dialog, do the following:

    Set the **Brush Density** to between 20 and 40. This will increase the amount of feathering and soften the distortion that occurs at the edge of the brush.

    Set the **Brush Pressure** to between 20 and 40 to decrease the speed at which the distortion occurs.

    ▶ If you're using a stylus, check the Stylus Pressure option and lower the Brush Pressure value.

6. To trim the waistline, position the edge of the brush pointer on the left edge of the figure, choose a brush diameter by pressing] or [, then drag downward.**B–D** Drag in the same direction as many times as necessary to reshape the area.

7. For the right side of the figure, drag upward.

    ▶ To compare the original Background with the liquified layer, check Show Backdrop, choose All Layers from the Use menu, and set the Opacity to 30%. Uncheck and recheck Show Backdrop to toggle the two views.

Continued on the following page

A The shirt and pants on this fellow are poufing out in an unflattering way.

B With the **Push Left** tool, we dragged downward along the left side of the shirt a few times (here, the Show Backdrop option is on).

C We used the same tool and a smaller brush to slim down the right side of the shirt...

D ...and to narrow the hip area (here, the Show Backdrop option is off).

8. If the figure has an area that you want to tighten, such as a belt, blouse, or exposed belly, choose the **Pucker** tool 🔲 (S). Change the Brush Density to 40 and the Brush Pressure to 40. Increase the brush diameter so it covers the area that you want to shrink, then click and hold just once or twice. Instant liposuction! **A**

9. Click OK. **B–C**

➤ To view the Liquify layer as an overlay on top of the Background, lower the layer opacity.

➤ To push pixels in the opposite direction from the Push Left tool's normal behavior, hold down Alt/Option as you drag.

HOW TO UNLIQUIFY

To restore pixels to their pre-Liquify state, do any of the following:

➤ In the Reconstruct Options area, choose **Revert** from the Mode menu, then either choose the **Reconstruct** tool 🖌 (R) and drag across the areas you want to restore, or click — and keep clicking — **Reconstruct** to undo your edits in reverse order.

➤ To restore the whole preview image to its undoctored state, click **Restore All** — and of course you can always Cancel out of the dialog…

A With the **Pucker** tool, we click and hold on the poufy shirt to contract it inward.

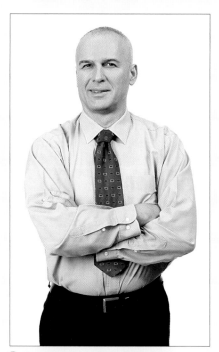

B The original image

C After using the **Liquify** filter

USING LIQUIFY TO TIGHTEN UP A CHIN

A Another good use for the **Liquify** filter is to tighten up a chin.

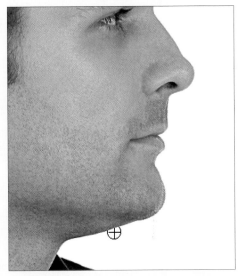

B We dragged the **Push Left** tool a couple of times from left to right (Brush Size 25, Brush Pressure 50).

C Although Liquify has a lot of distortion power, we like to use it to make subtle improvements, such as the "chin lift" that we gave this gentleman.

PROTECTING AREAS FROM LIQUIFY

➤ To paint a mask to protect areas of the image from distortion (or to add to an existing mask), choose the **Freeze Mask** tool (F), choose Tool Options (including a high Brush Pressure), then paint over areas in the preview.

➤ To remove the protection from any frozen areas, choose the **Thaw Mask** tool (D), then paint over areas in the preview.

➤ To create a mask based on layer transparency, a layer mask, or an alpha channel in the original image and thereby prevent those areas from being "liquified," choose that option from the first menu under **Mask Options**. If you want to reverse what's masked and what's not, click Invert All; or to unmask the entire image at any time (make all pixels editable again), click None.

Whitening teeth

In this exercise, you'll **whiten teeth** by using a Quick Mask and the Hue/Saturation dialog—instant bleaching.

To whiten teeth:

1. Open an RGB image of a smiling figure.**A**

2. Zoom in on the mouth area.

3. Click the **Edit in Quick Mask Mode** button ⬚ on the Tools palette (Q).

4. Choose the **Brush** tool 🖌 (B or Shift-B), a small Soft Round brush, Normal mode, and 100% opacity. Press D to make the Foreground color black.

5. Paint a Quick Mask over the teeth.**B** To remove areas of the Quick Mask, where needed, press X and paint with white.

6. Click the **Edit in Standard Mode** button ⬛ (Q) to turn the mask into a selection.

7. Press Ctrl-Shift-I/Cmd-Shift-I to invert the selection. Now just the teeth are selected.

8. Create a **Hue/Saturation** adjustment layer. Choose Edit: **Yellows**, reduce the **Saturation** and increase the **Lightness**, then click OK.**C–D**

▶ In our *Visual QuickStart Guide* to Photoshop, we show another (equally good) way to whiten teeth—via the Replace Color command.

A The teeth in this portrait could use some whitening.

B We painted a mask onto the teeth in **Quick Mask** mode with the Brush tool (13 px diameter).

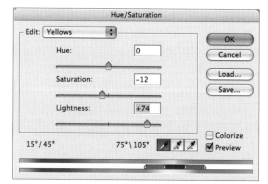

C In the **Hue/Saturation** dialog, we chose Edit: **Yellows**, then lowered the **Saturation** and raised the **Lightness**.

D Whiter, brighter (but still natural-looking) teeth...

Removing blemishes

You can easily zap pimples, moles, or crow's-feet with the **Spot Healing Brush** tool. Using the same photo as in the previous exercise, we'll remove a mole from the man's cheek.

To remove a blemish:

1. Open a portrait in which the figure has a blemish or wrinkle that you want to remove,**A** and press Ctrl-J/Cmd-J to duplicate the Background image.

2. Choose the **Spot Healing Brush** tool  (J or Shift-J).

3. On the Options bar, choose Mode: Normal and click Type: **Create Texture.** Click the Brush preset picker, and lower the brush Hardness to 0% to create a soft tip.

4. Press [or] to make the brush tip about double the diameter of the blemish.

5. Drag once across the blemish.**B** A dark mark will appear, then will disappear when the correction is done processing.**C** How easy was that?

➤ A list of shortcuts for changing brush settings, such as the mode, diameter, and hardness, is on page 230.

A We want to remove the mole from this man's cheek.

B With the **Spot Healing Brush** tool (40 px diameter), we drag a short distance — just once.

C The mole is gone. Now, anybody got a razor?!

"Curing" a sunburn

In this exercise, you'll use a Hue/Saturation adjustment layer and a layer mask to **correct a sunburn**, tone down a ruddy complexion, or neutralize the color in any overly red area, such as the cheeks.

To correct sunburned areas:

1. Open an RGB image.

2. Create a **Hue/Saturation** adjustment layer.

3. In the Hue/Saturation dialog, use the sliders to correct the sunburned areas. Choose the **Reds** color range from the **Edit** menu, then lower the **Saturation.** You can also increase the **Lightness** or adjust the **Yellows** color range, if needed. Click OK.**B**

4. Click the adjustment layer mask thumbnail, then press Ctrl-I/Cmd-I to make the mask black.

5. Choose the **Brush** tool 🖌 (B or Shift-B), a Soft Round tip, Normal mode, and an Opacity of 50% or lower. If necessary, press X to make the Foreground color white.

6. Make sure the adjustment layer mask thumbnail is still selected, adjust the brush diameter by pressing [or], then draw strokes where you want to apply the adjustment, such as on the cheeks, forehead, nose, or ears (**A–C**, next page).

7. *Optional:* To reduce the effect of the adjustment layer, lower the layer opacity.

A We want to tone down the ruddiness of this man's complexion without lightening his rich skin tones.

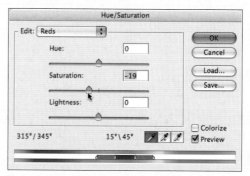

B We lowered the **Saturation** of the **Reds** color range for a **Hue/Saturation** adjustment layer.

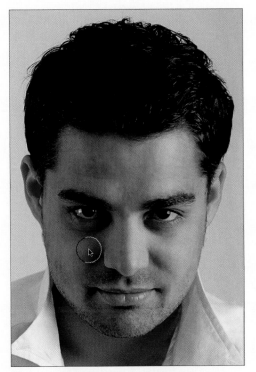

A With the **Brush** tool and a large Soft Round brush, and with the **adjustment layer mask** selected, we drew broad strokes on the areas that needed correction.

B The reds are diminished where needed, and the rest of the image is unaltered.

C The adjustment effect is revealed by the strokes that we applied to the **black mask** on the **Hue/Saturation** adjustment layer.

Smoothing out small areas

In this last retouching exercise, we'll show you how to **smooth out** small areas of a face (or any subject for that matter) by using a feathered selection and the Gaussian Blur filter. In this case, we'll smooth out the ridges on a woman's eyelids.

To smooth out skin texture:

1. Open a portrait image,**A** and press Ctrl-J/Cmd-J to duplicate the Background.

2. Do either of the following:

   With the **Lasso** tool ⌀ (L or Shift-L), drag a selection around the area you want to correct, and Shift-drag if you need to select additional areas, such as the second eyelid in a portrait.

   In **Quick Mask** mode,⬚ paint a Quick Mask over the areas to be corrected (as in steps 3–7 on page 160).**B**

3. Click any selection tool, then click **Refine Edge** on the Options bar. In the dialog, click Default, feather the selection slightly, and also expand it, if needed. As you make adjustments, click between the Quick Mask and On White preview options. Click OK.

4. *Optional:* To reshape the selection in specific areas, click the Add Layer Mask button ⬚ on the Layers palette to convert it to a mask, then use the Brush tool with a Soft Round tip.

5. With the layer thumbnail selected, choose Filter > Blur > **Gaussian Blur.** Choose a low Radius value, then click OK. Deselect.**C–D**

6. *Optional:* To diminish the smoothing effect, lower the opacity of the duplicate layer.

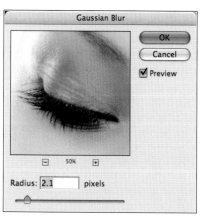

A We want to even out the crepe like texture of her eyelids without removing the iridescent eye shadow.

B We paint over the eyelids in **Quick Mask** mode.

C We chose a Radius of 3.3 pixels in the **Gaussian Blur** dialog.

D Now the eyelids look smoother.

Images can be combined using various techniques for different goals. In a photo illustration, you can create illusions by hiding the seams between layers, whereas in an artistic collage, you can leave conspicuous seams "on purpose" to emphasize differences in subject matter, scale, color, and texture. This chapter covers the gamut of compositing tools and techniques, including the Auto-Align layers command, the Background Eraser tool, drag-and-drop, the Move tool, the Clone Source palette, and the Vanishing Point filter—plus our old standby, layer masks.

Tips for creating montages

➤ Depending on the effect you're after, you can make the edges between image layers rough or jagged with the Brush tool or filters, or fuse them together via gradients in layer masks.

➤ If you're creating an artistic montage, venture out of your comfort zone. For source materials, fine artists have been known to scan everything but the kitchen sink: objects, drawings, paintings, fabric, handmade papers—even their own face or hands. Fiddle with that distortion filter you've always been curious about or apply a surreal color cast via the Color Balance (Color Imbalance!) command. Ultimately, of course, whatever techniques you settle on should serve the greater good of the overall image. We're not advocating a lapse of good taste!

➤ Once all the components are scaled, manipulated, and positioned where you want them, use such features as layer style controls (Blending Options or layer effects), color adjustments, or lighting for unity and cohesiveness.

➤ To add a handmade touch to your montages, incorporate some of the techniques we explore in Chapter 11, Fine Art Media.

➤ For inspiration, study the work by montage pros. Look for images labeled "photo illustration" in newsweekly magazines and other media; or browse the websites of our favorite Photoshop "montagists": oldtin.com (Clifford Alejandro), aliciabuelow.com, jeffbrice.com, daltoncowan.com (Stephanie Dalton Cowan), dianefenster.com, naomishea.com, and kerismith.com.

COMBINING IMAGES

8

IN THIS CHAPTER

Aligning and blending shots of the same scene

It can be a challenge to get a whole group of people to smile simultaneously for a portrait (unless there happens to be a comedian in the crowd)—and to keep everyone from blinking when you click the shutter. If you take multiple shots of the same scene, you can blend the choice areas of two of the best photos in Photoshop via the **Auto-Align Layers** command and a layer mask.

To align and blend two shots of a scene:

1. Open two RGB photos from the same shoot that contain figures or areas that you want to combine the best features of.**A** (We'll use a portrait for our illustrations, but you can use other subject matter.)

2. With the **Move** tool ⊹ (V), Shift-drag the Background from the Layers palette of one photo onto the document window of the other.**B** Holding down Shift will ensure that the copy will appear in the correct position.

3. On the Layers palette, Shift-click to select both layers, then choose Edit > **Auto-Align Layers.**

4. In the Auto-Align Layers dialog (**A**, next page), click a **Projection** option: **Reposition Only** if you used a tripod, or **Auto** for all other shooting situations to let Photoshop choose the best alignment option.

   Click OK. The Background will be converted to a layer.

A We want to combine the mother and child on the left from this photo...

B ...with the father and child on the right from this photo. The first step is to drag the image layer from one photo into the document window of the other.

5. *Optional:* Click the top layer, lower its **opacity** (to around 50%) to check the position of elements relative to the underlying layer, then restore its opacity to 100%.

6. Click the top layer, Alt-click/Option-click the **Add Layer Mask** button ◙ at the bottom of the Layers palette, and keep the mask thumb-nail selected. For the moment, the mask is hiding the top layer completely. **B**

7. Choose the **Brush** tool ✏ (B or Shift-B), a Soft Round tip, Normal mode, and 100% opacity. Zoom in, then paint strokes with white as the Foreground color to reveal the more desirable parts of the top layer. **C–D**

Continued on the following page

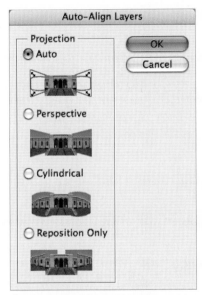

A In the **Auto-Align Layers** dialog, we clicked **Auto** as the **Projection** option.

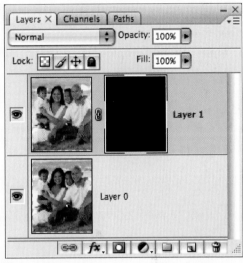

B The Auto-Align Layers command converted the Background to a layer and matched up the two layers. Next, we created a black layer mask, which for the moment is fully blocking the top layer.

C With the **Brush** tool, we're adding **white** strokes to the black layer mask to expose just the faces of the father and child from the top layer.

D In the process, we also revealed some of the light background along the edge of the child's face; we'll remedy that next.

8. To touch up the mask, decrease the brush diameter and zoom in even more. Paint along the edges of the shapes to reveal more of the top layer, or press X to paint with black to reduce the mask and reveal more areas of the underlying layer.**A–B**

A We zoomed in, reduced the brush diameter and then, with the layer mask still selected, painted with white (and then black) to correct the mask area between the mother and child.

B The final image is a seamless composite of the two photos, achieved by using the Auto-Align Layers command and brush strokes on a layer mask.

USING AUTO-BLEND LAYERS

You can also use **Auto-Blend Layers** (a cousin of the Auto-Align Layers command) to combine two portraits. Our best results have been with photos in which there's space between the figures and the background is soft or blurry.**C–D**

C **Drag and drop** a layer from one document into another. Double-click the Background (to convert it to a layer), then click OK. With the **Rectangular Marquee** tool, select and then delete the unwanted portion of each layer (shown as lightened areas here for illustration purposes), making sure to allow the portions that remain to partially **overlap.**

D Shift-click the two layers, then choose Edit > **Auto-Blend Layers.** The command will create a layer mask for each layer to blend the overlapping area between them (it does all the work for you).

Erasing to an underlying layer

When you click or drag with the **Background Eraser** tool, colored pixels are replaced with transparent ones. This tool gives you greater control than the plain old Eraser, because it lets you sample the color you want to erase and also lets you choose whether it will erase adjacent colors within a specific range of the sampled color.

To use the Background Eraser tool:

1. Open an RGB image. **A** Press Ctrl-J/Cmd-J to duplicate the Background, then hide the original Background.

2. Choose the **Background Eraser** tool ⬚ (E or Shift-E) and a brush tip. If you have a pressure-sensitive tablet, via the Brush preset picker, set the brush Size and Tolerance to Pen Pressure.

3. On the Options bar, click a **Sampling** button to control the tool behavior:

   Continuous ⬚ to replace all the colors directly under the pointer with transparent pixels, as well as adjacent colors that are within the current Tolerance range.

   Once ⬚ to replace only pixels that closely match the first color you click, with transparent pixels.

   Background Swatch ⬚ to erase only pixels that match the current Background color. For this option, pick a Background color before erasing.

4. To control which pixels can be erased, choose from the **Limits** menu:

   Discontiguous to erase all pixels within the current Tolerance range that the tool passes over; pixels don't have to be adjacent to one another.

   Contiguous to erase only pixels adjacent to the one you click, within the Tolerance range.

   Find Edges to erase pixels contiguous to the one you click, while preserving shape edges.

5. Choose a **Tolerance** percentage to control how widely the colors to be erased can differ from the first color you click. For the Continuous sampling option, use a low Tolerance (below 8%); for the Once option, use a moderate Tolerance of 20–30%.

6. Click or drag in the document window **B** (also **A–E**, next page, and **A–D**, page 171). You can change the Sampling option, Tolerance, brush Diameter, or brush Hardness between clicks or strokes.

A To replace the sky in the top photo (taken in Angkor, Cambodia) with the sky in the bottom photo, our first step was to drag and drop the sky image into the temple document.

B With the **Background Eraser** tool, we dragged horizontally from the sky into the trees. Because the tool setting is **Sampling: Once**, it sampled the sky color only from the point where we started dragging and erased only colors that were close in value to the sampled color, within the **Tolerance** range that we chose of 30%.

ERASING SKY BEHIND FOLIAGE

A The **Background Eraser** tool successfully removed the sky colors while preserving the leaves. Since the sky contained multiple colors, we needed to click and drag multiple times to sample and erase.

B Next, we clicked the left side of the image with the **Background Eraser** tool to sample that part of the sky.

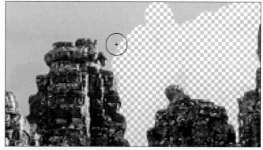

C Dragging across the tree removed sky colors within the chosen Tolerance range, while preserving the leaves.

D Using a smaller brush (and a lower Tolerance range, to avoid erasing the highlight colors on the buildings), we erased the sky near the buildings, then dragged from the sky toward the buildings to sample the sky color.

E An image of clouds on an underlying layer is now visible below the areas that we erased to transparency. However, the new sky looks too bright and saturated, so we'll fix that next.

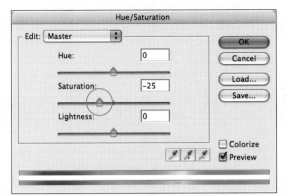

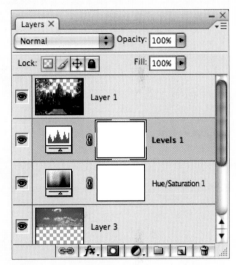

A We created a **Hue/ Saturation** adjustment layer above the sky layer and lowered the **Saturation.**

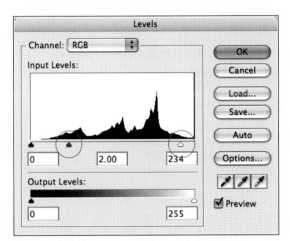

B To lighten the sky, we created a **Levels** adjustment layer and moved the **gray** and **white Input Levels** sliders.

C This is the **Layers** palette for the final image, which is shown below.

D In the final image, the two layers meld together successfully: the trees and temple from the original image and the new sky image behind it.

Enlarging the canvas area

Before creating a montage, you may want to enlarge the canvas area—that is, add a blank area to one or more sides of the image—to accommodate more imagery. When you draw a **marquee** with the **Crop** tool that's larger than the image, you effectively increase the canvas size. Unlike the Canvas Size command, this technique gives you manual control over the size and location of the additional canvas area. Another use for this technique is to reveal imagery that extends beyond the live canvas area, which may result when you drag and drop or paste in a layer from another document.

To enlarge the canvas area using the Crop tool:

1. Open an image, then choose a Background color. **A**

2. To reveal more of the work canvas (gray area) around the image, either press F for Maximized Screen Mode or enlarge the document window by dragging the lower right corner.

3. Choose the **Crop** tool (C). ⌗

4. Drag a crop marquee within the image.

5. Drag any of the handles of the marquee into the work canvas, beyond the live canvas area (**A–B**, next page).

6. To accept the crop, do one of the following (**C**, next page):

   Double-click inside the marquee.

   Press Enter/Return.

   Right-click/Control-click the image and choose Crop.

   If the image has a Background (Layers palette), the added canvas area will fill with the current Background color; if not, the added canvas area will fill with transparent pixels. Furthermore, pixels on any layer that were formerly hidden outside the live canvas area may now fall within it and become visible.

➤ To cancel the crop marquee before accepting it, press Esc.

A We want to add blank space around this image to accommodate other image layers that we're going to add to it.

OVERRIDING THE SNAP

Normally, if you resize a crop marquee near the edge of the canvas area and View > Snap To > **Document Bounds** is on, the crop edges will snap to the edge of the canvas area. To override this snap function (say you want to crop ever so slightly inside or outside the edge of the image), either turn Snap To > Document Bounds off, or start dragging a marquee handle, then hold down Ctrl/Control as you drag a handle near the edge of the canvas area.

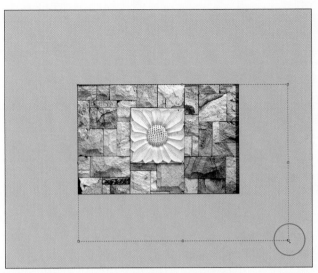

A We put our document into **Maximized Screen Mode** and chose white as the Background color. With the **Crop** tool, we drew a crop marquee within the image, then dragged the lower right corner of the marquee to enlarge it.

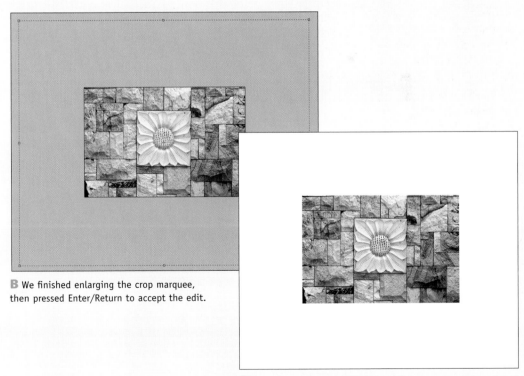

B We finished enlarging the crop marquee, then pressed Enter/Return to accept the edit.

C The canvas area now includes a white area around the original imagery.

Blending imagery via layer masks

When you create a montage from multiple image layers, you can keep the seams visible or you can use a **gradient** in the **layer mask** for each layer to meld the imagery together, as in these instructions.

To combine images into a composite:

1. Open an RGB image to be used as a background for your composite image (e.g., a soft-focus image or a photo of a texture). Make sure it's large enough to contain the other images that you're going to add. If you need to enlarge the canvas area, see page 172. Another option is to create a blank document and fill it with a solid color or gradient.

2. Open two or more smaller RGB images to be placed on top of the master background image. To make your job easier, make sure all the files have the same resolution (Image > Image Size).

3. Click in one of the smaller images, then drag the Background or a layer from the Layers palette into the document window of the master image. If desired, use the Move tool (V) to scale any of the imported layers.*

   Repeat to add imagery from the other files, then close all but the master file. **A–B**

4. Save the master file, then hide all but one of the new layers.

5. Click the visible image layer and then, with the **Move** tool ⊹ (V), drag it to one side of the document. Click the **Add Layer Mask** button ⬛ on the Layers palette.

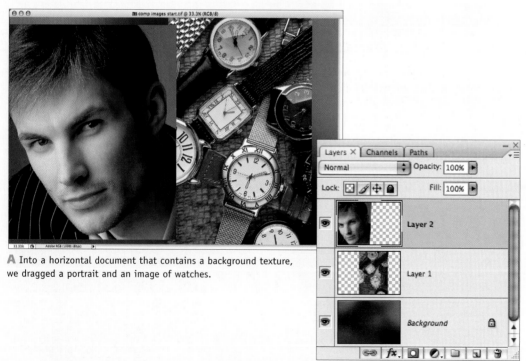

A Into a horizontal document that contains a background texture, we dragged a portrait and an image of watches.

B The two layers that we imported appear on the **Layers** palette.

If you need to enlarge any layer by a substantial amount, do so in the original file via Image > Image Size, and then reimport it.

6. Choose the **Gradient** tool ▣ (G). On the Options bar, click the **Linear Gradient** button, ▣ set the Mode to Normal and the Opacity to 100%, and click the **Black, White** preset in the Gradient preset picker. **A**

7. In the document window, start dragging horizontally from where you want the imagery to become transparent (the black area of the mask), and stop dragging where you want the image to remain fully opaque (the white area of the mask). **B** A representation of the gradient will appear in layer mask thumbnail. **C**

8. Redisplay the hidden image layer(s), and repeat steps 5–7 to add another layer mask and gradient.

Continued on the following page

A Choose the **Gradient** tool, then on the Options bar, click the **Black, White** preset on the Gradient picker and click the **Linear Gradient** button.

B We scaled and repositioned the face, then hid the watches layer. Next, we added a **layer mask** to the portrait layer, then dragged with the **Gradient** tool to fade the right side of the man's face.

C The linear **gradient** appears in the **layer mask** thumbnail for the face layer.

9. To transform the mask to control where the fadeout occurs on any of the layers, do the following:

Click the **Link** button 🖇 between the layer and layer mask thumbnails.

Choose the **Move** tool ⊹ (V). On the Options bar, check **Show Transform Controls**. Drag the middle handle on the transform box (where the fadeout is),**A** then double-click inside the transform box to accept the edit.

Click between the image and mask thumbnails to **relink** them.

10. To fade a corner of any layer, do the following:

Click the layer mask thumbnail. Choose the **Gradient** tool and the same settings as in step 6, except this time choose **Multiply** as the tool Mode (Normal mode would replace any existing gradient, whereas Multiply mode will combine the new and existing gradients).

Drag from the edge of the imagery to the middle.**B–C**

➤ If you need to redo a gradient, press Ctrl-Z/Cmd-Z to remove the current one, then reapply it.

A We **unlinked** the layer mask from the layer and then, with the **Move** tool, adjusted the position of the fadeout by dragging a handle on the transform box (as shown by the white arrow).

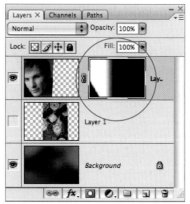

C The diagonal gradient appears in the layer mask for the portrait layer.

B With the **Gradient** tool Mode set to **Multiply,** we added another gradient to the layer mask to fade out the bottom left corner.

To fade a layer from its center:

1. Click a layer on the Layers palette, then click the **Add Layer Mask** button.

2. Choose the **Gradient** tool. On the Options bar, click the **Reflected Gradient** button, set the Mode to Normal and the Opacity to 100%, and check **Reverse**; also click the **Black, White** preset on the Gradient preset picker.

3. In the document window, drag horizontally from the center to the edge of the imagery.**A** Note how the gradient looks in the layer mask thumbnail.**B**

4. To blend the imagery, lower the layer **opacity.C** You can also try choosing a different layer **blending mode,** such as Soft Light.

See also the instructions on the following page.

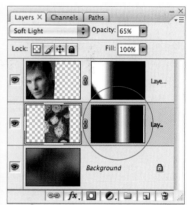

B The reflected gradient style fades to black on both sides of the layer mask.

A We made the watches layer visible and repositioned and scaled it. Next, we added a layer mask, then dragged the **Gradient** tool (with the Reflected Gradient style chosen) to fade both sides of the watches layer.

C Finally, we changed the layer blending mode to **Soft Light** and reduced the layer **opacity** to 65%. The layer could use some lighting refinements (see the following page).

To refine the lighting on an image layer:

1. To edit the layer that contains the reflected gradient in its mask without ruining its faded edge, select it, lower its opacity to around 50–60%, then press Ctrl-J/Cmd-J to copy it.

2. To make the duplicate layer look brighter, increase its **opacity** to 100%.**A**

3. Click the layer mask thumbnail for the duplicate layer. To intensify the light in the center by making the white area in the gradient narrower, do either of the following:

Choose Filter > Other > **Minimum.** In the Minimum dialog, click the zoom out button ⊟ to lower the zoom level in the preview, drag the slider to the far right, then click OK.

Choose the **Gradient** tool,▢ click the **Reflected Gradient** button ▬ on the Options bar, then drag a short distance on the image.**B**

4. *Optional:* To further intensify the light, choose a different blending mode for the duplicate layer, such as Overlay, Hard Light, or Luminosity, and adjust the layer opacity.**C**

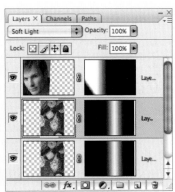

A We **duplicated** the watches layer and increased the **opacity** of the duplicate layer to 100%.

B The narrower **reflected gradient** that we applied to the layer mask lightened the middle of the watches layer.

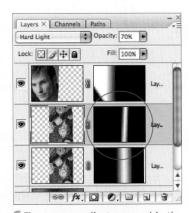

C The narrow gradient appeared in the layer mask. We chose **Hard Light** as the blending mode for the duplicate layer and reduced the layer **opacity** to 70%.

QUICK SUMMARY: USING THE MOVE TOOL

Once your imagery has been collected into one document — whether via the Clone Stamp tool, drag-and-drop, or copy-and-paste — you can use the **Move** tool ⊕ to move and transform each layer individually.

TASK	METHOD
Temporary Move tool (this works with most tools)	Ctrl/Cmd
Temporary Move tool, drag-copy a selection	Ctrl-Shift-drag/Cmd-Option-drag
Move imagery or a layer mask separately	Click the link icon between the two thumbnails to unlink them, then drag
Copy a layer or selection	Alt-drag/Option-drag with Move tool
Nudge a layer or selection	Arrow keys (or Shift-arrow keys)
Align or distribute multiple layers	Ctrl-click/Cmd-click multiple layers, then click one or more align or distribute buttons on the Options bar
Select (and move) the uppermost layer or layer group that contains the most opaque pixels below the pointer	Check Auto-Select on the Options bar, choose Layer or Group from the menu, then click or drag
Turn on Auto Select Layer mode for the Move tool temporarily when that option is unchecked	Ctrl/Cmd click or drag
Select a layer via a menu	Right-click/Control-click in the document window and choose a layer from the context menu
Transform a layer or selection	Check Show Transform controls on the Options bar, then manipulate the control handles: to scale proportionally, Shift-drag any handle; to skew, Ctrl/Cmd drag a side handle; to distort, Ctrl/Cmd drag a corner handle; to apply perspective, Ctrl-Alt-Shift/Cmd-Option-Shift drag a corner handle; or to rotate, position the pointer just outside the transform box then drag. To accept the transformation, press Enter/Return.

Using the Clone Source palette

To gather fragments of multiple images, you can use the Copy and Paste commands, drag and drop a selection or layer from other documents, or use the **Clone Stamp** tool, which is featured here. With this tool, you can clone imagery from one layer to another in the same file or between files. The **Clone Source** palette lets you keep track of up to five different clone sources (represented by a row of buttons at the top of the palette); assign different sources; clone repeatedly from the same source; and best of all, scale, rotate, or reposition the source pixels before or as you clone them.

To use the Clone Stamp tool and the Clone Source palette:

1. Open one or more RGB documents to use as source imagery, and create or open the document that you want to clone to.**A**

2. Choose the **Clone Stamp** tool 🖺 (S or Shift-S) and then, from the Options bar, choose a large Soft Round brush tip, a Mode, and Opacity and Flow values; also check Aligned.

3. Display the **Clone Source** palette.🖺 By default, the first clone source button is selected.

4. Check **Show Overlay** and **Auto Hide**, then set the **Opacity** to 35–40% so you'll be able to preview the source as an overlay (a faint version of the source layer below the pointer) while you clone.

5. In the document you're going to clone to, create a new layer, and keep it selected.

6. Click in the document that you want to clone from and then, from the **Sample** menu on the Options bar, choose **Current Layer**, **Current & Below**, or **All Layers**, depending on what you want to clone, and click a layer.

   Alt-click/Option-click an area to set the source point for cloning. The document and layer name will be assigned to, and listed below, the first clone source button on the palette.**B**

7. Click in the document you're going to clone to.

8. Move the pointer over the image without clicking to position the clone overlay, then drag to start cloning (**A–B**, next page). The overlay will disappear temporarily (because you checked Auto Hide), and then will reappear when you release the mouse. Note: When you start dragging, the position of the source overlay will

A We opened three files to use as source material for a piece on green energy.

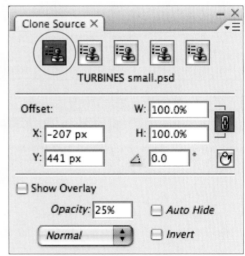

B We clicked the first clone source button on the **Clone Source** palette, then Alt/Option clicked to set a source point in another document; the name of the source document appeared below the buttons.

become fixed. To reposition it, see the instructions on the next page.

9. To rotate, flip, or scale the current clone source while cloning, do any of the following:

At any time while cloning, change the **Rotate** value △ on the Clone Source palette, or hold down Alt-Shift/Option-Shift and press < or >.

To **scale** the current clone source before or while cloning, change the **W** or **H** value on the Clone Source palette, or hold down Alt-Shift/Option-Shift and press [or]. Select the

Maintain Aspect Ratio button ⬚ to preserve the current aspect ratio as you change the W or H value. Avoid scaling beyond 150 or –150%.

To **flip** the current source, choose negative **W** and/or **H** values on the palette.

➤ To restore the default scale and rotation settings at any time, click the Reset Transform button on the palette. ↻

➤ To change values quickly on the Clone Source palette, use the scrubby sliders.

Continued on the following page

A With the **Clone Stamp** tool, we Alt/Option clicked in a clone source image, positioned the overlay in our destination file...

B ...then dragged with the tool to make part of the clone source image appear.

10. To clone from more sources, click the second source button,**A** create a new layer in the target document, and repeat steps 6–9.**B–C**

Note! The Clone Source palette keeps the links active only while the source document is open.

➤ To switch between source files while cloning, click a different source button. The new source will display in the overlay.

➤ When using the Clone Stamp tool, check the Ignore Adjustment Layers While Cloning button ▨ on the Options bar if you want to exclude adjustment layer data from the source file.

As soon as you begin cloning, the position of the source overlay becomes fixed. However, you can clone the source imagery in a new location by **repositioning** the **source overlay**.

To reposition the source overlay after you've begun cloning:

1. With the overlay visible in the document you're cloning to, change the **Offset X** and/or **Y** value on the Clone Source palette, or Alt-Shift-drag/Option-Shift-drag the overlay.

2. Click, then drag to clone in the new location.

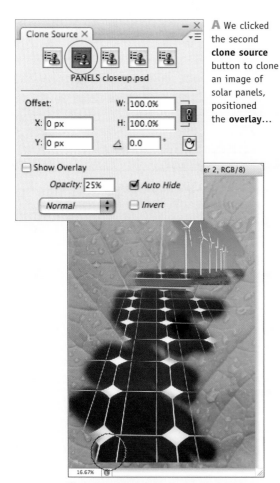

A We clicked the second **clone source** button to clone an image of solar panels, positioned the **overlay**...

B ...then dragged in long strokes to make part of the second clone source image appear.

C We also added editable type, drag-and-dropped silhouetted image layers from 3 other files (the recycle symbol, wind turbine, and bamboo), and used a Hue/Saturation adjustment layer to make the Background (the large leaf) lighter and less saturated.

ADDING FINISHING TOUCHES TO A MONTAGE

To create depth, we applied the Drop Shadow **layer effect** to the recycle symbol layer and then, to create unity in the image, Alt/Option dragged to copy the effect to the type layer.

To hide the middle of the solar panels layer, we added a **layer mask** and then, with the Gradient tool, applied a **radial gradient** to the mask.

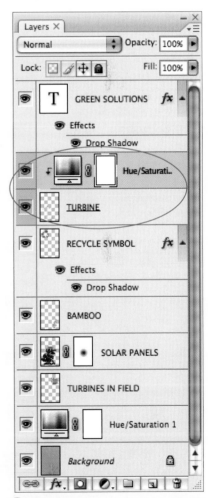

A With a few alterations, the image is now complete.

For an interesting color shift, we chose the **Luminosity blending mode** for the bamboo layer.

B We used an **adjustment layer** to make the TURBINE layer whiter. To **limit** the effect of the adjustment layer to just the layer below it, we Alt/Option clicked the line between them (this created a clipping group).

Using the Vanishing Point filter

The **Vanishing Point** filter lets you paste imagery or a pattern into a perspective plane, such as a building facade, wall, floor, or object. It can't compare to a dedicated drafting or 3D modeling program that an interior designer, architect, or package designer might use—and it doesn't always work perfectly because it's a relatively new feature—but you still might find a use for it. New options let you work with multiple source and destination surfaces.

To place imagery into perspective:

1. Open the file that contains the imagery that you want to paste, and make sure it has a similar resolution as the destination document. With a selection tool, select the area to be pasted, then **copy** it (Ctrl-C/Cmd-C).**A** Or to select editable text instead, Ctrl-click/Cmd-click the T icon on the Layers palette.

2. Open a document that you want to paste imagery into. Create a new, blank layer, and keep it selected. *Optional:* Select an area of the layer that you want the imagery or type to fit into.**B**

3. Choose Filter > **Vanishing Point** (Ctrl-Alt-V/Cmd-Option-V). The Vanishing Point dialog opens. Press Ctrl- –/Cmd- – to reduce the preview size.**C**

A We want to paste the striped "wallpaper" onto the side and back walls of the kitchen image. We created the stripes in Adobe Illustrator, placed the file into a blank Photoshop doc, then selected and copied it.

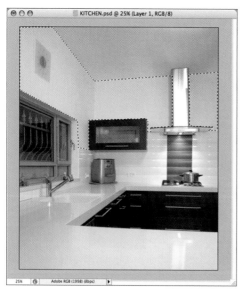

B With the Polygonal Lasso tool, we selected the areas that we want to apply the wallpaper to.

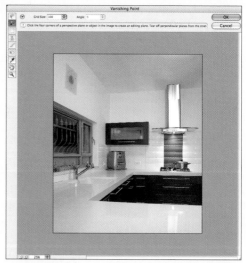

C The image displays in the preview in the **Vanishing Point** dialog.

4. To define the perspective grid for the image to be pasted onto, choose the **Create Plane** tool (C), click in the preview to place the first corner node for the perspective grid, then click to place three more nodes to complete the four-sided blue grid.**A** The Edit Plane tool becomes selected automatically.

> Press and hold down X to zoom in temporarily, click to place a node, then release X. (To delete the last node, press Backspace/Delete, then click to place new nodes.)

5. With the **Edit Plane** tool, do any of the following (Note: To undo any of these edits, press Ctrl-Z/Cmd-Z):

To **reshape** the grid, drag a corner point.

To **reposition** the whole grid, drag it.

The grid should still be **blue** (signifying that it's a valid plane). If it's yellow or red, drag a corner handle until it becomes blue.**B–C**

Continued on the following page

A With the **Create Plane** tool, we placed four corner points to create a **grid**.

B With the **Edit Plane** tool, we dragged a corner of the **yellow** grid...

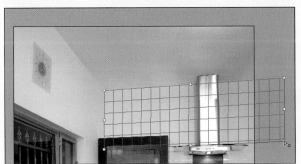

C ... until it turned **blue**.

To connect a **new plane** to the existing one, Ctrl-drag/Cmd-drag a midpoint handle from the edge of the grid. **A**

To change the **angle** of the new plane relative to the first one, Alt-drag/Option-drag a midpoint handle. **B**

6. Press Ctrl-V/Cmd-V to **paste** the imagery from the Clipboard. Don't deselect the new floating selection! The **Marquee** tool ⌷ becomes selected automatically. Drag the pasted image onto the grid or grids (**A**, next page).

7. Choose the **Transform** tool ⧉ (T), then do either or both of the following:

   Reposition the pasted image within the planes by dragging it (**B–C**, next page).

   Scale the pasted image by dragging any of the small white handles on its edge. (If you don't

see any of the white handles, drag the image to bring one or more into view.)

➤ To blend the pasted image into the background, choose the Marquee tool, then choose Luminance from the Heal menu to blend lights and darks, or On to blend lights, darks, and colors. These options take time to process.

8. Click OK. For a few ways to enhance the Vanishing Point results, see page 188.

➤ To hide and show the grid and any selection while in the Vanishing Point dialog, press Ctrl-H/Cmd-H.

➤ Read the tool hints in the Vanishing Point dialog to learn more.

A We Ctrl/Cmd dragged the left midpoint on the grid to add a **second** (connected) **plane** to define the left wall. Then we fine-tuned the angle of the new plane by Alt/ Option dragging a midpoint (the plane swung like a door).

B Now the grid is ready for us to paste in the imagery.

A We pressed Ctrl-V/Cmd-V to **paste** the image we copied into the grid and then, with the **Marquee** tool, dragged the image into the planes that we defined.

B With the **Transform** tool, we repositioned the image to reveal the white midpoint handle on the right edge, then dragged the midpoint handle to the right to fill the grid. After doing so, we discovered a shortcoming of the Vanishing Point filter: the stripes on the back wall are larger than those on the left—the reverse of natural perspective.

C The solution, in this case, was to paste the same image again into the right part of the grid, so we could then transform it separately from the left part.

See also the figures on the following page

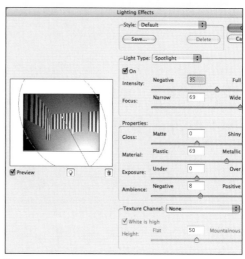

A This is the result of using the **Vanishing Point** filter. We think it could use a lighting enhancement, though, to make the wallpaper look more realistic.

B To add realism to the scene, we applied Filter > Render > **Lighting Effects,** using the default Spotlight type (we widened the lighting ellipse slightly).

➤ As an alternative to using the Lighting Effects filter, try changing the **mode** of the layer you applied the Vanishing Point filter to (try Screen or Multiply).

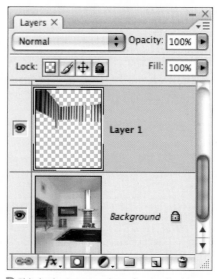

C Ahhh...that's better!

D This is the **Layers** palette for the final image.

➤ If you want to reveal an area of the underlying layer (such as an object on the wall or floor), after exiting the Vanishing Point dialog, add a **layer mask** to the vanishing point layer. Lower the layer opacity temporarily so you can see part of the underlying layer and then, with the mask selected, paint with black.

THERE'S A LOT MORE TO VANISHING POINT

To learn more about the Vanishing Point filter, see Adobe Photoshop CS3 Help.

The difference between a sharpened photo and an unsharpened one may be subtle, but the former will look blah and undefined and the latter will have that extra, well, edge. In this chapter, you'll learn how to use three sharpening filters in Photoshop: Unsharp Mask, High Pass, and Smart Sharpen.

If you're wondering whether to use the sharpening controls in Camera Raw or in Photoshop, the answer is "both": Use Camera Raw to apply a moderate amount of "capture" sharpening to your image as desscribed in Chapter 3; then after you've done all your tonal and color correction, image edits, and noise reduction work and any scaling or transformations that cause resampling, sharpen it again in Photoshop. For this, follow the instructions in this chapter.

A last round of sharpening should be applied to a copy of your file before you export it (see page 323). For Web output, do this after downsizing the image to 72 ppi. For print output, the extra sharpening will help compensate for the fact that details are softened slightly when pixels are converted to dots of ink.

The two powerhouse sharpening filters that we use most often are Unsharp Mask and Smart Sharpen. We'll show you how to use Unsharp Mask once for overall sharpening and then a second time to sharpen a specific tonal range further, and how to use the Smart Sharpen filter to target image sharpening to specific tonal ranges. We've also included instructions for applying the High Pass filter and Unsharp Mask to sharpen edges.

In Photoshop, you can apply sharpening to the entire image or, as we'll show you in this chapter, to target areas or tonal ranges. You'll learn how to control where the sharpening is applied and how to regulate the intensity of the sharpening effect.

9

IN THIS CHAPTER

Note: Settings listed in the captions in this chapter were chosen for photos that are approximately 3000 x 2000 pixels.

Sharpening a whole image with the Unsharp Mask filter

The best time to sharpen the overall image with the **Unsharp Mask** filter is after you apply capture sharpening in Camera Raw, reduce noise, and perform color corrections and other image edits, and before outputting or exporting your file. To achieve a sharpening effect, Unsharp Mask increases the contrast between adjacent pixels. Dialog settings let you control the increase in contrast (the Amount), how wide an area of surrounding pixels the filter affects (the Radius), and the minimum level of contrast needed between adjacent pixels for an area to be sharpened (the Threshold).

To apply the Unsharp Mask filter:

1. Open an RGB image, and flatten it if it contains layers. Choose a zoom level of 50% (**A**, next page).

2. Press Ctrl-J/Cmd-J to duplicate the Background. Change the blending mode of the duplicate layer to **Luminosity** to allow the sharpening to affect only tonal values, not the color. Keep the layer selected.

3. Choose Filter > Sharpen > **Unsharp Mask.**

4. In the Unsharp Mask dialog, choose an **Amount** value to control the intensity of the sharpening (**B**, next page). For a high-resolution image (2000 x 3000 pixels or higher) that contains figures or natural objects, use a low setting of around 80–120; for an image that contains hard-edged objects, use a higher setting of 150–170.

5. The **Radius** setting controls how wide an area of pixels surrounding high-contrast edges will be sharpened (**C**, next page). Determining the right Radius value is tricky, because you have to consider the total number of pixels in the file and the subject matter. The more pixels the image contains, the higher the Radius value needed. For a low-contrast image that contains large, simple objects and smooth color transitions, a high Radius of 1.5–2 is usually effective; for an

intricate, high-contrast image with sharp transitions, a lower Radius of around 1 will probably work better.

➤ Think of the Amount and Radius settings as interdependent. If you adjust one value, you should also readjust the other (**A**, page 192).

6. Choose a **Threshold** value to control the degree of contrast an area must have in order to be sharpened. Start with a Threshold of 0 (which would sharpen the entire image), then raise the value slowly. At a Threshold of 5–10, high-contrast areas will be sharpened and areas of lesser contrast will receive very little sharpening. At higher Threshold values, only high-contrast edges will be sharpened, in which case you can also increase the Amount and Radius to apply more sharpening to just those areas without oversharpening any of the lower-contrast areas (**B**, page 192).

7. Uncheck, then recheck Preview to compare the original and sharpened versions of the image.

➤ To inspect a different part of the image, click in the document window; that area will display in the preview window in the dialog.

8. Click OK, then flatten the document (choose Flatten Image from the Layers palette menu).

CHOOSING A ZOOM LEVEL FOR SHARPENING

When judging the effects of sharpening on images that are 3000 x 2000 pixels or larger, we recommend using a zoom level of 50%. At this level, you'll see just the right amount of detail, whereas at 100%, you would see too much detail (would be viewing the image at a much closer range than you'd normally look at a printout). Zoom to 100% only in the event that you need to judge whether sharpening has added noise to the midtone and shadow areas.

A The details in the original image look too soft.

B We chose a high **Amount** value of 200 in the **Unsharp Mask** dialog temporarily to better judge the Radius and Threshold values that we'll set next.

C We can see that a **Radius** value of 2.5 is too high, because it produced halos along the edges of some of the shapes.

See also the figures on the following page

A We lowered the **Amount** value to 160 to lessen the overall sharpening and lowered the **Radius** value to 1.3 to remove the halos.

B Our final **Unsharp Mask** filter edits were to raise the **Threshold** value to 3 to restrict the sharpening to just high-contrast edges and to raise the **Amount** value to 170 to slightly increase the sharpening on those edges. Now you can almost smell the chile powder.

SUGGESTED UNSHARP MASK FILTER SETTINGS FOR DIFFERENT TYPES OF IMAGES*

Landscapes that have sharp details

A For "high-frequency" images that contain a lot of fine details, try an **Amount** of **120–170**, a **Radius** just below **1.0**, and a **Threshold** of **3** or **4**.

Subjects that have soft edges

B For images that contain mostly soft textures with a few distinct edges here or there, try a high **Threshold** of **6–8** to preserve the softness, an **Amount** of **100–150**, and a **Radius** of **1**.

Buildings and other high-contrast subjects

C To preserve the contrast, surface detail, and well-defined edges in a subject like this one, try a high **Amount** of **170**, a high **Radius** of **2–3**, and a low **Threshold** of **0–3** to keep the edges nice and crisp.

Portraits

D To control the softness or sharpness of a portrait, try an **Amount** of **90–120**. Set the **Radius** to **1–2** to make the hair and facial details crisp, and set the **Threshold** to **3–6** (to the point where the skin begins to look smoother).

* These settings apply to high-resolution images.

SHARPENING MIDTONES WITH THE UNSHARP MASK FILTER

After using the **Unsharp Mask** filter once, you can refine the results by further sharpening just the midtone areas (not the highlights and shadows). In the second round, apply the filter to a duplicate layer, then use the **Blend If** sliders in the Layer Style dialog to control which more-sharpened pixels in the duplicate layer stay visible and which less-sharpened pixels from the Background show through.

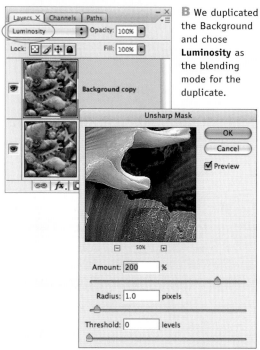

B We duplicated the Background and chose **Luminosity** as the blending mode for the duplicate.

A This image is sharpened adequately, but we want to enhance the surface detail even more in the midtones.

C Next, we applied the **Unsharp Mask** filter to the duplicate layer (settings shown above).

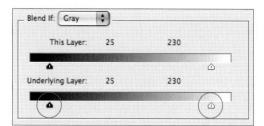

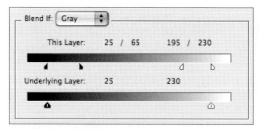

D We double-clicked the duplicate layer to open the Layer Style dialog, then clicked Blending Options on the left side. In the **Blend If** area, we set both black sliders to 25 and both white sliders to 230, which enabled the less sharp shadow and highlight pixels from the Background to show through the duplicate layer.

E We held down Alt/Option and dragged the right part of the **black This Layer** slider to 65 and the left part of the **white This Layer** slider to 195. These changes enable the extra sharp midtone areas on the duplicate layer to stay visible but also fade into the less sharpened areas.

A In this close-up of the image after applying the Unsharp Mask filter, you can see that highlight and shadow areas look **oversharpened** (it's especially noticeable on the two shells in the center).

B After the **Blend If** adjustments, the midtones are still very sharp and the highlights and shadows display neither oversharpening nor unwanted noise. Compare the red shell on the left side and the interior of the striped shell with the same areas in figure **A**, above.

Enhancing details with the High Pass filter

The **High Pass** filter is a simple but effective tool for increasing edge contrast and enhancing details. If you apply the filter to a duplicate layer, you'll be able to control not only the intensity of the sharpening, but also which areas are sharpened.

To apply sharpening using the High Pass filter:

1. In an RGB image that needs sharpening,**A** press Ctrl-J/Cmd-J to duplicate the Background, and keep the duplicate layer selected.

2. Choose Filter > Other > **High Pass.** The High Pass dialog opens.**B**

3. For a high-resolution image (300 ppi, or 2000 x 3000 pixels or larger), choose a **Radius** of 4; for a low-resolution image (150 ppi or lower), set the Radius to 2. Click OK.

4. To restore color to the image and control the effect of the High Pass filter, choose one of the following blending modes for the duplicate layer:

   To restore the color and show the sharpening effect, choose **Overlay** (**A**, next page).

   To restore the color and intensify the sharpening, choose **Hard Light** or **Vivid Light** (**B**, next page).

   To restore the color and soften the sharpening effect, choose **Soft Light.**

A This image could use some extra sharpening.

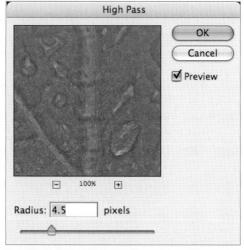

B We duplicated the Background, then applied the **High Pass** filter, choosing a **Radius** of 4.5 pixels.

5. Set the zoom level to 50% or 100% to judge the amount of sharpening and then, if needed, lower the layer **opacity** to compensate for any oversharpening.**C**

6. *Optional:* To limit where the sharpening occurs, Alt-click/Option-click the Add Layer Mask button ▢ at the bottom of the Layers palette to add a black mask. Choose the Brush tool 🖌 (B or Shift-B), a Soft Round tip, Normal mode, and 80% opacity, and press X to make the Foreground color white. Draw strokes where you want to reveal the sharpening effect. If you need to remask any of the sharpened areas, press X to paint with black.

A Choosing **Overlay** blending mode for the High Pass layer restored the color and displayed the effect of the High Pass sharpening.

B We settled on **Vivid Light** blending mode for the High Pass layer to increase the sharpening effect...

C ...but lowered the High Pass layer **opacity** to 50% to soften the sharpening amount by half.

Sharpening areas selectively

To give an image more punch, try applying a **sharpening** boost to **selective areas**. To control where the extra sharpening is applied, you'll use a layer mask (of course!). You can exercise some creative license with this approach, depending on the image content—or in a commercial setting, how much latitude you're allowed.

To sharpen areas selectively:

1. Open an RGB image that has areas that could benefit from an extra sharpening boost.

2. If you already applied some capture sharpening via Camera Raw, skip this step. If not, choose Filter > **Unsharp Mask** and apply a moderate amount of sharpening.

3. Press Ctrl-J/Cmd-J to duplicate the Background. Change the blending mode of the duplicate layer to **Luminosity**, and keep the layer selected.

4. Choose Filter > Sharpen > **Unsharp Mask.** In the dialog, set the **Amount** to 200%, the **Radius** to 1–1.5, and the **Threshold** to 3, then click OK.**B** Don't worry if the image now looks too sharp.

A Some capture sharpening was applied to this photo in Camera Raw. To emphasize the food details in the center, we'll apply more sharpening in a selective manner.

B We duplicated the Background, chose **Luminosity** as the blending mode for the duplicate layer, and applied the **Unsharp Mask** filter using the settings shown at right.

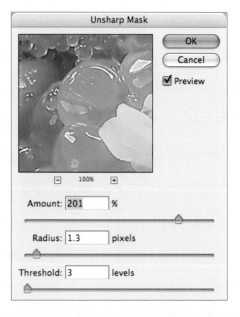

5. Alt-click/Option-click the **Add Layer Mask** button ▣ on the Layers palette to add a black mask, which will hide the extra sharpening that you just applied.

6. Choose the **Brush** tool 🖌 (B or Shift-B), a Soft Round tip, Normal mode, and 80% opacity.

Press X to make the Foreground color white. Draw strokes in areas where you want to reveal the extra sharpening. **A–B** Reapply your brush strokes to any areas that need an extra boost. And if you need to remask any sharpened areas, press X to paint with black.

A We added a **layer mask**, then painted with a soft-edged brush (Foreground color white) to reveal the extra sharpening along the edges of the flowers, roe, cucumber, and pieces of sushi.

B The extra sharpening heightened the edge details and textures in the center of this image. (Question: Are the flowers edible?)

Using the Smart Sharpen filter

Although the Unsharp Mask filter is fast, powerful, and a good choice for sharpening an overall image, when you want to apply selective sharpening without having to use a selection or mask, we recommend using the **Smart Sharpen** filter instead. Via the Smart Sharpen controls, you can target more sharpening to a particular tonal range, such as the midtones, and less sharpening to the highlights and shadows. It's particularly useful when you want to sharpen some areas in an image more than others, such as in a portrait.

Smart Sharpen offers several advantages:

➤ **More control:** Via the Tonal Width control in the Smart Sharpen dialog, you can widen or narrow the tonal range that receives sharpening. Also, Smart Sharpen lets you fade the sharpening in the shadow and highlight areas separately, whereas Unsharp Mask does not.

➤ **More muscle:** The More Accurate option in the Smart Sharpen dialog applies sharpening in multiple passes.

➤ **Fewer halos:** Because it has the ability to detect edges, Smart Sharpen produces fewer color halos.

➤ **Flexibility:** Smart Sharpen will correct Gaussian blur, lens blur, or motion blur, depending on your choice of three algorithms, whereas Unsharp Mask corrects only Gaussian blur.

➤ **Improved workflow:** With the option to save and reuse your settings, Smart Sharpen lets you apply the same settings to multiple images.

Continued on the following page

To sharpen areas selectively with the Smart Sharpen filter:

1. Open an RGB image that needs sharpening.  On the Layers palette, click an image layer or the Background, then press Ctrl-J/Cmd-J to duplicate it. Right-click/Control-click the duplicate layer and choose **Convert to Smart Object**, then click OK if an alert dialog appears.

2. Choose Filter > Sharpen > **Smart Sharpen.** In the Smart Sharpen dialog, **B** keep the zoom level for the preview at 100%.

3. Check **More Accurate** to allow multiple passes of the filter, for higher-quality sharpening (it may take longer, but it's worth the wait).

4. From the **Remove** menu, choose an algorithm for the correction:

   Gaussian Blur uses a sharpening method similar to the one used by the Unsharp Mask filter.

   Lens Blur (our favorite) does a better job of detecting edges and produces fewer color halos.

   Motion Blur is useful if the blurring was caused by a slight movement of the camera or subject and you know the angle at which the movement occurred.

A This image looks too soft.

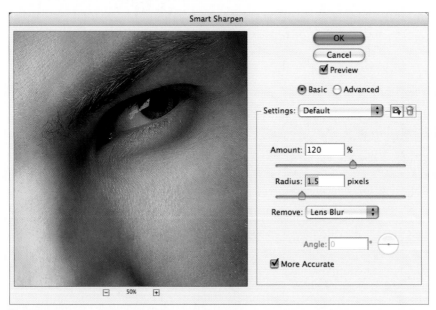

B The settings we used in the **Basic** pane of the **Smart Sharpen** dialog (shown above) properly sharpened the facial details (eyes, teeth, and lips) but oversharpened the skin.

5. Try a **Radius** value of 1–2 pixels and an **Amount** of 60–120% (you can use the scrubby slider to set all the values in this dialog). The image should now look slightly oversharpened.**A**

6. Next, you'll fade the effect. To control the amount of sharpening in the shadow and highlight areas, click **Advanced**, then click the **Shadow** tab. Drag in the preview to display an area of the image that contains both shadows and midtones, then do the following:

Raise the **Fade Amount** to reduce oversharpening in the shadows.

Choose a **Tonal Width** to control the range of midtones that are affected by the Fade Amount. The higher the Tonal Width, the wider the range of midtones in which the sharpening will be reduced, and the more smoothly the reduction will fade to no sharpening in the shadows.

Choose a **Radius** between 5 and 15 to control how many neighboring pixels will be compared to a sharpened pixel. The higher the Radius, the larger the area to be compared.

7. Click the **Highlight** tab. Drag the image in the preview to display an area that contains both highlights and midtones. Adjust the Fade Amount, Tonal Width, and Radius settings, as in the previous step.

8. Hopefully, now the details (e.g., the eyes and mouth, in a portrait) are sharpened properly, and the larger expanses (e.g., cheeks and forehead) are smooth. If the overall image now looks too sharp, click the **Sharpen** tab and lower the **Amount** value slightly. After making adjustments in one tab, you may need to readjust the settings in the other two.

➤ To save your Smart Sharpen settings for future use, click the Save a Copy of the Current Settings button, type a name in the New Filter Settings dialog, then click OK. Saved settings can be chosen from the Settings menu for any image.

9. To compare the unsharpened and sharpened images, click and hold on the dialog preview, then release. Click OK (**A–C**, next page).

➤ To restore all the options in the dialog box to the default settings, either hold down Alt/Option and click Reset or choose Default from the Settings menu.

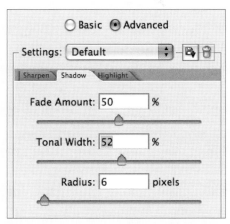

A To apply the **Smart Sharpen** filter selectively and fade the sharpening, we clicked the **Shadow** tab and chose the settings shown above. A **Tonal Width** of 52% reduced the sharpening completely in the shadow areas (the side of the face and around the eyes) but preserved it in the midtones.

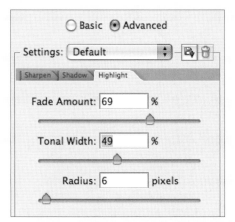

A In the **Highlight** tab of the **Smart Sharpen** dialog, we chose a high **Fade Amount** to reduce the sharpening and a medium **Tonal Width** value to fade the sharpening partially in the lighter midtones and completely in the highlights. With these settings, less sharpening is being applied to the cheeks and lower eyelids. The final image is shown at right and in figure **C**.

B This is the original image, before we applied the Smart Sharpen filter.

C With Smart Sharpen, we were able to successfully sharpen the eyes, eyebrows, nose, lips, and hair without oversharpening the skin.

Selecting edges for sharpening

Sometimes you can achieve better sharpening results if you limit the correction to just the edges of shapes (the areas of highest contrast) while leaving the lower contrast areas unsharpened. The following method for **selecting** only **high-contrast edges** works best on images that have large swaths of low-contrast color, such as a hazy sky or a portrait with soft skin tones, and a small proportion of contrasty edges. If used on an image that contains many intricate details, too many edges will become selected.

To select the edges of shapes:

1. Open an RGB image that needs sharpening.**A** Click the Background layer, then press Ctrl-J/ Cmd-J to duplicate it, and rename the duplicate "find edges."

2. Choose Filter > Stylize > **Find Edges** to reduce the image to line work.**B**

3. To increase the contrast and discard the thinnest edges, choose Image > Adjustments > **Levels** (don't create an adjustment layer), then do the following:

    Move the **white Input Levels** slider to the left to remove the thinnest lines in areas of low contrast (e.g., the cheeks and forehead or details on the ground). The three Input Levels sliders should now be closer together.

    Move the **black Input Levels** slider to the right to darken the line work.

    Move the **gray Input Levels** slider slightly to the right to further darken the line work.**C**

Continued on the following page

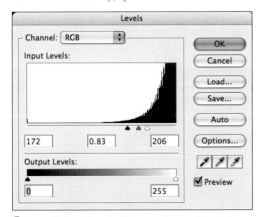

A We want to select just the high-contrast edges in this image, for targeted sharpening.

B We applied the **Find Edges** filter to a duplicate layer to reduce it to line work.

C We used these **Levels** dialog settings to boost the contrast in our "find edges" layer.

Click OK.

4. Choose Image > Adjustments > **Black & White** (Ctrl-Alt-Shift-B/Cmd-Option-Shift-B) to convert the layer to grayscale. In the Black & White dialog, do the following:

   For a portrait, move just the **Yellows** slider to the right (to around 130) to remove the thinnest lines.

   For a landscape, move the **Yellows** slider to the right to remove the finest lines and the **Blues** slider to the left to darken the line work.

   Click OK.**A**

5. Choose the **Magic Wand** tool (W or Shift-W). On the Options bar, set the Tolerance to around 60 and uncheck Contiguous.

6. Click one of the thick black lines in the image, then choose Select > **Similar** to select all the other medium to heavyweight lines.

7. On the Options bar, click **Refine Edge.** In the Refine Edge dialog, click Default, then do the following: (**A**, next page)

   Click the **Mask** (last) preview button to see how your selection will look after you save it to an alpha channel (in step 8).

   To preserve fine details, such as strands of hair, choose a **Radius** value of around 2 but keep the Contrast value at 0.

   To eliminate thin edges in areas of low contrast, choose a **Smooth** value between 5 and 10.

   To soften the transition between selected and unselected areas, choose a **Feather** value of 1.

   To expand the width of the selection lines, choose a **Contract/Expand** value between +5 and +10 (**B**, next page).

   ➤ Your selection is going to be used as a mask to limit further edits. By feathering and expanding the selection edges, you created a wider area for those edits, which will result in a smoother transition between the edited and unedited areas.

Instructions continue on page 206

A **Levels** and **Black & White** adjustments further reduced the image to just high-contrast line work.

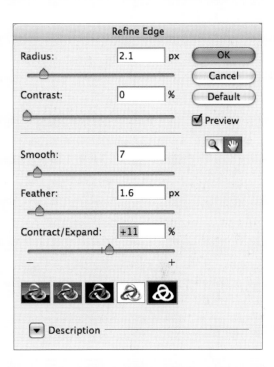

A In the **Refine Edges** dialog, we clicked the Mask preview button (because we're creating a mask). Setting the **Radius** value to 2.1 and the **Contrast** value to 0 preserved the fine details, such as the hair, and setting the **Smooth** value to 7 eliminated edges from low-contrast areas.

B For our final **Refine Edge** adjustments, we set the **Feather** value to 1.6 to soften the transition from selected to unselected areas (this is similar to applying Gaussian Blur to an alpha channel), and the **Contract/Expand** value to 11 to widen the edge selection.

8. Click OK. **A–C**

9. On the Channels palette,⬚ click the **Save Selection as Channel** button ⬚ to save the selection to a new alpha channel.

10. Press Ctrl-D/Cmd-D to deselect the selection and then, on the Layers palette, hide the "find edges" layer.

To sharpen the image using your saved selection, follow the instructions on the next page.

A This is our final **selection** of **edges**, which we'll save to an alpha channel.

B For the sake of comparison, we saved the selection (from step 6 in this exercise) to an alpha channel without the Refine Edge adjustments. Both moderate and high-contrast edges were saved, and there are no soft edge transitions.

C In the alpha channel that we created from our **Refine Edge** selection, on the other hand, there are fewer lines in the broad areas and the remaining line work is softer. Using this refined selection, the sharpening will affect only the areas of sharp detail and will blend smoothly into the low-contrast areas.

Sharpening edges

In the previous instructions, we showed you how to select just high-contrast edges in an image and then save that selection to an alpha channel. Here, we'll show you how to use that selection to limit sharpening to the **edges** of **shapes** when applying the **Unsharp Mask** filter. This method works well for sharpening a portrait, in which you usually want to emphasize facial details (edges) and deemphasize the skin texture (pores and blemishes).

To sharpen edges:

1. Open an RGB image, then follow the steps on pages 203–206 to create an edge selection. Press Ctrl-J/Cmd-J to duplicate the Background.

2. On the **Channels** palette, Ctrl-click/Cmd-click the alpha channel to load the selection.

3. On the Layers palette, click the **Add Layer Mask** button. The selection will be converted to white areas in the layer mask.

4. Click the layer thumbnail and zoom in to 50% view.

A We'll apply some targeted sharpening to this image using our saved selection.

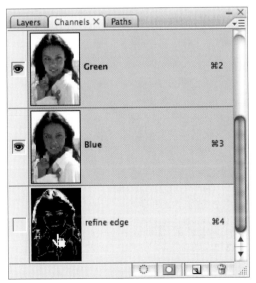

B We Ctrl-click/Cmd-click the **alpha channel** that we created in step 9 (on the previous page) to load it as a selection.

C We duplicated the Background, then added a **layer mask**. The selection became the white areas in the layer mask.

5. Choose **Filter > Sharpen > Unsharp Mask.**

6. You can use higher Amount and Radius values in the Unsharp Mask dialog than usual **A** because the filter will be applied only to edges:

   Set the **Amount** to 150–180%.

   Set the **Radius** to 1.3 pixels.

   Set the **Threshold** value to between 1 and 4. Judge the Threshold effect in the document window, not in the dialog; the preview can't show the effect of a layer mask.

   Optional: Increase the Amount value if you want to increase the edge sharpening.

   Click OK.**B**

7. *Optional:* To soften the overall sharpening effect, lower the opacity of the duplicate layer.**C**

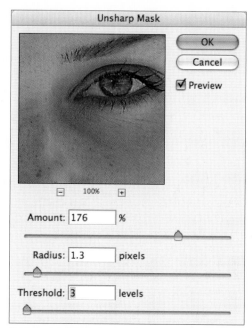

A In the **Unsharp Mask** dialog, we set the **Amount** and **Radius** to these values. Note that although the dialog preview displays sharpening in the whole image, the layer mask will actually limit the effect.

B With the **Threshold** value at **0**, full sharpening is applied to all the edges.

C With the **Threshold** value at **3**, soft, low-contrast edges are sharpened less. We lowered the layer opacity to 80% to soften the overall sharpening.

Sometimes a photo speaks for itself and is best left as is, and sometimes a little extra processing, such as applying a tint or a photo filter, can elevate an ordinary photo into an extraordinary one or help your viewers see a subject from a new perspective.

A few of the tasks in this chapter, such as layering gradients in the background with the Gradient tool, involve adding colors to an image to round out the scene. Most of the tasks, however, involve paring colors down to grayscale in one way or another, and then judiciously reintroducing color by using adjustment commands, such as Hue/Saturation or Black & White, or filters, such as Lighting Effects or the Photo Filter. The final task involves choosing settings for commercial duotone printing, a technique in which a subtle color tint is added to a grayscale print by using an extra plate and ink color.

What formerly took many hours of experimentation in the darkroom can now be accomplished with a few clicks of the mouse in Photoshop. But to get good results with the techniques you'll learn in this chapter, try to make good matches between the subject matter of the image, the method you choose, and your ultimate goal. For example, it would be overkill to apply a gradient to a photo of a brightly colored or complex object, but it might add just the right kick to a simple or ordinary one. If you want to showcase a particular area in a landscape or product shot, try the "Restoring colors selectively" method on page 220.

Although the technical aspects of photography, such as lighting, exposure, focus, depth of field, and timing—and equipment—do affect the outcome dramatically, no amount of postcapture processing and image editing can compensate for a poorly framed shot. A photo that has "good bones"—meaning a good composition and strong linear elements—will be a great candidate for one of the color reduction methods in this chapter, such as the faux infrared effect, whereas the same technique might just accentuate and magnify the flaws in a weaker photo. When browsing through prospective photos for tinting or color reduction, try to imagine what they would look like in grayscale (see them as a cat would!).

Note: Settings listed in the captions in this chapter were chosen for photos that are approximately 3000 x 2000 pixels.

TINTING & BLENDING

10

IN THIS CHAPTER

Layering gradients

In this task, you'll learn how to create a complex, blended background using multiple **Gradient Fill layers**. A subject that is silhouetted on a white background, such as a high-tech product shot or portrait, would be an excellent candidate for this treatment. The advantage of using Gradient Fill layers is that you can reopen the Gradient Fill dialog to edit the gradients at any time.

To layer multiple gradients:

1. Create an RGB document that has a white Background and a silhouetted object on a layer. On the Layers palette, click the Background.**A**

2. Click the Foreground color square on the **Color** palette. Click a color on the Swatches palette; or create a color via the Color palette, then add it to the **Swatches** palette by clicking the **New Swatch of Foreground Color** button.

3. From the New Fill/Adjustment Layer menu on the Layers palette, choose **Gradient**. The Gradient Fill dialog opens.

4. Click the arrowhead to the right of the gradient thumbnail to open the Gradient preset picker, click the **Foreground to Transparent** preset,**B** then click again in the dialog.

   Choose **Linear** from the Style menu, rotate the **Angle** dial to set the angle of the gradient, adjust the **Scale** value to control where the color transitions to transparency on the image,**C** keep Dither checked for better printing, and click OK.**D**

A This photo of a compact fluorescent bulb consists of a silhouetted object on a layer and a white Background below it.

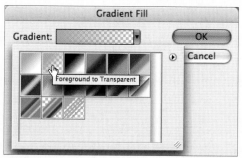

B After choosing a **Foreground** color, we created a **Gradient Fill** layer, then chose the **Foreground to Transparent** preset from the Gradient preset picker.

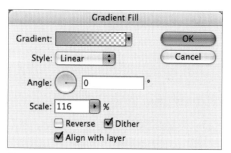

C We also chose these **Style**, **Angle**, and **Scale** settings for the first Gradient Fill layer.

D The first Gradient Fill layer (**Linear** style) is visible behind the bulb.

5. To create more fill layers, click the Background again, then choose a new Foreground color (you can't choose a Foreground color when an adjustment layer is selected). Click the Gradient Fill layer, and repeat steps 3–4 on the previous page to add another one. Experiment with different Style, Angle, and Scale settings.**A–B**

➤ For added depth or contrast, apply layer effects.**C–D**

➤ To change the Foreground color in the Gradient Fill layer, double-click the icon for the layer, click the gradient thumbnail in the Gradient Fill dialog, click the left color stop below the gradient bar in the Gradient Editor dialog, then click the Color swatch at the bottom of the dialog to open the Color Picker.

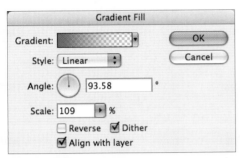

A We chose a new Foreground color for our second **Gradient Fill** layer.

B The two gradient fill layers create a beautiful glow in the background.

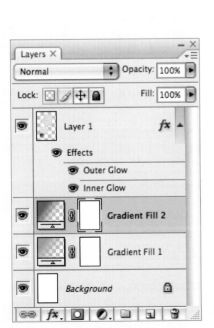

C This is the **Layers** palette for the final image, shown at right.

D To add depth and contrast to the final image, we added two layer effects — **Inner Glow** and **Outer Glow**.

Lighting a background

Another way to enhance a silhouetted object is by adding dramatic background lighting. The **Lighting Effects** filter makes this easy to achieve.

To apply lighting and create a reflection:

1. Create an RGB document that consists of a Background plus a silhouetted object positioned on a layer about two-thirds of the way down from the top.

2. On the **Color** palette, 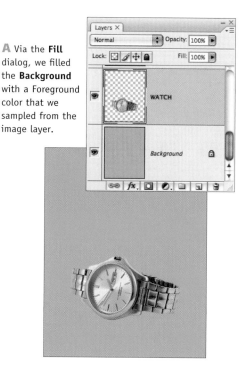 click the Foreground color square to open the Color Picker. Click to sample a medium light color in the image, then click OK.

3. On the **Layers** palette, click the Background.

4. Press Shift-Backspace/Shift-Delete to open the **Fill** dialog. Choose Use: Foreground Color, Mode: Normal, and Opacity: 100%. Click OK.**A**

5. To apply lighting, choose Filter > Render > **Lighting Effects.** The Lighting Effects dialog opens.**B**

6. From the **Style** menu, choose **Soft Omni.** In the lighting preview, drag the bottom handle on the circle downward or upward until the side handles touch the edges of the dark area, then drag the white center point to just above the center of the dark area. Click OK.**C**

A Via the **Fill** dialog, we filled the **Background** with a Foreground color that we sampled from the image layer.

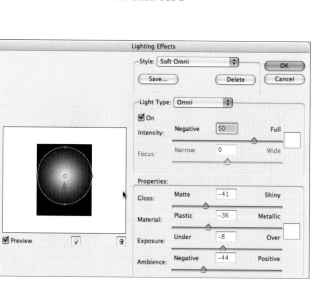

B In the **Lighting Effects** dialog, we chose Style: **Soft Omni.** We dragged the bottom handle of the circle until the side handles touched the edges of the preview and repositioned the center of the circle slightly above the middle of the preview.

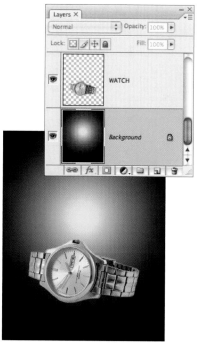

C The results of the **Lighting Effects** filter appeared on the Background.

7. Press Ctrl-J/Cmd-J to duplicate the Background.

8. For the duplicate layer, change the blending mode to **Lighten.** Choose the **Move** tool (V) and uncheck Show Transform Controls on the Options bar. Start dragging in the document window, then hold down Shift and continue to drag to move the duplicate lighting layer downward until you see a subtle dark seam.**A** Lower the layer opacity to a value that looks good.

9. Finally, you'll create a reflection of the object to create the appearance of a shiny surface:

Click the object silhouette layer, press Ctrl-J/ Cmd-J to duplicate it, then choose Edit > Transform > **Flip Vertical.**

With the **Move** tool, drag the reflection downward until the bottom lines up with the bottom of the duplicate object.

Choose **Overlay** as the layer blending mode, and lower the layer **opacity** to 20–40%. Voilà! **B**

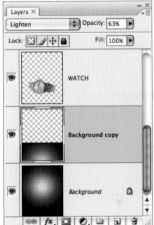

A We changed the blending mode of the duplicate lighting layer to **Lighten,** then moved it downward until a subtle seam appeared (see the arrow at left). We also lowered the layer opacity.

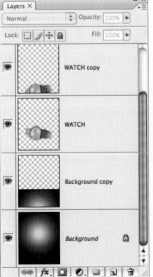

B We duplicated the object layer, applied Transform > **Flip Vertical,** and dragged the duplicate layer downward. We then chose **Overlay** as the blending mode and lowered the layer opacity to 40%.

Desaturating colors selectively

One way to add emphasis to part of an image is by desaturating most of the colors while preserving, or even heightening, the saturation in a specific color range. In this task, you'll use a **Hue/Saturation** adjustment layer to subdue the less important colors and intensify the colors that you want to emphasize.

To desaturate colors selectively:

1. Open an RGB image that has strong coloration.**A**

2. From the New Fill/Adjustment Layer menu ⬤. on the Layers palette, choose **Hue/Saturation**. The Hue/Saturation dialog opens.

3. Just to demonstrate a point, with Edit: **Master** chosen, move the **Saturation** slider to the left. As you can see, this generalized approach to desaturation won't allow you to deemphasize some colors while selectively preserving others.**B** Reset the Saturation to 0.

A Because this whole image is highly saturated, no area is taking center stage. Our goal is to tone down the greens and yellows while preserving some of the reds in the most important part of the image: the flower petals.

B Via a Hue/Saturation adjustment layer, we tried reducing the Saturation for the **Master** color range (all colors). Now the whole image looks dull, including the rose petals, so we'll reset the Saturation for the Master range to 0 and try a more selective approach instead.

A To subdue the colors of the leaves, we reduced the **Saturation** for the **Greens** color range to −80 and reduced the **Saturation** for the **Yellows** color range to −60.

4. From the **Edit** menu, choose a color range that you want to desaturate, then lower the **Saturation.A** Repeat for any other ranges.

5. If the color range that you want to emphasize looks too intense, select it, then reduce the **Saturation** slightly and increase the **Lightness** slightly.**B**

6. Click OK.

7. *Optional:* To enhance the saturation and desaturation effect, choose **Saturation** as the blending mode for the Hue/Saturation adjustment layer.**C**

➤ These steps also work well on downloadable image number 30 (the woman with daisies in her hair).

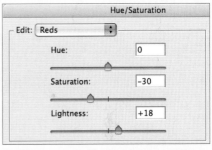

B Next, we reduced the saturation for the **Reds** color range, using the settings shown above. This improved the coloration in the rose petals.

C Finally, we chose **Saturation** as the **blending mode** for the Hue/Saturation adjustment layer, which muted the greens even more and softened the transition between the strong reds and desaturated yellows on the rose petals.

Tinting an image

When you replace all the color in an image with a **color tint**, instead of the color drawing the eye through the composition, the pattern of lights and darks orchestrates the scene. Here, you'll use a Black & White adjustment layer to convert the image to grayscale, intensify contrast, and apply a tint and a Photo Filter to neutralize the highlights.

To apply a tint to an image:

1. Open an RGB image.**A**

2. From the New Fill/Adjustment Layer menu ⬤. on the Layers palette, choose **Black & White**.

3. The dialog opens and the image is converted to grayscale. Heighten the contrast by moving the sliders.**B–C** Or in the document window, drag to the right or left over a grayscale shade that you want to lighten or darken; this will move the corresponding color slider in the dialog.

A This image is a good candidate for tinting because the tonal contrast is strong in the two main color areas — the stone pillars and the sky — and it has strong sculptural forms.

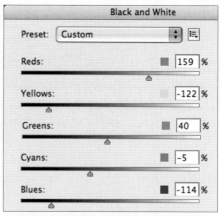

B The **Black & White** command converted the photo to grayscale. We reduced the **Cyans** and **Blues** values to intensify the contrast in the sky.

Reds:	■	159	%
Yellows:	■	-122	%
Greens:	■	40	%

C Next, we moved the **Reds** and **Yellows** sliders in opposite directions to create subtle contrast and enhance the detail in the columns.

4. Check **Tint.A**

5. Move the **Hue** slider to select a tint color, and use the **Saturation** slider to moderate the intensity of that color (we like to keep the Saturation around 15–22%).

6. Click OK. *Optional:* Click the Black & White layer, and lower its opacity slightly.**B**

7. From the New Fill/Adjustment Layer menu,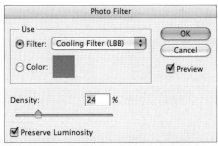. choose **Photo Filter.** From the **Filter** menu in

the dialog, choose a filter that has an opposite color temperature (warm or cool) from the tint color that you applied.

Set the **Density** slider to 20–30% and keep **Preserve Luminosity** checked, then click OK.

8. Lower the **Opacity** of the Photo Filter layer to around 50–60%.**C**

See also the optional step and illustrations on the following page, and see also page 219.

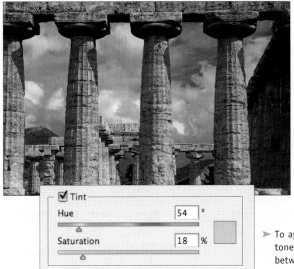

B We lowered the **Opacity** of the adjustment layer to 82% to reveal a little color from the original photo.

➤ To apply a sepia or earth-toned Hue, use a value between 34 and 54.

A With the **Black & White** dialog still open, we applied a **Tint.**

C Finally, to neutralize the colors and counter-balance the warm Tint, we applied a cooling filter via a **Photo Filter** adjustment layer, then lowered the adjustment layer opacity to 50%. The tints enhance the stunning architecture.

9. *Optional:* Restack the Photo Filter adjustment layer below the Black & White adjustment layer, and see if you like how it alters the colors.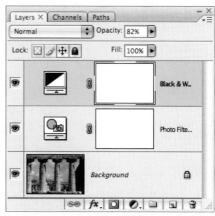

A We discovered that the simple step of **restacking** the Photo Filter layer below the Black & White layer produced better contrast and added a silvery quality to the highlights.

ANOTHER IMAGE TINTED THE SAME WAY

B We'll apply the same "silver" tinting method to this photo, which has two main color ranges (oranges and blues) plus white, and strong lighting contrasts.

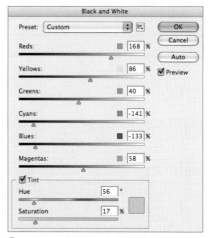

C In the **Black & White** dialog, we lowered the **Cyans** and **Blues** to intensify the contrast in the sky (as in **B** on page 216), and also increased the **Reds** and **Yellows** to lighten the midtones and highlights.

D We created a **Photo Filter** adjustment layer, using the same settings and opacity as in **C** on the previous page, except this time we kept it stacked above the Black & White layer.

To add more impact to a tinted image, you can **colorize** the **highlights** with an additional color.

To recolorize the highlights in a tinted image:

1. Open the RGB image that you applied a tint to, and click the topmost layer.

2. Choose any selection tool.

3. Choose Select > **Color Range.** In the dialog, choose Select: **Highlights,** then click OK.**A**

4. Click **Refine Edge** on the Options bar. Click Default, set the Feather slider to 15–20 px., then click OK. Keep the selection active.

5. From the New Fill/Adjustment Layer menu **⊘.** on the Layers palette, choose **Hue/Saturation.**

6. In the Hue/Saturation dialog,**B** check **Colorize,** then move the **Hue** slider to the desired color. We recommend choosing a cool color if you applied a warm color tint via the Black & White dialog, and vice versa. Move the **Saturation** slider to the left to lower the saturation of the colorization, then click OK.**C**

7. Choose **Hue** or **Color** as the blending mode for the Hue/Saturation layer and lower the layer **opacity** to 60–70%.**D**

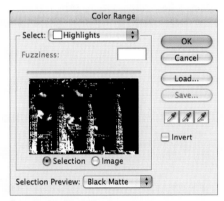

A In the **Color Range** dialog, we chose **Highlights** from the Select menu to select only the highlight areas in the image.

B With the selection active, we created a **Hue/Saturation** adjustment layer. We checked **Colorize** and chose a blue **Hue** of 240, and to keep the colorization effect subtle, lowered the **Saturation.**

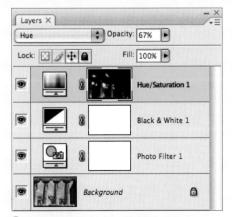

C The selected areas (the highlights) became white areas on the **layer mask** for the **Hue/Saturation** layer.

D Finally, we chose **Hue** as the mode for the Hue/Saturation layer (which lightened the highlights) and lowered the layer opacity to 67% to further soften the colorization effect. The new cool highlight color helps differentiate the stone from the sky.

Restoring color selectively

In the photo shown at right, the path is a strong geometric element that anchors the whole image, but it's overpowered by all the greenery. We'll enhance it with a sympathetic **color tint** while **desaturating** the rest of the photo.

To restore a color to a desaturated image:

1. Open an RGB photo that contains a distinct color area that you want to emphasize.

2. To make it easier to select the area to be tinted, increase the image contrast: From the New Fill/ Adjustment Layer menu, choose **Black & White**. In the dialog, move the sliders to intensify the contrast between the area to be tinted and the surrounding areas, then click OK.

3. Choose the **Quick Selection** tool or the **Magic Wand** tool. Click or drag to select the area to be tinted.

4. Press Ctrl-Shift-I/Cmd-Shift-I to reverse the selected and unselected areas, and keep the selection active.

5. On the Layers palette, drag the **mask** for the Black & White adjustment layer over the **Delete Layer** button, then click Delete in the alert.

6. Click the **Add Layer Mask** button to create a new mask for the Black & White adjustment layer. The selected area became the white area in the layer mask.

A The path in this photo is a strong compositional element. We'll heighten its color to emphasize it and convert the rest of the photo to grayscale.

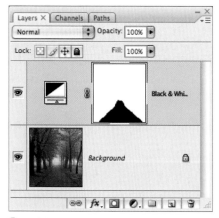

C We deleted the original Black & White **layer mask** and then, with the selection active, added a new mask. The selected area (grass and trees) corresponds to the white area in the mask, whereas the black area is masking the path.

B We used a **Black & White** adjustment layer to increase the contrast, to make it easier to select the path via the **Quick Selection** tool; then we reversed the selected and unselected areas.

7. Double-click the **Black & White** layer thumbnail to reopen the dialog, then readjust the sliders to create a well-balanced black and white conversion.**A**

Click **Tint** and move the **Hue** slider to apply a tint. Choose a low **Saturation** value so the tint doesn't compete with the color that's being preserved by the mask. Click OK.**B**

8. *Optional:* To boost the contrast and intensity, create a Brightness/Contrast adjustment layer. In the dialog, increase the Brightness value to the desired level, then click OK. For the adjustment layer, change the blending mode to Soft Light and the opacity to 70–80%.**C**

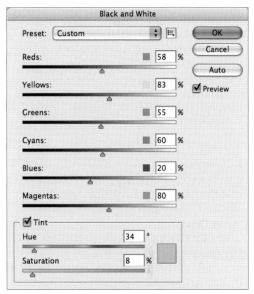

A We reopened the **Black & White** adjustment dialog, used the color sliders to lighten the grays in the leaves and grass, and applied a **Tint** similar to the original path color to unify the image (at a low Saturation so as not to compete with the focal point, the path).

B This is the image after we applied the last **Black & White** adjustment, including a subtle tint.

C Finally, we used a **Brightness/Contrast** adjustment layer (Brightness +100) to lighten the entire photo and chose **Soft Light** mode for the layer (80% opacity) to enrich the color and tint. Now the delicate, intricate trees are balanced by the solid geometric path.

Creating an infrared effect

Normally, infrared light waves aren't visible to the human eye, but photographers can capture images in this wavelength by using special infrared filters. In Photoshop, you can simulate the surreal effect of **infrared** photography by using the Monochrome option in the Channel Mixer, followed by the Diffuse Glow filter.

To create an infrared effect:

1. Open an RGB landscape photo that has some green areas and good contrast, and is sharp.**A** Press Ctrl-J/Cmd-J to duplicate the Background, and keep the duplicate layer selected.

2. From the New Fill/Adjustment Layer menu **⬤.** on the Layers palette, choose **Channel Mixer.**

3. In the Channel Mixer dialog, check **Monochrome** to convert the photo to grayscale. Move the **Green** slider almost all the way to the right to lighten the greens, move the **Red** slider slightly to the left or right, and move the **Blue** slider to the left. Try to create contrast between the light greens and the other colors. We've gotten good results by keeping the Total of the three sliders (listed below the sliders) at or below 100%.**B**

> ### INFRARED IN A LITTLE NUTSHELL
> The specialized filters used in infrared photography block blue wavelengths while allowing near infrared (IR) light to pass through. Fun factoid: With thermal imaging equipment, scientists also can capture far infrared wavelengths.

If you also want to darken the entire photo, drag the **Constant** slider to between –1 and –5. Click OK (**A**, next page).

4. *Optional:* You're going to have to merge the adjustment layer downward in the next step, but before doing so, you may want to duplicate it and then hide the duplicate, to preserve the option to choose different settings for it later.

5. Press Ctrl-E/Cmd-E to **merge** the adjustment layer with the duplicate of the Background.

6. Convert the duplicate layer into a Smart Object layer by choosing Filter > **Convert for Smart Filters** (click OK if an alert dialog appears). This conversion will enable the filter that you're going to apply next to remain editable.

A An infrared treatment is going to transform this image from ordinary to dramatic.

B In the **Channel Mixer** dialog, we checked **Monochrome**, then increased the contrast by moving the **Green** slider to the far right and moving the **Red** and **Blue** sliders to the left by differing amounts.

7. To simulate the glow that infrared photos develop (due to the required long exposure times), choose Filter > Distort > **Diffuse Glow.**

8. In the **Filter Gallery**, do the following: **B**

   Click the **Hide Thumbnails** ⏷ button to hide the pane of thumbnails, and lower the zoom level for the preview.

Adjust the three sliders to achieve the desired amount of graininess and glow. As you raise the Glow Amount, you'll also need to raise the Clear Amount. Click OK (**A**, next page). Don't worry if the highlights now lack detail; you can correct that somewhat in the next step.

Continued on the following page

A Our **Channel Mixer** adjustment produced this grayscale image and a simplified composition. Now the strong highlights (former green areas) are taking center stage.

B In the **Filter Gallery**, we chose these settings for the **Diffuse Glow** filter: Graininess 2; Glow Amount 5 (to create a glow without clipping too many highlights); and Clear Amount 8 (to lighten the entire photo).

9. If the Diffuse Glow filter clipped the highlights, double-click the **Edit Blending Options** button ⭮ (to the right of the filter name listing) **A** to open the Blending Options [filter name] dialog.

10. Reduce the zoom level in the dialog, lower the Opacity to restore some detail to the highlight areas,**B** then click OK.**C**

▶ Each Smart Filter can be edited individually: Double-click the filter name to edit the filter settings; or choose a different blending mode or opacity via the Blending Options dialog; or hide the filter effect via the visibility icon.

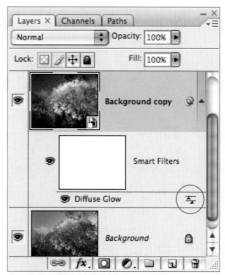

A On the Layers palette, we'll double-click the **Edit Blend Options** button to open the Blending Options dialog.

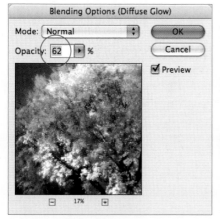

B In the **Blending Options** dialog, we lowered the **Opacity** for the Diffuse Glow filter to restore some detail to the highlights.

C By simplifying and intensifying the lights and darks, the **infrared** effect produced this luminous, surreal image.

A VARIATION ON THE INFRARED EFFECT

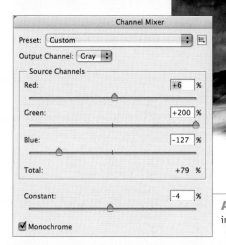

Channel Mixer

Preset: Custom

Output Channel: Gray

Source Channels

Red: +6 %

Green: +200 %

Blue: -127 %

Total: +79 %

Constant: -4 %

☑ Monochrome

A We followed the same steps as on pages 222–224 to create this infrared effect.

B To restore some color to the distant mountains and sky (the nongreen areas, in the original photo), we changed the blending mode of the Smart Object layer to **Lighter Color**.

Creating a duotone

To create a **duotone**, commercial printers use one or more additional plates and ink colors to give a grayscale image added depth and richness and to extend its tonal range (especially in the midtones). Via the Duotone Options dialog, you can specify settings for printing a duotone (two plates), tritone (three plates), or quadtone (four plates). Although you could choose custom colors and control how they're distributed across the tonal range, it will be easier—and, more important, will help prevent printing problems—if you use a preset.

Note: The only way to proof a duotone is via a press proof (not from a PostScript color printer).

To create a duotone by using a preset:

1. Open an RGB image that has good contrast.**A** To adjust or increase the contrast to get a good grayscale conversion (see the next step), use a **Black & White** adjustment layer, then merge it downward.

2. Choose Image > Mode > **Grayscale** to convert the image to grayscale.**B** Click OK in the first alert, then click Discard in the second alert.

3. Choose Image > Mode > **Duotone.** The Duotone Options dialog opens.

4. Choose **Duotone** from the **Type** menu to create a duotone that uses Black and one color.

5. Click **Load**, navigate to Program Files > Adobe in Windows or Applications in the Mac OS, then choose Adobe Photoshop CS3 > Presets > Duotones > Duotones > **PANTONE Duotones.** Click one of the presets that ends in **1**, then click Load. A tint will be applied to the image (**A**, next page), and swatches will display for the Ink 1 and Ink 2 colors (**B**, next page).

6. To view a preset that has a more muted color scheme for comparison, click **Load** again, click a preset that ends with **2**, then click Load.

7. Sample other duotone presets, if desired. When you settle on one that you like, click OK to close the Duotone Options dialog (**C–D**, next page).

➤ The duotone presets that end with a 1 apply the most color, and the presets ending in 2, 3, and 4 apply progressively less color to a smaller range of midtones.

A This is the original image.

B We used a **Black & White** adjustment layer to correct the contrast before converting the image mode to **Grayscale.**

➤ To edit the existing duotone settings for an image, reopen the Duotone Options dialog by choosing Image > Mode > Duotone.

➤ The presets differ not only in the color that they apply, but also in how the curves are shaped, as shown in the Ink 1 and Ink 2 thumbnails.**B, D**

Continued on the following page

A We converted the image to Duotone mode, and applied the **478 brown (100%) bl 1** duotone preset, as shown in figure **B**, below.

C In this **478 brown (100%) bl 2** duotone (well... simulated duotone), the gray shades are replaced with shades of a warm tint, as shown in figure **D**, below.

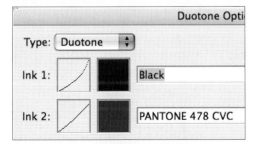

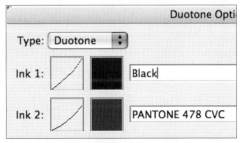

B The settings for the **478 brown (100%) bl 1** preset display in the **Duotone Options** dialog.

D Note that although the same PANTONE color is being used for this **478 brown (100%) bl 2** preset as the one shown at left, the Ink 1 and Ink 2 curves have a different shape. This preset applies less color to the midtones (the Ink 2 curve is lower).

Choosing a file format for a duotone

If you're going to print your duotone file directly from Photoshop, save it in the PSD format.

If you're going to import the duotone file into a page layout program, do either of the following:

► To import the file into an InDesign CS3 layout for two-color printing (black plus one color), save it in either the PSD or PDF format. For other layout programs, use the EPS format (see step 6 in the instructions below).

► To import the file into a page layout program for printing with four-color process inks, first convert it to CMYK mode (Image > Mode > CMYK Color), then save it in the PSD, PDF, or TIFF format, depending on which format the layout program supports.

To have your commercial printer output your duotone using two plates, tell them the duotone is set up with black as Ink 1 and ask which format you should save the file in. The order of inks and the screen angles will affect the outcome, so also ask if they'll take care of choosing **screen angles** for the colored ink, or if they would rather provide you with the necessary information so you can do it. In the latter case, follow the instructions below.

To choose options for duotone printing:

1. With the duotone file open, choose File > **Print**.

2. In the Print dialog, choose **Output** from the menu in the upper right, then click **Screen.A**

3. The Halftone Screen dialog opens.**B** Uncheck **Use Printer's Default Screen**, then click **Auto**.

4. In the Auto Screens dialog,**C** enter the **Printer** resolution and lines/inch **Screen** setting as specified by your print shop, check **Use Accurate Screens**, then click OK.

5. Click OK to close the Halftone Screen dialog, then click Done to close the Print dialog.

6. Save the file in the format your print shop has specified, which will be either **PSD** (so the print shop can make screen adjustments) or **EPS.** For the latter, choose Photoshop EPS from the Format menu in the Save As dialog. In the EPS Options dialog,**D** check Include Halftone Screen to embed the screen info into the file, then click OK.

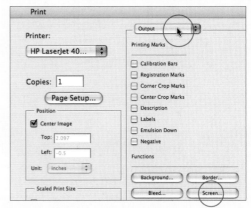

A To establish the necessary screen angles for duotone printing, go to the Print dialog, choose **Output** from the menu in the upper right, then click **Screen**.

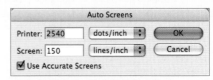

B In the **Halftone Screen** dialog, uncheck **Use Printer's Default Screen**, then click **Auto**.

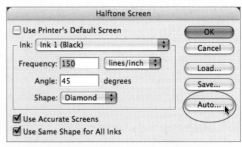

C In the **Auto Screens** dialog, enter the **Printer** resolution and **Screen** frequency and check **Use Accurate Screens**.

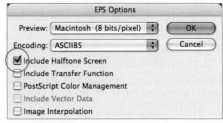

D If you're told to save the file in the Photoshop EPS format, check **Include Halftone Screen** in the EPS Options dialog.

This chapter covers painting techniques that are the antithesis of high tech—well, except that they're all done in Photoshop. One advantage to working electronically is that you can create images that have a handmade look without slavishly trying to mimic a specific medium.

This chapter begins with an introduction (or rehash, if you're already experienced with brushes in Photoshop) to brushes and painting techniques, which you can use as a reference guide. The first exercise is to create a brush from imagery and use it in a composition. This is a great way to apply a single shape repetitively or to apply a texture.

If you're not confident about your artistic skills or your ability to handle a brush, don't worry: you can easily simulate a fine art look by using filters. For example, we'll show you how to create a sketch by using the Gaussian Blur and Glowing Edges filters, then polish it off with a few brush strokes on a layer mask. To simulate pastels, you'll combine the Rough Pastels and Sprayed Strokes filters. For a more painterly look (similar to gouache or crayon), you'll use a combination of the Colored Pencil, Paint Daubs, and Smudge Stick filters. And finally, to create a watercolor look, you'll use the Noise Median, Poster Edges, and Glowing Edges filters. In all of the exercises, you'll apply multiple filters to a single image. Our experience has been that with filters, the more the merrier: when you apply them in twos, threes, or more, you get better results.

We like the effects that can be achieved with brushes and filters in Photoshop but tend to shy away from simulating thick surfaces, such as oil paint or impasto, because the faux version lacks three-dimensionality. Working on the flat plane of a computer screen, we gravitate to media that are traditionally applied to paper, such as pencil, charcoal, watercolor, and gouache (but hey, that's just our bias).

There are no hard and fast rules in the world of electronic or traditional art-making. You can develop your own electronic art media in any way that appeals to you. And remember that in addition to giving whole images a more handmade look, you can apply the techniques that you learn in this chapter (or your own variations thereof) to sections of an image, such as to individual layers in a collage.

Note: Settings listed in the captions in this chapter were chosen for photos that are approximately 3000 x 2000 pixels.

FINE ART MEDIA

11

IN THIS CHAPTER

QUICK SUMMARY: USING BRUSHES

TASK	METHOD
Using and choosing brushes	
Display the Brushes palette	Choose Window > Brushes (F5) or click the Brushes palette icon, 🖌 if it's in a dock
Open a temporary Brush preset picker	Choose a tool that uses brushes, then click the Brush preset picker ▪▪ on the Options bar or right-click/Control-click in the document window
Load brush tips	Choose from the Brush preset picker menu
Change the brush size	Press [or] (bracket key)
Select the next brush tip on the Brushes palette	. (period)
Select the previous brush tip on the Brushes palette	, (comma)
Select the first tip on the Brushes palette	Shift-, (comma)
Select the last tip on the Brushes palette	Shift-. (period)
Save all the tips on the Brushes palette	Choose Save Brushes from the Brushes palette menu
Save select brush tips on the Brushes palette	Use Edit > Preset Manager (see page 92)
Save brush settings, including the tip, mode, opacity, flow, etc., as a preset to the Tool preset picker	Open a temporary Tool preset picker from the left side of the Options bar or display the Tool Presets palette, ✳ then click the New Tool Preset button ⬒
Create a brush tip from an image	Select an area of an image, then choose Edit > Define Brush Preset
Delete a brush tip from the Brushes palette	Alt-click/Option-click the tip
Changing brush variables	
Control the rate of buildup	Change the Flow and Airbrush settings on the Options bar (use a higher Flow for quick strokes)
Control the softness of the edge of the brush stroke	Change the Hardness setting on the Brush preset picker; or check or uncheck Noise, Wet Edges, or Smoothing on the Brushes palette; or try Dissolve mode on the Options bar
Control the color variation	Change the Jitter values in the Color Dynamics panel of the Brushes palette
Choose a color from the image using a temporary Eyedropper tool	Alt-click/Option-click a color in the document window
Choose settings for a stylus	Use the Control menus on the Brushes palette panels

SHORTCUTS FOR CHANGING TOOL SETTINGS

You can use shortcuts to change settings for many tools, such as the Brush, Pencil, Color Replacement, Clone Stamp, Pattern Stamp, Smudge, Dodge, Burn, History Brush, Art History Brush, Spot Healing Brush, Healing Brush, Eraser, Magic Eraser, or Background Eraser, if the tool has that feature:

Cycle through the **blending modes** for the tool	Shift-+ (plus) or Shift -- (minus)
Decrease or increase the **Master Diameter** for a brush preset	[or]
Decrease or increase the **Hardness** for a brush preset	Shift-[or Shift-]
Change the **Opacity, Exposure,** or **Strength** percentage (Shift-press a number to change the Flow level)*	0–9 (e.g., 2 = 20%), or quickly type a percentage (e.g., "38")

*If the Airbrush option is on, press a number to change the Flow percentage or Shift-press a number to change the Opacity percentage. And when Shift-pressing in Windows, use the numbers on the main keyboard, not on the keypad.

QUICK SUMMARY: PAINTING TECHNIQUES

TASK	METHOD
Restore areas	Set the History Source icon to a snapshot or state on the History palette, then draw strokes with the History Brush tool (Y) (create snapshots periodically as you work); or use the Eraser tool (E) with the Erase to History option on
Erase areas to transparency	Use the Eraser (drag), Background Eraser (click), or Magic Eraser (click) tool
Repaint an image in stylized strokes	Add a new blank layer above an image layer, then draw strokes with the Art History Brush tool; or use the Pattern Stamp tool with the Impressionist option on
Smudge colors	Use the Smudge tool on a new layer with the Finger Painting option on
Add an overall paper color or texture	Apply a Solid Color or Pattern Fill layer via the New Fill/Adjustment Layer menu on the Layers palette; change the layer blending mode and/or lower the layer opacity

Creating brush tips from imagery

After **creating** a **brush tip** from a selected area of an **image,** you can click or drag with the Brush tool to quickly create multiple monochromatic repeats of that tip in the current Foreground color.

To create a brush tip from an image:

1. With the **Quick Selection** or **Magic Wand** tool, select a small area of a picture.**A**

2. Choose Edit > **Define Brush Preset.** The Brush Name dialog opens.**B** Enter a Name, then click OK.

3. To practice using the tip, choose the **Brush** tool and a Foreground color, click the tip on the Brush preset picker (the last preset on the picker),**C** turn on the Airbrush option, if desired, then click or drag in the image (see the illustrations on the next two pages).

➤ When you use a brush tip that you've created from an image, you can reset the brush diameter to the original sample size by clicking Use Sample Size in the Brush preset picker.

A We selected some leaf shapes, which will be made into a brush tip.

B We chose Edit > Define Brush Preset and then, in the **Brush Name** dialog, entered a name for the custom brush.

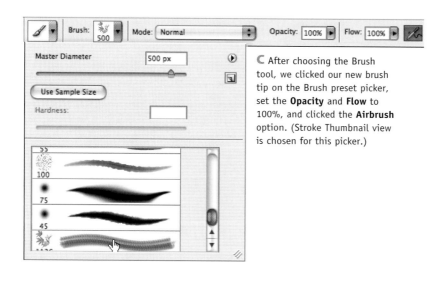

C After choosing the Brush tool, we clicked our new brush tip on the Brush preset picker, set the **Opacity** and **Flow** to 100%, and clicked the **Airbrush** option. (Stroke Thumbnail view is chosen for this picker.)

PAINTING WITH A BRUSH MADE FROM AN IMAGE

A To create the semitransparent brush mark (leaf shapes) in the center of this image, we created a new, blank layer, chose a Foreground color, then **clicked** with the Brush tool. To create the more opaque marks in the lower right, we **held** the **mouse down** (the marks gradually became darker, due to the **Airbrush** function).

B We changed the Foreground color to gold, then clicked again to create another brush mark. To rotate all the marks on that layer, we chose the Move tool, then dragged a corner handle on the transform box.

See also the figures on the following page

A Next, we created a second new layer and stacked it below the first one. We pressed [to reduce the brush diameter, changed the Foreground color to tan and then, to create a trail of leaves and a feeling of movement, **dragged** horizontally across the bottom of the image.

B We created one more layer, pressed] to increase the brush diameter, then added the green, orange, and red brush marks. Finally, to change the orientation of that layer and make the leaves look as though they're swirling in an autumn breeze, we chose Edit > Transform > **Flip Horizontal** and **Flip Vertical**.

Creating a sketch by using filters

In the remaining exercises in this chapter, you'll reinterpret a photo as a sketch, painting, or watercolor. In this exercise and the next, you'll reduce an image to a **line art sketch** by using filters and by drawing a few strokes on a layer mask.

To create a line art sketch:

1. Open an RGB image.**A** Press Ctrl-J/Cmd-J to duplicate the Background. Rename the layer "blur," and keep it selected.

2. Choose Filter > Blur > **Gaussian Blur.** Set the Radius slider to around 20 pixels, then click OK.

3. Lower the opacity of the blurred layer to 50%.**B**

4. The blur layer will supply the color; a line art layer will supply the necessary details. Duplicate the Background again, then drag the new duplicate layer to the top of the stack.

Continued on the following page

A This image will convert well to a sketch because it has strong contrast and broad color areas.

B To create a layer of soft color, we applied the **Gaussian Blur** filter (Radius 20 px) to a duplicate layer, then lowered the opacity of that layer to 50%.

5. Choose Filter > Stylize > **Glowing Edges.** In the Filter Gallery dialog, click the Hide Thumbnails button to expand the preview panel. Raise the **Edge Brightness** and **Smoothness** values to create bright, crisp lines without too many tiny details. Click OK.**A**

6. Press Ctrl-I/Cmd-I to **invert** the layer (the background switches to white).**B** And to allow some color from the blurred layer to show through, choose **Overlay** as the layer mode.**C**

7. To restore some underlying color by hand, with the topmost layer still selected, click the **Add Layer Mask** button. With the **Brush** tool, a large, Soft Round, low-opacity tip, and Black as the Foreground color, drag across areas that you want to restore color to (**A–B**, next page). To remove any of your strokes, paint with white.

➤ If you need to brighten the sketch, see **C** on the next page.

A In the Filter > Stylize > **Glowing Edges** dialog, we increased the **Edge Brightness** to make the line work brighter and set the **Smoothness** to eliminate superfluous lines from low-contrast areas.

B Next, we pressed Ctrl-I/Cmd-I to **invert** the colors.

C **Overlay**, the blending mode of the line art layer, allows color from the blurred layer to show through.

A To restore more color and detail, we added a **layer mask** and then, with the **Brush** tool (Soft Round 200 Pixels tip, Opacity 65%, Flow 50%), drew horizontal strokes across the face to partially remove the mask. Next, we lowered the brush opacity to 30% and painted a stroke across the eyes and the mouth (see the layer mask insert at right).

B By partially removing the layer mask, we were able to restore line work to the facial features.

C Finally, to brighten the sketch, we created a **Levels** adjustment layer. In the Levels dialog, we set the gray Input Levels slider to 1.06 and the white Input Levels slider to 246. We also chose **Soft Light** as the blending mode for the adjustment layer and lowered the layer **Opacity** to 55%.

CREATING A LINE ART SKETCH: A VARIATION ON THE PRIOR EXERCISE

The main difference between this method for converting a photo to a line art sketch and the previous one is that here you'll restore colors from the original Background image, whereas in the previous exercise colors were restored from a blurred layer.

WHICH FILTER HAS THE EDGE?

When converting a photo to a sketch, we use the Glowing Edges filter instead of Find Edges because the former lets us eliminate extraneous fine lines and control the line thickness, whereas the latter has no dialog or controls.

A With its strong geometry, color, and linear details, this photo of Nyhavn harbor in Copenhagen, Denmark will translate beautifully into a sketch.

 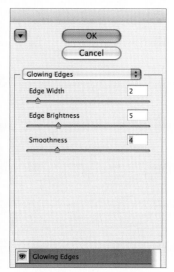

B We duplicated the Background, then used the **Glowing Edges** filter to convert the duplicate layer to line art. In this image (unlike the portrait on the previous page), we wanted to preserve most of the delicate lines, so we chose low settings for all three options.

A As in the previous exercise, we **inverted** the line art (Glowing Edges) layer to produce dark lines on a light background.

B We added a **layer mask** to the line art layer. Then we chose the Brush tool, the brush tip called "Chalk 60 Pixels," and 50% Flow, and added strokes. We varied the brush opacity between 25% and 50%.

C The strokes that we applied to the layer mask restored color from the Background, which added a **watercolor** effect to the line art.

Simulating pastels

Another fine art medium that you can simulate in Photoshop is **pastels**. The way we suggest doing so is to desaturate a copy of the Background, apply the Rough Pastels and Sprayed Strokes filters, and change the layer mode to allow colors from the Background to show through.

To create a pastel sketch:

1. Open an RGB image. Press Ctrl-J/Cmd-J to duplicate the Background, and keep the duplicate layer selected.

2. Create a **Black & White** adjustment layer. In the dialog, use the sliders to create good contrast in the grayscale layer, then click OK.**B**

3. Press Ctrl-E/Cmd-E to merge the adjustment layer into the duplicate layer.

4. Change the blending mode of the grayscale layer to **Luminosity** to blend its lights and darks with colors in the Background.

5. To enable editing of the filters you're going to apply, choose Filter > **Convert for Smart Filters** (click OK in any alerts).

A With its clearly defined color areas and strong contrast, this photo will convert well to a pastel.

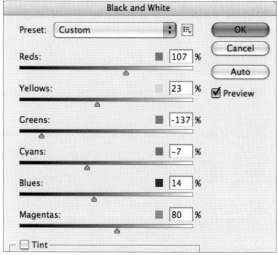

B We converted a duplicate image layer to grayscale via a **Black & White** adjustment layer. To darken the midtones, we moved most of the sliders slightly to the left; to lighten the face, we moved the Reds slider to the right; then we merged the Black & White adjustment layer into the duplicate layer.

6. Choose Filter > Filter Gallery. In the dialog, choose **Rough Pastels** from the menu, and drag a key area of the image into view.**A** Adjust the Stroke Length and Stroke Detail values, and use the Texture sliders to control the graininess and roughness of the strokes.

7. To make the Rough Pastel filter strokes look less uniform, apply an additional filter. Click the **New Effect** button ⬒ at the bottom of the dialog, then choose Brush Strokes > **Sprayed Strokes.B** Choose settings, then click OK.

A We changed the mode of the duplicate layer to Luminosity and converted it to a Smart Object. Via the Filter Gallery, we applied the **Rough Pastels** filter, increasing these values: Stroke Length and Stroke Detail to make the strokes more clearly defined; Scaling to make the Canvas texture more prominent; and Relief to accentuate the strokes.

B Next, we added the **Sprayed Strokes** filter to add randomness to the strokes. We chose a high Stroke Length to accentuate the strokes, and a low Spray Radius to make the strokes thin enough to provide detail to the image.

See also the figures on the following page

ADDING LINE WORK TO THE PASTEL

A To compare this final **pastels** image with a line art sketch from the same original image, see figure **C** on page 237.

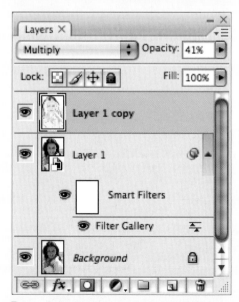

SMART FILTERS: SOLO OR ON ONE LAYER

➤ One advantage of applying multiple filters to a single Smart Object layer is that you have to open the Filter Gallery only once to edit the filter visibility, stacking order, or settings. This is faster than it would be to open the Filter Gallery separately for individual Smart Filter listings. Another advantage is that the preview in the dialog shows the combined effect of all the filters.

➤ A disadvantage of applying multiple filters to a single layer is that you can't change the blending mode or opacity for the Smart Filters individually. You can't have everything!

B To add crisp lines to the pastels image (shown above), we followed steps 4–6 on pages 235–236, but chose **Multiply** mode for the line art layer instead of Overlay, and also lowered the layer **opacity**.

Turning a photo into a painting

To create a **painting**, you'll start with a grayscale layer, as in the previous exercise, but apply a different series of filters and then add a texture. You won't have to use the Brush tool!

To turn a photo into a painting:

1. Open an RGB photo that has bright, clearly defined color areas.**A**

2. Follow steps 1–5 on page 240 to create a grayscale **Smart Object** layer. To preserve the color in the Background image, you'll apply your Smart Filters to the grayscale layer.

3. Choose Filter > **Filter Gallery.** In the dialog, click the Hide Thumbnails button ▾ to expand the preview panel and choose **Paint Daubs** from the menu. Set the sliders to convert existing shapes into smooth, blocky areas.**B** Don't close the dialog yet!

Continued on the following page

A We'll use this photo again because its vivid colors and geometric shapes will translate well into a painting.

B We converted a duplicate image layer to grayscale and chose **Luminosity** as the layer blending mode. Next, after converting the layer to a **Smart Object**, we chose Filter > Filter Gallery and applied the **Paint Daubs** filter. To soften the details while preserving shapes, we chose low Brush Size and Sharpness settings.

4. Click the **New Effect** button  at the bottom of the dialog, then choose **Colored Pencil** from the menu. Choose settings to turn the paint daubs into a collection of strokes **A**.

5. Click the **New Effect** button once more, and choose **Smudge Stick** from the menu. Choose settings to increase the contrast and make the strokes look more expressive.**B** Click OK (**A**, next page).

A Next, we applied the **Colored Pencil** filter to break up the paint daubs into strokes: a Pencil Width value of 8 for moderately thick strokes, a Stroke Pressure value of 8 for good contrast, and a very high Paper Brightness value of 43 to lighten the image.

B The last filter effect we applied was **Smudge Stick**, to boost the contrast and make the strokes look more expressive. We chose a low Stroke Length because the line work was already present, a low Highlight Area value to produce fewer highlights, and a high Intensity value to preserve the contrast.

6. *Optional:* To add texture to the image, click the filter effects mask thumbnail on the Layers palette. Choose Filter > Sketch > Conté Crayon. Set the Foreground Level slider to around 7 and the Background Level slider to a low value of 2 or 3.

Choose a Texture option and a Light direction option **B** (we like Bottom Left). Click OK.**C**

7. *Optional:* To restore more color from the Background image, lower the opacity of the Smart Object layer to around 70%.

A This is the result after we applied the three filters via the Filter Gallery and lowered the opacity of the Smart Object layer to 70%. The image has an Impressionist feel but still plenty of detail.

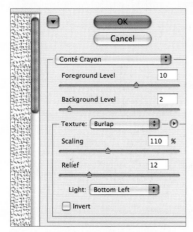

B To add a texture to the image, we clicked the **filter effects mask** thumbnail on the Layers palette, then applied the **Conté Crayon** filter.

C In this closeup view of the image, you can see that the Conté Crayon filter (burlap texture) added a "tactile" quality to the painting.

Creating a watercolor

You don't have the time, patience, or skill to paint a watercolor with a brush? We'll show you how to simulate a **watercolor** effect by using filters (and no brushes).

To create a watercolor by using filters:

1. Open an RGB image, preferably one that has clearly defined color areas.**A** Press Ctrl-J/Cmd-J to duplicate the Background, and keep the duplicate layer selected.

2. To keep the filters you're going to apply editable, choose **Convert to Smart Object** from the Layers palette menu.

3. To convert the colors into blocky shapes, choose Filter > Noise > **Median.** In the dialog, choose a Radius of 10–12 pixels, then click OK.

4. To posterize the colors, choose Filter > Artistic > **Poster Edges.** In the Filter Gallery dialog, set the Edge Thickness and Edge Intensity to 0 and the Posterization to 2, then click OK.**B**

A The watercolor effect will work well on this image because it has clearly defined colors.

B After creating a Smart Object layer, we applied the **Median** and **Poster Edges** filters. The color transitions are no longer smooth or continuous, and color areas are now separate, distinct shapes.

5. *Optional:* To lighten areas and restore some of the white of the "paper" background, choose Filter > Sharpen > Unsharp Mask. In the dialog, set the Amount to 125, the Radius to 20 and the Threshold to 3–4, then click OK. To soften the sharpening effect, on the Layers palette, drag Unsharp Mask to the bottom of the stack of Smart Filters.**A** Note: If the Unsharp Mask filter made the highlights too bright, double-click the Edit Blend Options icon ⬇ for that filter on the Layers palette, lower the Opacity to 60–70%, then click OK.

6. To add lines along the edges of the shapes, click the Background, press Ctrl-J/Cmd-J to duplicate it once more, then choose Filter > Stylize > **Glowing Edges.** Set the Edge Width to around 3, the Edge Brightness to around 5, and the Smoothness to around 7–9, then click OK.

7. Press Ctrl-I/Cmd-I to **invert** the Glowing Edges layer, then drag it to the top of the layer stack. Change the layer blending mode to **Multiply**, and adjust the layer opacity as needed.**B** Done!

A We applied the **Unsharp Mask** filter to intensify the brightness and contrast, but restacked it to the bottom of the list of Smart Filters to soften its effect.

B Finally, we applied the **Glowing Edges** filter to a duplicate of the Background, inverted the duplicate layer, dragged it to the top of the layer stack, changed its mode to **Multiply**, and lowered its **opacity** to 60%. Now the line work blends beautifully with the colors on the Smart Object layer.

In traditional **watercolors,** pigment tends to pool, or collect, at the edges of the brush strokes. In Photoshop, you can mimic this effect in a unique way: Create a pattern preset from an entire photo, then with the **Pattern Stamp** tool and a variety of brushes, paint (stamp) the image onto a new layer.

To create a watercolor with the Pattern Stamp tool:

1. Open an RGB photo that has broad color areas.**A**

2. Choose Edit > **Define Pattern,** without selecting anything first. The Pattern Name dialog opens. Enter a name or keep the default name, then click OK.

3. Choose the **Pattern Stamp** tool 🏝 (S or Shift-S).

4. On the Options bar,**B** do all of the following:

   Click the brush thumbnail to open the Brush preset picker. From the preset picker menu,⊙ choose **Wet Media Brushes.** In the alert, click Append to add the brush library to the existing presets.

   Scroll to the bottom of the picker, then click the last brush tip, which is **Watercolor Light Opacity.** (You'll be using the last five "Watercolor" brushes in this exercise.)

   Choose Mode: Normal, Opacity 60%, and Flow 50%, and check **Aligned** and **Impressionist.**

   Click the Pattern thumbnail to open the **Pattern preset** picker. Click the pattern you defined (now the last preset on the picker).

A To reinterpret this still life as a watercolor, the first step will be to create a pattern preset from the whole image.

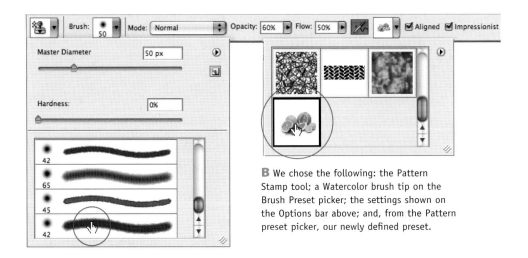

B We chose the following: the Pattern Stamp tool; a Watercolor brush tip on the Brush Preset picker; the settings shown on the Options bar above; and, from the Pattern preset picker, our newly defined preset.

5. Create a new, blank layer. Press Shift-Backspace/Shift-Delete to open the **Fill** dialog. Choose these settings: Use: White, Mode: Normal, and Opacity: 100%. Click OK.

6. Lower the layer opacity to 85%. You'll use this faint version of the image as a guide when you apply strokes.

7. Press] to enlarge the brush tip, then fill in the main shapes in the image.**A** For an authentic watercolor look, leave some of the white (paper) showing and keep the strokes distinct and separate.**B**

8. Once the main areas have been blocked in, right-click/Control-click on the image to open the Brush preset picker, then click the **Watercolor Textured Surface** brush tip.

9. Increase the brush opacity via the Options bar, then paint in details on the edges or interiors of the shapes. You can switch to other Watercolor brushes and brush settings between strokes (**A–B**, next page) and periodically raise, then lower, the layer opacity to check your progress.

Instructions continue on page 251

A To use a faint version of the image as a guide for painting, we created a new layer, filled it with white, and lowered its opacity to 85%. We chose the **Watercolor Light Opacity** brush tip, increased the brush size, and then "painted in" the grapefruit (the color derived from the pattern preset automatically).

B We continued to paint in the other large fruit shapes, pressing [or] as needed to resize the brush tip in order to fit the size of the shapes.

SEEING DOUBLE
If your display is large enough, open (or save as, then open) the original image and keep it onscreen, to refer to as you stamp in the details. Don't be a slave to the original image, though; you can be selective about which details you decide to omit or restore.

A We switched to the **Watercolor Textured Surface** brush tip to add details along the edges and surfaces of the fruit.

B To concentrate more on the watercolor that is starting to take form, we reset the layer opacity to 100% to hide the Background. We chose the **Watercolor Heavy Pigments** brush tip, lowered the brush opacity, and increased the brush size, then added a light color wash along each fruit shape. To add final details, we used the Watercolor Textured Surface brush tip again.

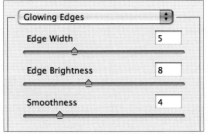

C We duplicated the paint layer, applied the Stylize > **Glowing Edges** filter to the duplicate (settings shown above), then **inverted** the layer to restore the white background.

10. When you're done painting in the image, press Ctrl-J/Cmd-J to duplicate the paint layer, and keep the duplicate selected (**C**, previous page).

11. To enhance the watercolor look, choose Filter > Stylize > **Glowing Edges**, choose settings, then click OK. Press Ctrl-I/Cmd-I to **invert** colors on the layer, change the layer blending mode to **Multiply** to blend the lines with the paint layer,**A** then press Ctrl-E/Cmd-E to merge the line art layer into the paint layer.

12. To heighten the color contrast and saturation, create a **Levels** adjustment layer. In the dialog, move the black and gray Input Levels sliders to the right, then click OK. To adjust its impact, lower the opacity of the adjustment layer.**B**

13. Your watercolor is almost done. To add a texture to the white "paper" background, double-click the paint layer to open the Layer Style dialog, then click **Pattern Overlay.**

14. In the Pattern Overlay panel, click the pattern thumbnail to open the Pattern preset picker. From the picker menu, choose **Artist Surfaces,** then click Append to add the pattern library to the existing presets. Scroll down in the picker and click the **Watercolor** pattern thumbnail. Set the Scale to around 132, the blending mode to Multiply (to blend the pattern with the paint layer), and the Opacity to 100%, then click OK.

Your watercolor is finished (**A–B**, next page).

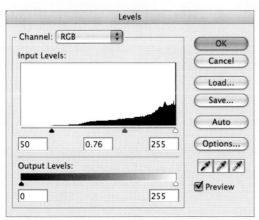

A We chose **Multiply** mode for the line art layer to blend the line work with the underlying paint layer. Now the edges and details look more crisp and provide a needed counterpoint to the broad shapes.

B To heighten the color contrast and saturation, we used a **Levels** adjustment layer.

A This is the final watercolor, complete with a subtle **Pattern Overlay** paper texture.

A VARIATION ON THE WATERCOLOR TECHNIQUE

B Instead of using the Glowing Edges filter (step 11 on the previous page), we created these black lines by applying the Artistic > **Poster Edges** filter (Edge Thickness 6, Edge Intensity 1, and Posterization 2) to the duplicate paint layer, and chose **Multiply** as the layer mode.

In this chapter, you'll learn how to make type characters look as if they're carved into granite, embossed into leather, punched into metal, stamped onto a cracker, illuminated, scratched away, spray painted, written in the sky, cut out of paper, made of neon, and printed on porcelain. To accomplish these feats, you'll use a variety of Photoshop features, such as layer styles, filters, masks, and gradients. You can use these methods as a springboard for developing a personal repertoire of type treatments.

Note: This chapter requires familiarity with the basic typesetting features of Photoshop, which we cover thoroughly in our *Visual QuickStart Guide* to Photoshop.

Tips for designing with type

➤ Think thematically. Choose a font—be it formal, casual, high-tech, calligraphic, historical, simple, or ornate—that suits the background image.

➤ Chubby is good. Chunky letters will give you more surface area to alter or apply effects to.

➤ For a sophisticated, cohesive look, take your color cues from the background image. You can sample a type color in the image with the Eyedropper tool.

➤ Make sure the type is legible, not a struggle to decipher.

➤ Improvise with Photoshop features in unconventional ways. For example, to create informal "hand" lettering, such as spray paint or chalk, instead of using the Type tool, you could draw the letters by hand with the Pencil or Brush tool (preferably with a graphics tablet and stylus).

➤ Be concise. To create more than a few words or a short phrase for print output, export your Photoshop image to a page layout program and typeset the text there.

➤ Keep your type treatments editable, if possible, by using flexible features, such as layer effects.

➤ Keep a record. Take notes of your editing sequences and settings, for future reference. Save your favorite layer style settings to the Styles palette, for future use. Record your successful editing steps in an action (see Chapter 14).

CREATIVE TYPE

12

IN THIS CHAPTER

Using layer effects

Layer styles encompass all the settings that you can apply via the **Layer Style** dialog (**A–B**, next page), including **Blending Options,** such as Layer Opacity and Fill Opacity, and **layer effects,** such as a Drop Shadow or Inner Glow. Although layer effects can be applied to any kind of layer (image layer, shape layer, Smart Object, etc.), we feature them in this chapter because they work magic on type. They're easy to apply and edit, singly or in combination, and will transform automatically if you transform the layer that they're applied to.

➤ As you'll see from many of the exercises in this chapter, we think applying layer effects in twos, threes, or more produces the best results. And don't be afraid to use nondefault settings. For example, you can lighten the shadow for a bevel by changing its mode.

CHOOSING IMAGERY FOR LAYER EFFECTS

➤ Apply the layer effects that work inward or outward from edges — Drop Shadow, Inner Shadow, Outer Glow, Inner Glow, Bevel and Emboss, and Stroke — to a type layer, shape layer, or any layer imagery that's surrounded by transparent pixels. You can select an area of a layer, then use Layer via Copy (Ctrl-J/Cmd-J) to isolate a subject from its background before applying an effect.

➤ You can apply the Satin, Color Overlay, Gradient Overlay, and Pattern Overlay effects either to fully opaque layers or to layers that contain transparency.

QUICK SUMMARY: LAYER EFFECTS

TASK	METHOD
Apply a layer effect (you don't need to create a selection first; the effect will ignore the selection)	Double-click next to any layer name (not a locked layer or the Background); or double-click the thumbnail for an image layer; or click a layer, then choose from the Add Layer Style menu *fx* on the Layers palette. Click an effect name and choose settings.
Change the layer effect settings or add more effects	Double-click next to or below the layer name; or double-click the "Effects" bar or an effect name that's nested below the layer name.
Restore settings that were in place (in all the panels) when you opened the Layer Style dialog	Alt-click/Option-click Reset.
Copy an individual effect from one layer to another	Alt-drag/Option-drag an effect name from one layer to another (to move an effect without copying it, don't use Alt/Option).
Move all the effects from one layer to another (replacing the existing effects)	Drag the "Effects" bar from one layer to another.
Change the opacity of a layer and its effects	Adjust the Opacity slider on the Layers palette (the Fill slider controls the opacity of only layer imagery, not of layer effects).
Make the lighting consistent for multiple layer effects	Use the Angle to control the direction and the Altitude (if available) to control the height of the light source, to create highlights and shading. To unify the lighting for all effects, adjust the Angle for an individual effect, then check Use Global Light; other effects for which Use Global Light is enabled will update accordingly.
Scale a layer effect (except those defined by a percentage)	Right-click/Control-click the *fx* icon on the layer and choose Scale Effects (a dialog opens).
Remove a layer effect or effects	Drag the effect name or Effects bar to the Delete Layer button. 🗑

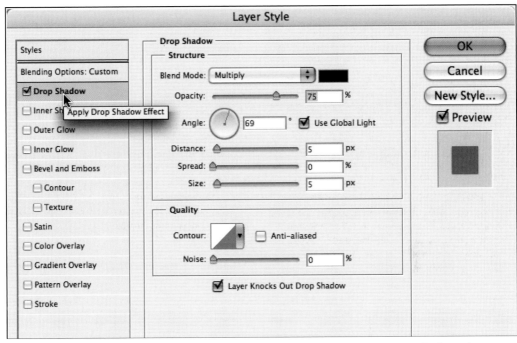

A In the **Layer Style** dialog, click an **effect** name (the box checks automatically) to view and edit the settings.

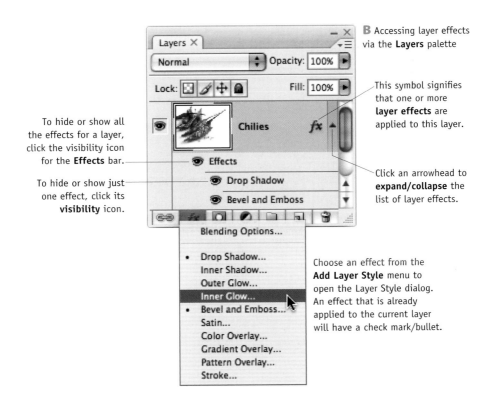

B Accessing layer effects via the **Layers** palette

This symbol signifies that one or more **layer effects** are applied to this layer.

To hide or show all the effects for a layer, click the visibility icon for the **Effects** bar.

To hide or show just one effect, click its **visibility** icon.

Click an arrowhead to **expand/collapse** the list of layer effects.

Choose an effect from the **Add Layer Style** menu to open the Layer Style dialog. An effect that is already applied to the current layer will have a check mark/bullet.

One way to modify the edges of a layer effect (except for Overlay or Stroke) is by choosing a different **contour** in the Contour Picker.

To choose a contour for a layer effect:

1. On the Layers palette, double-click a layer or an effect name to open the Layer Style dialog.

2. Apply one of the first six effects, and click the arrowhead next to the **Contour** thumbnail (or for the Bevel and Emboss effect, click the **Gloss Contour** arrowhead) to open the Contour preset picker.

   ➤ For the Bevel and Emboss effect, you can also click the nested Contour option on the left side of the Layer Style dialog to add an extra contour.**A–D**

3. Click a contour thumbnail.

4. Click away from the picker to close the menu.

➤ When applying multiple layer effects, we recommend the following strategy. Change the contour in just one or two of the effects. If Bevel and Emboss is applied, change its contour first; if Inner Glow is applied, change its contour next; if neither of those effects are applied, change the contour in one of the other "Inner" effects. The contours for Drop Shadow and Outer Glow control how the "Outer" effects follow the edge of an object; change the contour for only one of the two effects.

USING THE CONTOUR OPTION THAT'S NESTED UNDER THE BEVEL AND EMBOSS EFFECT

—Opaque pixels

A This is the default **Linear** contour for the Bevel and Emboss layer effect (Inner Bevel style).

B The **Cone** contour reversed the highlights and shadows in the bevel and moved the bevel inward.

C The **Gaussian** contour rounded and softened the bevel.

D The **Ring** contour sharpened the edge of the bevel and moved it inward.

Using layer styles

You can conveniently store any collection of Blending Options and layer effects (Layer Style dialog settings) for future use as a **layer style** on the **Styles** palette. A saved style can be applied quickly to any layer in any document. To acquaint yourself with this palette, apply a preset style first.

To apply a style to a layer:

1. Show the **Styles** palette.*fx*

   ➤ From the palette menu, choose a thumbnail size or a list display mode for the palette.

2. Do either of the following:

   Click a layer (not the Background) on the **Layers** palette, then click a style on the **Styles** palette.**A–C**

   Drag a style name or thumbnail from the **Styles** palette over any selected or unselected layer on the **Layers** palette.

   ➤ Styles can also be applied via the Layer Styles dialog (click Styles at the top of the dialog).

   ➤ Normally, when you apply a style, it replaces any existing effects on the current layer. To add a style without replacing existing effects, Shift-click or Shift-drag the style. Whether you hold down Shift or not, if the new and existing effects have the same name, the new effects will replace the old.

As you **save** a **layer style** to the Styles palette, you have the option to include the layer effects and/ or Blending Options settings (such as layer opacity, blending mode, and fill opacity) that are currently applied to the selected layer.

To save a style to the Styles palette:

1. *Optional:* To give yourself a head start, apply an existing style to type, then modify the settings or apply additional effects.

2. Do either of the following:

   On the **Layers** palette, click a layer that contains the desired layer style settings (layer effects, layer opacity, blending mode, fill opacity, etc.) then click a blank area on the **Styles** palette *fx* or click the **New Style** button.

   On the **Layers** palette, double-click a layer that contains the desired layer style settings. In the Layer Style dialog, click **New Style.**

3. In the New Style dialog, type a **Name** for the new style, check whether you want to **Include Layer Effects** and/or **Include Layer Blending Options** in the style, then click OK. If the Layer Style dialog is open, click OK to exit that dialog. Your new style will appear as the last listing or thumbnail on the Styles palette.

   ➤ You can load other style libraries from the bottom of the Styles palette menu or from the Styles menu in the Layer Style dialog. To create a library of style presets, see page 92. The preset styles that ship with Photoshop are stored in Adobe Photoshop CS3/Presets/Styles.

   ➤ To remove a style from a layer (and thereby revert the layer blending mode to None and the layer opacity to 100%), right-click/Control-click a layer and choose Clear Layer Style.

A This is the original editable type.

B With the type layer selected, we clicked a style thumbnail on the **Styles** palette.

C The Swimming Pool **layer style** in the Text Effects library is applied.

Applying layer effects to type

Next, we'll show you ways to use **layer effects** to add depth and volume to type, to make it look three-dimensional. For good-quality print results, choose a resolution for your file of 250–300 ppi.

To create beveled type:

1. Create editable type.

2. From the **Add Layer Style** menu *fx* on the Layers palette, choose **Drop Shadow.**

3. In the Layer Style dialog, Drop Shadow is selected; choose **Drop Shadow** settings.**A**

4. Click **Bevel and Emboss.** Choose Style: Inner Bevel and Technique: Chisel Hard, and choose Depth, Size, and Soften settings.**B**

5. Click **Inner Glow** and choose settings (**A**, next page).

6. Click OK. If desired, you can also apply a gradient to the Background. (**B–D**, next page).

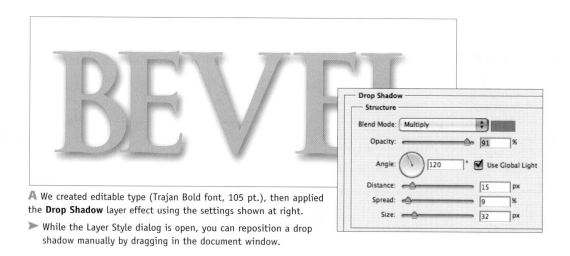

A We created editable type (Trajan Bold font, 105 pt.), then applied the **Drop Shadow** layer effect using the settings shown at right.

▶ While the Layer Style dialog is open, you can reposition a drop shadow manually by dragging in the document window.

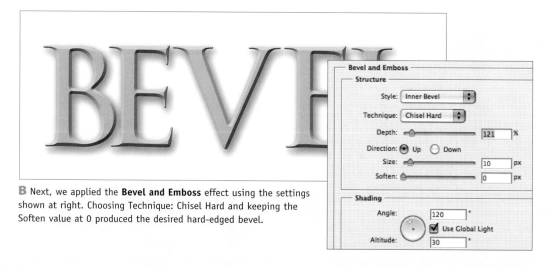

B Next, we applied the **Bevel and Emboss** effect using the settings shown at right. Choosing Technique: Chisel Hard and keeping the Soften value at 0 produced the desired hard-edged bevel.

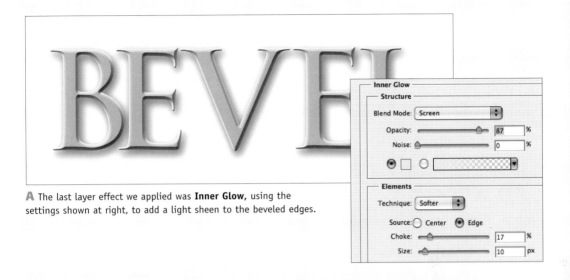

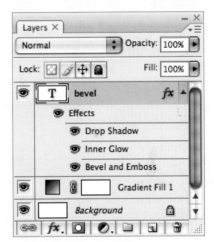

A The last layer effect we applied was **Inner Glow,** using the settings shown at right, to add a light sheen to the beveled edges.

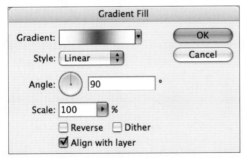

B Finally, we added a gradient above the background in coordinating colors via a **Gradient Fill** layer (see also page 210).

C This is the **Layers** palette for the image shown below.

D The final image has three layer effects, plus a Gradient Fill layer above the Background.

Now that you know how to apply layer effects, you can explore some variations. You'll need to adjust the settings for your document dimensions and resolution, the colors in the background image, and your font, point size, and type color. The type images in this chapter have a file resolution of 300 ppi.

CARVING LETTERS IN STONE

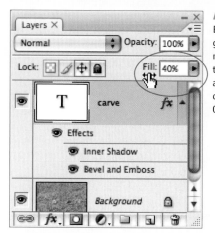

A We created editable type (Trajan Bold font, 93 pt.) above a photo of granite on the Background. To reveal more of the underlying layer inside the type, we lowered the **Fill** percentage on the Layers palette (this setting can also be accessed in the Blending Options area of the Layer Style dialog).

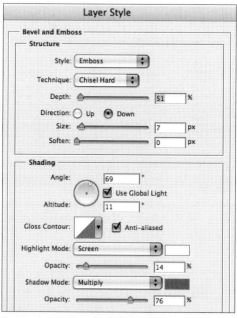

B Then we applied the **Inner Shadow** and **Emboss** layer effects.

C The type looks as if it's carved into the stone texture.

WARPING THE CARVED LETTERS

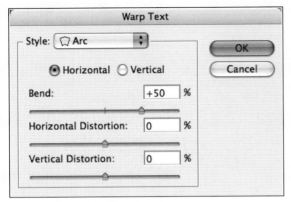

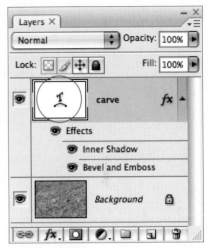

A After applying the Inner Shadow and Emboss effects, we chose Layer > Type > **Warp Text** and the settings shown above.

B The **warp text** icon appeared in the layer thumbnail.

C To reopen the **Warp Text** dialog at any time to edit the settings, click the type layer thumbnail, then click this button on the Options bar.

D This is the same image as shown on the previous page, with the **Warp Text** command applied (Arc style).

STAMPING LETTERS INTO METAL

A We created an editable type layer (Helvetica Bold Condensed font, 64 pt.) above a photo of a metal plate on the Background.

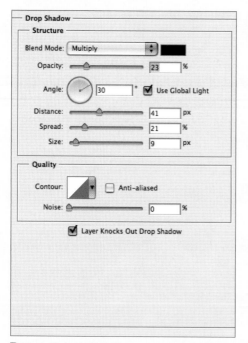

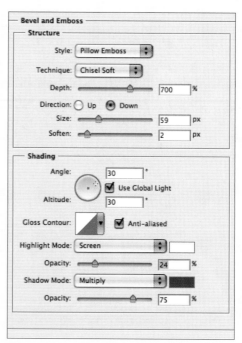

B We applied the **Drop Shadow** and **Pillow Emboss** effects to the type layer using the settings shown above.

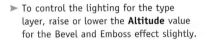

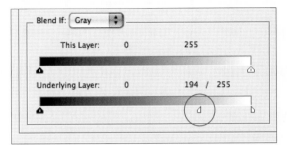

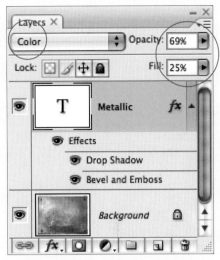

A In the **Blending Options** panel of the Layer Style dialog, we Alt/Option dragged the left part of the **white Underlying Layer** slider to reveal part of the underlying layer.

► To control the lighting for the type layer, raise or lower the **Altitude** value for the Bevel and Emboss effect slightly.

B For the type layer, we chose **Color** blending mode, and lowered the **Opacity** and **Fill** settings.

C The final type looks as if it's been stamped onto metal.

MAKING TYPE LOOK LIKE RUSTED METAL

A We created editable type (Bauhaus 93 Regular font, 223 pt.) above a photo of a rusted metal texture.

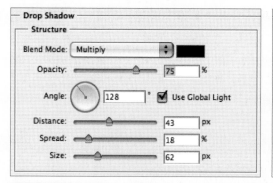

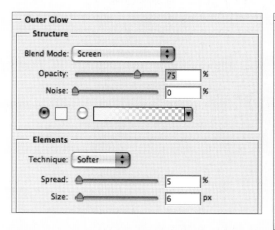

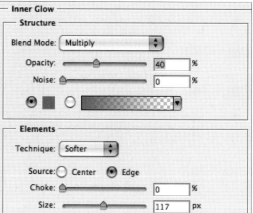

B We applied the **Drop Shadow**, **Inner Shadow**, **Outer Glow**, and **Inner Glow** effects, using the settings shown above.

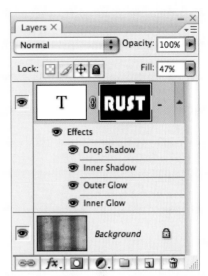

A To reveal some of the underlying layer, we lowered the **Fill** percentage of the type layer. The results are acceptable, but we want to make the letters look more corroded.

B To "corrode" the edges of the type, we Ctrl/Cmd clicked the type layer thumbnail, clicked the **Add Layer Mask** button, then applied Filter > Brush Strokes > **Spatter**. This is the Layers palette for the final image, which is shown below.

C The Spatter filter added just the finishing touch we were after. (The Distort > Glass filter would also work well.)

Note: If you followed along with these steps, save your the file and keep it open for the instructions on the following page.

FILLING TYPE WITH A RUSTED METAL TEXTURE

As a variation on the previous task, we'll show you how to fill the type characters with a texture by using a **clipping mask** and intensify the texture by applying the **Lighting Effects** filter in a texture channel.

1. Save a copy of the file from the exercise on pages 264–265. Double-click the **Effects** bar to open the Layer Style dialog, uncheck the Inner Glow effect, then click OK.

2. On the Layers palette, reset the **Fill** value to 100%.

3. Duplicate the Background (Ctrl-J/Cmd-J), hide the original Background, and restack the duplicate layer above the type layer.

4. Click the Background. Choose a new Foreground color, create a new blank layer, press Alt-Backspace/Option-Delete to fill the layer with the current Foreground color.

5. Alt-click/Option-click the line between the top two layers to create a clipping mask.**A**

6. Click the Background copy (topmost) layer, then choose Filter > Render > **Lighting Effects**.

7. In the Lighting Effects dialog, choose **Style: 2 O'clock Spotlight** and **Texture Channel: Blue**, then click OK.

8. To make the edges of the type look more rough, click the mask thumbnail on the type layer, then choose Filter > Distort > **Glass**. Adjust the sliders, then click OK.

9. Double-click the **Effects** bar for the type layer. For the Drop Shadow, lower the opacity to around 55% and increase the Size to 85 px. For the Inner Shadow effect, set the Distance to 7 px and the Size to 16 px. For the Outer Glow effect, set both the Spread and Size to 7. Also apply the Bevel and Emboss effect (**A–C**, next page).

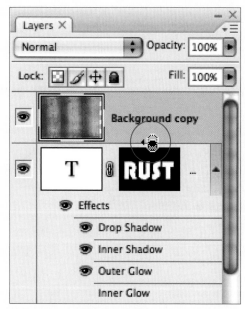

A To create a **clipping mask**, Alt/Option click the line between two layers.

MOVING THE IMAGE IN A CLIPPING MASK

Click the image layer and then, with the **Move** tool, drag the image to a different position within the type shapes. (In the Layers palette at left, you can see transparent areas in the topmost layer thumbnail because we moved the imagery.)

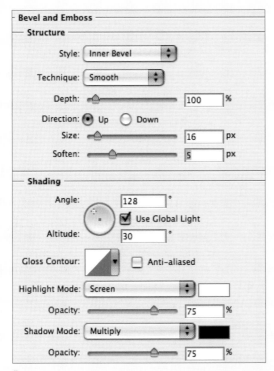

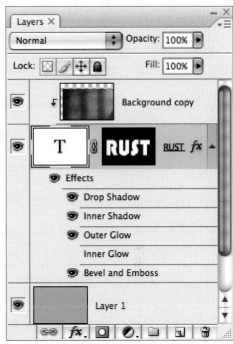

A Choose these settings for the **Bevel and Emboss** effect.

B This is the **Layers** palette for the final image, which is shown below.

C In this final image, the metal looks more corroded than in **C** on page 265.

EMBOSSING LEATHER

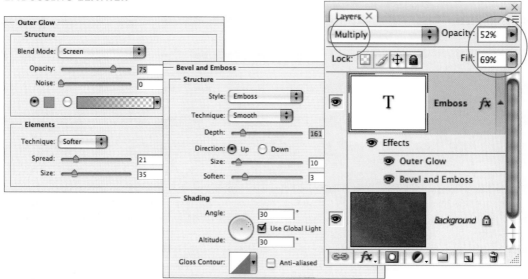

A To create these embossed letters, we opened a photo of leather, created type (Trajan Bold font, 112 pt.), then chose a color for the type by clicking in the image with the Eyedropper tool (I). We chose the **Bevel and Emboss** and **Outer Glow** settings (shown above), chose **Multiply** mode for the type layer, and lowered the layer **Opacity** and **Fill** settings.

B We saved the settings shown above as a **layer style** (see page 257), then applied it to a type layer above a Background photo of a leather-covered book.

➤ We added the fleur-de-lis at the top of this image by using the Custom Shape tool and the Fleur-De-Lis shape preset (see pages 304–305). We copied the layer effects from the type layer to the shape layer by Alt/Option dragging the Effects bar and then we lowered the layer opacity.

CREATING A METALLIC SHEEN USING GRADIENTS

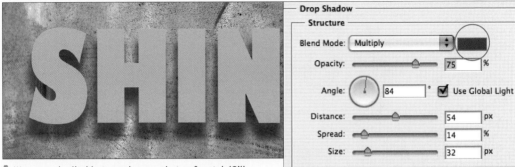

A We created editable type above a photo of metal (Gill Sans Ultra Bold Condensed font, 109 pt.), then applied the **Drop Shadow** effect to the type.

B For the Drop Shadow, we clicked the color swatch, then clicked a dark color in the document window.

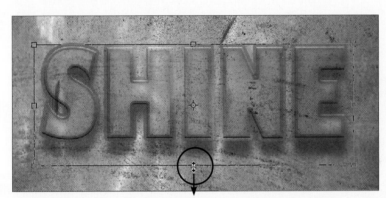

C We transferred the shadow effect to its own layer via Layer > Layer Style > **Create Layer**. Then we chose Edit > **Free Transform** (Ctrl-T/Cmd-T), and transformed the new drop shadow layer by dragging the midpoint handle downward (the result is shown in **C** on the next page).

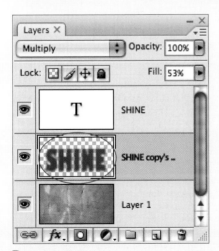

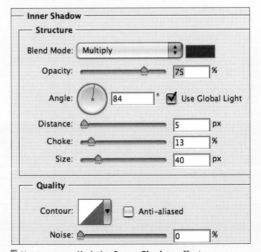

D The drop shadow appeared as a new rasterized layer above the image layer. We changed the layer blending mode of the shadow layer to **Multiply** and set the **Fill** value to 53%.

E Next, we applied the **Inner Shadow** effect.

See also the figures on the following page

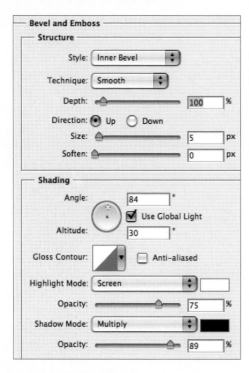

A We applied the **Bevel and Emboss** effect (Inner Bevel style).

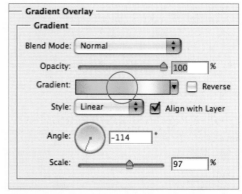

B For the **Gradient Overlay** style, we clicked the **Gradient** bar, which opened the Gradient Editor dialog.

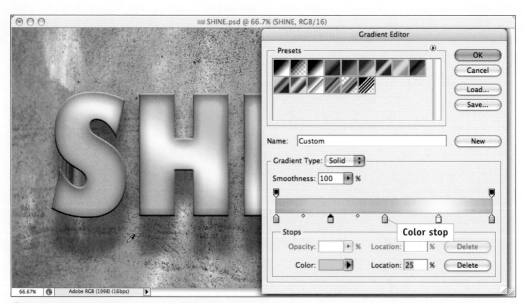

C In the **Gradient Editor** dialog for the **Gradient Overlay** style, we clicked below the gradient bar to add color stops and, for each stop, clicked a color in the document window.

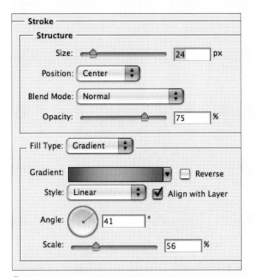

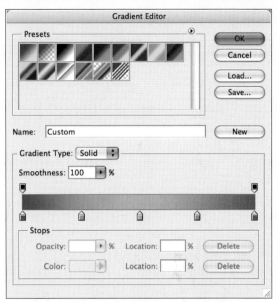

A For the Stroke effect, we chose Fill Type: **Gradient**.

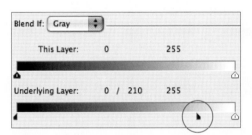

B In the **Gradient Editor** dialog for the **Stroke** effect, we added color stops below the gradient bar, and for each stop, we chose a color by clicking a dark, medium, or light color in the document window.

C Finally, in **Blending Options**, we held down Alt/ Option and dragged the right part of the **black Underlying Layer** slider to reveal some of the image layer within the type (depending on the type color, you may not need to drag your slider as far as we did).

D The shiny metallic type is completed.

CREATING METALLIC TYPE WITH GROMMETS

1. Open an image to serve as a background, then create editable type.**A**

2. To create the metal texture, open a photograph of metal and then, with the **Rectangular Marquee** tool, select all or most of the image.

3. Choose Edit > **Define Pattern**.

4. In the **Pattern Name** dialog, enter a descriptive name, then click OK.**B**

5. Click in the image that contains the type, and click the type layer. Apply the **Drop Shadow**, **Emboss**, and **Pattern Overlay** layer effects (settings shown below).**C** For the Pattern Overlay

A Create editable type (This is the Helvetica Bold Condensed font, 196 pt.).

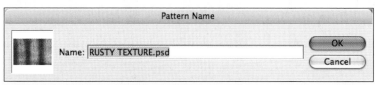

B Define an area of a background image as a **pattern preset**.

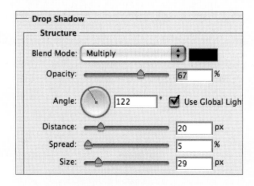

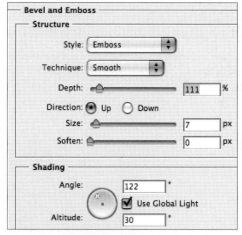

C Apply the **Drop Shadow**, **Emboss**, and **Pattern Overlay** effects.

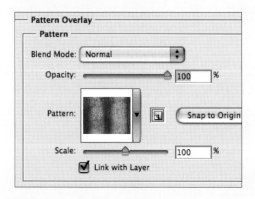

USING PATTERN OVERLAY

When you apply a pattern via the **Pattern Overlay** effect, you can adjust the **Blend Mode**, **Opacity**, and **Scale** for the effect. You can also **drag** the pattern in the document window while the Layer Style dialog is open.

effect, choose your custom pattern from the Pattern preset picker.

6. To create one of the grommets, click the type layer, then create a new blank layer. Choose the **Elliptical Marquee** tool, ○ then drag to create a small circle. Choose a Foreground color (we chose a deep russet), then press Alt-Backspace/Option-Delete to fill the selection with the current Foreground color. Don't deselect!

7. Choose the **Move** tool ⤴ (V), then Alt-drag/Option-drag as many copies of the selection as you need. To keep the copies on the same axis, also hold down Shift. Now you can deselect.

8. Alt-drag/Option-drag the **Effects** bar from the type layer to the "grommets" layer.

9. For the "grommets" layer, hide the Pattern Overlay effect. Double-click the **Bevel and Emboss** effect, change the Style to Pillow Emboss and click the Down button, then click OK.

10. Apply the **Outer Glow** effect to the "grommets" layer (settings shown below). **A–C**

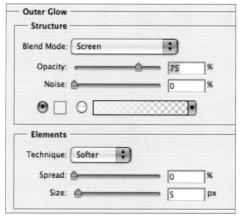

A In addition to the effects that you copy from the type layer to the "grommets" layer, also apply the **Outer Glow** effect.

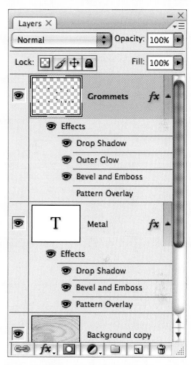

B This is the **Layers** palette for the final image, which is shown below.

C For the final image, we happen to like the contrast that the photo of wood provides as a background image, but other kinds of textures would be suitable.

CREATING A NEON SIGN

A We chose this photo of a shop window to serve as a backdrop for the neon lettering, and added some type (Orator Std font, 209 pt.).

➤ For this exercise, use a dark-toned image and create light-colored type.

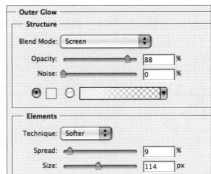

B We applied the **Outer Glow** effect, using the settings shown at right to create a glow around the "neon" fixture.

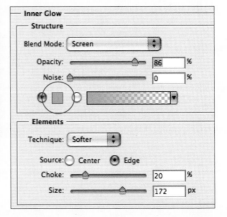

C Next, we applied the **Inner Glow** effect to lighten the type color. We clicked the color square, and chose a light gray from the Color Picker.

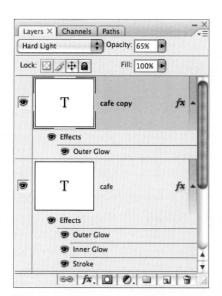

A We applied the **Stroke** effect, which made the letters look narrower. We clicked the color swatch, changed the Stroke color to H51, S25, and B99 in the Color Picker (for your type, choose a Hue close to the type color but use the same S and B values as ours). We also increased the Size value until the type looked like glowing neon tubing, then exited the dialog.

B To intensify the neon effect and restore some of the original type color, we duplicated the type layer, deleted all the layer effects from the duplicate layer except Outer Glow, chose **Hard Light** as the layer blending mode, and chose an **Opacity** of 65%. Finally, we double-clicked the Outer Glow effect on the duplicate layer and raised the Size value slightly.

STAMPING A PRODUCT NAME

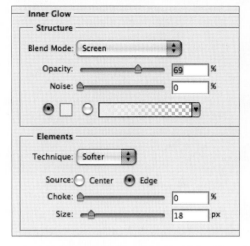

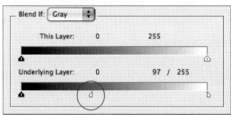

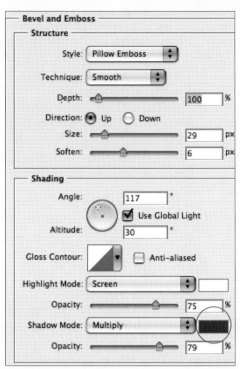

A We created editable type above an image layer (a photo of a cracker) in the Helvetica Extra Compressed font, 165 pt. To choose a color for the type, we clicked a medium tan color in the image. Next, we applied the **Inner Glow** and **Bevel and Emboss** effects. For the Bevel and Emboss effect, we chose the Pillow Emboss style, clicked the Shadow Mode color swatch, then clicked a dark color in the image. Finally, in Blending Options, we Alt/Option dragged the left part of the **white Underlying Layer** slider to the left.

B The type looks as if it's been stamped into the cracker.

Applying filters and gradients to type

Another way to manipulate type in Photoshop is by applying **filters** and/or **gradients**. The possible variations are virtually unlimited. On this page and the next two pages are a few ideas, for inspiration.

To illuminate type with gradients and a filter:

1. Create editable type for the top word in an orange color. Copy the type layer, then hide the original (keep it for potential future edits).

2. Click the copy, choose Filter > **Convert for Smart Filters,** then choose Filter > Blur > **Gaussian Blur.** Adjust the Radius slider to blur the type, **A** then click OK.

3. Choose the **Horizontal Type** tool, **T** type the bottom word, then press Ctrl-Enter/Cmd-Return. Right-click/Control-click the type layer and choose **Rasterize Type** from the context menu.

4. Choose the **Gradient** tool ▇ (G or Shift-G) and click the Linear Gradient button on the Options bar. From the Gradient preset picker menu, choose **Color Harmonies 1,** then click Append. Click the **Orange, Blue** gradient on the picker. **B**

5. Click the **Lock Transparent Pixels** button on the Layers palette, then Shift-drag a short distance from the top of the new word downward.

6. *Optional:* Click the Background, then apply a light-toned gradient via a Gradient Fill layer. **C**

▶ To customize a gradient, double-click the Gradient preset picker thumbnail on the Options bar, click any gradient stop below the bar in the Gradient Editor, click the Color swatch, then click a color in the Color Picker (or sample a color in the document window).

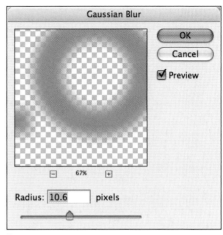

A Blur the type layer via the **Gaussian Blur** dialog.

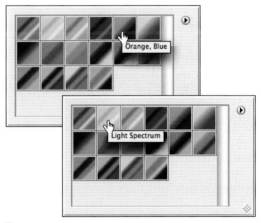

B We applied the **Orange**, **Blue** gradient preset to the type and the **Light Spectrum** gradient to the Background.

C You can easily create variations on this idea by changing the colors in the gradients (we used the Futura Extra Bold font, 86 pt.).

To create skywriting:

1. Create a layer above a background image, choose the **Pencil** tool,✎ then draw letters.

2. Duplicate the new layer, keep the duplicate selected, and hide the original type layer. Choose Filter > **Convert for Smart Filters.** Click OK if an alert appears.

3. *Optional:* If you want to make the letters thinner, apply Filter > Other > **Maximum.**

4. Choose Filter > Blur > **Motion Blur,** choose a Distance setting of 20–30 pixels, then click OK.

5. Choose Filter > Stylize > **Wind,*** click Wind and From the Right, then click OK.

6. Next, you'll make the blur gradually fade. Choose the **Gradient** tool ▮ (G or Shift-G) and then, on the Options bar, click the Black,White preset on the Gradient preset picker, click the Linear Gradient button, set the Mode to Normal, set the Opacity to 100%, and uncheck Reverse.

   Click the filter effects mask thumbnail (to the left of "Smart Filters"), then drag from the right edge of the document window halfway to two-thirds of the way across the type.**A–B**

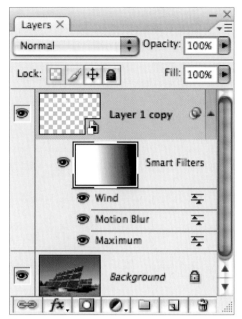

A This is the Layers palette for the final image. Note the **gradient** in the **filter effects** mask. If you need to edit the settings for any filter, double-click the filter name.

B To produce this skywriting, we drew letters with the **Pencil** tool (15 px. diameter tip), applied three **filters,** and masked part of the effect by applying a **gradient** to the filter effects mask.

To apply the Wind filter to type:

1. Create a type layer, duplicate it, and keep the duplicate layer selected. **A**

2. Hide the original type layer.

3. Choose Filter > **Convert for Smart Filters**, and click OK if an alert appears.

4. Choose Filter > Stylize > **Wind.*** In the Wind dialog, click Method: **Blast** and **From the Left**, then click OK.

5. Apply the **Wind** filter once more, but this time click Direction: **From the Right.B–C**

A We created type (Brush Script Std Medium font, 109 pt.) on a layer above a Background photograph of painted wood boards.

***Alas, some Windows users have run into a bug that makes this filter inaccessible for a Smart Object layer. If you find this to be the case, don't convert the layer to a Smart Object.*

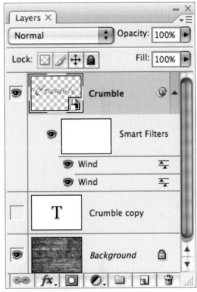

B After converting a copy of the type layer to a **Smart Object**, we applied the **Wind** filter twice, using different Direction settings.

C The **Wind** filter made the edges of the type look as if they've been scratched away. Note that the wind direction matches the horizontal direction of the wood grain.

Creating graffiti

To create graffiti:

1. Open a background image, and create a new, blank layer.

2. Choose the **Brush** tool ✎ (B or Shift-B), choose a rough-edged brush tip, **A** click the **Airbrush** option on the Options bar (to make the letters look spray painted), and choose a Foreground color. Scrawl some letters on the new layer.

3. To create another layer of graffiti, create a new, blank layer, choose a new Foreground color, then draw more letters.

4. To make the letters look slightly corroded, double-click a graffiti layer and then, in the **Blend If** area of the Layer Style dialog, Alt-drag/Option-drag the black or white **Underlying Layer** slider a long or short distance, depending on which works best for the type color and background colors. **B–D** Repeat for the other graffiti layer.

5. *Optional:* To make the paint "drip," choose Filter > Liquify (Ctrl-Shift-X/Cmd-Shift-X). In the dialog, choose the Forward Warp Tool ✎ (W), choose Brush Size, Density, and Pressure settings, then drag from the end of a few characters downward, multiple times if necessary, to mimic the pull of gravity (**A–B**, next page).

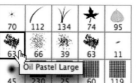

A Click a brush preset on the **Brush preset** picker. We chose the Oil Pastel Large preset for the white graffiti and the Watercolor Loaded Wet Flat Tip for the red graffiti.

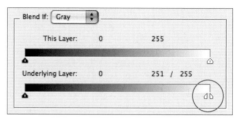

B We moved the left part of the **white Underlying Layer** slider slightly to the left for the red letters...

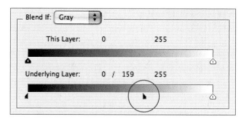

C ...and moved the right part of the **black Underlying Layer** slider to the right for the white letters.

D To create the graffiti in this image, we drew letters with the **Brush** tool, then used the **Blend If** sliders in the **Layer Style** dialog for each graffiti layer to partially reveal the image layer.

MAKING DRIP MARKS

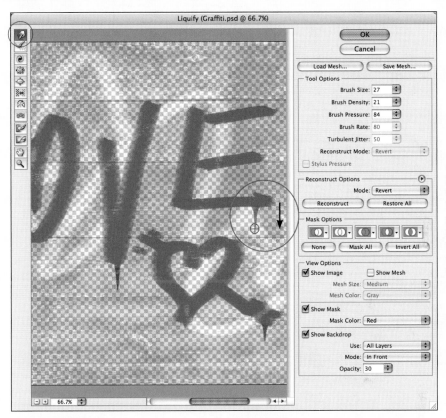

A To make the paint drips, we opened the **Liquify** dialog and dragged downward several times with the **Forward Warp** tool in a few areas.

B The final graffiti image has paint drips, and the letters look as if they've been slightly weathered by the elements.

Corroding type

By hiding pixels from a type layer, you can make the type look as if it's been worn away or **eroded**. We'll show you two different ways to do this: by using a layer mask and by using the Blend If sliders in the Layer Style dialog. Shop and compare.

To create corroded type:

Method 1

1. Open a photo of a surface texture, create editable type in a contrasting color,**A** then click the **Add Layer Mask** button ▣ on the Layers palette.

2. Do one of the following:

   Choose the **Pencil** tool ✐ and a very small brush tip.

   Choose the **Brush** tool ✐ and a small rough-edged brush tip, such as one of the Spatter tips.

Click the Background, create a small, rectangular feathered selection, choose Edit > **Define Brush Preset**, enter a name for the preset, then click OK. Deselect, choose the **Brush** tool,✐ and, on the Options bar, choose your new preset from the Brush preset picker (the last tip on the picker).**B**

3. Choose an Opacity of 40–50% on the Options bar, click the layer mask thumbnail, press D to make the Foreground color black, then draw quick scribbles in the document window.**C** To add variety, switch your tools and/or brush tip and draw more strokes.

   ➤ To undo the last stroke, either click an earlier state on the History palette or press X and paint over any unwanted strokes with white (100% opacity brush).

A We created an editable type layer (Brush Script font, 109 pt.) on top of a Background photo of a textured wall.

B Next, we created a **custom brush preset** from a selection of the Background, chose the Brush tool and the new preset from the Brush preset picker, and set the brush Diameter to 32 px.

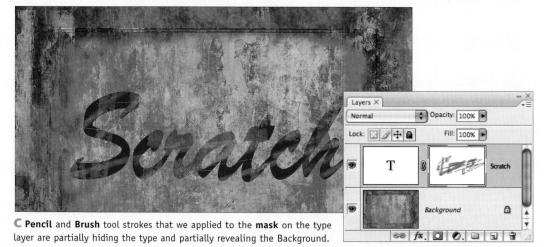

C **Pencil** and **Brush** tool strokes that we applied to the **mask** on the type layer are partially hiding the type and partially revealing the Background.

Method 2

1. Open a photo of a surface texture, then create editable type in a contrasting color.

2. To distress the type, you'll force dark or light colors from the image to show through the type. Double-click the type layer (below the layer name) to open the **Layer Style** dialog.

3. If the type is dark, in the **Blend If** area, drag the **black Underlying Layer** slider to the right until some dark (underlying) texture color starts to show through the type layer,A then Alt-drag/Option-drag the right half of the black slider further to the right.B If the type is light, do the same thing with the **white Underlying Layer** slider instead.

4. Click OK.

A In the **Blend If** area of the Layer Style dialog, we dragged the **black Underlying Layer** slider to the right. Darks from the texture layer now show through the type layer.

B Next, we Alt/Option dragged the **Underlying Layer** sliders to enable midtone colors from the underlying texture layer to show through the type layer. (If you want to enable highlight areas to show through, drag the white Underlying Layer slider.)

Cutting up a rasterized type layer

If you can't produced the desired type treatment by using layer effects, filters, or masks, you can rasterize the type layer, then "attack" the type characters with knives (well, actually, one of the **Lasso** tools)!

To create a cut paper effect:

1. Create an editable type layer, duplicate it, and choose Layer > **Rasterize** > **Type.**
2. Hide the editable type layer.
3. Choose the **Lasso** tool or the **Polygonal Lasso** tool (L or Shift-L).**A**
4. Drag with the Lasso tool or click with the Polygonal Lasso tool to select a portion of a type character. Choose the **Move** tool (V), then drag the selection in the document window or press any arrow key.**B–D**
5. Repeat steps 3–4 for other characters (**A**, next page).

A We created editable type (Futura Extra Bold font, 102 pt.), duplicated and hid the type layer, and rasterized the duplicate. With the **Polygonal Lasso** tool, we created a straight-edged selection of the stem on the letter P.

B We repositioned the selection with the **Move** tool.

C We used the **Lasso** tool to create an irregular selection of the top of the letter A...

D ...then repositioned the selection by pressing the up and right arrow keys.

A This is the final "cut paper" image after we moved more straight-edged and irregularly-shaped selections of the rasterized type layer.

PUTTING SECTIONS OF RASTERIZED TYPE ON SEPARATE LAYERS

B We clicked each piece of "paper" with the Magic Wand tool, then pressed Ctrl-J/Cmd-J to put it on a separate layer.

C This enabled us to apply a different color and the Drop Shadow layer effect to each layer, and move each layer individually. Live a little!

Transforming type to fit onto a perspective plane

In this example, we'll "adhere" type to a photo of a porcelain bowl, but these steps would also work with a photo of a vehicle, package, billboard, interior wall, etc.

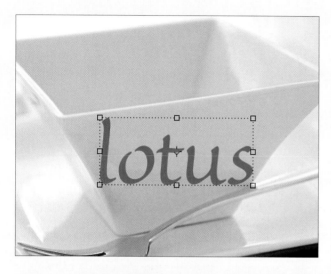

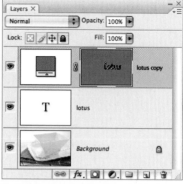

A We entered type (Sanvito Roman font, 81 pt.) above an image layer, then chose the Move tool. To apply a color to the type, we clicked the color swatch on the **Character** palette, clicked a green on the napkin in the image (not shown), then clicked OK to exit the Color Picker. Next, we duplicated the type layer, kept the duplicate layer selected, chose Layer > Type > **Convert to Shape,** then hid the original type layer.

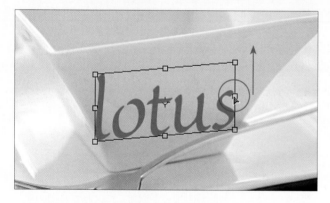

B After pressing Ctrl-T/Cmd-T to display the transform box for the **Free Transform** command, we Ctrl/Cmd dragged the middle handle on the right side upward to **skew** the type, to make it conform with the angle of the top of the bowl.

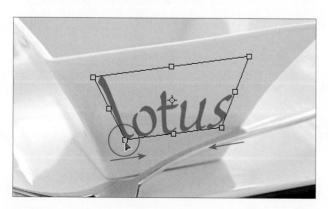

C Next, we Ctrl-Alt-Shift/Cmd-Option-Shift dragged a bottom corner handle of the transform box inward to apply **perspective** to the type to make it conform more closely to the bowl shape.

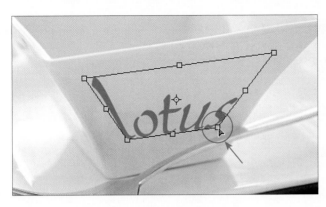

A For the final transformation, we Ctrl-dragged/Cmd-dragged the bottom right and left corner handles diagonally inward to **distort** the type, to make it conform with the inward slant of the bowl, then double-clicked inside the transform box to accept the transformation.

➤ If you need to scale your type horizontally, drag either of the side middle handles.

B To blend the type with the surface of the bowl, we applied the **Outer Glow** and **Satin** layer effects and moved the **Blend If** sliders to add reflections and shadows (settings shown below).

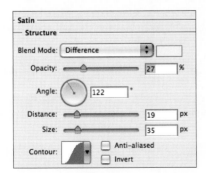

C For the **Outer Glow** effect, we changed the Outer Glow color to a medium dark gray to match the bowl color and adjusted the Opacity.

D Applying the **Satin** effect at a low opacity and with Difference mode chosen added subtle lights and darks and more surface reflection. We changed the Satin color to a very light gray to match the bowl and dragged the Size slider just far enough to minimize the dark areas in the effect.

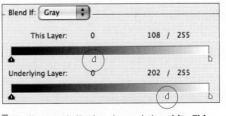

E Finally, we Alt/Option dragged the **white This Layer** and **white Underlying Layer** sliders to reveal light colors and surface reflections from the image layer through the type layer.

Putting screened-back type on a bar

To create screened-back type on a bar:

1. Open a background image, then create editable type.

2. Ctrl-click/Cmd-click the type layer, then hide it.

3. From the **New Fill/Adjustment Layer** menu, ◐ choose **Levels**. In the Levels dialog, move the gray **Input Levels** slider slightly to the left. **A** Click OK.

4. Choose the **Rectangular Marquee** tool, ⬚ then drag a rectangle for the bar. Create another Levels adjustment layer, but this time move the gray **Input Levels** slider to the right instead of to the left. **B**

5. *Optional:* Readjust the Levels settings, if needed, or apply layer effects to, or change the opacity settings for, the "bar" layer. **C**

6. *Optional:* Shift-click the two adjustment layers, then click the Link button ⚭ at the bottom of the palette (note the Link icons) so you can transform (e.g., scale, move) them as a unit. **D**

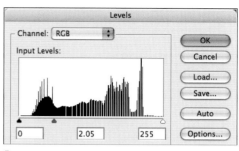

A We chose **Levels** settings for the "imagine" layer...

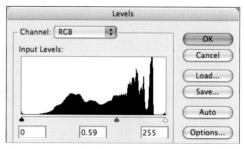

B ...and for the "bar" layer.

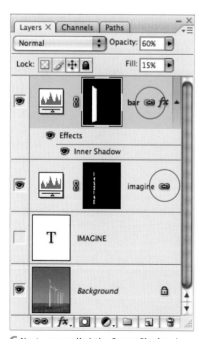

C Next, we applied the **Inner Shadow** layer effect to the "bar" adjustment layer and lowered its **Opacity** and **Fill** settings. We also **linked** the two adjustment layers.

D Finally, to **transform** the linked bar and type layers to conform to the same angle of perspective as the wind turbines, we pressed Ctrl-T/Cmd-T and then, with Ctrl-Alt-Shift/Cmd-Option-Shift held down, dragged the upper right handle on the transform box downward.

In this chapter, you'll learn how to create vector outlines, called paths, with the Pen tool and shape tools. All paths consist of anchor points connected by curved and/or straight segments, and can be reshaped and filled.**A** You'll also learn how to create vector masks, which serve the same purpose as layer masks except that they can be used on any kind of layer; have sharp, precise edges; and take up less storage space than layer masks or channels.

To create a path, you use a pen or shape tool with the **Paths** button 🔳 selected on the Options bar. You can also convert a selection to a path. The Paths palette 🔳 lets you display, activate, deactivate, restack, save, and delete paths.

To create a shape layer, you use a pen or shape tool with the **Shape Layers** button 🔳 selected on the Options bar. Every shape layer has a vector mask that controls which parts of the layer are visible and hidden. When a shape layer is selected, a listing for its vector mask also appears on the Paths palette.

PATHS & SHAPES

13

THE COMPONENTS OF A PATH A

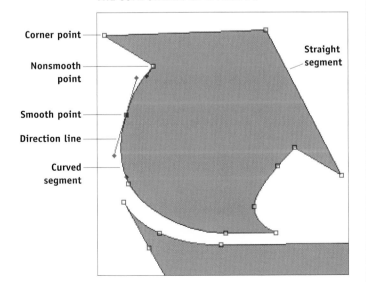

Corner point

Nonsmooth point

Smooth point

Direction line

Curved segment

Straight segment

Converting selections to paths

Before delving into using the pen tools, we'll show you how to create a **path** from a **selection**. After converting a selection to a path, you can reshape it with precision and then use it as either a standard path or a vector mask. You can also convert a path back to a selection at any time (see page 299).

To convert a selection to a path:

1. Create a selection, and display the **Paths** palette ▢.**A**

2. Do either of the following:

   To choose a Tolerance setting as you convert the selection to a path, hold down **Alt/Option** as you click the **Work Path from Selection** button ◌ at the bottom of the Paths palette (or choose Make Work Path from the Paths palette menu). In the Make Work Path dialog,**B** enter a **Tolerance** value (the range is 0.5–10; try 3–4), then click OK.**C–D** A path created with a low Tolerance setting will closely match the original selection marquee, but its high number of anchor points could cause a printing error. A path created with a high Tolerance value will be smoother due to its fewer anchor points but won't match the selection as precisely.

   To convert the selection to a path using the current Tolerance setting, click the **Work Path from Selection** button ◌ at the bottom of the Paths palette.

3. A new Work Path listing will appear on the Paths palette. Don't leave it as a temporary work path! Save it by double-clicking the path name, entering a name in the Save Path dialog, then clicking OK.

4. To reshape the path, see pages 295–298.

THE VECTOR ADVANTAGE

Paths and shapes are resolution independent, which means they will print at the resolution of the output device, not at the file resolution. Also unlike pixel layers, they remain sharp when transformed.

A We created this selection with the Magnetic Lasso tool, but you can use any selection tool.

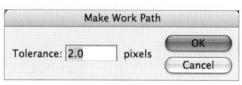

B In the **Make Work Path** dialog, we entered a **Tolerance** value of 2.0 to control the number of points on the resulting path.

C The selection is converted to a **path** using our chosen **Tolerance** setting of 2. (We clicked this path with the Path Selection tool.)

D A higher **Tolerance** setting of **6** would have produced fewer points and a less precise path, as shown at left.

Using the Pen tool

It takes practice to master the **Pen** tool. If you can't get the hang of it, remember that you can always start by creating a preset path using a shape tool and then reshape the path (see pages 295–298).

To draw a path with the Pen tool:

1. Choose the **Pen** tool 🖋 (P or Shift-P).

2. Click the **New Path** button 🔲 on the Paths palette, or to add the new path to an existing one, click the path name on the palette.

3. On the Options bar, click the **Paths** button.🖾 To preview the line segments as you draw them, click the **Geometry** options arrowhead,🖾🔽 then check **Rubber Band.A**

4. Do any of the following:

   Click in the document window, reposition the mouse, then click again to create a straight segment (Shift-click to draw the line at a multiple of 45°).**B**

   Drag to create a curved segment. Direction lines will appear.**C–D**

   To create a nonsmooth point, starting from on top of the last anchor point, **Alt-drag/Option-drag** in the direction you want the next curve to follow, release Alt/Option and the mouse, then drag in the direction of the new curve.**E**

5. Repeat any of the options in the previous step as necessary to complete the shape.

   ➤ As you draw, press Backspace/Delete once to erase the last anchor point you created, or twice (watch out!) to delete the entire path.

6. Do either of the following:

   To end the path but keep it **open**, Ctrl-click/Cmd-click outside the path or click any tool.

   To **close** the path, click the starting point (a small circle appears in the pointer).

7. Deselect the path listing unless you want the next path you draw to share the same listing.

➤ You can use the Convert Point tool to convert smooth points into nonsmooth points. In fact, you could draw your initial path as all smooth points, then use the Convert Point tool to convert any of the smooth points to nonsmooth or corner points (see page 298).

➤ To move the last point while drawing a path, drag the point with Ctrl/Cmd held down.

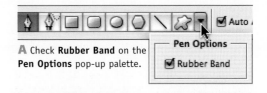

A Check **Rubber Band** on the Pen Options pop-up palette.

B Click to create **straight** sides...

C ...or **drag** to create **curved** segments.

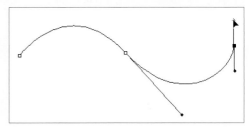

D Drag in the direction you want the curve to follow. To create **smooth,** graceful curves, use as few anchor points as possible and try to place anchor points at the ends of each curve, not at the peak.

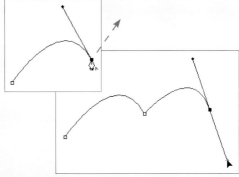

E To draw a **nonsmooth** curve, Alt-drag/Option-drag from the last anchor point in the direction you want the next curve to follow.

Using the Freeform Pen tool

With the **Freeform Pen** tool, you can draw a free-form path by eye or trace shapes in an image. With its **Magnetic** option unchecked on the Options bar, you drag with the tool to create a path. With this option checked (as in the instructions below), as you move or drag the mouse, the tool snaps a path to the nearest high-contrast edge that it detects in the image and creates the anchor points for you. The Freeform Pen is easier to use than the Pen tool, though the latter tool is a better choice when you need to create smooth, geometric curves.

To trace part of an image using the Freeform Pen tool with its Magnetic option:

1. Open an image, and hide any layers you don't want to trace.

2. Choose the **Freeform Pen** tool ✒ (P or Shift-P).

3. Deselect all the paths on the Paths palette.

4. On the Options bar, click the **Paths** button 🔲 and check **Magnetic**. To choose other options, see the following page.

5. Click the edge of the shape you want to trace to establish a starting point for the path, then slowly move the mouse—with or without pressing down the mouse button—along the edge.**A** As you move or drag, the path will snap to the nearest edge. If you move the mouse too quickly, the tool might not keep pace with you.

6. If the path snaps to any shapes that you don't want to include, get it back on track by clicking the edge of a shape (to create an anchor point), then continue to move or drag the mouse. You can reshape the path later.

7. Do one of the following:

   To **close** the path,**B** double-click anywhere over the shape to close the path with magnetic seg-ments; or Alt-double-click/Option-double-click to close it with a straight segment; or click the starting point (a small circle appears in the tool pointer).

   To end the path but keep it **open,** press Enter/Return.

8. Save the new Work Path (see page 294).

➤ Press Esc to delete a path while drawing it.

A When using the **Freeform Pen** tool with its **Magnetic** option, click to start the path, then move the mouse around the object you want to trace.

B The path is closed.

DRAWING STRAIGHT LINES

To draw **straight segments** with a temporary Pen tool while using the Freeform Pen tool, Alt-click/Option-click, and keep clicking. Release Alt/Option, then drag to return to the normal Freeform Pen behavior.

To choose options for the Freeform Pen tool:

1. With the **Freeform Pen** tool  selected, click the **Geometry Options** arrowhead on the Options bar to display the Freeform Pen Options palette.**A**

2. When using the tool with the Magnetic option off, choose a **Curve Fit** value (0.5–10 pixels) to control how closely the path will match the movement of your mouse as you drag. The higher the Curve Fit, the fewer the points and the smoother the path, but the less precisely it will match the edge of the shape.

3. Check **Magnetic** to activate that function of the tool and allow you to choose related settings:

   Width (1–256 pixels) for the width of the area under the pointer that the tool will consider when creating points. Use a wide Width for a high-contrast image in which the shapes are clearly delineated, or a narrow Width for more exact line placement in a low-contrast image that has subtle gradations or closely spaced shapes.

   ▶ To decrease the Width incrementally while creating a path, press [; or to increase the Width, press].

   Contrast (0–100%) for the degree of contrast needed between shapes for the tool to discern an edge. Use a higher Contrast setting to trace low-contrast shapes that have poorly defined edges.

   Frequency (0–100) for the speed at which points will be placed as you draw a path. The lower the Frequency, the fewer points are created.

4. Check **Pen Pressure** if you have a graphic tablet and want to control the width with stylus pressure. As you apply more pressure, the width decreases.

A Choose options for the **Freeform Pen** tool.

Working with paths

When you draw a path, Photoshop labels it "Work Path" automatically. Although it will save with your file, you should think of it as temporary, because it will be replaced by the next work path you create. We recommend that you **save each path** you create, as in the following instructions. When you edit a saved path, Photoshop resaves it for you.

To save a Work Path:

On the Paths palette, do either of the following:

To name the path as you save it, double-click the **Work Path** listing,**A** enter a name in the Save Path dialog,**B** then click OK.**C**

To save the path with a generic name, drag the Work Path over the **New Path** button.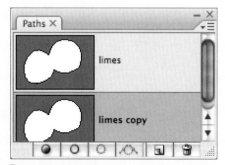

➤ To rename a saved path, double-click the path name.

Later in this chapter you'll learn how to display and select individual anchor points on a path. Here, we describe how to work with the **overall path** shape in the document window.

To display or hide a path in the document window:

To **display** a path, click the path name or thumbnail on the Paths palette.

To **hide** a path, on the Paths palette, Shift-click the path listing or click below all the path names.

➤ To change the size of the palette thumbnails, right-click/Control-click below the path listings and choose None, Small, Medium, or Large.

To move a path in the document window:

1. On the Paths palette, click a path name.
2. Choose the **Path Selection** tool (A or Shift-A).
3. In the document window, drag the path.

To duplicate a saved path:

Drag the path name over the **New Path** button on the Paths palette.**D**

➤ To change the stacking position of a path, drag the path name upward or downward on the palette. The Work Path listing always stays at the bottom.

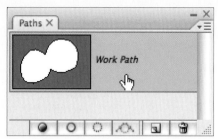

A Double-click the **Work Path** on the **Paths** palette.

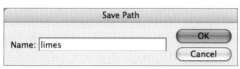

B Type a name in the **Save Path** dialog.

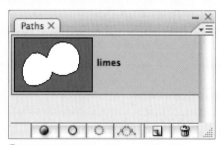

C The Work Path becomes a **saved** path.

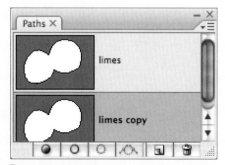

D We dragged the "limes" path listing over the **New Path** button, and a copy appeared on the palette.

To delete a saved path:

On the Paths palette, do either of the following:

Right-click/Control-click the path listing and choose **Delete Path.**

Click a path listing to be deleted, click the **Delete Current Path** button, 🗑 then click Yes; or to bypass the prompt, drag the path name over the button.

Reshaping paths

Not even the most seasoned Pen tool artists can draw a perfect path from scratch every time. In this section, you'll learn how to add segments to a path; transform a path; select points on a path; and, finally, reshape a path by adding, deleting, converting, or manipulating its anchor points.

To add segments to an existing, open path:

1. Choose the **Freeform Pen** tool (with the Magnetic option unchecked) 🖊 or **Pen tool** 🖊 (P or Shift-P).

2. On the Paths palette, click a listing that contains at least one open (unclosed) path.

3. Drag from either **endpoint** of the path.**A–B** To close the path, drag over the other endpoint, or to keep it open, click the tool again.

To transform an entire path:

1. Choose the **Path Selection** tool ▶ (A or Shift-A).

2. Click a path name on the Paths palette. Note: If multiple paths are saved under that path name, they will all be transformed.

3. Do one of the following to make the bounding box appear for the path:

Press Ctrl-T/Cmd-T or right-click/Control-click in the document window and choose **Free Transform Path.**

Click on or inside the path in the document window, then check **Show Bounding Box** on the Options bar.

4. Transform the path via the handles on its bounding box (for modifier keys, see the sidebar on page 179), then press Enter/Return to accept the transformation.**C**

➤ To repeat the last transformation, press Ctrl-Shift-T/Cmd-Shift-T.

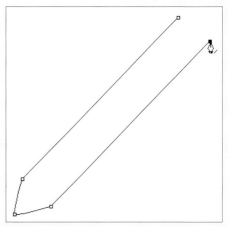

A To **add** to a **path,** drag from an **endpoint** with the Pen or Freeform Pen tool.

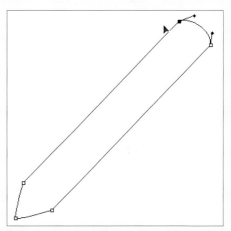

B The addition is completed.

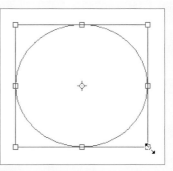

C A path is **scaled.**

Before you can manipulate individual **anchor points** on a path, you have to display them.

To select a whole path:

1. Click a path name on the Paths palette.

2. Choose the **Path Selection** tool ▶ (A or Shift-A).

3. Click the path in the document window. All the anchor points on the path will become selected.**A**

To select anchor points on a path:

1. Click a path name on the Paths palette.

2. Choose the **Direct Selection** tool ▶ (A or Shift-A).

3. Click the path, then click an anchor point. To select additional points, Shift-click them or drag a marquee around them. The direction lines on the selected points, if any, will become visible.**B**

   To deselect any points, Shift-click them.

To deselect all the points on a path:

1. Choose the **Direct Selection** tool ▶ or the **Path Selection** tool ▶ (A or Shift-A).

2. Click outside the path in the document window. The path will remain visible, but its anchor points and direction lines will now be hidden.

A Click a path with the **Path Selection** tool to select **all** its anchor points.

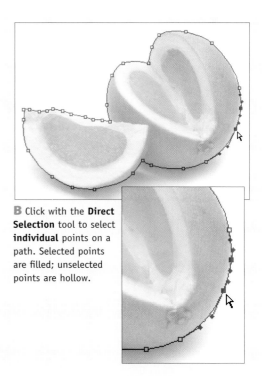

B Click with the **Direct Selection** tool to select **individual** points on a path. Selected points are filled; unselected points are hollow.

To **reshape a path** that you created by using a pen or shape tool, you can move, add, or delete anchor points; move segments; or convert points from smooth to corner and vice versa. To change the shape of a curved line segment, you can move a direction line toward or away from its anchor point or rotate it around its anchor point.

To reshape a path:

1. On the **Paths** palette, click a path listing; or to edit a shape layer, click the vector mask thumbnail on the **Layers** palette (see pages 304–305).
2. Choose the **Direct Selection** tool (A or Shift-A).
3. Click the path in the document window.**A**
4. To reshape the path using the existing points, do any of the following:

   Drag an **anchor point.B**

   Select a **segment** by Shift-clicking both of its endpoints, then drag the segment.

   Drag or rotate a **direction line** that stems from an anchor point.**C** If you move a direction line on a smooth point, both segments that are connected to that point will reshape; if you move a direction line on a nonsmooth point, only one curve segment will move.
5. To add or delete anchor points, choose the **Pen** tool, check **Auto Add/Delete** on the Options bar, then do either of the following:

   To **add** an **anchor point**, click a line segment (note the plus sign in the pointer).**D**

Continued on the following page

TEMPORARY SELECTION TOOL

To turn a pen tool into a temporary Path Selection tool or Direct Selection tool (whichever one was used last), press Ctrl/Cmd.

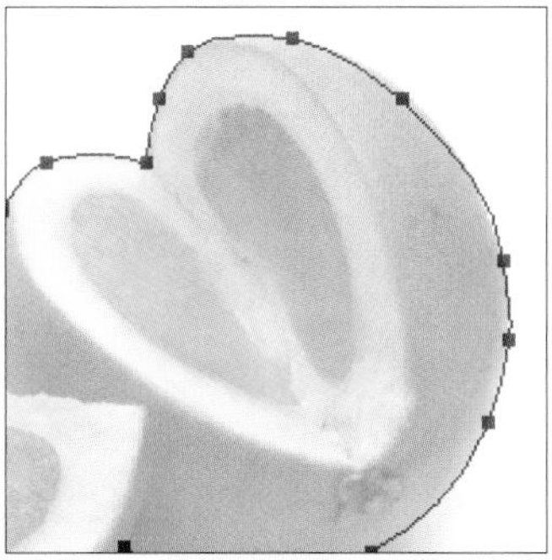

A A path is selected.

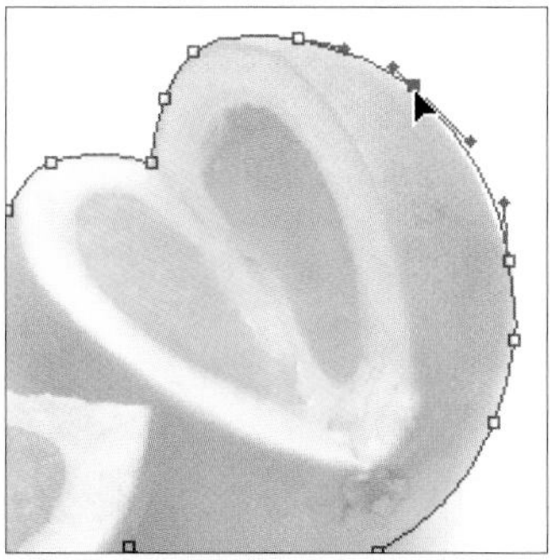

B An anchor point is dragged.

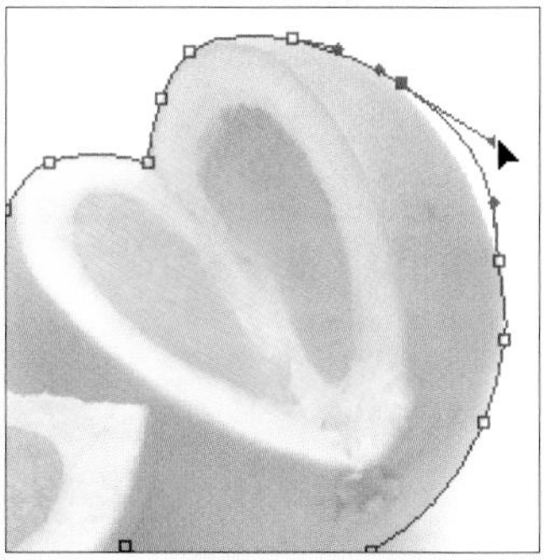

C A direction line is dragged.

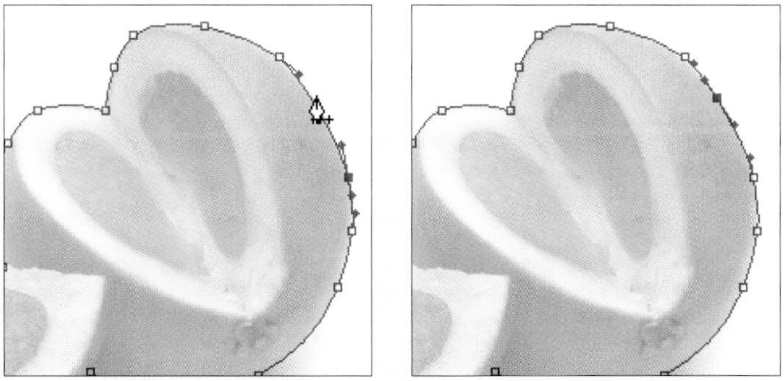

D An anchor point is added.

To **delete** an **anchor point**, click on it (note the minus sign in the pointer).**A–B**

To convert a smooth point to a corner point, choose the **Convert Point** tool,⊠ then click the **anchor point.** To convert a corner point to a smooth point, use the same tool, but drag away from the anchor point. (Remember to choose a different tool when you're done with the Convert Point tool.)

▶ To access a temporary Convert Point tool when you're using the Direct Selection tool, hold down Ctrl-Alt/Cmd-Option with the pointer over an anchor point; or when using one of the pen tools, hold down Alt/Option.

To rotate a **direction line** independently of its counterpart, drag it with the **Convert Point** tool.**C** Once you do so, you can use either the same tool or the Direct Selection tool to rotate the other direction line in the pair.

6. Click outside the path to deselect it.

▶ To turn off the Add/Delete function of the Pen tool temporarily, hold down Shift. If this option is off, you can use the Add Anchor Point tool or Delete Anchor Point tool to add or delete points, respectively.

Recoloring paths

To recolor a path:

1. Choose a Foreground color, and select an image layer (not a type or shape layer, and not a layer mask thumbnail).

2. Click a path listing on the **Paths** palette.

3. To apply a fill, Alt-click/Option-click the **Fill Path with Foreground Color** button ◔ on the Paths palette (or choose Fill Path from the palette menu). In the dialog, choose from the Use menu for the contents of the fill, choose Blending and Rendering options, then click OK.

▶ To fill a path using the last-used Fill Path dialog settings, click the button without holding down Alt/Option.

4. To apply a stroke, click the tool you would like the stroke to be applied with (e.g., Brush tool), choose Options bar settings, then click the **Stroke Path with Brush** button ◯ on the Paths palette. (An alternative method is to Alt-click/Option-click the Stroke Path with Brush button ◯ and then, in the Stroke Path dialog, choose the desired tool from the menu.)

A An anchor point is being **deleted.**

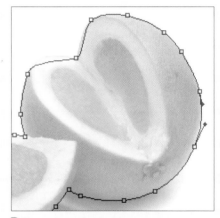

B The anchor point is gone.

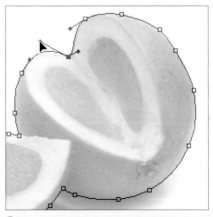

C A smooth point is being **converted** to a nonsmooth point.

Converting paths to selections

To convert a path to a selection:

1. *Optional:* Create a selection to add, delete, or intersect with the new path selection.

2. On the Paths palette, do one of the following:

   Ctrl-click/Cmd-click the listing for the path that you want to convert to a selection.

   Click the listing for the path you want to convert to a selection, then click the **Load Path as Selection** button.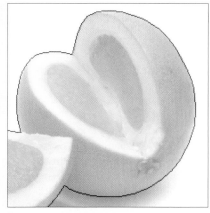 **A** The last-used Make Selection settings will apply (see the next paragraph).

   To choose options as you load a path as a selection, right-click/Control-click the path listing and choose **Make Selection** from the context menu.**B** In the Make Selection dialog,**C** you can apply a **Feather Radius** to the selection (if you check Anti-aliased, keep the Feather Radius at 0). You can also add the path to, subtract it from, or intersect it with an existing selection in the image by clicking an **Operation** option. Click OK.

   ➤ To access an Operation option by way of a shortcut, see the sidebar on this page.

3. On the Layers palette, click the layer you're going to use the selection for.

A A path is selected.

B The **path** is **converted** to a **selection**.

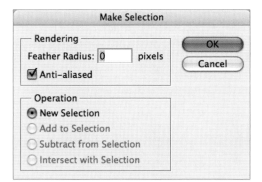

C When converting a path to a selection, you can choose options in the **Make Selection** dialog.

CONVERTING A PATH TO A SELECTION	
TASK	METHOD
Convert a path to a selection	Ctrl-click/Cmd-click the path name
Combine a path with an active selection	Create a selection, then Ctrl-Shift-click/Cmd-Shift-click the path name
Subtract a path from an active selection	Create a selection, then Ctrl-Alt-click/Cmd-Option-click the path name
Intersect a path with an active selection	Create a selection, then Ctrl-Alt-Shift-click/Cmd-Option-Shift-click the path name

Creating vector masks

A **vector mask** works like a layer mask in that it hides pixels on a layer, except in this case, a clean, sharp-edged path delineates the visible and masked areas. You can create the path to be used for a vector mask by using the Pen tool, the Freeform Pen tool, or a shape tool, or from a selection that you convert to a path. You can reshape the path that is being used for the mask, or discard the mask entirely, at any time.

A vector mask displays as a thumbnail on the Layers palette and also appears on the Paths palette temporarily when the layer that contains the mask is selected. Like a layer mask, each vector mask belongs to only one layer.

To create a vector mask using a new path:

1. On the Layers palette,🖤 click the layer to which you want to add a vector mask.**A**

2. Do either of the following:

   To create a mask that **reveals** all the layer pixels, Ctrl-click/Cmd-click the **Add Vector Mask** button 🔲 on the Layers palette (or choose Layer > Vector Mask > Reveal All).

   To create a mask that **hides** the layer pixels, Ctrl-Alt-click/Cmd-Option-click the **Add Vector Mask** button 🔲 on the Layers palette (or choose Layer > Vector Mask > Hide All).

3. Choose the **Pen** tool, the **Freeform Pen** tool, or a **shape** tool (Rectangle, Rounded Rectangle, Ellipse, Polygon, or Custom Shape), then draw a path to reveal the layer content.**B–D**

To create a vector mask from an existing path:

1. On the Layers palette, click the layer to which you want to add a vector mask.

2. On the Paths palette, click the path within which you want to reveal the layer content, then choose Layer > Vector Mask > **Current Path**.

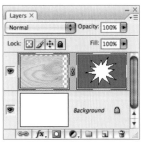

C The star that we drew appears in the vector mask thumbnail on the Layers palette.

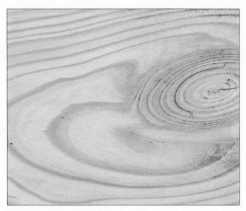

A This is the original image layer.

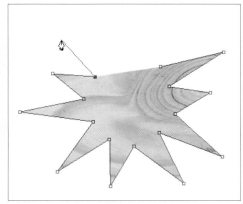

B After adding a **vector mask** using the **Hide All** option to the image layer, we're now drawing a path with the Pen tool to partially reveal the layer content.

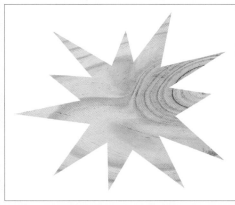

D The **vector mask** is hiding part of the wood image layer.

You can **convert** a **layer mask** to a **vector mask**, should you decide that you want to use a hard-edged mask to define the layer content.

To convert a layer mask to a vector mask:

1. Ctrl-click/Cmd-click a layer mask thumbnail on the Layers palette to display the mask as a selection.

2. On the Paths palette, click the **Work Path from Selection** button.

3. Keep the path selected, and choose Layer > Vector Mask > **Current Path.A**

4. *Optional:* To remove the layer mask, right-click/ Control-click the layer mask thumbnail and choose Delete Layer Mask (the vector mask will remain).

By using a vector mask, you can make it appear as if **type shapes** are filled with **imagery**.

To create a vector mask from type:

1. Have an image layer available (you won't be able to use the Background). Create a type layer, duplicate it, hide the duplicate, then click the original one.

2. Right-click/Control-click the type layer listing and choose **Convert to Shape**.

3. Drag the **vector mask thumbnail** to an image layer to move it, then delete the original type shape layer.**B–C**

➤ To reveal a different part of the image layer, follow the first set of instructions on the next page. To reverse the hidden and revealed areas of the image layer, see page 303.

A The selection from a **layer mask** has become the path for a **vector mask**.

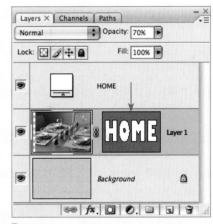

B We converted a type layer to a **shape** layer, then dragged the **vector mask thumbnail** to an image layer (Layer 1).

C The image is visible only within the confines of the **vector mask**.

Working with vector masks

A **vector mask** can be **moved** independently of its layer pixels at any time. It stays on its designated layer.

To reposition a vector mask:

1. Choose the **Path Selection** tool ⬉ (A or Shift-A).

2. On the Layers palette, click a vector mask thumbnail.

3. If the mask consists of multiple paths (such as type shapes) and you want to reposition them all, marquee them. Drag the vector mask in the document window.**A** A different part of the image will now be visible within the path shapes.**B**

You can **reshape** a **vector mask** as you would reshape any path.

To reshape a vector mask:

1. Choose the **Direct Selection** tool ⬉ (A or Shift-A).

2. Click a **vector mask thumbnail** on the Layers palette. The path that defines the vector mask should now be visible in the document window.

3. Click the edge of any vector mask shape to make its anchor points visible.

4. Reshape the path by following any of the instructions on pages 297–298.

To deactivate a vector mask:

Shift-click the **vector mask thumbnail** on the Layers palette. A red X will appear over the thumbnail, and the entire layer will now be visible.**C** Shift-click the vector mask thumbnail again to remove the X and restore the masking effect.

To copy a vector mask to another layer:

Alt-drag/Option-drag a vector mask thumbnail to another layer (not the Background). A duplicate vector mask will appear.

A A vector mask is moved.

B Now a different part of the image is visible within the mask shape.

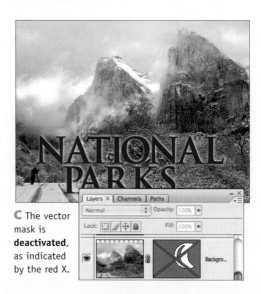

C The vector mask is **deactivated**, as indicated by the red X.

To reverse the visible and hidden areas in a vector mask:

1. Choose the **Path Selection** tool (A or Shift-A).

2. On the Layers palette, click a **vector mask** thumbnail to display the edge of the vector in the document window.

3. Click the vector mask in the document window, or if the mask contains multiple shapes, marquee them. Its anchor points and segments will become selected. **A**

4. Click the **Subtract from Shape Area** button on the Options bar, or press – (the minus key). **B**

   To switch the revealed and hidden areas again, click the **Add to Shape Area** button on the Options bar, or press + (plus key).

You can **delete** any **vector masks** that you no longer need, though you won't recoup much file storage space by doing so, since masks don't gobble up space (like channels do).

To discard a vector mask:

On the Layers palette, click the thumbnail for the vector mask that you want to remove, click the **Delete Layer** button, then click OK. Or to bypass the prompt, Alt-click/Option-click the **Delete Layer** button; or right-click/Control-click the mask thumbnail and choose **Delete Vector Mask**, then click OK.

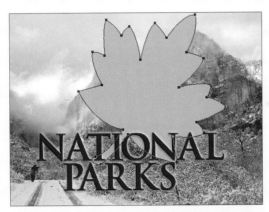

A We selected a vector mask.

B Then we switched the hidden and visible (masked and unmasked) areas by pressing – (the minus key).

Using the shape tools

In this section, you'll learn the three basic functions of the **shape tools:** creating a shape layer, creating a Work Path, and defining an area of pixels. We'll explore shape layers first.

A **shape layer** is a precise geometric or custom-shaped clipping path that reveals a solid-color, gradient, or pattern fill within its contour.**A** At any time, you can reposition, transform, or reshape a shape layer; modify its fill content or change it to a different type; and apply the usual Layers palette settings, such as layer effects and blending modes.

To create a shape layer, you can either choose the Pen tool, click the Shape Layers button 🔲 on the Options bar, then draw a path, or you can do it the easy way by using a ready-made shape, as in the instructions below.

To create a shape layer:

1. Click a layer on the Layers palette for the new shape layer to appear above.

2. Choose a Foreground color for the fill of the shape.

3. Choose one of the **shape** tools on the Tools palette (U or Shift-U).**B** Once a shape tool is selected, you can switch to a different shape tool by clicking one of the six shape tool buttons on the Options bar.**C**

4. On the Options bar:

   Click the **Shape Layers** button.🔲

   For the Rounded Rectangle tool,🔲 choose a **Radius** value; for the Polygon tool,🔵 choose the desired number of **Sides;** for the Line tool,╲ choose a **Weight;** or for the Custom Shape tool, 🔳 choose a shape from the **Custom Shape** preset picker.**D**

A A shape is a predefined path that can be filled with a solid color (as shown here) or a gradient or pattern.

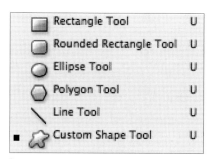

B Choose one of the **shape** tools.

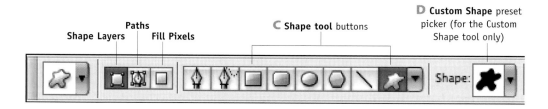

D Custom Shape preset picker (for the Custom Shape tool only)

Paths

Shape Layers   **Fill Pixels**   **C Shape tool** buttons

5. Drag in the document window to create the shape.**A** While dragging, you can hold down Shift to preserve the proportions of the shape; or hold down Alt/Option to draw it from its center; or hold down Alt-Shift/Option-Shift to do both.

A new "Shape 1" layer will be listed on the Layers palette.**B** It will have an adjustment layer thumbnail that controls its fill content and a vector mask thumbnail that controls its contour and location. You can choose Layers palette settings (blending mode, opacity, fill) for this new layer.

➤ When the Custom Shape tool 🎨 is selected, you can right-click/Control-click the image to open an "on-the-fly" shape preset picker.

➤ To append other libraries to the Custom Shape preset picker, choose a library name from the bottom of the Custom Shape picker menu, then click Append.

➤ To choose options for one of the shape tools, click the Geometry Options arrowhead 🔽 on the Options bar. For example, we like to keep the Defined Proportions option on for our Custom Shape tool, so we don't have to bother using the Shift key.

A We chose the **Custom Shape** tool, clicked the Sun 1 preset on the **Custom Shape** preset picker (it's in the Nature library), chose a Foreground color, then dragged in the document window to create this shape.

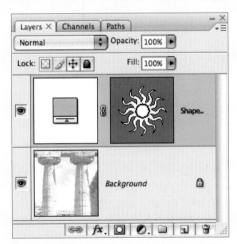

B The **shape** layer appears on the Layers palette, complete with its own vector mask.

GETTING SHAPE LAYERS FROM ILLUSTRATOR

To paste a path from Illustrator to Photoshop as a shape layer, in Adobe Illustrator, copy a vector object. In Photoshop, choose Edit > Paste. In the Paste dialog, click Paste As: **Shape Layer,** then click OK. The shape layer will be filled with the current Foreground color, without a stroke; you've just pasted the vector mask outline for the shape layer.

Recoloring shape layers

To recolor a shape layer:

Do either of the following:

To apply a new **solid-color** fill, double-click a shape layer thumbnail on the Layers palette; or choose the Custom Shape tool, click the shape layer, then click the Color swatch on the Options bar. Choose a color from the color picker, then click OK.**A**

To apply a stroke color or a gradient or pattern fill, double-click the layer to open the Layer Style dialog, then apply the **Stroke** effect or one of the **Overlay** effects.

➤ To apply a layer style to a shape layer, click the layer, make sure the link icon is selected on the Options bar, choose the Custom Shape tool, then click a style on the Style preset picker.**B**

Saving shapes

After editing the contour of a preset shape, pasting in a shape from Adobe Illustrator, or drawing a custom shape, you can **save** the results to the **Custom Shape preset picker** for future use.

To save a shape as a preset:

1. On the Layers palette, click the vector mask thumbnail on a shape layer that you created or edited in Photoshop or pasted from Adobe Illustrator. The shape will become selected in the document window.

2. Choose Edit > Define **Custom Shape**, enter a Name in the Shape Name dialog, then click OK. The new shape will appear at the bottom of the Custom Shape preset picker and is now available for any document.

   If you subsequently load in another shape library, to prevent the new shape from being deleted, click Append. Or if you prefer to click Replace, in the alert dialog, click Save to save the current library as a file; the new library will be listed on the Custom Shape preset picker menu.

A We double-clicked the **shape layer** thumbnail, then chose an orange color from the Color Picker.

B Then on the **Style** preset picker, we clicked the Overspray style (in the default style library).

Using shapes to create pixel areas

Finally, using the **Fill Pixels** function for any shape tool, you can create an area of pixels on an image layer in any predefined shape—without having to use a selection marquee or draw a path.

To create an area of pixels by using a shape:

1. On the Layers palette, create a new layer, and keep it selected.

2. Choose a Foreground color.

3. Choose a **shape** tool (U or Shift-U).

4. On the Options bar, do the following:

   Click the **Fill Pixels** button.■

   If you're using the Rounded Rectangle tool,▢ choose a **Radius** value; for the Polygon tool,⬭ choose the desired number of **Sides;** for the Line tool,╲ choose a **Weight;** or for the Custom Shape tool,🎨 choose a shape from the **Custom Shape** preset picker.

5. Drag across the document window to create the shape (or Shift-drag to maintain its proportions). A filled area of pixels will be created.**A**

   You can use brushes, editing tools, filters—whatever—to modify the pixels, or change the Layers palette settings (e.g., blending mode or opacity). It's just a regular ol' layer.

➤ To add a shape to a layer mask, first Alt-click/Option-click the Add Layer Mask button (on the Layers palette) to create a black mask. Choose a shape tool, click the Fill Pixels button on the Options bar, choose white as the Foreground color, then drag or Shift-drag in the document window.**B**

A The bird, which we created by using the **Custom Shape** tool with the **Fill Pixels** button clicked on the Options bar, is a standard image layer. (We chose the Bird preset from the Animals shape library, which we loaded from the Custom Shape preset picker menu.)

B To add a white area to a **layer mask,** we created a Hide All layer mask, made the Foreground color white, chose the Custom Shape tool, clicked the Fill Pixels button, then Shift-dragged in the document window.

Rasterizing shape layers

If you want to apply pixel edits to a shape layer (such as applying brush strokes or a filter) or convert a vector mask into a layer (pixel) mask, you have to **rasterize** it first.

Note: If you used a shape tool to create a pixel area (see the previous page) instead of a shape layer, it's already rasterized and this step is unnecessary.

To rasterize a shape layer:

1. Click a shape layer on the Layers palette.**A**

2. From the Layer > **Rasterize** submenu, choose:

   Shape to convert the shape layer into a filled pixel shape surrounded by transparency, without a vector mask.**B**

   Fill Content to convert the fill content of the shape layer into a pixel area, clipped by the same vector mask.**C**

   Vector Mask to convert the vector mask to a pixel-based layer mask in the same shape and position as the vector mask. The fill content

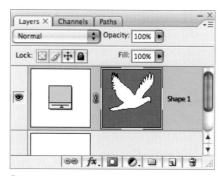

A This is the original shape layer.

remains an editable solid-color fill. The layer mask can be repositioned on the layer.**D**

   Layer to convert a shape layer into a filled pixel shape without a vector mask.**E**

   Note: If you chose the Shape, Fill Content, or Layer option, you can now edit the layer (apply paint strokes, filters, etc.).

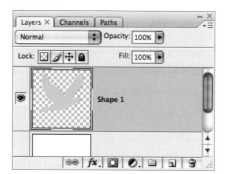

B Layer > Rasterize > **Shape** removed the vector mask and the editable fill icon.

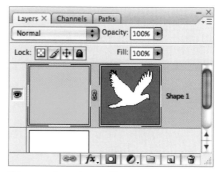

C Layer > Rasterize > **Fill Content** converted the editable fill to image pixels.

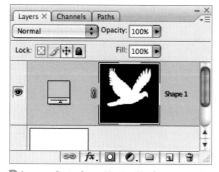

D Layer > Rasterize > **Vector Mask** converted the former vector mask to a layer mask.

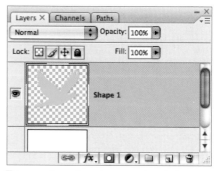

E Layer > Rasterize > **Layer** produced the same results as **B** (above left).

To automate repetitive (and boring!) editing steps and tasks, you can record a sequence of commands in an action and then replay your action on one image or on a batch of images. Actions can be used to execute anything from one simple editing step, such as converting files to a different format or color mode, to a complex sequence of commands, such as running a series of adjustment commands or filters or a series of preflight steps to prepare files for output. Actions can boost your productivity, relieve your life of drudgery, and standardize your edits. Photoshop ships with dozens of ready-made actions, some of which you may find useful (including those in the Default Actions set on the palette). In this chapter, you'll learn how to create, play, and edit custom actions.

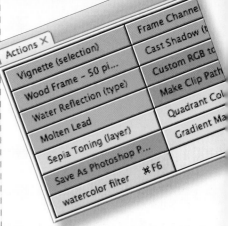

Features of the Actions palette

Using the Actions palette, ▶ you can record, store, edit, play, delete, save, and load actions. The palette has two modes: **List** (edit) **A** and **Button** (**A**, page 311). In List mode, you can expand or collapse a listing of all the commands in an action; toggle a dialog control on or off; add, exclude, delete, rerecord, or change the order of commands; or save actions and/or sets to an actions file. To switch to List mode, uncheck **Button Mode** on the palette menu.

A This **Actions** palette is in **List** mode.

Actions **set**

Action

Dialog control
(allows input from user during playback)

Recorded **command**
(within an action)

Toggle action or command **on** or **off**

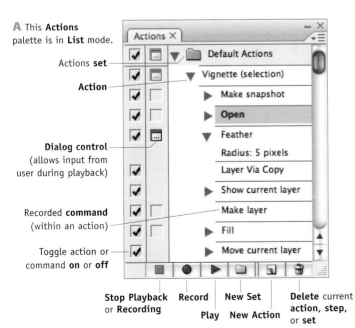

Stop Playback or **Recording**

Record

Play

New Set

New Action

Delete current action, **step,** or **set**

Recording actions

To **create** an **action**, you click the Record button, execute a series of commands, then click the Stop button. Recorded commands are nested below the action name on the Actions palette; actions, in turn, are saved in sets.

To record an action:

1. *Optional:* To create a new set for the action you're going to record, click the **New Set** button ▢ at the bottom of the **Actions** palette,▶ type a Name (preferably a broad but descriptive category), then click OK.

2. Open a document or create a new one. Just to be on the safe side, copy the document, using File > Save As.

3. Click the **New Action** button ▣ at the bottom of the Actions palette (or choose New Action from the Actions palette menu). The New Action dialog opens.**A**

4. Enter a **Name** for the action, and from the **Set** menu, choose the set you created in step 1 or a previously existing set.

5. *Optional:* Assign a Function Key (keyboard shortcut) and/or display Color to the action. These options will display when the palette is in Button mode.

6. Click **Record.**

7. Execute the commands that you want to record, as you would normally apply them to any image. When you enter values in a dialog and click OK, your settings will be recorded (unless you click Cancel).

8. When you're done recording, click the **Stop** button ▣ or press **Esc.**

9. The new action will appear at the bottom of the palette. (With the palette in List mode, click the arrowhead next to the action name to expand or collapse the list of commands.)

   To play the new action (or any other action), see the following page.

➤ When recording the Save As command in an action, be especially careful not to enter specific file names that could be written over when the action is played. We recommend either not changing the name or adding a modal control to make the action pause at the Save As command (see page 317).

RECORDING THE USE OF TOOLS

Some edits are not recordable, such as the following: specific strokes made by tools that use a brush (such as the Brush, Pencil, Healing Brush, Clone Stamp, Blur, and Dodge tools); some menu commands; and some Options bar and palette fields, menus, and sliders. However, you can record the selection of a specific tool, then insert a Stop into the action that includes a message instructing the user to choose specific settings for the tool and describing how to use it (see page 315). Text and audio annotations made with the Annotation tools are recordable (see the sidebar on the next page).

Note also that an action can't include conditional logic, meaning you can't tell an action to perform one command if one situation exists and another command when it doesn't. Also, Photoshop actions work only in Photoshop.

UNITS OR PERCENT?

Position-related operations (such as using a selection tool or the Gradient, Magic Wand, Path, Slice, or Notes tool) are recorded based on the current ruler units. The units can be **actual** (e.g., inches or picas) or **relative** (percentages). An action recorded when the default measurement unit is actual can be played back on a file of the same size or smaller relative to the one in which it was recorded, provided there's enough canvas area to execute the action. An action recorded when a relative unit is chosen will work in any other relative space and on a file of any dimensions. To change the units, go to Preferences > Units & Rulers and then, from the Units: Rulers menu, choose either a specific unit or Percent.

A Use the **New Action** dialog to assign a name and set to your action, as well as an optional function key or color, and to begin recording.

Playing actions

Actions can be **triggered** in various ways: via the Play button on the Actions palette (see below); via the keyboard shortcut that has been assigned to it; by dragging a file or folder full of files onto a droplet icon (a mini-application that was created from an action); or by using the Batch command. We'll discuss the Play button first.

To play an action on one image:

1. Open an image.

2. *Optional:* Create a snapshot of your document (History palette). This will give you the option to restore it quickly to its preaction state.

3. Do one of the following:

   If the Actions palette is in **List** mode, click an action name, then click the **Play** button.

   If the palette is in **Button** mode, 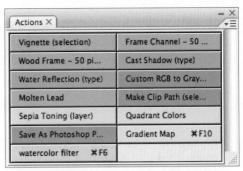 click the button for the action you want to play.

   Execute the keyboard shortcut, if one has been assigned to the desired action.

   ► To play an action starting from a specific command in the action, put the palette in List mode, click the command name, then click the Play button. Or to play just one command in an action, click the command name, then Ctrl-click/Cmd-click the Play button, or simply Ctrl-double-click/Cmd-double-click the command.

   ► When creating layers or alpha channels in a document, assign them descriptive, nongeneric names to prevent the wrong edits from occurring when the action is played.

To exclude a command from playback:

1. Put the Actions palette in List mode (actions can't be edited in Button mode).

2. Expand the list for the action you want to edit.

3. Click in the leftmost column for the command you want to **exclude** from playback to remove the check mark. **B**

   Beware! If you click the check mark for an entire action or actions set, as an alert will tell you, any individual commands that you've painstakingly checked will become unchecked.

   ► To reinclude a command at any time, click in the same spot again (to restore the check mark).

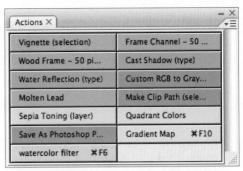

A When the Actions palette is in **Button** mode, it displays a brightly colored button for each action, as well as shortcuts, if you assigned any via the New Action or Action Options dialog.

PLAYBACK OPTIONS

To choose a playback option, put the Actions palette in List mode, choose **Playback Options** from the palette menu, then click one of the following in the dialog:

► **Accelerated:** The fastest playback option.

► **Step by Step:** The list for the action expands on the palette, and the name of each command or edit becomes highlighted as it's executed.

► **Pause for [ ] seconds:** This option works like Step by Step, except that a user-defined pause is inserted at each step.

With the **Pause for Audio Annotation** option on, the playback pauses when it encounters an audio annotation, then resumes when the audio message is completed.

B The Unsharp Mask step within this action is unchecked, so it's **excluded** from playback.

The ability to play an action on multiple files is a super timesaver. You can do this quickly by dragging a folder of files onto a droplet (see "To create a droplet for an action" on page 314). Or if you want to choose a destination, a file naming scheme, or other options for the files to be processed by the action, use the **Batch** command, as described below.

Note: If you follow the first option in step 1 and choose Folder as the Destination in step 4, further options will become available for naming the resulting files. For example, you can specify that the files be named sequentially using serial numbers or letters, so they don't replace one another in their new folder. Another option adds the proper extensions to make your files compatible with other operating systems.

To play an action on a batch of images:

1. Follow the instructions in the first paragraph below if you want to access and use the File Naming options; otherwise, do the second set:

   In Bridge, put all the files to be processed into one folder and display the folder contents, then choose Tools > Photoshop > **Batch.** In the Batch dialog, choose Source: **Folder,** click **Browse/Choose,** locate the desired folder, then click Choose.

   In Bridge, select the thumbnails for the images that you want to process, then choose Tools > Photoshop > **Batch.** The Batch dialog opens (**A,** next page). Choose a set from the **Set** menu and an action from the **Action** menu and then, from the **Source** menu, choose **Bridge.**

2. *Optional:* If the action contains an Open command and you check Override Action "Open" Commands, the batch command will ignore the specific file name in the Open step.

3. Check **Suppress File Open Options Dialogs** and/or **Suppress Color Profile Warnings** to have the command bypass any dialogs or alerts that appear onscreen as source files are opened.

4. From the **Destination** menu, choose one of the following options:

   None to keep all the files open after processing.

   Save and Close to have the files save after processing and then close.

   Folder to have the files save to a new folder and to access the file naming options. Click Browse/ Choose, then choose a destination folder.

   Optional: If the action contains a Save As command and you check Override Action "Save As" Commands, the batch command will ignore the specific file name and location during the Save As step.

5. *Optional:* By default, Photoshop will end the Batch process if it encounters an error. To have it play without stopping and keep track of error messages in a text file instead, from the Errors menu, choose Log Errors to File, then click Save As. A Save dialog opens. Type a name for the text file, choose a location, then click Save. If errors are encountered, you'll be alerted via a prompt that errors were logged into the designated error log file.

6. If you chose Folder as the Destination, you can do the following:

   Choose options from the menus in the **File Naming** area, or simply type in any text you want included in the name. Make sure the **Example** name shows the desired naming convention.

   If you chose a naming option that uses sequential (serial) numbers, enter a 1- to 4-digit starting number in the **Starting Serial #** field.

   Check any or all of the file name **Compatibility** options for the platforms you want the files to be compatible with.

7. Click OK to start the batch processing.

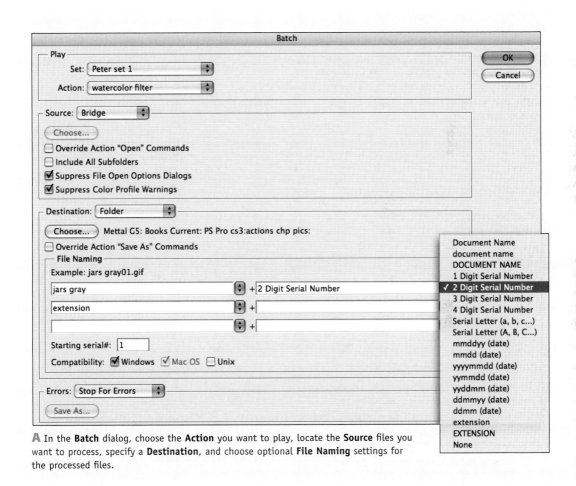

A In the **Batch** dialog, choose the **Action** you want to play, locate the **Source** files you want to process, specify a **Destination**, and choose optional **File Naming** settings for the processed files.

An action can be turned into its own little mini-application, called a **droplet,**  that sits out on the Desktop or in a folder, waiting to be triggered. If you drag a file or a folder full of files onto a droplet icon, Photoshop will launch (if it's not yet running), and the action that the droplet represents will be played on those files. Droplets can be shared with other Photoshop users.

To create a droplet for an action:

1. Choose File > Automate > **Create Droplet.** The Create Droplet dialog opens. **B**

2. Click **Choose.** A Save dialog opens. Enter a name in the Save As field, choose a convenient location for the droplet, then click Save.

A This is a **droplet** icon for an action.

wood frame

MAKING DROPLETS COMPATIBLE

➤ To make a droplet that was created in Windows usable in **Macintosh**, drag it onto the Macintosh Photoshop CS3 application icon.

➤ To make a droplet that was created in Macintosh usable in **Windows**, save it with an ".exe" extension.

---

3. Back in the Create Droplet dialog, choose a set from the **Set** menu, then choose the **Action** that you want to save as a droplet.

4. Check any **Play** options you want included in the droplet, and choose **Destination** and **Errors** options for the processed files (see steps 4–6 on page 312).

5. Click OK. The droplet will appear in the designated location.

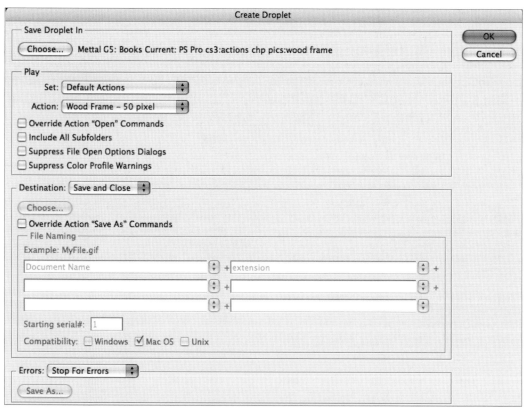

B Use the **Create Droplet** dialog to choose a location and other options for an action droplet.

Editing actions

You can insert a variety of special commands into your actions. For example, if you insert a **Stop**, the playback will pause at that point in the action to allow the user to perform a manual or nonrecordable edit, such as the use of the Brush or Clone Stamp tool. When the manual edit is completed, the user clicks the Play button again to resume the playback. A Stop can also include a text message for the user, which will display in an alert dialog.

To insert a Stop in an action:

1. Do either of the following:

   As you're creating an action, pause at the point at which you want the Stop to appear.

   To add a Stop to an existing action, on the Actions palette, click the command name after which you want it to appear.

2. Choose **Insert Stop** from the Actions palette menu. The Record Stop dialog opens.

3. Type an instructional or alert message.**A** We recommend spelling out in the message that after performing the desired edit, the user should click the Play button to resume the playback if their Actions palette is in List mode, or click the action name if their palette is in Button mode.

4. *Optional:* Check Allow Continue to include a Continue button in the alert dialog.**B** This will give the user an easy way to continue the action playback without performing the requested manual edits. Without this option, the user will still be able to resume the playback by clicking Stop when the alert dialog appears, followed by clicking the Play button on the palette.

5. Click OK. The Stop listing will appear below the command you paused after or clicked on in step 1.**C**

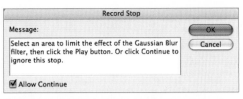

A In the **Record Stop** dialog, type an instructional message for the user. The **Allow Continue** option creates a Continue button that the person replaying the action can click to quickly resume the playback.

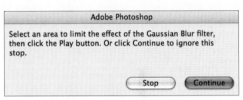

B The **Continue** button lets the user continue the action playback without performing any manual tasks.

C The **Stop** command appears as a listing within the action.

If you forgot to include a particular command or editing step in an action, or you want to **add** a **command** to improve it, here's your second chance.

To add a command or edit to an action:

1. On the Actions palette, expand the list for the action that you want to add the edit to, then click the command name after which you want the new one to appear.

2. Click the **Record** button.

3. Perform the steps required to record the command(s) that you want to add. Note: You can't add a command that's available only under certain conditions (e.g., the Feather command requires an active selection) unless the creation of those conditions is also included as steps in the action.

4. Click the **Stop** button ■ to stop recording.

▶ To expand or collapse all the steps in an action, Alt-click/Option-click the arrowhead next to the action name.

Some dialog features aren't recordable, but there's a next best option. Via the **Insert Menu Item** command, you can force the dialog for a particular menu command to open onscreen during playback, allowing the user to choose custom settings.

To insert a menu item in an action:

1. Expand the listing for an existing action, then click the command name after which you want the new menu command to be inserted.

2. Choose **Insert Menu Item** from the Actions palette menu. The Insert Menu Item dialog opens.

3. From the Photoshop menu bar, choose the command that you want to add to the action. The command name will appear in the Insert Menu Item dialog.**A**

4. Click OK.**B** The ability to display a dialog and allow user input is disabled for inserted menu commands. To provide this capability, use a modal control, discussed on the following page.

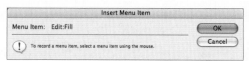

A When we chose the Fill command from the Edit menu, the command name magically appeared in the **Insert Menu Item** dialog.

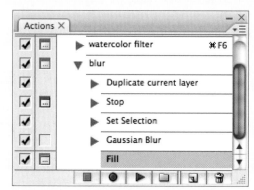

B The menu item that we **inserted** appears as a listing on the **Actions** palette.

COPYING COMMANDS BETWEEN ACTIONS

To copy a command from one action to another, expand both action lists, then Alt-drag/Option-drag the command you want to copy from one list to the other (if you don't hold down Alt/Option, you'll cut the command from the original action). Be careful when copying a Save command, as it may contain information that pertains only to the original action.

A **modal control,** or pause, in an action, can be enabled for any command that uses a dialog or any tool that requires pressing Enter/Return in order to be executed. If users encounter a modal control upon playing an action, they can either enter different settings in the dialog or just click OK to proceed with the settings that were originally recorded for that dialog.

To add a modal control for a command in an action:

1. With the Actions palette in List mode, expand the list for an action.

2. For any individual listing within the action, click in the second column; the **dialog** icon ⊡ will appear.**A** When the action is played, it will pause when it reaches a command with a dialog icon, and the dialog for that command will appear onscreen. The user can then enter new values, accept the existing values by just clicking OK, or click Cancel. After the dialog is exited, the playback resumes.

➤ To remove a modal control, click the dialog icon.

To enable or disable all modal controls for an action:

Click in the dialog column for an action name to turn all the modal controls in that action on or off. If the action has a red dialog icon, it means that some modal controls in the action are turned off and some are still on; click the red icon, then click OK in the alert dialog.

A Via the **dialog** icon, you give the user an opportunity to enter different settings in a dialog while playing the action.

If you want to experiment with an action or add to it without messing around with the original, work on a **duplicate**.

To duplicate an action:

Do either of the following:

Click an action, then choose **Duplicate** from the Actions palette menu.

Drag an action over the **New Action** button ⬛ on the Actions palette.

➤ To rename an action, double-click the name.

To rerecord an action using different dialog settings:

1. Click the name of the action that contains the settings you want to edit.

2. Choose **Record Again** from the Actions palette menu. The action will play back, stopping at any command that uses a dialog.

3. When each dialog opens in succession, enter new settings, if desired, then click OK. Each time you close a dialog, the rerecording continues.

4. To stop the rerecording, click Cancel in a dialog or click the **Stop** button ⬛ on the palette.

To change the settings for a command in an action:

1. Expand the listing for an action on the Actions palette, then double-click a command that uses a dialog (or alert dialog) that you want to change the settings for.

2. Enter new settings.

3. Click OK. (Click Cancel to have your revisions disregarded.)

BEING RESPONSIBLE FOR YOUR ACTIONS

Before editing an action, we recommend that you **duplicate** it first and edit the duplicate (see the instructions at left). Barring that, you should at least save the set to a file beforehand (see page 320). To reset or replace all the actions that are currently on the palette, see page 320.

This may seem obvious, but remember that if you **change** the **order** of **edits** in an action, the revised action may produce different results from the original.

To change the order of edits in an action:

1. On the Actions palette, expand the list for an action, if it's not already expanded.

2. Drag a command upward or downward on the list. Simple.

➤ To duplicate a command in an action, drag the command over the New Action button ▣ or Alt-drag/Option-drag the step to the desired location.

Deleting commands and actions

You can **delete** a whole **action**, or merely **delete** individual **commands** from an action.

To delete an action or delete a command from an action:

1. *Optional:* To save the current list of actions as a set for future use, before deleting any actions or commands, follow the instructions on the next page.

2. Do either of the following:

   Click the **action** that you want to delete.

   Click the name of the individual **command** that you want to delete. Ctrl-click/Cmd-click to highlight additional commands, if desired.

3. Click the **Delete** button 🗑 on the Actions palette, then click OK (or to bypass the prompt, Alt-click/Option-click the Delete button).

Saving and loading actions sets

Each time you create a new action, you have to choose a set for it to be stored in. You can also **save** a whole **actions set** to a **separate file** for use on another computer or as a backup for safekeeping.

To save an actions set to a file:

1. Click the actions set that you want to save.

2. Choose **Save Actions** from the palette menu.

3. In the **Save** dialog, type a name for the actions set file, keep the default location (see the sidebar at right), then click **Save**. The new file will be regarded as one set, irrespective of the number of actions it contains.

4. When you relaunch Photoshop, your newly saved set will appear on the Actions palette menu. Note: If you edit any actions in the set, save the set again by following the steps above.

Photoshop includes many useful actions that don't appear on the palette by default. You can **load** them by following the instructions below, plus you can also load any user set.

To load a set onto the Actions palette:

1. Click the **set** name that you want the loaded set to appear below.

2. Choose a Photoshop **actions set** from the Actions palette menu (Commands, Frames, Image Effects, Production, Text Effects, Textures, or Video Actions), or choose a user-saved set from the bottom of the menu.

If you like to list only one set on the Actions palette at a time, use the **Replace Actions** command instead of the Load Actions command.

To replace the current actions set with a different set:

1. Choose **Replace Actions** from the Actions palette menu.

2. Locate and click the actions set file that you want to replace the existing sets with, then click **Load**.

To load the default actions set:

Choose **Reset Actions** from the palette menu, then click **Append** in the alert dialog to add the default set to the existing sets on the palette, or click **OK** to replace the existing sets with the default set.

WHERE ARE ACTIONS STORED?

► There are several places where Photoshop expects to find Actions files, but the easiest place to find them is Adobe Photoshop CS3 > Presets > Actions. User-saved sets are listed at the bottom of the Actions palette menu.

► To save a text (TXT) listing of all the actions sets that are currently listed on the palette, hold down Ctrl-Alt/Cmd-Option while choosing Save Actions from the Actions palette menu, then enter a name and choose a location in the Save dialog.

Whether you're planning to print your document directly from Photoshop to a desktop printer, place it in a page layout application for commercial printing, or import it into a Web page layout application for display online, Photoshop provides a variety of formatting options.

To obtain a quality color print from an **inkjet printer** that closely matches your onscreen image, you'll need to follow up on the color management workflow that you began in Chapter 1 by selecting the proper printer profile. Once that is in place, you'll be ready to choose options for your printer and send your document to print.

If you're planning to export your file to a **page layout** application that can read Photoshop PSD files, see page 332. If, on the other hand, your target application doesn't read Photoshop PSD files, find out from your client or output service provider which format (and settings) are right for your particular output scenario, then follow the instructions in this chapter to save the file in the Photoshop PDF, Photoshop EPS, or TIFF format.

If your document is headed for a **Web page layout** application, on the other hand, refer to the section beginning with "Optimizing files for the Web" on page 340. Read about the GIF and JPEG formats, and decide which one is right for your file.

The **Adobe Media Gallery** command lets you create a gallery, or slideshow, for viewing your photos on a website. Not only does it give you many options for creating and customizing slideshows, but it also has an optional feature that will upload your photos to a website of your choice.

With so many print and output options available in Photoshop, your files can be prepped for use in a wide variety of media. In fact, multiple versions of the same file can be saved in various sizes and formats for different purposes.

OUTPUT FOR PRINT & WEB

15

IN THIS CHAPTER

Preparing a file for print output

By now, your "master" Photoshop document may contain multiple image, adjustment, shape, or Smart Object layers, and possibly also a few masks. Before reaching for the Print command, you need to prepare the file for printing (or, rather, prepare a copy of the file) by **flattening layers**, changing the **bit depth**, possibly changing the **dimensions**, and applying output **sharpening**.

To prepare an RGB file for printing:

1. Open a high-resolution RGB file that you're going to print. Choose File > **Save As.** Choose a location in which to save the new file, then enter a different name in the File name/Save As field.

   Leave as is any options in the Save area that are already checked. In the Color area, check **ICC Profile/Embed Color Profile** [profile name] to preserve the profile in the new file. Click Save.

2. If the Photoshop Format Options alert displays, uncheck Maximize Compatibility, then click OK.

3. The new file will appear in the document window. You need to flatten the layers to prepare the file for sharpening. Choose **Flatten Image** from the Layers palette menu, and click OK in any alert dialogs.

4. On the Image > **Mode** submenu, make sure 8 Bits/Channel is checked (not 16 Bits/Channel).

5. To make sure the image has the proper dimensions for the chosen paper size, choose Image > **Image Size,** and note the Width and Height under Document Size.**A** If that size will fit on the paper size, you're all set; click Cancel.

   If you need to modify the dimensions, check Resample Image to prevent the Resolution value from changing (it should already be set to the necessary high resolution for your printer). Change just the **Width** or the **Height** value to fit the paper size. From the menu at the bottom, choose **Bicubic Smoother (Best for Enlargement)** if you enlarged the dimensions, or **Bicubic Sharper (Best for Reduction)** if you reduced the dimensions, then click OK.

6. Apply output sharpening, as per the instructions on the following page.

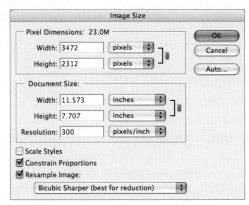

A To fit the image to your paper size, check Resample Image in the **Image Size** dialog, change the Width or Height, then choose an interpolation method from the menu at the bottom.

On pages 50–52, we showed you how to apply capture sharpening in Camera Raw and in Chapter 9, we showed you how to apply sharpening in Photoshop. Before printing your file, you should apply a last round of **output sharpening** to help compensate for potential "softening" from dot gain (the slight spreading of printing inks on paper).

To apply output sharpening:

1. Keep the high-res RGB file that you prepared for printing (see the previous page) open onscreen.

2. Press Ctrl-J/Cmd-J to duplicate the Background.

3. Double-click below the duplicate layer name to open the **Layer Style** dialog.

4. Next, you'll use the **Blend If** sliders **A** to hide the highlight and shadow pixels on the duplicate layer to prevent any sharpening from affecting those areas (this technique was also used on pages 194–195):

   Move the **black Underlying Layer** slider to 10, then Alt-drag/Option-drag the right part of the slider to 20.

   Move the **white Underlying Layer** slider to 245, then Alt-drag/Option-drag the left part of the slider to 235.

   Click OK.

5. Next, you'll set the **zoom** level to help you judge the sharpening. Alt-click/Option-click the status bar at the bottom of the document window and note the pixel dimensions of your file.**B** If it's 2000 x 3000 pixels (6 megapixels) or smaller, zoom to **100%**; if it's 2400 x 3600 pixels (8 megapixels) or larger, zoom to **50%**.

6. Choose Filter > Sharpen > **Unsharp Mask**. In the Unsharp Mask dialog,**C** set the **Amount** slider to between 200 and 250, the **Radius** slider to between 0.7 and 1.0, and the **Threshold** slider to 3 or 4. Don't worry if the image now looks too sharp. This final sharpening should be judged from the print output, not on how the image looks onscreen. Click OK.

7. Immediately choose Edit > **Fade Unsharp Mask**. In the Fade dialog, choose Mode: Luminosity to limit the sharpening to just tonalities,**D** then click OK.

8. Save your file, then print it (see the next section). If the image looks too sharp on the printout, lower the **opacity** of the duplicate layer to lessen the sharpening effect, then print again.

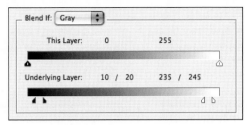

A In the **Layer Style** dialog, set the **Blend If** sliders to the positions shown above.

B Alt-click/Option-click the **status** bar to view the pixel dimensions (Width and Height).

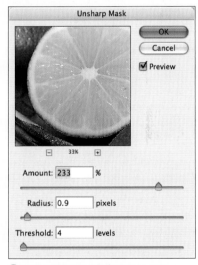

C In the **Unsharp Mask** dialog, choose values similar to those shown above.

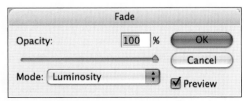

D In the **Fade Unsharp Mask** dialog, choose **Luminosity** from the Mode menu.

Printing from Photoshop

Before you print a document on any type of device, you need to specify which printer model and paper size you're going to use via the **Properties/Page Setup** dialog. Options will vary depending on your printer driver and operating system.

In this section, we'll focus on desktop inkjet color printers, which can be used to produce either an initial "test" print before a commercial print run or photo prints from a quality photo inkjet printer as final output.

In Windows, the Page Setup command opens the confusingly named "[your printer model] Properties" dialog, which has many printer-specific options beyond the basic page size and paper type. In the Mac OS, you'll find equivalent options in the Print dialog for your system, which opens when you click the Print button in the Print dialog in Photoshop. (Hey… we don't design these things; we just try to help you make sense of them.)

To choose a paper size and orientation for inkjet printing:

1. Choose File > **Print** (Ctrl-P/Cmd-P). The Print dialog opens (**A**, next page).

2. From the **Printer** menu, choose the printer you want to use.

3. Click **Page Setup** to open the **[printer name] Properties** dialog in Windows **A** or the **Page Setup** dialog in the Mac OS.**B**

4. In Windows, from the **Source** menu, choose the tray that holds the media you want to print on, and from the **Type** menu, choose the specific kind of media you want to use (the menu names may differ, depending on your printer model).

   In the Mac OS, from the **Format For** menu, choose your inkjet printer once again.

5. From the **Size** or **Paper Size** menu, choose a paper size for printing. If your device can print borderless pictures, choose one of the sizes that is listed as "(borderless)."

   Leave the Scale value at 100% (because you already adjusted the image size on page 322).

6. Click OK. To choose settings for your printer, follow the instructions that begin on the next page.

A This is the **Properties** dialog (Epson printer) in **Windows.**

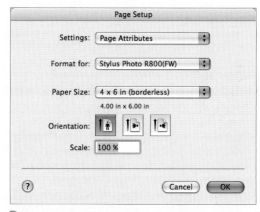

B This is the **Page Setup** dialog (Epson printer) in the **Mac OS.**

In these instructions, you'll choose settings for your printer via the **Print** dialog in Photoshop, incorporating color management as you do so. In addition to showing you a preview of the image on your chosen paper size, this dialog lets you choose print size, color management, and output settings, and also lets you control the position of the image on the paper.

To choose settings for an inkjet printer:

1. Choose File > **Print** (Ctrl-P/Cmd-P). The Print dialog opens,**A** complete with a preview. The white area represents the paper.

2. Make sure the correct output device is listed on the **Printer** menu.

3. If you haven't chosen page settings yet, click **Page Setup** (see the previous page). After using the [printer name] Properties/Page Setup dialog, click OK to return to the Print dialog.

4. Check **Center Image** to position the image in the center of the paper, or uncheck this option and enter new **Top** and **Left** values to change

the position of the image on the paper; the preview will update accordingly. If the default margins of the printer cause your images to print off-center, you can compensate for this by changing the Top and Left values.

5. You could change the Scale, Height, or Width fields in the **Scaled Print Size** area to reduce or enlarge the printed image (by a small amount), but if you followed our instructions on page 322, you've properly scaled the image already, so skip this step.

Continued on the following page

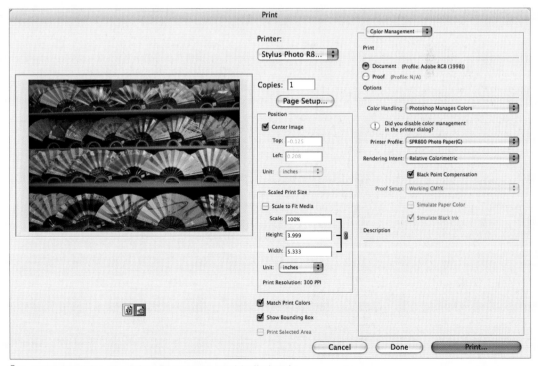

A In this **Print** dialog, the **Color Management** panel is displayed.

➤ Although we prefer to use the Image Size and Position options to adjust the size and position of the image for printing, this can also be done manually. To scale the image slightly, check Show Bounding Box, then drag a handle or the edge of the boundary in the preview. Or to reposition the image on the paper, uncheck Center Image, then drag the whole bounding box.

6. From the menu in the upper right corner of the dialog, choose **Color Management** (**A**, next page). In this pane, you'll tell Photoshop which profile to use for your chosen printer and paper.

7. In the Print area, click **Document** [Profile] to use the color profile that's embedded in the image, which will be Adobe RGB (1998) if you're continuing with the color management workflow from Chapter 1.

8. From the **Color Handling** menu in the Options area, choose **Photoshop Manages Colors** to let Photoshop handle the color conversion. Assuming you installed a profile for your specific printer, ink, and paper (as per the instructions on page 8), this option will ensure optimal color management.

9. Next, choose that same printer, ink, and paper profile from the **Printer Profile** menu.

10. From the **Rendering Intent** menu, choose the same intent that you used when you created the soft-proof setting for your inkjet printer, which is most likely either Perceptual or Relative Colorimetric (see pages 9–10).

   ➤ Run one test print for the Perceptual intent and one for the Relative Colorimetric intent, and see which one gives better results.

11. Check **Black Point Compensation.** This option preserves the darkest blacks and shadow details by mapping the full color range of the document profile to the full range of the printer profile, and is recommended when printing an image from RGB Color mode.

12. In the central area of the dialog, toward the bottom, check **Match Print Colors** to display a color-managed soft proof of the image in the preview, based on the chosen printer and printer profile settings.

13. Do one of the following:

   Click **Print** to access the system-wide Print dialog, then carefully follow the steps on page 328 or 329 to turn off color management for the printer before sending the file to print.

   Press Alt/Option and click **Remember** to save your custom settings with the file. The Print dialog will remain open. Click **Print**, then follow the steps on page 328 or 329 to turn off color management for the printer before sending the file to print. Note: Don't click Reset, or you'll lose all your custom settings—ouch!

   Click **Done** to preserve your settings and close the dialog. You'll see these settings when you reopen the dialog, but unlike the Remember option, they won't save with the file that was open when you chose them.

➤ For technical information and documentation on specific printer models, see Photoshop Help.

OTHER COLOR HANDLING CHOICES

Other options on the **Color Handling** menu in the **Color Management** pane of the Print dialog are as follows:

➤ **Printer Manages Colors** sends all of the file's color information to the printer along with the document profile, and the printer, not Photoshop, manages the color conversion. This isn't a good choice if you use either custom profiles or paper from a company other than the printer manufacturer, because (depending on the features and quality of the printer driver) the printer may not be aware of your custom choices. If you do use this option, be sure to enable color management options in the printer driver for the chosen printer.

➤ **No Color Management** prevents color values from being converted by Photoshop or the printer. Choose this option if you're planning to print a color target from which a color reading device will scan and generate a custom printer and paper profile. (We don't mean to be cryptic, but to explain color targets fully would take a whole chapter in itself…)

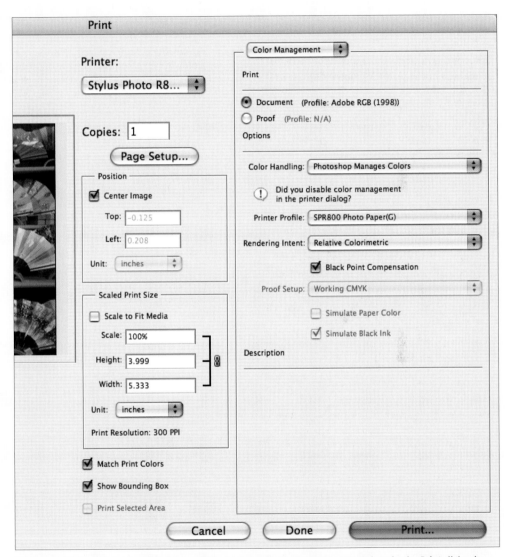

A To optimize the color accuracy of your printout, choose **Color Management** settings in the **Print** dialog in Photoshop.

The last step before outputting your file from an inkjet printer is to **turn off color management** for that device to allow Photoshop to manage the color conversion.

In **Windows**, the dialog that contains color management settings for printing is part of the printer driver software, not part of the system software. Therefore, the names and locations of the controls will vary depending on the manufacturer. In these instructions, printer color management will be turned off for an Epson printer driver. If you have a different printer model, research how to access print quality and color management settings for it, and use our steps as general guidelines.

To turn off color management for your printer in Windows, and print the file:

1. Open the File > **Print** dialog in Photoshop, then click **Print** to get to the Print dialog for your system.

2. In the **Select Printer** area of the **General** tab, click the name of your inkjet printer.

3. Click **Preferences A** to open the **Printing Preferences** dialog for your printer, which is identical to the Properties dialog that you used to specify the size and media type.

4. In the **Main** tab of the Printing Preferences dialog, click **Advanced.B** A different set of options will appear, including controls for color management.

5. In the **Color Management** area, click **ICM C** to switch color management from the Epson driver to the color management system that's built into Windows XP.

6. In the **ICC/ICM Profile** area, click **Off (No Color Adjustment)** to turn off color management for the printer (**A**, next page).

7. Click **OK** to close the Printing Preferences dialog and return to the Print dialog. Now you're ready to click **Print.** Phew!

➤ When you need to enable printer-based color management in Windows, follow steps 1–6 above, except in step 6, click Applied by Printer Software.

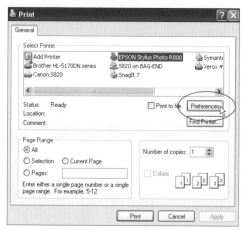

A In the **Print** dialog in Windows (here, for an Epson printer), click **Preferences** to open the next dialog.

B In the Main tab of the **Printing Preferences** dialog for an **Epson** printer, click **Advanced.**

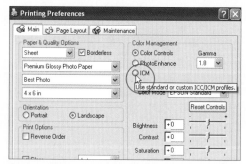

C These **Color Management** options are revealed when you click the Advanced button.

In the **Mac OS**, the dialog that contains **color management** settings for the printer builds its list of options from both the system and the printer driver. Therefore, option names in the dialog will vary depending on the printer manufacturer. In these instructions, printer color management will be turned off for a Canon or Epson printer driver. If you have a different printer model, research how to access print quality and color management settings for it, and use our steps as general guidelines.

To turn off color management for your printer in the Mac OS, and print the file:

1. Open the File > **Print** dialog in Photoshop, then click **Print** to get to the Print dialog for your system.

2. From the **Printer** menu, choose the name of your inkjet printer.

3. From the third menu, for a Canon printer choose **Quality & Media** B or for an Epson printer choose **Print Settings**.

4. Choose the **Media Type** (your chosen paper type) and the **Paper Source** (how the paper will be fed into the printer).C

5. In the **Print Mode** area, click an option for the print quality.

6. Returning to the third menu from the top, choose **Color Options** (Canon) D or **Color Management** (Epson). A new set of options displays in the dialog. Choose **None** from the **Color Correction** menu (Canon), or click **Off (No Color Adjustment)** (Epson).

7. Click **Print**. Congratulations!

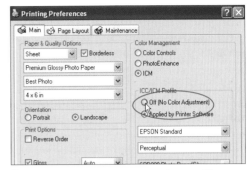

A In **Windows,** click **Off** in the **ICC/ICM Profile** area to turn off color management.

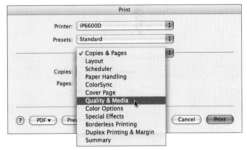

B In the **Print** dialog, we chose the Canon Pixma **iP6600D** printer from the Printer menu and are now choosing **Quality & Media** from the third menu.

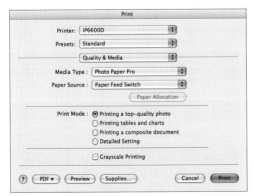

C For the **Quality & Media** settings, choose your paper type and source, and click the desired Print Mode.

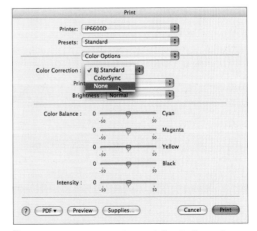

D From the third menu, choose **Color Options**, then choose **Color Correction: None.**

The **Proof** option in the Print dialog instructs your desktop printer to simulate the output of a commercial, four-color press. This "hard" proof won't match the press output exactly, but it will give you an idea of how the image will look in the restricted color range (color gamut) of a commercial press.

To output a CMYK proof from an inkjet printer:

1. For the best results, create a custom CMYK proof setup for your RGB file via View > Proof > **Custom** (see pages 9–10).**A**

2. With the File > **Print** dialog open and the **Color Management** pane showing, click **Proof.B**

3. Make sure the **Color Handling** menu is set to **Photoshop Manages Colors** and the **Printer Profile** menu is set to the profile for your inkjet printer.

> ### GIVE THE PRINT TIME TO MATURE
> To judge the true colors in an inkjet print, especially when printing on matte paper, wait an hour for the inks to stabilize and the final colors to develop.

4. From the **Proof Setup** menu, **C** choose a profile for proofing, preferably the one you saved via View > Proof > Custom (the same profile will also appear on the View > Proof Setup submenu).

5. Below the Proof Setup menu, check **Simulate Paper Color** (see page 9) and/or **Simulate Black Ink** to mimic those commercial printing conditions. See also Photoshop Help.

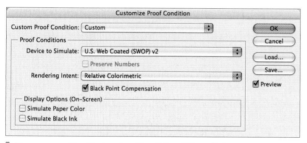

A You can use the **Customize Proof Condition** dialog to create a custom CMYK proof.

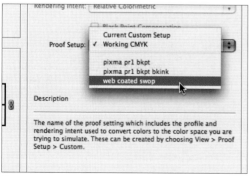

C Choose a proofing profile from the **Proof Setup** menu in the **Print** dialog.

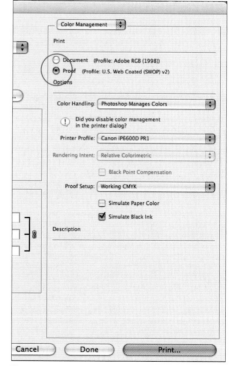

B Click **Proof** in the **Color Management** pane of the Print dialog, then choose **Color Handling** and **Printer Profile** menu options.

Preparing a file for commercial printing

A computer monitor displays additive colors by projecting red, green, and blue (RGB) light, whereas a commercial press prints subtractive colors using CMYK (cyan, magenta, yellow, and black) and/or spot color inks. Obtaining good CMYK color reproduction of a digital file from a commercial press is an art, but nowadays, print shops create their own profiles for their commercial presses, so you don't need to concern yourself with creating a custom profile; you can leave this step to the pros.

Do concern yourself with saving the custom file or profile from your print shop to the correct folder so it can be accessed from the Color Settings dialog in Photoshop. The profile will control the CMYK conversion and can be used to create a soft proof. (In Chapter 1, we showed you where to save a .csf file and custom profile, and how to create a soft proof.)

When you're ready to convert your file for a commercial press, the first step is to set the current

Working Spaces: CMYK menu in the Edit > Color Settings dialog in Photoshop to either a custom profile your print shop has provided or to a pre-press profile that they've requested you use. This **CMYK profile** will control the conversion of your images from RGB to CMYK color mode.

To choose a predefined CMYK profile:

1. Choose Edit > **Color Settings** (Ctrl-Shift-K/Cmd-Shift-K).

2. Do either of the following:

   From the **Settings** menu, choose the .csf file that you received from your print shop and installed.**A**

   From the **CMYK** menu in the Working Spaces area, choose a custom .icc profile that you received from your print shop and installed; or choose a prepress profile that they recommend for the specific press and paper type they're going use for your job.**B**

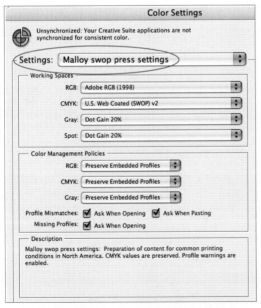

A From the **Settings** menu in the **Color Settings** dialog, choose the **.csf profile** you received from your print shop.

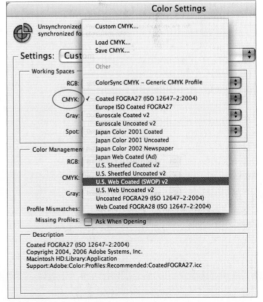

B From the CMYK menu in the **Color Settings** dialog, choose either a custom **.icc profile** that you received from your print shop or a preset **CMYK profile** that they recommend.

Exporting Photoshop files to Adobe InDesign and Adobe Illustrator

If you're going to export your Photoshop file to Adobe InDesign or Adobe Illustrator, be aware that **Photoshop (PSD), TIFF**, and **Photoshop PDF**, and the less practical **Large Document (PSB)** are the only formats that preserve Photoshop features such as multiple layers, Smart Objects, adjustment layers, etc. (A list of these features appears on page 76.) You can import a Photoshop PSD file into InDesign or Illustrator via the Place command, or via the open command into Illustrator, which makes exporting files to those programs as easy as pie.

To speed up performance when importing Photoshop files into InDesign, save a flattened, composite preview of a Photoshop PSD file with the layered version. To ensure that a flattened, composite preview of a layered file is always included when the Save or Save As command is used, go to Preferences > File Handling, and on the **Maximize PSD and PSB File Compatibility** menu, choose **Always**. With this option on, a rasterized copy of any vector art will also be included for applications that don't support vector data. This option produces larger files that take longer to save, but it ensures compatibility for applications that don't support the Photoshop features listed above.

If you'd rather decide on a file-by-file basis whether to include the additional flattened version with your layered file, choose **Ask** from the Maximize PSD and PSB File Compatibility menu instead. With this setting, if you create one or more layers and then choose the Save or Save As command, an alert dialog will appear, giving you the option to include the composite preview or not.

If you need to preserve the possibility of editing a 16 bits/channel Photoshop file after importing it into InDesign, don't change the bit depth. Or if you're prepared to lower the bit depth now, before exporting the file, choose 8 Bits/Channel from the Image > Mode submenu.

Photoshop to Adobe InDesign

Adobe InDesign can import Photoshop PSD files and color-separate them (RGB or CMYK), and it can also read embedded ICC color profiles. In InDesign, you can turn the visibility of Photoshop layers on or off at any time, as well as view layer comps. Since alpha channels, layer masks, and transparency are preserved, you won't need to create a clipping mask when you want to block areas of an image from printing. And like other programs in the Adobe Creative Suite, InDesign lets you use Bridge for file and color management.

Photoshop to Adobe Illustrator

It's also easy to get Photoshop files into Adobe Illustrator.

➤ If you **drag and drop** a Photoshop selection or layer into an Illustrator document, the imagery will appear either as an image layer on the Layers palette or as a group with a generic clipping path and an image layer. Transparent areas will be filled with white, the opacity will be reset to 100%, the blending mode will be reset to Normal, and any layer and vector masks will be applied to their respective layers.

➤ Via File > **Place** in Illustrator, you can place either a whole Photoshop image or just a single layer comp. If you place a Photoshop image with the Link option checked, the image will appear on the Layers palette on a single image layer, and any masks in the file will be applied. If you embed the Photoshop image as you place it (uncheck the Link option), you'll be given the option to convert layers into objects or flatten them into one layer.

➤ Any layers below an **adjustment layer** in the Photoshop file won't arrive as individual layers in Illustrator. To work around this restriction, merge all the adjustment layers into their underlying layers before opening or placing the file into Illustrator.

➤ If you **flatten** the Photoshop layers into one layer, all transparency, blending modes, and layer mask effects will be preserved—but only visually; they won't be editable in Illustrator.

Exporting a silhouetted image from Photoshop

To place just a portion of a Photoshop PSD image into InDesign CS3 or Illustrator CS3, the first step is to isolate it to a separate layer.

To create a silhouetted image in Photoshop:

1. Do either of the following:

    With an area of a layer selected, create a layer mask.**A**

    Select the area that you want to silhouette, and put it on its own layer via Ctrl-J/Cmd-J.**B**

2. *Optional:* Click the visibility icon to hide the Background. You'll also have the option to hide the Background in InDesign or Illustrator once the file is imported (see the next page).

3. Choose File > Save As, check Save a Copy in the dialog to save a copy of the file, then follow either set of instructions on the next page.

COPYING A PATH TO ADOBE ILLUSTRATOR

To copy a Photoshop path to an Adobe Illustrator file or to another Photoshop file, we find the drag-and-drop or copy-and-paste method to be easier than the File > Export > Paths to Illustrator command. Regardless of the original state of the path, when it arrives in Illustrator, it will have neither a stroke nor a fill. Open the source and target documents, position them so they're both visible, click in the source document window, then do either of the following: Click a path name on the Paths palette, choose the **Path Selection** tool, then **drag** the path from the source document window into the target document window. Or click a path listing on the Paths palette, press Ctrl-C/Cmd-C to copy it, then **paste** it into the target document window (Ctrl-V/Cmd-V); in the Paste Options dialog, click Paste As: **Compound Shape**.

➤ As an alternative to creating a path or text in Photoshop, consider using the File > Place command in Adobe Illustrator to import your Photoshop image, then use Illustrator to create your vector paths or text on top of the image.

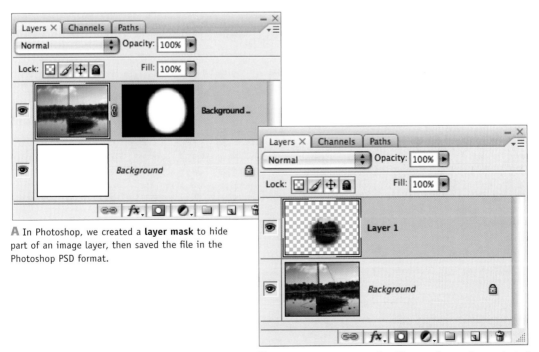

A In Photoshop, we created a **layer mask** to hide part of an image layer, then saved the file in the Photoshop PSD format.

B In Photoshop, we created a silhouette by copying a selected area to a **new layer**, then saved the file in the Photoshop PSD format.

To place a Photoshop file into InDesign as a silhouette:

1. In InDesign, import the file via File > **Place.**

2. Choose Object > **Object Layer Options.**

3. In the dialog,**A** check Preview, show the layer that contains the **layer mask** and hide any other layers, then click OK.**C–D**

To import a Photoshop file into Illustrator as a silhouette:

1. In Illustrator, open the file via File > **Open** or import it via File > **Place.**

2. In the Photoshop Import Options dialog, click **Convert Photoshop Layers to Objects,** then click OK. On the Layers palette, the image will appear on editable nested layers, within a group.**B–D** Note: When a Photoshop layer is converted into an Illustrator object, transparency and blending mode settings are preserved (and are listed as editable appearances), and any layer masks become opacity masks, as identified by a dashed line under the layer name.

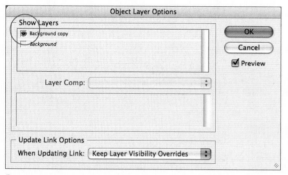

A In the **Object Layer Options** dialog in **InDesign,** we clicked the visibility icon for the Background to hide it.

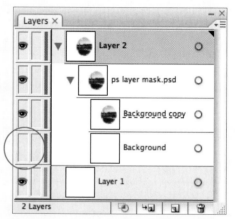

B In **Illustrator,** we chose **Convert Photoshop Layers to Objects** in the Photoshop Import Options dialog. Then, on the Layers palette, we clicked the visibility icon to hide the Background.

C This is the imported Photoshop PSD file with the **Background visible.**

D Here it is with the **Background hidden.**

E And here it is with **both layers hidden.** ;0)

Saving files in the TIFF format

TIFF files are versatile in that they can be imported into most applications and are usable in many color management scenarios. Both InDesign and QuarkXPress can color-separate a CMYK color TIFF.

To save a file in the TIFF format:

1. If the document will be printed on a four-color press and your print shop requests a CMYK file, choose Image > Mode > CMYK Color.

2. Choose File > **Save As.**

3. In the Save As dialog, do the following:

   Enter a name and choose a location for the file.

   Choose Format: **TIFF.**

   Optional: Although you could check Layers to preserve any layers in your file, few image or layout programs can work with layered TIFF files, and those that don't will flatten layers upon import. You can also choose to save Alpha Channels, Annotations, or Spot Colors; or check ICC Profile/Embed Color Profile [profile name] to include the currently embedded color profile with the file.

   Click Save. The TIFF Options dialog opens.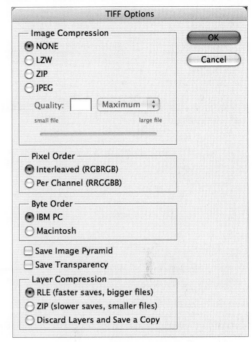

4. In the **TIFF Options** dialog, do the following:

   If the file is going to be color-separated, click **None** under **Image Compression** because output service providers usually prefer uncompressed files. If you do need to compress the file, LZW is the best method because it's nonlossy. Note that some programs can't open TIFF files that are saved with ZIP or JPEG compression.

   For the **Pixel Order,** keep the default setting of **Interleaved (RGBRGB).**

   For the **Byte Order,** click **IBM PC** or **Macintosh** (the platform the file will be used on).

   Optional: Check Save Image Pyramid to include multiple resolutions in one file. Photoshop doesn't offer options for opening image pyramids, whereas Adobe InDesign does.

   Optional: If the file contains transparency that you want to preserve, check Save Transparency. Bear in mind that some applications can't open TIFF files that contain transparency.

   If the file contains layers, click a **Layer Compression** option.

   Click OK.

A Choose settings in the **TIFF Options** dialog.

Saving files in the Adobe PDF format

PDF (Portable Document Format) files can be opened in many Windows and Macintosh applications, and in Adobe Reader (available as a free download), Acrobat Standard, and Acrobat Professional.

There are two different PDF formats to choose from. The default format, **Photoshop PDF**, preserves image, font, layer, and vector data but saves only one image per file. To create this type of file, check Preserve Photoshop Editing Capabilities in the Save Adobe PDF dialog.

The other format is a **generic PDF** file, which is similar to a PDF from a graphics or page layout application. To create this type of file, uncheck Preserve Photoshop Editing Capabilities in the Save Adobe PDF dialog. The file will be flattened and rasterized, which will make your reediting choices in Photoshop quite limited.

Adobe has simplified the process of choosing settings for a PDF file by offering an array of presets.

To save a file as a PDF using a preset:

1. Open an 8-bit or 16-bit file (not a 32-bit file), choose File > **Save As**, enter a file name, choose a location, choose Format: **Photoshop PDF**, then click Save. If an alert appears, click OK.

2. The Save Adobe PDF dialog opens. **A** From the **Adobe PDF Preset** menu, choose a settings preset that's appropriate for the intended output medium (press, Web, etc.). The High Quality Print and Press Quality presets embed all fonts automatically, compress your files using JPEG at Maximum quality, and create large Photoshop PDF files that are compatible with Adobe Acrobat 5 and later. Also, the Preserve Photoshop Editing Capabilities option (discussed at left) is selected for these two presets automatically.

High Quality Print (the default preset) is for desktop printers and color proofing devices. The printer driver handles the color conversion; the profile for the chosen printer is included.

Press Quality is for high-quality prepress output. Colors are converted to CMYK, using the current CMYK workspace profile.

For the following presets, Preserve Photoshop Editing Capabilities is unchecked, so they produce generic PDF files:

PDF/X-1a: 2001, PDF/X-3: 2002, and **PDF/X-4: 2007** files are checked for compliance with specific printing standards, to help prevent printing errors. These files are compatible with Acrobat 4; PDF/X-4 files are also compatible with Acrobat 5 and later.

Smallest File Size uses higher levels of JPEG compression to produce very compact files for the Web, e-mail, and other onscreen uses.

➤ You can read about the currently selected preset in the Description field.

3. Click **Save PDF.** If an alert appears, click Yes.

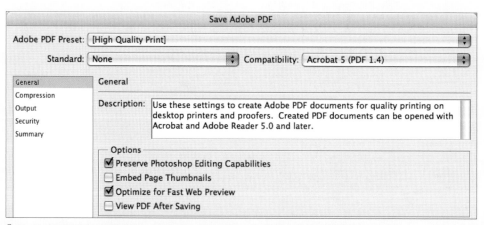

A In the **Save Adobe PDF** dialog, choose a preset from the **Adobe PDF Preset** menu.

To save a file as a PDF using custom settings:

1. Via the **Standard** menu, you can apply a PDF/X compliance standard to any non-PDF/X preset to ensure printing compliance. If you opt not to choose a PDF/X compliance standard, from the Compatibility menu, choose which version of Adobe Acrobat you need your file to be compatible with, bearing in mind that not all applications can read Acrobat 7 or 8 files.

   If you change any settings from the preset defaults, "[Preset Name] (Modified)" will appear on the Adobe PDF Preset menu.

2. Under **Options**, check any of the following:

   Preserve Photoshop Editing Capabilities to allow the PDF file to be reopened and edited in Photoshop CS2 or later. This option limits how much the file can be compressed.

   Embed Page Thumbnails to save a thumbnail of the file for display in the Open and Place dialogs.

   Optimize for Fast Web Preview to enable the file to display quickly in a Web browser.

   View PDF After Saving to have your system's default PDF viewer (usually Adobe Reader or

Acrobat) launch automatically and display the file after you click Save PDF.

To choose more custom options, follow the remaining steps.

3. For online output (not print output), click **Compression** on the list of panels on the left side of the dialog, 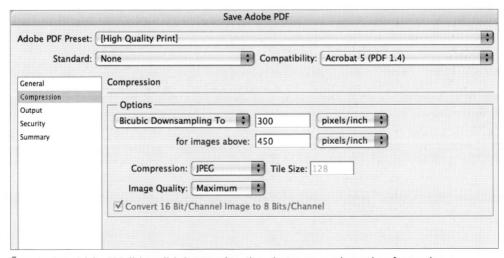 then choose options to control how your image will be compressed (downsampled) to reduce the file size. From the first menu, choose an interpolation method for downsampling:

   Do Not Downsample keeps the image at its present size.

   Average Downsampling To divides the image invisibly into sample areas, averages the pixels in each area, and substitutes the average values for the original ones.

   Subsampling To replaces a sampled area with pixel data taken from the middle of that area, producing a smaller but possibly less accurate file.

   Bicubic Downsampling To replaces the sampled area with an average of the area's values,

Continued on the following page

A In the **Save Adobe PDF** dialog, click **Compression**, then choose compression options for your image.

which usually produces a more accurate result than average downsampling.

For any of the interpolation methods, enter the desired ppi resolution and the minimum resolution threshold an image must have for it to be downsampled.

Choose other **Compression** settings:

Choose a compression type from the **Compression** menu: None for no compression, ZIP, or either of the JPEG options. JPEG2000 is available only when Acrobat 6 or higher is chosen on the Compatibility menu.

The ZIP option is lossless. If you chose a JPEG option, choose an **Image Quality** for the amount of compression. Maximum applies very little compression and produces a higher-quality image with a larger file size, whereas Minimum applies a lot of compression and produces a lower-quality image with a smaller file size. All the JPEG options are lossy (cause data loss), except for JPEG2000 with the Lossless option chosen. (See Saving & Exporting Images > Saving PDF Files in Photoshop Help.)

If Acrobat 6 or higher is chosen on the Compatibility menu, you can convert your file to a lower color depth by checking **Convert 16 Bit/Channel Image to 8 Bits/Channel.**

4. You can click **Output** on the left side of the dialog to view options for controlling the color conversion and profile inclusion in the PDF file. Unless you're experienced with using a color-managed workflow, it's best to leave these menus on the default settings. (For Web output, we suggest choosing Smallest File Size from the preset menu in the General panel, in which case the Output options will be set correctly for you.)

Ask your print shop what settings to choose from the menus in the **Color** area. When No Conversion is chosen on the Color Conversion menu, the output device converts colors to a destination profile; when Convert to Destination is chosen, Photoshop performs the conversion.

Note: Although the PDF/X options will be available if you chose a PDF/X preset from the Standard menu, you should leave the default settings in these fields unless your press shop instructs you otherwise.

(To learn more about the Output options, see Saving and Exporting Images > Saving PDF Files in Photoshop Help.)

5. *Optional:* Click **Security** on the left side of the dialog to view features for restricting user access to the PDF (these are available only if None is chosen on the Standard menu):

Check **Require a Password to Open the Document** to have the file be password protected; type a password in the Document Open Password field.

➤ The password can't be recovered from a document, so make a note of it in a separate location.

Check **Use a Password to Restrict Printing, Editing and Other Tasks** if you want to maintain control over these options. Type a password in the Permissions Password field. The following Permissions become available:

Choose an option from the **Printing Allowed** menu to control whether users can print the file: None, Low Resolution (150 dpi), or High Resolution.

Use the **Changes Allowed** menu to control precisely what users can and cannot alter.

Check **Enable Copying of Text, Images and Other Content** to permit users to alter text or images.

Check **Enable Text Access of Screen Reader Devices for the Visually Impaired** to permit screen readers to view and read the file.

Check **Enable Plaintext Metadata** to enable the file's metadata to be searchable by other applications (available only for Acrobat versions 6 through 8).

6. Click **Summary** on the left side of the dialog, then expand any category to view a list of settings that you've chosen for that category.

7. Click **Save PDF**, click Yes in the alert dialog, then give yourself a nice pat on the back.

Saving files in the EPS format

For drawing and page layout programs that can't import Photoshop PSD or PDF files (and when TIFF isn't an option), consider the **Photoshop EPS** format, but note its limitations: When you save a file in this format, layers are flattened and alpha channels and spot channels are discarded; it's available only for 8-bit files (in any color mode except Multichannel). Also, to print an EPS file, you must use a PostScript or PostScript-emulation device.

To save a file in the Photoshop EPS format:

1. *Optional:* If the image is going to be color-separated by another application and your display is calibrated properly, you can choose View > Proof Setup > Working CMYK to see how the mode conversion will affect the image.

2. Choose File > **Save As** (Ctrl-Shift-S/Cmd-Shift-S). The Save As dialog opens.

3. Enter a file name, choose Format: **Photoshop EPS**, and choose a location for the file.

   Optional: Check ICC Profile/Embed Color Profile [profile name] to embed the document's color profile or current working color space into the file.

   Click Save. The EPS Options dialog opens.**A–B**

4. From the **Preview** menu, choose **TIFF (1 bit/ pixel)** to save the file with a black-and-white preview or **TIFF (8 bits/pixel)** to save the file with a grayscale or color preview. Macintosh users, choose one of the Macintosh previews only if you're sure you won't be opening the file on another platform.

5. In the Mac OS, choose **Encoding: Binary**, the default method used by PostScript printers. Binary-encoded files are smaller and process more quickly than ASCII files. For printing in Windows and for applications, PostScript printers, or printing utilities that can't handle binary files, you must choose **ASCII** or **ASCII85**. JPEG is the fastest encoding method but causes data loss; a JPEG file can be output only from a PostScript Level 2 or higher printer.

6. If you changed the frequency, angle, or dot shape settings in the Halftone Screen dialog in Photoshop, check **Include Halftone Screen**. (To get to the Halftone Screen dialog, you would choose File > Print, then Output from the menu in the upper right corner, then click Screen.)

7. If the file is to be imported into another color-managed application (e.g., InDesign), don't check PostScript Color Management. This option would convert the file's color data to the color space for the printer, and could produce unpredictable color shifts.

8. If your page contains vector elements, such as shapes or type, check **Include Vector Data**. Although saved vector data in EPS files is available to other applications, as an alert will inform you when you reopen the file in Photoshop, the vector data will be rasterized.

9. The **Image Interpolation** option allows other applications to resample pixels in an effort to reduce jagged edges on low-resolution printouts.

10. Click OK.

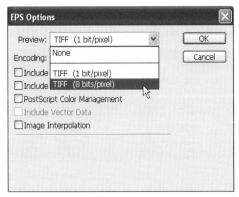

A In the **EPS Options** dialog in Windows, choose Preview and Encoding options.

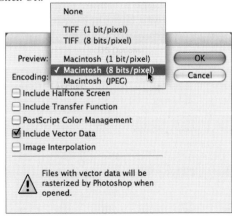

B In the **EPS Options** dialog in the Mac OS, choose Preview and Encoding options.

Optimizing files for the Web

When resaving, or "optimizing," images for viewing online, the two main variables that you'll need to address are the file size (dimensions and compression options) and the file format (GIF or JPEG). Two factors that influence the format choice are whether the image contains flat or continuous-tone colors, and whether it contains transparency. The challenge is to compress an image to the point that it will download quickly on the Web, but not so much that its quality becomes unacceptably low.

Image size

The length of time it takes for an image to download to a Web page is related directly to its **file size.** Its size, in turn, is governed by its pixel dimensions and the amount and kind of compression that it has undergone.

The browser windows that most viewers surf in are approximately 800 pixels wide by 600 pixels high. Two factors to consider when choosing dimensions for your file are the maximum browser and the fact that Web browsers always display images at a magnification of 100%. To judge the image size onscreen, choose View > **Actual Pixels** and then, in the Image > **Image Size** dialog, set the image resolution to **72 ppi** and choose the desired **Pixel Dimensions.**

Although both the GIF and JPEG formats (discussed next) lower the image quality slightly due to their compression methods, their smaller file sizes download quickly on the Web. Note that some types of images are more compressible than others. For example, an image with a solid background color and a few assorted solid-color shapes will be much more compressible than a large image that contains many color areas, textures, or patterns. The file format choice also affects how much an image can be compressed.

File formats

GIF and **JPEG**, the two most common file format choices for optimizing Web graphics, have different strengths and weaknesses and are appropriate for different types of images.

➤ **GIF** is an 8-bit format, meaning that a GIF file can contain up to 256 colors. It's a good choice when color fidelity is a priority, such as for images that contain solid-color areas or shapes with crisp edges, such as type. Since images like these tend to contain fewer colors to begin with than continuous-tone (photographic) images, the color restriction won't have an adverse impact. GIF is the only format option for images that contain transparency.

You don't have to use the full complement of 256 colors when saving a file in the GIF format. You can lower the color depth of a GIF file to make its color table smaller (reduce the number of colors it contains), which in turn will shrink the file size and allow the image to download more quickly. Although such a color reduction may make the edges look grainy (dithered) and the colors a bit dull, it's a worthwhile tradeoff.

➤ Because of its capacity to save 24-bit color, the **JPEG** format does a better job than GIF of preserving color fidelity in continuous-tone images, such as photographs and montages. Another advantage of JPEG is its superior compression methods, which can shrink images significantly without lowering their quality. When saving an image in this format, you have a choice of quality settings; higher-quality settings produce larger files and lower-quality settings produce smaller files. Unfortunately, the JPEG format doesn't preserve transparency.

Next, we'll introduce the Save for Web & Devices dialog, then outline the actual steps for optimizing files in the GIF and JPEG formats.

ALWAYS OPTIMIZE A COPY

Regardless of which format you choose, always remember to create a copy of your file for safekeeping (and a backup, too) before optimizing it!

Previewing optimized files

In the **Save for Web & Devices** dialog, you'll find all the controls you need to optimize your images for the Web, and with its multiple-preview layout you can compare the results of different optimization settings.

To use the Save for Web & Devices previews:

1. With your file open, choose File > **Save for Web & Devices** (Ctrl-Alt-Shift-S/Cmd-Option-Shift-S). The dialog opens.**A**

2. Click the **4-Up** tab to display the original image and three previews. Based on the current optimization settings, Photoshop will generate the first preview (to the right of the original) and then two more preview variations. You can click any preview and change the optimization settings for just that one.

▶ For a more definitive test of the chosen settings, click the Preview In [default browser] button ● ▼ at the bottom of the dialog to open your optimized image in the default Web browser application on your computer. Or to choose a nondefault browser application that's installed in your system, from the menu next to the button, choose a browser name, or choose Other and locate a browser via the dialog.

Preview tabs   Optimization options

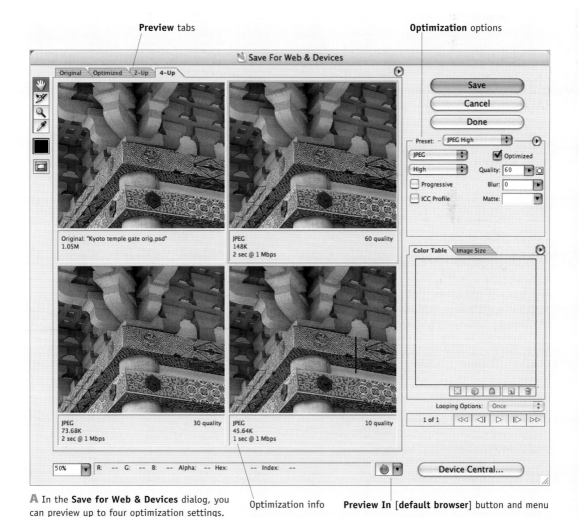

A In the **Save for Web & Devices** dialog, you can preview up to four optimization settings.

Optimization info   **Preview In [default browser]** button and menu

Optimizing files in the GIF format

GIF is an appropriate file format choice if the image contains solid-color areas, or if it contains transparent areas that you need to preserve.

To optimize a file in the GIF format:

1. Via the Image > **Image Size** dialog, change the file resolution to 72 ppi, which is the screen resolution, and resize it to the desired final Pixel Dimensions, then save your file.

2. Choose File > **Save for Web & Devices** (Ctrl-Alt-Shift-S/Cmd-Opt-Shift-S).

3. Click the **2-Up** tab at the top of the dialog to display the original and optimized previews.

4. Do either of the following:

   From the **Preset** menu, choose one of the GIF "Dithered" options; the number in the name, such as "GIF 32 Dithered," corresponds to the number of colors that will be preserved in the image. Leave the preset settings as is, then click Save. The Save Optimized As dialog opens. Leave the name as is, choose a location, click Save, and you're done.

   Follow the remaining steps to choose custom optimization settings. As you do so, note the file size value below the preview. Your goal is to reduce the file size as much as possible while keeping its quality at an acceptable level.

5. From the **Optimized File Format** menu, choose GIF.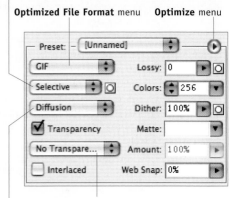

6. From the **Color Reduction Algorithm** menu, choose a method for reducing the number of colors in the image (see the sidebar at right and **A**, next page).

7. Specify the maximum number of **Colors** to be generated for the color table by choosing a preset number from the menu or by entering an exact number in the field. By lowering the number of colors, you reduce the file size.

8. From the **Dither Algorithm** menu, choose the Diffusion, Pattern, or Noise method. The dither process simulates a wider color range by mixing dots of different colors. The Diffusion option produces a higher-quality image but also a larger file size. If you choose None (no dither option), any gradients in the image may show visible bands in the browser.

Color Reduction Algorithm menu

Optimized File Format menu   **Optimize** menu

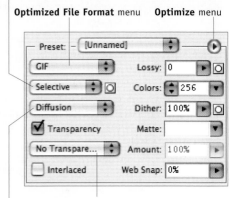

Transparency Dither Algorithm menu

Dither Algorithm menu

A Choose **optimization** options for the **GIF** format in the **Save for Web & Devices** dialog.

THE COLOR REDUCTION ALGORITHMS

▶ **Restrictive (Web)** changes the image colors to standard Web-safe colors (from among the 216 colors that the Windows and Macintosh browser palettes have in common). This option yields the least number of colors and the smallest file size but not necessarily the best image quality.

▶ **Perceptual** generates a new color table based on existing colors in the document, with a bias toward how people actually perceive colors.

▶ **Selective,** the default option, generates a color table based on the colors currently in the image, with a bias toward preserving flat colors, Web-safe colors, and overall color integrity.

▶ **Adaptive** generates a color table based on the part of the color spectrum in which most of the colors in the document are situated. This option produces a slightly larger optimized file.

Also choose a **Dither** percentage. The higher the dither value, the more color simulation occurs, and the larger the file size.

9. Check **Transparency** to preserve any fully transparent pixels in the image and allow for the creation of nonrectangular image borders. With Transparency unchecked, transparent pixels will be filled with the color that's chosen on the Matte menu. Regardless of the Transparency setting, the GIF format doesn't preserve semitransparent pixels.

10. By using one of the options on the **Matte** menu, you can specify which color will be used to fill any semitransparent, soft-edged areas (such as a drop shadow) that border transparent areas. If you know the background color of the Web page and you choose that color, the image will blend in better with the background. If the background color is unknown, choose None from the Matte menu; the resulting edges will be hard and jagged.

Another option is to choose **Matte: None**, check Transparency, and choose one of three options from the **Transparency Dither Algorithm** menu. In this case, the results will look the same regardless of the background. **Diffusion** applies a random pattern to semitransparent pixels and diffuses it into adjacent pixels, usually producing the most subtle results; you can set a dither value. **Pattern** applies a halftone pattern to semitransparent pixels. **Noise** applies a pattern similar to Diffusion without affecting neighboring pixels.

11. *Optional:* You can adjust the Lossy value to further reduce the file size of the optimized image. As the name implies, this option discards some image data, but the savings in file size may justify the minor reduction in image quality.

12. Click Save. The Save Optimized As dialog opens. Leave the name as is, choose a location, then click Save.

A This image was optimized as a GIF with **32** colors by using the **Selective** algorithm but **no dither**...

B ...and here it is optimized with a 100% **Dither**.

C For this **GIF**, **Transparency** was checked and **Matte** was set to **black** (note the thin line of black on the edges of the shapes).

D For this **GIF**, **Transparency** was checked and **Matte** was set to **None** (here the shapes have hard edges).

Optimizing files in the JPEG format

JPEG is the best format for optimizing continuous-tone imagery, such as photographs or collages, or images that contain brush strokes or gradients. This format preserves the 24-bit colors in your file so they can be seen and enjoyed by any viewer whose display is set to thousands or millions of colors. Two drawbacks to JPEG are that its compression methods are lossy (they discard image data) and it doesn't preserve transparency.

To optimize an image in the JPEG format:

1. Via the Image > **Image Size** dialog, change the file resolution to 72 ppi, which is the screen resolution, and resize it to the desired Pixel Dimensions, then save your file.

2. Choose File > **Save for Web & Devices** (Ctrl-Alt-Shift-S/Cmd-Opt-Shift-S).

3. Click the **2-Up** tab at the top of the dialog to display the original and optimized previews.

4. Do either of the following:

   From the **Preset** menu,**A** choose one of the JPEG options, depending on the level of image quality needed. Leave the preset settings as is, then click Save. The Save Optimized As dialog opens. Leave the name as is, choose a location, click Save, and you're done.

   Follow the remaining steps to choose custom optimization settings. As you do so, note the file size value below the preview.

5. From the **Optimized File Format** menu, choose **JPEG**.

6. As you do either of the following, bear in mind that the higher the compression quality, the higher the resulting image quality and the larger the file size:

   From the **Compression Quality** menu, choose a quality level for the optimized image **B–C** (and **A**, next page).

   Move the **Quality** slider to the desired compression level.

7. Increase the **Blur** value to soften any JPEG artifacts that the JPEG compression method has produced and to reduce the file size—but not to the point where details are lost. (You can lower the Blur setting later to reclaim some sharpness.)

8. By using one of the options on the **Matte** menu, you can specify a color to replace areas

Compression Quality menu

Optimized File Format menu   Optimize menu

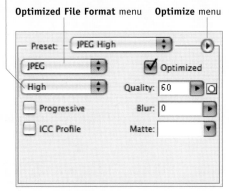

A Choose **optimization** options for a **JPEG** file in the **Save for Web & Devices** dialog.

B This **JPEG** was optimized using the **High Quality** setting.

C This **JPEG** was optimized using the **Medium Quality** setting.

of transparency (preferably the background color of the Web page, if that color is known), or choose None to have transparent areas become white. Although the JPEG format doesn't support transparency, the Matte color will simulate it if you make it the same solid color as the background of the Web page.

9. Keep Progressive and ICC Profile unchecked.

10. *Optional:* Check Optimized to produce the smallest possible file size, depending on your output needs.

11. Click **Save.** The Save Optimized As dialog opens. Keep the name as is, choose a location, then click Save.

Using the Adobe Media Gallery

One way to display your Photoshop images on the Web is via a gallery, or slideshow, in which the images display sequentially on a colored or neutral background, with viewer controls for stopping and proceeding. You can create a slideshow by using the Adobe Media Gallery plug-in, which is accessible from Bridge. The new and improved version, which requires the Bridge 2.1 upgrade, will probably become the preferred choice for most users.

Before you can create a slideshow, you have to **download** the **Adobe Media Gallery** plug-in from the Adobe website, if you haven't already done so.

To download the Adobe Media Gallery:

1. Via your browser, go to **adobe.com.**

2. On the **Communities** menu, choose **Adobe Labs.**

3. At the top of the Adobe Labs window, click **Wiki.** In the left navigation column, locate and click **Adobe Media Gallery** (scroll down if you don't see it).

4. In the Adobe Media Gallery panel, read the installation instructions in the Download and Installation section, then click the download link for your platform: either **Adobe Media Gallery for Windows** or **Adobe Media Gallery for Macintosh.**

5. Exit/Quit Photoshop and Bridge, then follow the installation instructions for your system. In the Mac OS, upon relaunching Bridge, click OK when the alert about enabling the Bridge extension/Media Gallery startup script appears. To learn how to use the Adobe Media Gallery, see the following page.

CREATE AN OPTIMIZATION PRESET

To save your settings in the **Save for Web & Devices** dialog as a preset, choose **Save Settings** from the Optimize menu. In the Save Optimization Settings dialog, enter a name (in Windows, include the .irs extension), make sure Adobe Photoshop CS3\Presets\Optimized Settings is chosen as the location, then click Save. Your saved preset is now available on the **Preset** menu for any document.

A This **JPEG** was optimized with the **Low Quality** setting.

B A **gallery** is being previewed in a Web browser.

To create a slideshow for the Web using the Adobe Media Gallery:

1. Go to Bridge, then from one of the workspace menus in the bottom right corner of the Bridge window, **1**, **2**, **3**, choose **Adobe Media Gallery.** The Adobe Media Gallery panel appears on the right side.

2. In the **Folders** panel on the left side, click a folder name to display its contents as thumbnails at the bottom of the Content panel. Cmd-click/Control-click just a couple of thumbnails in the **Content** panel so you don't have to wait for a lot of previews to render.

3. To make more room for the **AMG Preview** panel, double-click the vertical bar between the Favorites/Folders and AMG Preview panels; the Favorites/Folders pane will disappear.

4. In the fields in the **Style Information** area, enter information to appear in the title bar.

5. Click **AMG Preview** to generate a preview of the selected thumbnails and the personal data that you just entered. **A** Only the text, images, and navigation buttons in the AMG Preview panel will display on the Web.

6. Click any gallery thumbnail to view a large preview of that image.

7. Scroll down in the **Style Information** panel to display slideshow options (**A**, next page), then change any of the variables, such as the Slide Duration for each image, the Transition Effect between images, or the color for the Background, Title Bar, etc. (click a swatch to open the system color picker). Check Show File Names if you want to display file names in the slideshow.

➤ In the color picker in the Mac OS, you can click the second button at the top to display a grayscale slider.

A We chose the **Standard** (Medium Thumbnails) template for this slideshow and hid the left pane.

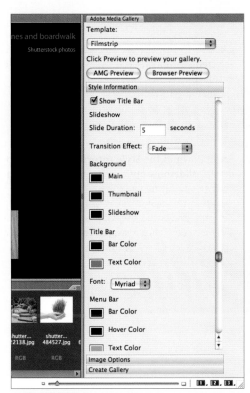

Continued on the following page

A Via the **Style Information** panel, we chose new colors for the two **Text Color** options.

8. To preview your Style Information changes, click **AMG Preview** again.

9. If you like, you can choose a different layout from the **Template** menu at the top of the Adobe Media Gallery panel, then click AMG Preview.**B** Possibilities include:

The **Standard** templates display the thumbnails to the left of the large preview image. You choose the thumbnail size.

The **Filmstrip** template displays the thumbnails below the preview image.**C**

The **Journal** templates list metadata information for the selected thumbnail.

B From the **Template** menu, choose a preset template (layout) for the slideshow.

C After choosing **Filmstrip** on the Template menu, we clicked **AMG Preview** to update the gallery.

10. Click the **View Slideshow** button ⬛ below the large preview image to enlarge the preview image and hide the thumbnails.

11. Click the **Play Slideshow** button ▮ to start the slideshow and preview your settings; click it again to stop the show.

12. Click the **Image Options** bar in the Adobe Media Gallery panel,**A** then choose from the **Preview** and/or **Thumbnail** menus to change the size of the preview or thumbnails. Click AMG Preview once again to update the gallery.

To view the slideshow in your default browser:

1. In the Adobe Media Gallery panel in Bridge, click **Browser Preview** (next to AMG Preview). The gallery will open in your default browser, conveniently scaled to fit the window.**B**

2. When you're done watching the show, exit/ quit the browser, then click in the Bridge window to get back to Bridge. To save the gallery, follow the instructions on the next page.

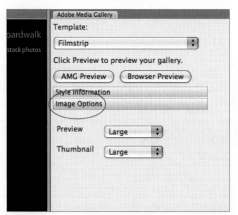

A Via the **Preview** and **Thumbnail** menus in the **Image Options** panel, you can choose a different size for the preview and thumbnail images. Note that Extra Large previews take longer to update.

B When you **preview** the Web gallery in your default browser, test out your slideshow by clicking either the thumbnails or the navigation buttons.

Once you've **finalized** your gallery, don't forget to **save** it!

To save a Web gallery:

1. Select all the thumbnails you've decided to include in the Web gallery.

2. Click the **Create Gallery** bar to open that panel.

3. Enter a Gallery Name for a folder to be created, click Save to Disk, click Browse and locate a destination folder, then click OK/Choose.

4. Back in the Create Gallery panel, click **Save.** All the necessary files for creating the Web gallery will be saved to the chosen folder.

You can even let Adobe Media Gallery **upload** your gallery to a Web server. What service!

To upload a Web gallery:

1. Verify that you've been authorized to upload data to a Web server.

2. Click the **Upload** button in the middle of the Create Gallery panel.

3. In the **FTP Server, User Name,** and **Password** fields, type the data for the FTP (file transfer) server that your Web administrator has instructed you to enter, and in the **Upload Folder** field, enter the name of the folder on the server to which the gallery files are to be uploaded (the Web administrator should also give you this folder name).

4. After entering all the necessary data, click the **Upload** button at the bottom of the panel. Your gallery files will be sent to the server.

5. Give your viewers the address of the website so they can view your gallery.

A In the **Create Gallery** bar, enter a **Gallery Name** for the folder to hold the images, click **Save to Disk**, choose a location, then click **Save**.

Using Zoomify

If you have a high-resolution image that you want to share with viewers, but you don't want to have to shrink it down to a speck in order to download it, check out **Zoomify**. This command creates an HTML file, along with a folder containing a Flash file and a series of JPEG tiles (slices) of the high-resolution image. When the files are uploaded to a Web server, the viewer will be able to zoom in on a detail. The slice for each area displays quickly because it's just a mere segment of the larger image.

To create a zoomify file:

1. With a high-resolution file open in Photoshop, choose File > Export > **Zoomify**. The Zoomify™ Export dialog opens.**A**

2. Do all of the following:

   Choose a preset **Template** for the background color behind the image in the browser. The Navigator templates include a blue frame that the viewer can click to display a different area of the image, which is very handy.

   For **Output Location**, click **Folder**, choose a location for the file, then click OK/Choose; also enter a one-word **Base Name** for the tile folder and HTML file.

Under **Image Tile Options**, choose a **Quality** setting for the tiles (slices).

For **Browser Options**, you can keep the default pixel **Width** and **Height** dimensions for the image when viewed in a browser or enter slightly larger values.

Check **Open in Web Browser** to have the file open in your default browser automatically after you click OK, so you can see how it looks.

Click OK.

3. The HTML page will open in your default Web browser.**B** To **zoom** in or out, use the plus and minus buttons or the slider. To **pan** (bring a different area of the image into view), use the arrows; or if you chose one of the Navigator templates, you can also click or drag the blue frame inside the thumbnail.

4. Upload the files to your Web server, making sure that the HTML file and [base name]_img folder are located in the same folder.

A In the **Zoomify™ Export** dialog, choose a template style, location, name, and quality, and choose image dimensions.

B In the browser, you can use the controls below the image to zoom and pan, or click or drag the navigation frame (if you chose a template with that option).

Note: The listings in this index pertain to Photoshop, except where noted as pertaining to Bridge or Camera Raw.

Photography credits

ShutterStock.com
Photographs on the following pages © ShutterStock.com

pp. i, 67, 88, 89, 348, 350, Catnap
pp. vii, 225, Pichugin Dmitry
pp. 1, 40, 95, 96, 189, 193–195, 214, 246, Ultimathule
p. 11, Jason Page
p. 39, Joe Gough
pp. 54, 68, 69, 94, Styve Reineck
pp. 56–58, 105–107, 209, 220, 233, 234, 286, Elena Elisseeva
p. 59, Andy Lim
p. 66, Alex Staroseltsev
p. 70, Mark Yuill
p. 71, Zastol'skiy Victor Leonidovich
pp. 96, 97, Magdalena Kucova
pp. 97, 111–113, 146, 147, iofoto
p. 100, Marc Goff
p. 101, Fedor A. Sidorov
pp. 108–110, Tiago Jorge de Silva Estima
pp. 114–117, Yuri Arcurs
p. 117, Andresr
pp. 119, 130, 131, Curtis Kautzer
p. 120, Vera Bogaerts
pp. 122–125, 238, 243, Kamil Sobócki
pp. 128, 129, Igor Dutina
pp. 132, 133, Jaroslaw Grudzinski
pp. 136–138, Carsten Reisinger
pp. 139, 150, 151, Kurhan
pp. 140, 141, Magdalena Bujak
pp. 142–145 Zina Seletskaya
pp. 148, 149, 226, 227, Sagasan

pp. 152, 153, 162, 163, Dori O'Connell
pp. 154, 164, Solovieva Ekaterina
pp. 155, 193, Adrian Moisei
p. 156, Coka
pp. 157, 158, 159, Aurelio
pp. 160, 161, 165, 174, 200–202, Andriy Solovyov
pp. 166–168, digitalskillet
pp. 169–171, Connors Bros.
pp. 172, 173, Chen Wei Seng
pp. 180, 196, 197, Szefei
pp. 180, 288, Tebenkova Svetiana
pp. 180, 182, Adrian Matthiassen
pp. 182, Trutta55
pp. 182, Prism 68
pp. 184–186, Dmitry Pistrov
pp. 191, 192, Igor Dutina
p. 193, Cristi Bastian
p. 193, Maxim S. Sokolov
pp. 198, 199, Laurin Rinder
pp. 203, 207, 208, 235, 240, John Bailey
p. 210, Danny E. Hooks
p. 212, Samsonov Juri
pp. 216, 305, 306, Laura Frenkel
p. 232, Dwight Smith
pp. 248, 296–299, Olga Shelego
pp. 260, Vladislav Gurfinkel
p. 262, Maxstockphoto
pp. 264, 267, 274, Jim Mills
p. 268, Kmitu

p. 268, Christophe Testi
pp. 269, Cheryl Casey
pp. 272, 300, Nat Ulrich
p. 276, PhotoCreate
p. 278, Tobias Machhaus
pp. 279, 280, Larisa Lofitskaya
pp. 282, 283, Marilyn Volan
p. 290, Douglas Freer
p. 291, Dhoxax
p. 292, Andrew F. Kazmierski
p. 301, Marciej Mamro
p. 301, Blaz Kure
pp. 302, Qinhe
p. 307, Al Khabazov
pp. 346, 347, Richard A. McGuirk

Photos.com
Photographs on the following pages © 2007 JupiterImages.com

pp. 102, 103
pp. 165, 174

Others
pp. 321, 325, 341, 343–345 © Victor Gavenda

All other photographs © Elaine Weinmann and © Peter Lourekas

pp. 44–45 © Elaine Weinmann, access to garden courtesy firstbornmultimedia.com